# RESEARCH METHODS IN PSYCHOLOGY

## Fourth Edition

# RESEARCH METHODS IN PSYCHOLOGY

## Fourth Edition

**David G. Elmes**
Washington and Lee University

**Barry H. Kantowitz**
Battelle Memorial Institute

**Henry L. Roediger III**
Rice University

WEST PUBLISHING COMPANY
St. Paul ■ New York ■ Los Angeles ■ San Francisco

**Copyeditor:** Kathleen Rae Pruno
**Cover image:** Stanislaw Fernandes, The Image Bank
**Composition:** Parkwood Composition Services, Inc.

LIBRARY OF CONGRESS CATALOGING-IN-PUBLICATION DATA

Elmes, David G.
    Research methods in psychology / David G. Elmes,
    Barry H. Kantowitz, Henry L. Roediger, III.—4th ed.
        p.    cm.
    Includes index.
    ISBN 0-314-92999-1 (hard)
        1. Psychology—Research—Methodology.    2. Psychology,
    Experimental.    I. Kantowitz, Barry H.    II. Roediger, Henry L.
    III Title.
    BF76.5.E44 1992
    150′.724—dc20                                                        91-28780
                                                             CIP

# CONTENTS

## PART II  EXPERIMENTATION IN PSYCHOLOGY  *101*

## Chapter 5  Basics of Experimentation  *103*

## Chapter 6  Experimental Design  *121*

# PREFACE

Presenting you with the fourth edition of a book first published in 1981 gives us great pleasure. The acceptance by earlier readers has allowed us to prepare this new version, which we hope you find rewarding. As with the other editions, the purpose of this book is to present the methods of psychological science so that you can understand the nature of valid and reliable research. Whether you become a producer or a consumer of research, it is vital that you be able to evaluate and appraise it.

## TEXT ORGANIZATION

The text is divided into three parts or sections. The first part focuses on the basics of scientific investigation, including the philosophy of science. The four chapters in the first section provide the groundwork for the remainder of the material. The second part contains five chapters, which focus on the design and execution of experiments. The final section and appendixes A and B treat the tactical aspects of conducting and analyzing research.

We recommend that the first section be read first. The chapters within a section are best read in the order given, except for those in the third section, which are self-contained and may be read at any time after reading the first four chapters.

### Pedagogical Features

Each chapter contains several features designed to improve comprehension and enhance interest. The **Facing Page** provides a summary of the upcoming chapter. The facing page will alert you to important concepts and will provide a convenient aid for review. The **Overview** introduces the substance of each chapter. Within the chapter there are frequent **Concept Summaries,** which are designed to drive home important concepts and to assist in study and review. The first eleven chapters include an **Application** section, which considers how some of the concepts discussed in that chapter can be used outside of the laboratory setting. At the end of each chapter are several features: a point-by-point **Summary;** a list of **Key Concepts;** thought-provoking **Exercises;** and **Suggested Readings.** These features will help you derive maximum benefit from the contents of the chapter—they will reinforce and extend your understanding. Most of the chapters are followed by a **Psychology in Action** section, which presents a project for you to undertake. These projects are intended to further your interest in scientific psychology.

As in earlier editions, many concepts are discussed more than once. The repeated discussion of important ideas in separate parts of the text is done to enhance understanding. We want to take advantage of the well-known benefits of distributed practice and varied rehearsal to maximize the efficiency of the learning process for our readers.

## CHANGES FROM THE THIRD EDITION

Users of the previous edition will notice several changes in this edition. The advice of our capable reviewers, the suggestions of readers, and our own experience have resulted in changes in organization and content. The knowledge explosion in science and the increasing importance of psychological research demand well-trained practitioners and consumers. In addition, we believe that our survival depends on improvements in the technological and scientific sophistication of society. Thus, the first four chapters have been heavily revised, placing more emphasis on conducting research and its philosophical background than was the case in earlier editions. The beginnings of a project are considered in chapter 1. Students participate as subjects in an experiment, and then many of the basics of research are examined in the light of their experience in the experiment. Chapter 2 focuses on the nature of theory construction and hypothesis testing. The next two chapters consider reliability and validity in the context of making scientific observations and measuring behavior. The intent of the first section is to make sure that the student is aware of the rationale of psychological science and will, therefore, be challenged to master the nuts and bolts of scientific investigation.

Part of the organizational changes have involved relocating the ethics chapter to the section on Tactical Aspects of Research. Our reviewers noted that the goals of the course may determine when ethical considerations are examined. Thus, the ethics chapter may be read at any point during the course, which is also true of the chapter on how to read and write laboratory reports. We believe that the current organization is very flexible, and it can be altered to suit the needs of most instructors.

In several places we have chosen new examples to illustrate concepts and principles. Students intrigued by nearly any aspect of scientific psychology will find examples to challenge and interest them. Research on a case of multiple personality illustrates small-$n$ research, and the tip-of-the-tongue phenomenon is used to illustrate the basics of experimentation. Several new examples have been used to illustrate the principles of descriptive research, including a case study of a famous scientist.

Our goals in choosing examples were threefold: to illustrate the proper ways to conduct research, to convey the importance and tremendous scope of psychological science, and to impart a sense of fun and excitement that can be found in undertaking psychological investigations. We hope that we have been successful in attaining those goals.

# ACKNOWLEDGEMENTS

Writing a textbook is a cooperative effort among the authors, readers, and users of earlier editions; the editors and production staff; and the sage advice of several capable reviewers. Many readers of the third edition and the professors who assigned it have written us with valuable suggestions and comments. We thank them for their help and hope that new readers will help us devise a fifth edition. We appreciate the help of the production staff at West—a group of competent people who made our job easier and the product better. Mary Schiller, our editor, deserves special recognition for her organizational skill and wit. We owe a debt to the following reviewers: E. C. Dalrymple-Alford, University of Guelph; Larry Hochhaus, Oklahoma State University; Phyllis Hornbuckle, Virginia Commonwealth University; John Limber, University of New Hampshire; Michael Moore, University of California at Davis; Michael Perone, West Virginia University; and Michael Stadler, Louisiana State University.

Others have provided invaluable technical help. It is a pleasure to recognize the contributions of Denny LeCompte, Heather Turner, and Jennifer Gladwell. They helped in many ways with such skill and efficiency that this edition would be in limbo without their fine assistance. The support of Washington and Lee University, especially its Department of Psychology, is gratefully acknowledged. Several authors and publishers have helped us reproduce important materials. We are grateful to the Literary Executor of the late Sir Ronald A. Fisher, F.R.S., to Dr. Frank Yates, F.R.S., and to Longman Group Ltd. London for permission to reprint Table C-5 from their book *Statistical Tables for Biological Agricultural and Medical Research* (6th edition, 1974).

Finally, we owe an incalculable debt to our teachers who encouraged us to pursue scientific psychology. We would like to dedicate this work to the memory of three outstanding individuals who shared the fun and excitement of experimental psychology with us: **David A. Grant, William M. Hinton,** and **L. Starling Reid.** Each, in his own way, encouraged students to engage in sound psychological research. Their enthusiasm led us into experimental psychology, and we hope that you find a similar model to lead you in the same direction.

David G. Elmes
Barry H. Kantowitz
Henry L. Roediger III

# ABOUT THE AUTHORS

**David G. Elmes** is a Professor of Psychology and Head of the Department of Psychology at Washington and Lee University, where he has taught since 1967. He earned his B.A. with high honors from the University of Virginia and continued on to complete the M.A. and Ph.D. degrees there. Elmes was Adjunct Professor at Hampden-Sydney College, was a research associate for a year in the Human Performance Center of the University of Michigan, and was a Visiting Fellow of University College at the University of Oxford, England. At Washington and Lee he is a codirector of the Cognitive Science Program. Professor Elmes edited *Readings in Experimental Psychology* and is coauthor of the fourth edition of *Experimental Psychology* (with B. H. Kantowitz and H. L. Roediger III). He has published numerous articles concerned with human and animal learning and memory in the *Journal of Comparative and Physiological Psychology, Memory & Cognition, Physiological Psychology,* and *Journal of Experimental Psychology: Learning, Memory, and Cognition,* among others. He frequently referees papers submitted to technical journals and was a Consulting Editor for the *Journal of Experimental Psychology: Learning, Memory and Cognition* for several years.

**Barry H. Kantowitz** is a Senior Staff Research Scientist at Battelle Memorial Institute, Seattle, in the Center for Human Factors and Organizational Effectiveness. He received the Ph.D. degree in Experimental Psychology from the University of Wisconsin in 1969. From 1969 to 1987 he held positions as Assistant, Associate, and Professor of Psychological Sciences, at Purdue University, West Lafayette, Indiana. Dr. Kantowitz was elected a Fellow of the American Psychological Association in 1974. He has been a National Institute of Mental Health Postdoctoral Fellow at the University of Oregon, a Senior Lecturer in Ergonomics at the Norwegian Institute of Technology, Trondheim, Norway, and a Visiting Professor of Technical Psychology at the University of Lulea, Sweden. He has written and edited more than one dozen books. His research on human attention, mental workload, reaction time, human-machine interaction, and human factors has been supported by the Office of Education, the National Institute of Mental Health, the National Aeronautics and Space Administration, and the Air Force Office of Scientific Research. He served a five-year term on the editorial board of *Organizational Behavior and Human Performance.* He has published over seventy scientific articles and book chapters.

**Henry L. Roediger III** is the Lynette S. Autrey Professor of Psychology at Rice University, where he has taught since 1988. He received a B.A. degree in psychology from Washington and Lee University in 1969 and a Ph.D. in cognitive psychology from Yale University in 1973. He has previously been on the faculty at Purdue University (1973–1988) and spent three years as a visiting professor at the University of Toronto. His research interests lie in cognitive psychology, particularly in human learning and memory. He has published over seventy chapters, articles, and reviews as well as two other textbooks: *Psychology* (coauthored with E. D. Capaldi, S. G. Paris, and J. Polivy) and *Experimental*

*Psychology* (with D. G. Elmes and B. H. Kantowitz). He also edited (with F. I. M. Craik) *Varieties of Memory and Consciousness: Essays in Honour of Endel Tulving*. Roediger serves as a Consulting editor for *Contemporary Psychology; Journal of Experimental Psychology: Learning, Memory, and Cognition;* and *Journal of Memory and Language*. He served as Editor of the *Journal of Experimental Psychology: Learning, Memory, and Cognition* from 1985–1989 and as its Associate Editor from 1981 to 1984. He is a member of the Governing Board of the Psychonomics Society (Chair, 1989–1990) and is Secretary-Treasurer of the Midwestern Psychological Association.

# RESEARCH METHODS IN PSYCHOLOGY

## Fourth Edition

# BASES OF PSYCHOLOGICAL RESEARCH

**Goals of Psychological Research**
Conducting Sound Research
Critically Evaluating Research

**Sources of Psychological Research**
Theories
Practical Problems

**Sources of Research Ideas**
Observation
Experts
Journals

**Steps in the Research Process**
Get an Idea
Formulate a Testable Hypothesis
Review the Literature
Conduct Pilot Research
Complete the Research
Conduct Statistical Tests
Interpret the Results
Prepare an Article

# BEGINNING PSYCHOLOGICAL RESEARCH

In this chapter you will participate in a demonstration experiment. Then you will discover that the focus of this book is on conducting sound research and critically evaluating the research of others. You will be introduced to the initial stages of the research process—getting ideas, formulating hypotheses, reviewing the literature, and conducting preliminary research.

Psychological research attempts to understand why people and animals behave as they do. Psychologists usually define **behavior** as overt activities, such as eating, recalling stories, and so on. What about covert psychological processes, such as thinking and feeling? Although thoughts and feelings are not directly observable, they influence such aspects of behavior as reaction time and blood pressure, which are often used to measure these covert processes.

Psychological research is very important. The astounding number of practical gains are too numerous to list, but include discoveries such as improved methods of treating psychologically disordered people, better designs of vehicles to make them easier and safer to use, and new ways of enhancing the performance and happiness of workers. Just as important are the scientific gains provided by psychological research. Scientific psychology is a relatively young science, having begun in earnest in the middle of the nineteenth century. Nevertheless, the 150 years of psychological research has led to a dramatic increase in the scientific understanding of behavior.

In this chapter you will first participate in an experiment. Then we examine how psychological research is begun by using the demonstration experiment as an example.

## AN INVESTIGATION OF READING

To start your study of psychological research, we want you to take part in an experiment. We hope that your participation in this project will elicit the kinds of questions about research that psychology students and experimental subjects often ask. We also will use the experiment to highlight many issues confronting a researcher in psychology as he or she begins to study and use the methods of scientific psychology.

## Introduction and Method

The following demonstration experiment is designed to decide whether aspects of reading and counting can occur automatically. You are a skilled reader, having spent a dozen or so years of your life practicing this skill. You probably believe that reading words and enumerating objects are rational, deliberate processes. Are they? Do you have to think about reading and naming while doing them, or do these processes occur automatically with little conscious effort? To find out whether reading can occur automatically, you will engage in a series of reading and naming tasks. The crucial part of the experiment is that the tasks differ. The behavior you will measure is how fast you do each. One task is set up so that if reading occurs automatically, you will do that task more slowly than the others.

To participate in this experiment, you will need a clock or a watch with a second hand (a watch that records elapsed time in seconds will do), and you also will need a pen or a pencil. You might want to do this experiment with a classmate, so you can accurately time each other. Your task is to read or name a series of digits or symbols as quickly and as accurately as you can. The digits and symbols are in a single column. You should start at the top and go to the bottom of the column without skipping any items. You will go through three different columns on three different pages. Be sure to do them in order. At the top of each page are directions—read them carefully, because the directions on each page are different. The phrase *Start Time* is also at the top of each page. If you are working alone and are using a clock or watch with a second hand, write down the exact time in minutes and seconds. Then start the task. If you are using a watch that records elapsed time, start the time and then begin the task. When you have finished the task on a particular page, either note your finishing time or stop your watch and write down the elapsed time. If you are doing this experiment with a classmate, have him or her time you as you go through each task. Your classmate then can serve as a subject, and you can do the timing for each task.

To begin the experiment, turn to page 20. Do not continue reading here until you have participated in the experiment.

## Results and Discussion

Let us consider the results of the experiment. For each column of digits or symbols, figure out how long it took you to do the task. If you recorded elapsed time, this is straightforward. If you wrote down your start and finish times, calculate the time to go through the column by subtracting the start time from the finish time. When you compare the results of the three tests, you probably will find that naming the number of numbers (the last task you did) took the longest time, and reading the digits took the shortest time.

FIGURE 1–1

Results of demonstration experiment.

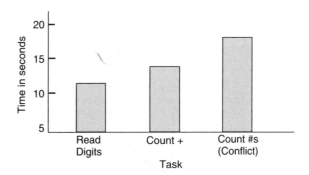

When we conducted this experiment, we obtained the results shown in figure 1–1. Students in our classes took an average of about two seconds longer to enumerate the pluses (the second task) than to read the digits (the first task). In the final task of naming the number of numbers, our students averaged about six seconds longer than simply reading the digits. If you combine your results with those of your classmates, statistical procedures described in appendix B will allow you to decide whether the differences in completion time among the tasks are large enough to be considered real or reliable ones worth considering.

An alternative way to think about the results is to examine how long on average it took people to respond to each item in each task. Because there were 32 items in each task, we can divide the mean time by 32 to find the average time per item. The students averaged .35 seconds to read a single digit, .43 seconds to count a row of pluses, and .57 seconds to count a row of numbers in the conflict task.

Time to read through the columns measures reading difficulty; the longer the time, the more difficult the task. Why is it difficult to name the number of digits when the response is different from the name of the digit? That is, why is it difficult to say "4" when you see 3 3 3 3?

To answer this question, we will outline a theory that seems to account for the results. Other researchers have found that people usually are slower in naming the quantity of digits when the names of those digits conflict with that quantity. Apparently, we automatically read the name of the digits as we are enumerating the quantity. So when we have to respond "2" when we see 3 3, we simultaneously have the responses "2" and "3" available, and because we cannot say two things at once, competition exists between the available responses.

You can think of this as a mental race between two processes that lead to different responses when you see 3 3. One process is naming the digits ("3"); the other is counting them and saying the number ("2"). Because the naming process is greatly practiced, it wins the race, and the naming response ("3") comes to mind before the correct counting response ("2"). Thus there is response competition, because you must inhibit the faster naming response to permit the slower counting response to be spoken. Even if you try to completely ignore the names of the digits, you will discover that you are slower in counting numbers than you were in counting pluses (check the results of the second test you took). This outcome can be interpreted as showing that reading is an automatic process, because even when you try to avoid reading the numbers 3 3, you cannot completely suppress the response "3." Put another way, you cannot not read. Try looking at a word and not reading it.

# GOALS OF PSYCHOLOGICAL RESEARCH

You have just participated in a demonstration experiment that was supposed to show that reading occurs even when we do not want it to under some circumstances. You could ask at this point why people bother to engage in research, or why you are taking a course that focuses on research. A recent survey of over 650 departments of psychology in colleges and universities showed that 73 percent required some combination of courses in statistics and research design as part of their major program (A. J. Golden, personal communication, January 2, 1991), and an additional 20 percent of these departments have research methods and statistics courses as optional components of the psychology major. Why the emphasis on research in 93 percent of the programs?

Two important reasons for the research focus are to teach you how to conduct sound research and to teach you how to evaluate the results of research. We examine each of these purposes in turn.

## Conducting Research

Science progresses when new facts lead to new theories. This progression begins with attempts to answer questions. Is reading a deliberate, reflective process? Not always, as our demonstration experiment shows. Scientific interest in reading is more than idle curiosity—it is curiosity guided by theories and data (facts). The finding that reading often does not require conscious attention must be considered by theories that attempt to explain some aspects of reading. For example, a recent theory of attention by Cohen, Dunbar, and McClelland (1990) tries to show how skilled reading develops. The theory predicts, for example, that highly practiced readers will be more disrupted by conflicts between reading and naming than will less fluent readers. Cohen and associates showed that this is the case, and their theory provides an account of the mechanisms underlying the effects of experience on automaticity. Thus, basic scientific research arises from curiosity and provides the data that allow the development of theoretical explanations.

Scientific progress is not only driven by basic questions and theories, but also motivated by practical problems. One aspect of the research by Cohen and his colleagues shows that automaticity in reading takes a substantial amount of practice. Some obvious practical questions include: How much practice leads to fluent reading? What is the best way to practice to become fluent? The application of scientific psychology to applied problems has had a tremendous impact on social welfare, and the development of improved ways to teach reading is no exception. The understanding of reading has benefited from attempts to determine its bases and solve some practical problems (Crowder, 1982).

Obviously, psychological research is neither necessarily practical in its focus nor necessarily theoretical in its focus. Psychological research can have an impact on scientific explanation and the amelioration of many applied problems. Many facets of human affairs involve psychological research, and a sample of careers using scientific psychology is summarized in the Application section.

# APPLICATION

### Research Careers in Psychology

Many of you may view a course about psychological research as a necessary hurdle for a major in psychology, but of little intrinsic interest. We hope that this book will convince you that psychological research is important and exciting. One reason you may not be particularly interested in psychological research is that you are unaware of the variety of fields open to qualified researchers. You do not have to have a Ph.D. to do good psychological research, and good psychological research does not necessarily deal with esoteric theoretical problems. In fact, we believe there are many careers that demand sound psychological research.

The range of opportunities for a person with training in psychological research is surprisingly broad. Most of these areas require an advanced degree in psychology, but that is not always the case. In any event, almost all aspects of our life need and use psychological research. Here is a list of some of the less obvious careers involving psychological research.

1. A police psychologist who serves as an expert witness on a variety of topics. The psychologist may do work on eyewitness testimony, profiles of criminals, and incentive programs for the department members.

2. A psychologist who does library and laboratory research on the causes of traffic accidents, and who evaluates safety programs. Or, a psychologist who does the same kind of work but specializes in industrial or home accidents.

3. A research psychologist who specializes in population trends: migration, fertility, marriage, and the effects of population density. Federal, state, and local governments often need qualified psychologists to conduct such research.

4. A research psychologist who designs effective computer displays and user-friendly components and software. Such psychologists are in high demand throughout private industry.

5. A research psychologist who determines effective ways of increasing energy conservation. These researchers might study personality dynamics, or they might examine ways to teach people to conserve energy.

6. A research psychologist who tries to determine the brain mechanisms involved in alcoholism and drug addiction. Such a researcher is likely to work in a government hospital or hold an academic position.

7. A research psychologist in human-factors engineering who is interested in one or more of the following: urban transportation, military training, hijacking, equipment design, or the effects of fatigue on performance.

If you are interested in additional descriptions, the following book may be helpful: Woods, P. J. (1976). *Career opportunities for psychologists.* Washington, DC: American Psychological Association.

## CONCEPT SUMMARY

Research helps
- *provide scientific understanding*
- *solve practical problems*

---

### Evaluating Research

Although you have diverse opportunities for a career in psychological research, conducting sound research is not the only focus of a course concerned with research methods. The second focus of such a course and this book is to help you evaluate the results of psychological research. Because the same research methods are used in many disciplines, much of the information you learn about the logic of research will generalize to other fields, such as biology, sociology, and medicine. As an involved member of society, you will be influenced by psychological research. To be a careful consumer of research findings, you need to be able to consider carefully the soundness of the research.

We hope that you will acquire the ideas necessary to think critically about research. A **critic** is a person who makes an informed or reasoned judgment about the value of something. So, to be a **critical thinker** does not mean just finding fault or criticizing unfavorably; it also means exercising careful judgment. Critical thinking is difficult. You probably accepted the results of the demonstration experiment without a second thought. Unfortunately, the design of the experiment does not permit an unequivocal answer to the original question.

Let us outline the principles of a good experiment and see how our experiment fails to meet those principles. In an ideal experiment, something is manipulated or changed, potential sources of influence are held constant, and some behavior is measured. The factor varied is called the **independent variable,** and the behavior measured is called the **dependent variable. Control variables** are those held constant. The researcher manipulates or changes the independent variable so that the effects of the different values or levels of the independent variable can be determined by changes in the dependent variable. In the demonstration experiment, the three tasks were the levels of the independent variable, and your time to go through the lists was the dependent variable. The order in which you and your classmates went through the tasks was constant. The constancy of order is the problem. A summary of the variables in experiments is presented in figure 1–2.

To see how the constant order presents difficulties, you need to recognize that another variable that could influence the dependent variable should not vary with or contaminate the independent variable in an experiment. Because order and task varied together, they are said to be confounded. **Confounding** here means that both the tasks and the order in which they were done varied together—order of the tasks and their nature were confused or confounded. The longer time required in the third task may have resulted from fatigue or boredom rather than from the nature of the task. More likely, people got better

FIGURE 1–2

The variables in an experiment.

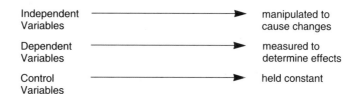

at doing the tasks as they went through them, which would underestimate the effect of the independent variable. In either case the independent variable may not have caused changes in reading time, and the results of the experiment may not be interpretable.

A critical view of the experiment questions the soundness of the results. A more careful research design would have different people go through the tasks in different orders, resulting in an unconfounding of order and task. Alternatively, different groups of people would each be exposed to one task, so order of experiencing the tasks is not a consideration. When either is done, approximately the same results are obtained—the conflict task still takes longest to complete. Because you did not know that until now, you should have been skeptical of the results. As a general rule, you should carefully evaluate research procedures so that potential problems such as confounding may be identified.

An important time for you to think critically about research is when the results may have personal importance. Let us consider a hypothetical example. Suppose that in a few years Doris, your child, is in the first grade. Her teacher calls you in for a conference and informs you that Doris has difficulty learning to read. The teacher then tells you that the school has several ways to provide remedial help. You and the teacher will choose what seems the best alternative to help Doris' progress. Can you make an informed judgment about the remedial reading methods? You probably are not an expert in teaching reading. Yet, can you decide that one method shows more promise than another? What do you need to know? At least some parts of the answers to these questions require that you can critically assess the research and theory underlying the various programs.

Most of this book tries to help you identify problems associated with conducting sound research and to help you develop the skills necessary to make informed judgments about the research process. You need to be able to identify weaknesses and to rectify them. Choosing a poor remedial reading program for your daughter could have dramatic effects—much more dramatic than getting a mediocre grade in a required course. The need to understand psychological research will last your whole life not just a single term of your undergraduate career.

## CONCEPT SUMMARY

Critical thinking about research involves
* *making informed judgments*
* *looking for design flaws such as confounding*

# SOURCES OF RESEARCH IDEAS

We emphasize conducting and evaluating research. What constitutes a research project? The typical research project proceeds as follows: get the research idea, formulate a testable hypothesis, review the pertinent literature, conduct preliminary research, design the project, collect the data, analyze the results statistically, interpret the data, and write the report. It sounds easy and straightforward, but it is not. In this chapter we focus on the initial stages of a research project, and the rest of the book will try to complete the picture.

## Observation

Science begins with observation—both as a source of data and as a source of ideas for further research. Look around with a critical eye, and you will likely generate a number of ideas for research. All you need to do is observe yourself, your classmates, your family, or even your pet. Then phrase your question so that you can make additional observations. Some typical questions might include: Do I study better in the library than in my dormitory room? Do students learn more in small classes than in large classes? Do students retain as much after studying with music on as without music? Do children work harder or less hard when given rewards such as candy? These and similar questions are easy to generate, and with some work they can be turned into manageable research projects. Your native curiosity or the need to solve a particular problem will serve you well in developing ideas for research.

## Experts

Both people, such as your professor, and textbooks, such as this one or your introductory psychology text, are usually good sources of research ideas. Often an idea presented in class or one that you read about will produce an interesting idea. Once you are titillated by a problem, you should seek a consultant. Within a particular course, your instructor is the obvious choice. Beyond a particular course, you may try to get advice from someone whose competence and interest match what you are interested in exploring. Many faculty members will be delighted to discuss research with you. If you have read about an interesting research project, you can try writing to the author.

We designed this text to be a source of possible research projects. If you carefully answer the design-related questions that appear at the end of most chapters, the germ of a good research project may be lurking in one or more of your answers. Many of the questions derive from problems in actual research, so it is apparent that even experts do not conduct perfect research. Why not profit from their mistakes? Another source of ideas in this book are the exercises presented at the end of each chapter in the Psychology in Action section. These exercises are usually easy to carry out. If you think critically about them, you will likely devise additional research projects.

## *Journals*

Ideas frequently come from reading journal articles. Part of the last chapter of this book considers how to read a journal article carefully. If you are going to be reading journal articles soon, we suggest that you read that part of the chapter before you get into the technical literature. After reading several journal articles, you will soon have a longer list of possible experiments than you could perform.

To keep track of ideas generated from your critical reading of journals or textbooks, you should keep records of your research ideas. Most psychologists have some sort of index file containing information about the articles they have read. On your file cards you should have several kinds of information: authors' names, journals, and article titles; and information about the procedure and results. It is probably best to supplement your article file with a file of research ideas. Most psychologists keep a file of such ideas, and you should too. Write down the reference that started you thinking, a short description of your idea for a project, and the date the idea occurred. You will find it interesting to go back through your files to see how your thinking about some topic has changed over time.

As your idea file gets larger because each article you read suggests at least one additional project to you, you are now confronted with another problem. At first an idea for any project was cause for celebration. Later the problem becomes one of deciding which of several ideas in your file should be tried. Some potential ideas will be eliminated because you do not have access to specialized equipment or special subject populations. Others will be too complicated or will take too long to carry out. After paring down your list, you probably still will have more than one alternative. Assuming that each idea is equally practical and feasible, given your resources, our advice is to tackle the project you think would be most fun. Psychological research is interesting, exciting, and often has important outcomes. However, interest, excitement, and importance will happen only if you do research (follow up on your idea file).

If you are unsure about what journals and other resources to examine for research ideas, you can refer to table 1–1 to help you along. The table lists several general sources of information as well as journals with particular topical emphases. Perhaps the most important general resource is *Psychological Abstracts,* which contains brief abstracts of articles from almost all journals that publish psychological research. After you have found an abstract of interest there, you can then read the entire article or send a note to the author requesting a reprint of the article or additional information. The other resources listed in table 1–1 have a variety of purposes, and we recommend that you familiarize yourself with each of the first seven general-purpose resources and as many of the research journals as seem to be of interest to you. We have included only a small number of research journals in the table, but the ones we have included are among the most widely read in psychological research. Others emphasizing education, clinical problems, sociology, law, and industrial concerns can be ferreted out of your school's library. Many libraries have a **computerized literature search** available. You provide the topic, and the computer scans standard abstracting sources (such as the *Psychological Abstracts)* as well as government documents and technical reports that often are not abstracted. Computer searches can be quick and thorough, but they also can be expensive. However, a computer search is much less costly than the value of time needed to accomplish the same search manually. It is possible for one hour of computer-search time

**TABLE 1–1   Some Important Resources for Psychological Research**

| Topic Area | Title of Resource | Comment |
|---|---|---|
| Article titles | *Current Contents* | Several specialty areas |
| Author citations | *Social Science Citation Index* | |
| Article abstracts | *Science Citation Index* | |
| | *Biological Abstracts* | |
| | *Ergonomics Abstracts* | |
| | *Index Medicus* | |
| | *Psychological Abstracts* | |
| Review articles | *American Psychologist* | |
| | *Annual Review of Psychology* | Book with chapter-length reviews |
| | *Journal of Experimental Psychology: General* | Contains original experiments |
| | *Psychological Bulletin* | |
| | *Psychological Review* | Often contains original studies |
| | *Psychological Science* | Contains original research |
| Laboratory experiments | *American Journal of Psychology* | |
| | *Animal Learning and Behavior* | Some field studies |
| | *Behavior Research Methods, Instrumentation and Computers* | Notes on apparatus and computers |
| | *Behavioral Neuroscience* | |
| | *Bulletin of the Psychonomic Society* | |
| | *Canadian Journal of Psychology* | |
| | *Cognition* | |
| | *Cognitive Psychology* | |
| | *Cognitive Science* | |
| | *Journal of Comparative Psychology* | |
| | *Journal of Experimental Child Psychology* | Some field studies |
| | *Journal of Experimental Psychology: Animal Behavior Processes* | |
| | *Journal of Experimental Psychology: Learning, Memory, and Cognition* | |
| | *Journal of Experimental Psychology: Human Perception & Performance* | |
| | *Journal of Experimental Social Psychology* | |
| | *Journal of the Experimental Analysis of Behavior* | Small-$n$ experiments |
| | *Journal of Memory and Language* | |
| | *Learning and Motivation* | |
| | *Memory & Cognition* | |
| | *Perception & Psychophysics* | |
| | *Psychobiology* | |
| | *Quarterly Journal of Experimental Psychology* | |
| Various research methods | *Applied Ergonomics* | |
| | *Behavior Therapy* | Case histories, small-$n$ |
| | *Child Development* | |
| | *Developmental Psychology* | |
| | *Developmental Psychobiology* | |
| | *Journal of Abnormal Psychology* | |
| | *Journal of Applied Behavioral Analysis* | Small-$n$ |
| | *Journal of Applied Psychology* | |
| | *Journal of Educational Psychology* | |
| | *Journal of Personality and Social Psychology* | |

to yield the same number of useful references as three to five days of intensive manual searching. Furthermore, some databases (such as Knowledge Index) have special low rates on nights and weekends that allow even students on tight budgets to afford computer services.

An excellent method for discovering new findings uses the *Social Science Citation Index,* which can be searched either by computer or manually. By entering a critical or key reference, you can obtain a list of more recent articles that have cited your critical reference. Because these articles contain a discussion of your key reference, it is very likely that they are directly related to your topic of interest. This is an extremely efficient way to bring yourself up to date in some specific content area.

## CONCEPT SUMMARY

Sources of ideas include
- *observation, experts, and*
- *journals*

## DEVELOPING TESTABLE HYPOTHESES

After you have developed an idea, you need to frame it in the form of a testable hypothesis. A **testable hypothesis** makes a statement about a presumed or theoretical relation between two or more variables (Kerlinger, 1986). According to Kerlinger, a testable hypothesis either states or implies that the variables are measurable. It also specifies the relation among the variables. Specifying measurements and relations sets the stage for the research project, because research requires that something can be observed and measured. Therefore, if a hypothesis is not testable, research on it is impossible.

Consider one of the possible ideas generated from observation that was considered above: Do I study better in the library than in my dormitory room? Is this a testable hypothesis? A relation is implied—better study in the library—but measurements are not specified. So at this point the hypothesis is not testable. How can you measure better study? One way would be to assess the outcome of study; namely, your grades on a test could be determined. Grades are observable and measurable, so they fit one of Kerlinger's criteria for a testable hypothesis. The reformulated question might become: Do I get better grades on tests after studying in the library than after studying in my dorm room? Because you might be interested in the generality of the research outcome, you can modify the initial question to develop the following hypothesis: Higher grades are obtained after studying in the library than after studying in the dorms. This hypothesis follows Kerlinger's guidelines, because it specifies both what will be measured and the expected relationship between study location and grades.

At this point you might want to practice developing testable hypotheses. Take some of the ideas or questions you have and see if you can put them in testable form. Any research that you undertake requires a testable hypothesis, so now is a good time to practice generating them. If you do not have many potential ideas to consider, several are available in one of the exercises at the end of this chapter.

Many hypotheses cannot be tested, because they either do not include variables that can be observed and measured or do not specify relations among variables. Thus, scientific research cannot be used to study many moral and religious issues. Research can be used to assess a person's attitude toward abortion, for example, but it cannot address the issue of whether abortion in principle is good or bad. The broad statement "Abortion is wrong" specifies neither what is to be measured nor relations among measurable variables. Testable hypotheses about the positive or negative impact of abortion in particular circumstances are possible, but encompassing hypotheses about the moral value of abortion are not. Many questions that you generate may not be testable, because they fail to include observable and measurable variables. Scientific research can be used to study how people respond to colors, but it cannot address the question of whether your experience of the color blue is the same as someone else's experience of the color blue. *Experience* in this context cannot be measured, but responding (behavior) can.

## CONCEPT SUMMARY

Testable hypotheses specify
- *how variables will be measured*
- *how variables will be related*

# REVIEWING THE LITERATURE

The next phase of the research process involves a review of the pertinent literature. Previously, we discussed using journals to obtain ideas. Now we will consider another important use of journals—determining what is known about your hypothesis. A literature review will reveal whether your research hypothesis has been tested, and it will indicate important things for you to consider in developing your research project.

You do not want to reinvent the wheel. The idea about the effects of study location on grades probably is not novel. So you must find out whether someone else has already tested your hypothesis. Thousands of research articles about psychological hypotheses are published each year, so you will probably find many articles related to your hypothesis. Even if those articles do not match your hypothesis precisely, you will probably discover many details that will allow you to devise your own research project more efficiently.

## An Example of a Literature Search

Suppose you have developed a testable hypothesis about reading based on our demonstration experiment. Because the experiment showed that it is difficult not to read words, you reasoned that the conflict effect might disappear if reading were made difficult, say by printing the materials upside down. Your hypothesis is: The time to read through lists with a conflict between the number of digits and their name will be less if the digits are presented upside down rather than right-side up. Has this experiment been done? What "tricks of the trade" can I discover in the literature?

Where does the literature search begin? You could start with the *Psychological Abstracts* or a computer search, but an easier way would be to use this textbook. We referenced an article concerned with the conflict effect by Cohen and others (1990). So, you might look up that article in the Reference section of this book, and then go to the library to read it. You can read about the research they did and the theory they proposed. You can use their reference list as a source of additional articles for your literature search (they reference over 70 research papers). One thing you will discover is that the conflict effect shown in the demonstration experiment is usually called the **Stroop effect** after the man who first demonstrated the phenomenon (Stroop, 1935). Generally, you should read the primary source of a research phenomenon, so examine Stroop's paper. If you are interested in the Stroop effect, you will find a recent review of 50 years of research on the Stroop effect by MacLeod (1991) to be very helpful. He cites about 400 studies, and he also summarizes them. For a person interested in the phenomenon, this journal article is an extremely important source of information.

Another efficient way to get background information is to examine the subject index of textbooks. If you look in the index of this book, you will find that the Stroop effect is discussed in two different places later in the text. In those discussions you will find additional references that might be valuable to read. A particularly important article is the one by Windes (1968). Windes apparently was the first researcher to use a task similar to the one used in the demonstration experiment.

Finally, you might consider searching the *Psychological Abstracts* or the *Social Science Citation Index*, or you might have a computer search done. These searches should provide you with sufficient information to allow you to design your research procedure.

## CONCEPT SUMMARY

To conduct a literature search use
- *Psychological Abstracts*
- *Social Science Citation Index*
- *computerized searches*
- *textbooks*

## CONDUCTING PILOT RESEARCH

Before undertaking a full-scale research project, you should do some preliminary research, which is usually called **pilot research**. A thorough literature search will help you devise a reasonable research plan, as well as help you figure out what kinds of material and apparatus you may need. However, you will probably find it necessary to try out various parts of your project. This is the purpose of pilot research.

In pilot research you test a small number of participants to try to ensure that you have all the bugs out of your research procedure. You will find out whether your subjects understand the instructions. You will learn how much time the experiment requires and whether the tasks you chose are too easy or too hard. You will be able to practice using the equipment and materials, and you will be able to practice observing and measuring the behavior of interest.

Frequently, pilot research is used to assess the levels of the independent variable to make sure that they have an effect on the dependent variable. If one level of the independent variable is presenting the conflicting digits upside down, you should try this out on a few people to ensure that there is less conflict than when the digits are right-side up. Suppose you find that there is less conflict when the digits are presented upside down. Is that a foolproof sign that you have an independent variable that works? Probably, but it may not be the case. One difficulty with pilot research is that you test your procedure on just a few participants. For whatever reason, this small sample of people may not be representative of the population of people you are interested in testing. To find out whether your pilot data are a fluke, you need to conduct the full-blown project with a large number of observations under each level of the independent variable. Although the small test sample is a problem, pilot research plays an important role in developing a sound research project.

## CONCEPT SUMMARY

Conduct pilot research to
- *refine the research procedures*
- *test the levels of your independent variable*

## FINISHING THE RESEARCH PROJECT

After completing the preliminary stages outlined above, you can now conduct the research, analyze and interpret the data, and then write a research paper. The remainder of this book focuses on these aspects of the research process. We hope you will be a critical reader and thinker, using the information we convey to conduct sound psychological research and to evaluate carefully the research of others.

Neither the practice nor the use of science is easy. The benefits that can be derived from scientific knowledge and understanding depend on critical and well-informed citizens and scientists. Unless you plan to hibernate or drop out of society in some other way, you are going to be affected by psychological research. As a citizen you are a consumer of the results of psychological research, and we hope that the material discussed in this book will help to make you a more intelligent consumer.

Some of you, we hope, will become scientists. We also hope that some of you budding scientists will focus on why people and animals think and act as they do. We wish you future scientists good fortune. Your scientific career will be exciting, and we hope that your endeavors will be positively influenced by the principles of psychological research presented in this text.

About a hundred years ago, T. H. Huxley, a British scientist, said: "The chessboard is the world, the pieces are the phenomena of the universe, the rules of the game are what we call the laws of Nature. The player on the other side is hidden from us. We know that his play is always fair, just, and patient. But we also know, to our cost, that he never overlooks a mistake, or makes the smallest allowance for ignorance."

## SUMMARY

1. One goal of psychological research is to provide scientific understanding about why people and animals behave as they do. Another goal of psychological research is to solve practical problems.

2. The goals of this book (and, likely, your course) are: to help teach you how to conduct sound research and to help you learn how to evaluate critically the research of others.

3. An experiment involves manipulating or changing the levels of an independent variable while trying to minimize the effects of confounding variables that may vary with the independent variable. Those factors that are held constant are called control variables. The behavior that is measured is called the dependent variable.

4. Research begins with observation, which is a source of data and ideas for research projects. Other sources of research ideas are journal articles and experts, such as your professor or your textbook.

5. Numerous journals report the results of psychological research. Two of the better sources for research ideas and background information are *Psychological Abstracts* and *Social Science Citation Index*.

6. A testable hypothesis makes a statement about a presumed or theoretical relation between two or more variables. A testable hypothesis implies or specifies how the variables are measured.

7. Prior to undertaking a research project, you should do a literature search to find out whether your hypothesis has been studied. Becoming acquainted with the literature also will help you to design your project carefully and efficiently.

8. Preliminary research, called pilot research, usually is done before conducting a research project. The pilot research will help you refine your procedure, and it may help you to choose appropriate levels of your independent variable.

## Key Concepts

| | |
|---|---|
| behavior | independent variable |
| computerized literature search | pilot research |
| confounding | *Psychological Abstracts* |
| control variable | *Social Science Citation Index* |
| critic | Stroop effect |
| critical thinker | testable hypothesis |
| dependent variable | |

## Exercises

1. [*Special Exercise.*] (Some of the exercises at the end of chapters ask that you critique a research project in some way. You are provided with enough information in the question to answer it. If some procedural detail is omitted—for example, the time of day the research was conducted—you may assume that the detail is irrelevant. Base your discussion on the information provided.) Do you listen to music as you are studying? A large percentage of college students do. A substantial amount of research concerns the effects of music on people's ability to learn and remember. The research has generated an interesting controversy. Some researchers find that listening to music disrupts learning, and others report that music does not disrupt learning. Generate several testable hypotheses as to why music might or might not have a negative effect on learning. One thing you might consider is the type of music. One of the authors of this book never studied in his dorm room as a freshman because his roommate regularly played Ravel's *Bolero* during the evening.

2. Look up the term *aggression* in the index of a recent issue of *Psychological Abstracts*, then read several of the abstracts. Note how articles with various emphases are organized in the *Abstracts*. Articles about animal aggression are grouped together and in a different section than those concerned with aggression in children.

3. Transform each of the following problems or statements into at least two testable hypotheses:

   a. You can't teach an old dog new tricks.

   b. Eating junk food lowers your grade point average.

   c. A penny saved is a penny earned.

   d. The best way to study is cramming the night before an exam.

   e. Out of sight, out of mind; or—Absence makes the heart grow fonder.

## Suggested Readings

The following two books contain additional information about the preliminary stages of a research project: Alsip, J. E., & Chezik, D. D. (1974). *Research guide in psychology.* Morristown, NJ: General Learning Press. Leedy, P. D. (1985). *Practical research: Planning and design* (3rd ed.). New York: Macmillan.

# PSYCHOLOGY IN ACTION
## Doing Research

This section does not contain a particular project for you to do. Rather, it is a plea to do research. Find something you did or read about recently that you considered really interesting. Examine it, study it, and learn about it. Suppose you find that you are more likely to study in a quiet place. You might ask yourself how that finding relates to the music and study question presented in this chapter. Is there a personally relevant research project waiting for you to do?

Have you been lucky or made a serendipitous finding? One thing you may have noticed when you participated in the experiment on reading and naming is that some mismatches between digits and quantity are more likely to slow down your naming time than are others. Is this true for everybody or just you? Does everyone have difficulty with the same mismatches, or do the difficult ones differ from person to person?

Most good scientists are intensely curious about many things. Where others may see commonplace occurrences, scientists may ask why and try to answer the question through research. According to the Nobel Prize-winning chemist Albert Szent-Györgyi, "Discovery consists of seeing what everybody has seen and thinking what nobody has thought."

**THE EXPERIMENT**   DIRECTIONS: Name the numbers below aloud as fast as you can.

START TIME

_____

| |
2
1
4
3
3
2
4
1
4
1
3
2
2
1
3
4
3
1
4
2
4
3
2
1
1
3
2
4
2
3
4
1

FINISH TIME

_____

ELAPSED TIME

_____

To continue the experiment, please go to next page.

**THE EXPERIMENT** DIRECTIONS: Count the number of +s aloud in each row as fast as you can.

START TIME

_____

```
+
+ + + +
+ + +
+ +
+ + + +
+ +
+ + +
+
+
+ +
+ + +
+ + + +
+ +
+ + + +
+
+ + +
+ + + +
+ + +
+
+ +
+ +
+ + +
+
+ + + +
+
+ + + +
+ +
+ + +
+ + +
+ + + +
+
+ +
```

FINISH TIME

_____

ELAPSED TIME

_____

To continue the experiment, please go to next page.

**THE EXPERIMENT**   DIRECTIONS: Count the number of digits aloud in each row as fast as you can.

START TIME

_____

|     |
| --- |
| 2 |
| 1 1 1 1 |
| 4 4 4 |
| 3 3 |
| 3 3 3 3 |
| 2 2 2 |
| 4 4 |
| 1 1 |
| 4 |
| 1 1 |
| 3 3 3 3 |
| 2 2 2 |
| 2 2 2 2 |
| 1 1 |
| 3 |
| 4 4 4 |
| 3 3 3 3 |
| 1 1 1 |
| 2 |
| 4 4 |
| 3 3 |
| 4 4 4 |
| 2 |
| 1 1 1 1 |
| 3 |
| 1 1 1 1 |
| 4 4 |
| 2 2 2 |
| 4 4 4 |
| 3 3 3 3 |
| 2 |
| 1 1 |

FINISH TIME

_____

ELAPSED TIME

_____

You are through participating in the experiment.
Please return to page 4.

**EXPLANATION IN SCIENTIFIC PSYCHOLOGY**

Why do people and animals behave as they do?

**Research**
  arises from curiosity
  solves basic and applied problems

**Sources of Belief**
  authority
  tenacity
  a priori assumptions
  empiricism

**Scientific Procedures**
  induction
  deduction
  strong inference

**Scientific Theories**
  organize and predict
  are: parsimonious
       precise
       testable

**Scientific Data**
  illustrate psychological processes
  demonstrate what can happen in controlled settings

# 2

# EXPLANATION IN SCIENTIFIC PSYCHOLOGY

How does science differ from other modes of understanding? What are some of the assumptions underlying the scientific method? How do psychologists use theory and data to explain behavior? We pursue these questions in this chapter by examining a social psychological phenomenon called social loafing. Because the answers to the questions provide a framework for the rest of the text, you need to understand what is meant by scientific explanation.

A scientist wants to discover how and why things work. In this desire he or she does not differ from anyone else who is also curious about the world we inhabit. The casual observer may not feel terribly frustrated if some observation cannot be explained. For example, the nonscientist may simply accept that water always goes down a sink drain counterclockwise or that individuals tend to work less hard in groups than when alone. However, the professional scientist has a strong desire to pursue an observation until an explanation is available or a problem is solved. By being unwilling to tolerate unanswered questions and unsolved problems, scientists use several techniques for obtaining relief from curiosity and developing explanations. Careful application of these techniques distinguishes scientific understanding from everyday understanding.

In this chapter we introduce scientific explanation from the viewpoint of a working scientist—in particular, an experimentally oriented psychologist. To do so we examine a series of research studies on social loafing. The purpose of the research is to understand why people work less hard in groups than when they work alone. Our discussion of scientific explanation leads to a consideration of aspects of the philosophy of science used for an understanding of behavior. Because abstract principles of science do not always make much sense when removed from specific topics, we relate the philosophy of science to research on social loafing. We intend to show how psychologists undertake to explain why people and animals behave as they do.

# MAKING SENSE OF THE WORLD

## Social Loafing

A common observation—one you probably have made yourself on many occasions—is that people working in a group often seem to "slack off" in their effort. Many people in groups seem willing to let a few do the work. Bibb Latané, a social psychologist, noticed this tendency and decided to study it experimentally. Initially, Latané examined the research literature to see if any evidence existed for this phenomenon of people's working less hard in groups, which he named **social loafing.** One of the earliest studies of social loafing was conducted by a French agricultural engineer (Ringelmann, 1913; Kravitz and Martin, 1986), who asked people to pull on a rope as hard as they could. The subjects pulled by themselves or with one, two, or seven others. A sensitive gauge was used to measure how strongly they pulled the rope. If people exert as much effort in groups as when alone, then the group performance should be the sum of the efforts of all individuals. Ringelmann discovered that groups of two pulled at only 95 percent of their capacity, and groups of three and eight sank to 85 percent and 49 percent, respectively. So, it is probably not just our imaginations when we notice others (and ourselves?) putting forth less effort when working in groups: Ringelmann's research provides us with a good example of social loafing.

Latané and his colleagues then performed a systematic series of experiments on the phenomenon of social loafing (Latané, 1981; Latané, Williams, and Harkins, 1979). They first showed that the phenomenon could be obtained in other experimental situations besides that of rope pulling. They also demonstrated that social loafing occurs in several different cultures (Gabrenya, Latané, and Wang, 1983) and even holds for young children. Thus social loafing is a pervasive characteristic of working in groups.

Latané related this work to a more general theory of human social behavior (Latané, 1981). The evidence from the experimental studies points to **diffusion of responsibility** as a possible reason for social loafing. People working by themselves think they are responsible for completing the task; when they work in groups, however, this feeling of responsibility diffuses to others. The same idea accounts for behavior in other group situations: if one of your professors asked a question in a class containing only two other people, you would probably feel responsible for trying to answer. However, if there were 200 other people in the class, you would likely feel much less responsible for answering. Similarly, people are more likely to help in an emergency when they feel the burden of responsibility than when there are several others about who could help.

One possible benefit of such basic research into a phenomenon is that the findings may be applied later to solve some practical problem. A problem in American society is the declining productivity of the work force. Although social loafing is, at best, only one factor involved in this complicated issue, Marriott (1949) showed that factory workers working in large groups produce less per individual than do those working in small groups. Thus, basic research that would show a way to overcome the problem of social loafing may be of great practical import. In fact, Williams, Harkins, and Latané (1981) found conditions that eliminated the effect of social loafing in their experimental situation. When individual performance (rather than just performance of the entire group) was monitored within the group situation, the individuals worked just as hard as they did when they worked alone. Certainly more research must be done, but simply measuring individual performance in group situations could help eliminate social loafing and increase productivity. The proposed solution may seem simple, but many jobs measure only group performance, not individual performance.

Research on social loafing by Latané and others shows how an interesting problem can be studied scientifically and be understood. The research will, when carefully conducted, promote a better explanation of the phenomenon of interest than will simple observation of events and reflection about them. Let us now examine the nature of scientific explanations.

# SOURCES OF UNDERSTANDING

## *Fixation of Belief*

Science and scientific psychology in particular are valid ways to acquire knowledge about the world around us. What characteristics of the scientific approach make it a desirable way to learn about and arrive at beliefs about the nature of things? Perhaps the best way to answer this question is to contrast science with other modes of fixing belief, since science is only one way that understanding is obtained.

More than a hundred years ago, the American philosopher Charles Sanders Peirce (1877) compared the scientific way of knowing with three other methods of developing beliefs. He called these the **authority, tenacity,** and **a priori** methods. According to Peirce, the simplest way of fixing belief is to take someone else's word on faith. A trusted authority tells you what is true and what is false. Young children believe what their parents tell them simply because Mommy and Daddy are always right. As children get older they may discover, unhappily, that Mom and Dad are not always correct when it comes to astrophysics, macroeconomics, computer technology, and other specialized fields of knowledge. Although this may cause children to doubt some of their parents' earlier proclamations, they may not completely reject this method of fixing belief. Instead, some other authority may be sought. Religious beliefs are formed by the method of authority. Long after children have rejected their parents as the source of all knowledge, they may still believe that the pope is infallible insofar as religious doctrine is concerned. Believing the evening news means that one accepts Dan Rather or some other news commentator as authority. You may believe your professors because they are authorities. Because people lack the resources to investigate everything they learn, much knowledge and many beliefs are fixed by the method of authority. Provided nothing happens to raise doubts about the competence of the authority setting the beliefs, this method offers the advantages of minimum effort and substantial security. It is most pleasant in a troubled world to have complete faith in beliefs handed down to you.

Another method of fixing belief is one in which a person steadfastly refuses to alter acquired knowledge, regardless of evidence to the contrary. The method of tenacity, as it was termed by Peirce, is commonly seen in racial bigots who rigidly cling to a stereotype even in the presence of a good counterexample. Although this method of maintaining a belief may not be entirely rational, we cannot say it is completely without value. Bigots are still around and somehow manage to find a few others to share their beliefs. The method of tenacity allows people to maintain a uniform and constant outlook on things, so it may relieve them from a certain amount of stress and psychological discomfort. For people who have difficulty handling stress, the method of tenacity may be a reasonable way to try to understand the world.

The third nonscientific method discussed by Peirce fixes belief a priori. In this context the term *a priori* refers to something that is believed without prior study or examination. Propositions that seem reasonable are believed. This is an extension of the method of authority. However, no one particular authority is being followed blindly in this method; rather, the general cultural outlook fixes belief a priori. People once believed the world was flat; and it did seem reasonable to suppose that the sun revolved around the earth as does the moon. Indeed, the world does look flat if you are not in a spacecraft.

The last of Peirce's methods, the **scientific method,** fixes belief on the basis of experience. If we define scientific psychology (as well as science in general) as a repeatable, self-correcting undertaking that seeks to understand phenomena on the basis of empirical observation, then we can see several advantages to science over the methods just outlined. Let us see what we mean by **empirical** and **self-correcting,** and examine the advantages associated with those aspects of science. First, none of those other methods relies on data (observations of the world) obtained by systematic observation. That is, the other methods do not have an empirical basis for fixing belief. The world *empirical* is derived from an old Greek word meaning *experience*. Having an empirical basis for beliefs means that experience rather than faith is the source of knowledge. Having one's beliefs fixed by authority carries no guarantee that the authority obtained data before forming an opinion. By definition, the method of tenacity refuses to consider data, as does the a priori method. Facts that are considered in these other modes of fixing belief are not ordinarily obtained by systematic procedures. For example, casual observation was the "method" that led to the ideas that the world was flat and that frogs spontaneously generated from the mud each spring, as Aristotle believed.

The second advantage of science is that it offers procedures for establishing the superiority of one belief over another. Persons holding different beliefs not based on science will find it difficult to reconcile their opinions. Science overcomes this problem. In principle, anyone can make an empirical observation, which means that scientific data can be public and can be repeatedly obtained. Through public observations, new beliefs are compared with old beliefs, and old beliefs are discarded if they do not fit the empirical facts. This does not mean that each and every scientist instantaneously drops outmoded beliefs in favor of new opinions. Changing scientific beliefs is usually a slow process, but eventually incorrect ideas are weeded out. Empirical, public observations are the cornerstone of the scientific method, because they make science a self-correcting endeavor and lead to scientific understanding.

## CONCEPT SUMMARY

Methods of fixing belief include
- *authority*
- *tenacity*
- *a priori*
- *scientific (empirical)*

---

# THE NATURE OF SCIENTIFIC EXPLANATION

Empirical observation and self-correction are the hallmarks of the scientific method. In this section we examine how these work in science and scientific psychology.

Let us first step back and look at the social loafing research in a general way. Casual observation and some applied work suggested the problem area to be investigated. Laboratory experiments indicated some characteristics of social loafing and tested some predictions about its nature. Eventually, the data from the experiments suggested a solution to the practical aspects of social loafing. The same data also were related to diffusion of responsibility, a more general theory in social psychology. This summary captures how science typically works: empirical observations made on the basis of either casual observations or more formal theories reveal something about those theories, which in turn can lead to further empirical work.

According to Harré (1983), this cyclical and self-correcting nature of science was first recognized by Francis Bacon (1561–1626). Bacon is credited with being the leading force in the scientific revolution that began in the seventeenth century (Jones, 1982). Although Bacon's analysis seems somewhat primitive today, he anticipated several important aspects of modern science that we explore in detail.

## Induction and Deduction

All approaches to science share certain basic elements. The most important of these are **data** (empirical observations) and **theory** (organization of concepts that permit prediction of data). Science needs and uses both data and theory, and our outline of research on social loafing indicates that they can be interlinked in a complex way. However, in the history of science, individual scientists have differed about which is more important and which comes first. Trying to decide this is a little like trying to decide whether the chicken or the egg comes first. Science attempts to understand why things work the way they do, and, as we will argue, understanding involves both data and theory.

Although Bacon recognized the importance of both data and theory, he believed in the primacy of empirical observations. Modern scientists also emphasize data and view progress in science as working from data to theory. Such an approach is an example of **induction**, in which reasoning proceeds from particular data to a general theory. The converse approach, which emphasizes theory predicting data, is called **deduction.** With deduction, reasoning proceeds from a general theory to particular data. Because many scientists and philosophers of science have argued for the primacy of one form of reasoning over the other, we will examine induction and deduction in some detail.

Because empirical observations distinguish science from other modes of fixing belief, many have argued that induction must be the way that science should work. As Harré (1983) states it, "observations and the results of experiments are said to be 'data,' which provide a sound and solid base for the erection of the fragile edifice of scientific thought" (p. 6). In the case of social loafing, the inductive position would be that the facts of social loafing derived from experimentation produced the theory of diffusion of responsibility.

One problem with a purely inductive approach has to do with the finality of empirical observations. Scientific observations are tied to the circumstances under which they are made. This means that the laws or theories that are induced from them also must be limited in scope. Subsequent experiments in different contexts may suggest another theory or modifications to an existing one. So, theories that are induced on the basis of particular observations can (and usually do) change when other observations are made. This, of course, is a problem only if one takes an authoritarian view of ideas and believes in clinging tenaciously to a particular theory. Theories induced from observations are tentative ideas not final truths. Changes in understanding that occur as a result of continued empirical work exemplify the self-correcting nature of science.

According to the deductive view, which emphasizes the primacy of theory, the important scientific aspect of the social loafing research is the empirical guidance provided by the formal theory of social loafing. Further, the more general theory, diffusion of responsibility, provides understanding of social loafing. The deductive approach holds well-developed theories in high regard. Casual observations, informal theories, and data take second place to broad theories that describe and predict a substantial number of observations.

From the standpoint of the deductive approach, scientific understanding means, in part, that a theory will predict that certain kinds of empirical observations should occur. In the case of social loafing, the theory of diffusion of responsibility suggests that monitoring individual performance in a group should reduce the diffusion of responsibility. In turn, measuring individual effort should reduce the amount of social loafing that is observed. Experimental tests of this prediction confirm it, as we have seen.

But what do correct predictions reveal? If a theory is verified by the results of experiments, a deductive scientist might have increased confidence in the veracity of the theory. However, empirical observations are not final and can change. The tentative nature of scientific understanding means that verifying or confirming a theory is not enough. Popper (1961), a philosopher of science, has suggested that good theories, like good hypotheses (see chapter 1), must be testable. The empirical predictions must be capable of tests that could show them to be false. This suggestion of Popper's has been called the **falsifiability view.** According to the falsifiability view, the temporary nature of induction makes negative evidence more important than positive support. If data confirm a prediction, one cannot say that the theory is true. However, if a theory leads to a prediction that is not supported by the data, then Popper would argue that the theory must be false, and it should be rejected. According to Popper, a theory can never be proven; it can only be disproven. The importance of falsification is discussed in the Application section.

One problem with the deductive approach has to do with the theories themselves. Most theories include many assumptions about the world that are difficult to test and may be wrong. In Latané's work one assumption underlying the general theory is that measuring a person's behavior in an experimental context does not change the behavior in question. Although this often is reasonable to assume, we will show later that people can react to being observed in unusual ways, which means that this assumption is sometimes wrong. If the untested assumptions are wrong, then a particular experiment that falsifies a theory may have falsified it for the wrong reasons. That is, the test of the theory

# APPLICATION

### The Importance of Falsification

Most students find the philosophical idea of falsifiability a difficult one to understand. Why is it important to try to disconfirm a hypothesis rather than simply confirm that it is correct? The primary reason is because confirming evidence could be consistent with any number of hypotheses or theories, but disconfirming evidence will rule out some. Negative evidence usually provides more meaningful information than does confirming evidence.

To see how this works, consider the following problem from an experiment by Wason (1977). Wason presented his subjects with the series 2 4 6, which was supposed to illustrate a particular rule. The people in Wason's experiment were to discover the rule by generating sequences that Wason would confirm or deny as being consistent with the rule he had in mind. One plausible hypothesis is that the rule is any series of even numbers increasing by two. Wason observed that people showed a persistent bias in selecting sequences confirming that hypothesis. They generated sequences such as: 8 10 12, 300 302 304, 620 622 624, and so on. Unfortunately, there are an infinite number of such strings, and although they confirm the theory of even numbers increasing by two, they do not rule out other hypotheses. Could the rule be any numbers increasing by two, such as 3 5 7? Could the rule be even more general, such as any three ascending numbers? To test the last hypothesis, the subjects would have to suggest a sequence such as 6 7 8. Participants rarely generated sequences like the last one, even though it would rule out the previous two hypotheses. Furthermore, any three ascending numbers was the rule.

In ordinary human reasoning, the bias to confirm hypotheses is striking even though it is not very productive. In scientific reasoning, the confirmation bias would limit scientific progress, because the bias would make self-correction unlikely. Why is there such a strong bias toward confirming hypotheses? Johnson-Laird (1988) notes that some confirmation is necessary, and he also notes that seeking ways to disconfirm a hypothesis is often difficult. Apparently, therefore, people take the easy way out and simply seek confirming evidence. If you are interested in pursuing this topic, Best (1989) reviews the large literature on reasoning and faulty reasoning.

may not have been fair or appropriate. One conclusion, then, is that the deductive approach by itself cannot lead to scientific understanding.

At this point you may be wondering whether scientific understanding is possible if both induction and deduction are not infallible. Do not despair. Science is self-correcting, and it can provide answers to problems, however temporary those answers may be. Scientific understanding changes as scientists ply their trade. We have a better understanding of social loafing now than we did before Latané and his coworkers undertook their research. Through a combination of induction and deduction, science progresses toward a more thorough understanding of its problems. Figure 2–1 illustrates how induction and deduction join to produce understanding.

By way of concluding this section, let us reexamine social loafing. Initially, positive experimental results bolstered our confidence in the general notion of social loafing. These results, in turn, suggested hypotheses about the nature of social loafing. Is it a general phenomenon that would influence even group-oriented individuals? Does it occur in the workplace as well as the laboratory? Positive answers to these questions are consistent with a diffusion-of-responsibility interpretation of social loafing.

In the next phase of the research, Latané and his colleagues attempted to eliminate other explanations of social loafing by falsifying predictions made by these alternative theories. In earlier work they tested a particular person's effort both when alone and when in a group. They subsequently reasoned that under these conditions a person might rest during the group test so he or she could allocate greater effort to the task when tested alone. To eliminate the possibility that allocation of effort rather than diffusion of responsibility accounted for social loafing, they conducted additional experiments in which a person was tested either alone or in a group—but not in both situations. Contrary to the allocation-of-effort hypothesis, the results showed that social loafing occurred when a person was tested in just that one condition of being in a group (Harkins, Latané, and Williams, 1980). Therefore, they concluded that diffusion of responsibility was a more appropriate account of social loafing than was allocation of effort.

Note the course of events here. Successive experiments pitted two possible outcomes against each other in the hopes that one possibility would be eliminated

**FIGURE 2–1**

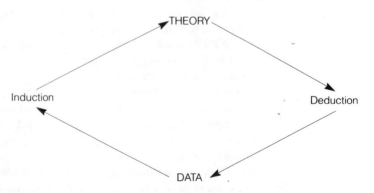

A theory organizes and predicts data. By means of deduction, particular observations (data) may be predicted. By means of induction, the data suggest organizing principles (theories). This circular relationship indicates that theories are tentative pictures of how data are organized.

and one supported by the outcome of the research. As Platt (1964) has noted, this eliminative procedure, which he calls **strong inference,** should, in the ideal case, yield one remaining theory (if the procedure of strong inference is used repeatedly). Of course, subsequent tests of the diffusion-of-responsibility theory might contradict it or add to it in some way. Thus, the theory might be revised or, with enough contradictions, rejected for an alternative explanation, itself supported by empirical observations. In any event, where we stand now is that we have constructed a reasonable view of what social loafing entails and what seems to cause it. The mixture of hypotheses induced from data and experimental tests deduced from testable hypotheses resulted in the theory that diffusion of responsibility leads to social loafing.

## CONCEPT SUMMARY

The scientific method involves
- *deduction*—reasoning from general to specific cases
- *induction*—reasoning from specific to general cases
- *strong inference*—eliminating possible alternative explanations

## What Is a Theory?

Thus far we have argued that scientific understanding is tentative: incorrect theories are modified and additional information is gathered through empirical tests about the problem at hand. In this section we focus on explaining theories.

A theory can be crudely defined as a set of related statements that explains a variety of occurrences. The more the occurrences, and the fewer the statements, the better the theory. The law of gravity explains falling apples, the behavior of roller coasters, and the position of bodies within the solar system. With a small number of statements about the mutual attraction of bodies, it explains a large number of events. It is therefore a powerful theory. (This does not necessarily mean it is a correct theory, because there are some events it cannot explain.)

Theory in psychology performs two major functions. First, it provides a framework for the systematic and orderly display of data—that is, it serves as a convenient way for the scientist to **organize** data. Even the most dedicated inductive scientist will eventually have difficulty remembering the outcomes of dozens of experiments. Theory can be used as a kind of filing system to help experimenters organize results. Second, it allows the scientist to generate **predictions** for situations in which no data have been obtained. As noted in chapter 1, these testable hypotheses guide research. The greater the degree of precision of these predictions, the better the theory. With the best of intentions, scientists who claim to be testing the same theory often derive from the theory different hypotheses about the same situation. This unfortunate circumstance is relatively more common in psychology, where many theories are stated in a loose verbal fashion, than in physics, where theories are more formal and better quantified through the use of mathematics. Although psychologists are rapidly becoming equipped to state their theories more precisely through such formal mechanisms as mathematics and computer simulations, the typical psychological theory still is not as precise as theories in other sciences.

Let us see how the theory devised by Latané to account for social loafing stacks up with regard to organization and prediction. The theory of diffusion of responsibility organizes a substantial amount of data about social loafing. More important, the theory seems to account for a remarkable variety of other observations. For example, Latané (1981) notes that the size of a tip left at a restaurant table is inversely related to the number of people in the dinner party. Likewise, proportionately more people committed themselves to Christ at smaller Billy Graham crusades than at larger ones. Finally, work by Latané and Darley (1970) shows that the willingness of people to help in a crisis is inversely related to the number of other bystanders present. The entire pattern of results can be subsumed under the notion of diffusion of responsibility, which asserts that people feel less responsibility for their own actions when they are in a group than when they are alone. So, people in groups are less likely to help in an emergency, they are less likely to leave a large tip, and so on. Latané's theory also makes rather precise predictions about the impact of the presence of other people on a person's actions. In fact, one version of the theory (Latané, 1981) presents its major assumptions in terms of mathematical equations.

Theories are devised to organize concepts and facts into a coherent pattern and to predict the results of future research. Sometimes the two functions of theory—organization and prediction—are called *description* and *explanation*, respectively. Unfortunately, formulating the roles of theory in this manner often leads to an argument about the relative superiority of deductive or inductive approaches to science—a discussion we have already dismissed as fruitless. According to the deductive scientist, the inductive scientist is concerned only with description. The inductive scientist defends against this charge by retorting that description is explanation. If a psychologist could correctly predict and control all behavior by referring to properly organized sets of results, then that psychologist would also be explaining behavior. The argument is futile because both views are correct. If all the necessary data were properly organized, predictions could be made without recourse to a formal body of theoretical statements. Because all the data are not properly organized as yet, and perhaps never will be, theories are required to bridge the gap between knowledge and ignorance. Remember, however, that theoretical explanation is tentative, because all the data will never be in. So, we have merely recast the argument between inductive and deductive views about which approach will more quickly and surely lead to truth. Ultimately, description and explanation may be equivalent. The two terms describe the path taken more than the eventual theoretical outcome. To avoid this pitfall, we refer to the two major functions of theory as **organization** and **prediction** rather than as description and explanation.

## CONCEPT SUMMARY

A theory
- *organizes data*
- *predicts new research*

## Intervening Variables

Theories often use constructs that summarize the effects of several variables. Variables are discussed at greater length in later chapters. Recall that in chapter 1 we discussed independent and dependent variables. Independent variables are those manipulated by the experimenter. For example, not allowing rats to have any water for several hours would create an independent variable called hours of deprivation. Dependent variables are those observed by the experimenter. For example, one could observe how much water a rat drinks.

Science tries to explain the world by relating independent and dependent variables. **Intervening variables** are abstract concepts that link independent variables to dependent variables. Gravity is a familiar construct that accomplishes this goal. It can relate an independent variable, how many feet of height an object is dropped, to a dependent variable, the speed of the object when it hits the ground. Gravity also summarizes the effects of height on speed for all manner of objects. Gravity explains falling apples as well as falling baseballs. Science progresses when a single construct, such as gravity, explains outcomes in many different environments. By connecting concepts to independent and dependent variables, scientists attempt to make their theories empirical and testable. Diffusion of responsibility is an intervening variable connected to group size on the one hand and individual behavior, such as work effort, on the other. If diffusion of responsibility were not measurable and producible, it would be a useless theoretical concept. Testable predictions concerning diffusion of responsibility can be made only if it can be varied (it is tied to an independent variable) and observed (it is tied to a dependent variable). The importance of testable concepts is considered further in the Psychology in Action section at the end of this chapter.

Miller (1959) has explained how a single intervening variable, thirst, organizes experimental results efficiently. Figure 2–2 shows a direct and an indirect way to relate an independent variable, hours of deprivation, to a dependent variable, rate of bar pressing. The dependent variable is obtained by placing a rat into a small chamber where it can press a bar to obtain drinking water. The experimenter observes the rate (how many presses per minute) that the rat presses the bar to get water. The direct relationship uses only one arrow to link hours of deprivation to rate of bar pressing. After doing the experiment, we could build a mathematical formula that directly related hours of deprivation to rate of bar pressing. The indirect method uses two arrows. The first arrow relates hours of deprivation to thirst, an intervening variable. The second arrow relates the intervening variable, thirst, to the rate of bar pressing. Because the

| FIGURE 2–2 | | | |
|---|---|---|---|

One set of variables.

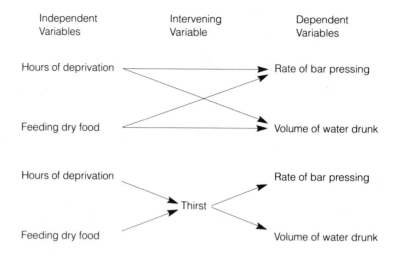

**FIGURE 2–3**

Two sets of variables.

indirect method is more complicated, requiring an extra arrow, you might expect the scientist to prefer the direct method of explanation. Indeed, if the only scientific goal were to relate hours of deprivation to rate of bar pressing, you would be correct because science prefers simple explanations to complex explanations. However, as we shall explain, the scientific goal is more general.

Figure 2–3 relates two independent variables, hours of deprivation and feeding dry food, to two dependent variables, rate of bar pressing and volume of water drunk. Again both direct and indirect explanations are shown. In figure 2–3 direct and indirect explanations are equally complex. Each requires four distinct arrows.

Figure 2–4 relates three independent variables, hours of deprivation, feeding dry food, and saline injection (giving a rat salt water through a tube inserted in its stomach), to three dependent variables, rate of bar pressing, volume of water drunk, and amount of quinine required to stop the rat from drinking. Again both direct and indirect explanations are shown. Now it is obvious that the indirect method is less complicated. It requires six distinct arrows, whereas the direct method requires nine arrows. So as science tries to relate more independent and dependent variables, intervening variables become more efficient.

Intervening variables have another advantage. Thirst, no matter how produced, should have the same effect on all dependent variables. This can be tested in experiments. If it is not true, we can reject the idea of a single intervening variable. Later chapters discuss this under the topic of converging operations.

## CONCEPT SUMMARY

Intervening variables
- *connect theoretical concepts to observables:*
  *independent variable* ⟶ *intervening variable* ⟶ *dependent variable*
- *provide economy in explanation*

| | | |
|---|---|---|
| **FIGURE 2–4** | | |

Three sets of variables.

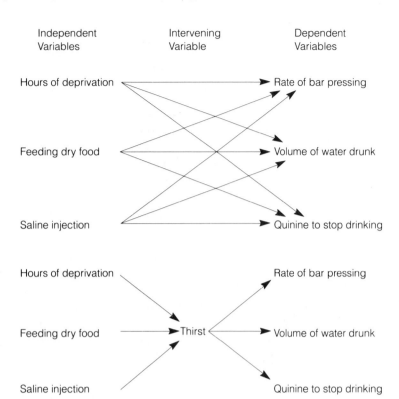

*Evaluating Theories*

The sophisticated scientist does not try to determine if a particular theory is true or false in an absolute sense. There is no black-and-white approach to theory evaluation. A theory may be known to be incorrect in some portion and yet continue to be used. In modern physics, light is represented, according to the theory chosen, either as discrete particles called quanta or as continuous waves. Logically, light cannot be both at the same time. Thus, you might think that at least one of these two theoretical views must necessarily be false. The physicist tolerates this ambiguity (although perhaps not cheerfully) and uses whichever representation—quantum or wave—is more appropriate. Instead of flatly stating that a theory is true, the scientist is much more likely to state that it is supported substantially by data, thereby leaving open the possibility that new data may not support the theory. Although scientists do not state that a theory is true, they must often decide which of several theories is best. As noted earlier, explanations are tentative; nevertheless, the scientist still needs to decide which theory is best for now. To do so, there must be explicit criteria for evaluating a theory. Three such criteria are **parsimony, precision,** and **testability.**

One criterion was hinted at earlier when we noted that the fewer the statements in a theory, the better the theory. This criterion is called parsimony, or sometimes Occam's razor, after William of Occam. If a theory needs a separate statement for every result it tries to explain, clearly no economy has been gained by the theory. Theories gain power when they can explain many results with few explanatory concepts. Thus, if two theories have the same number of concepts, the one that can explain more results is a better theory. If two theories can explain the same number of results, the one with fewer explanatory concepts is to be preferred. Here you can see the relationship between theories and intervening variables. Constructs, such as diffusion of responsibility, are intervening variables tied to several independent and dependent variables. The theoretical notion of diffusion of responsibility is parsimonious because it accounts for substantial amounts of data, as seen in our previous discussion.

Precision is another important criterion, especially in psychology, where it is often lacking. Theories that involve mathematical equations or computer programs are generally more precise, and hence better, than those that use loose verbal statements (all other things being equal, of course). Unless a theory is sufficiently precise so that different investigators can agree about its predictions, it is for all intents and purposes useless.

Testability goes beyond precision and is the most important aspect of a good theory, as we have emphasized in this chapter and the previous one. A theory can be very precise and yet not able to be tested. For example, when Einstein proposed the equivalence of matter and energy ($E = MC^2$), nuclear technology was not able to directly test this relationship. The scientist places a very high value on the criterion of testability, because a theory that cannot be tested can never be disproved. At first you might think this would be a good quality because it would be impossible to demonstrate that such a theory was incorrect. The scientist takes the opposite view, as we noted in the discussion of falsifiability. For example, consider ESP (extrasensory perception). Some believers in ESP claim that the presence of a disbeliever is sufficient to prevent a person gifted with ESP from performing, because the disbeliever puts out "bad vibes" that disrupt ESP. This means that ESP cannot be evaluated, because only believers can be present when it is demonstrated. The scientist takes a dim view of this logic, and most scientists, especially psychologists, are skeptical about ESP. Belief in a theory increases as it survives tests that could reject it. Because some future test possibly may find a flaw, belief in a theory is never absolute. If a theory cannot logically be tested, it cannot be evaluated; hence, it is useless to the scientist. If it is logically possible but not yet technically feasible, as was once the case with Einstein's theory, then evaluation of a theory is deferred.

## CONCEPT SUMMARY

Good theories are
- *parsimonious*
- *precise*
- *testable*

# THE SCIENCE OF PSYCHOLOGY

Some students find it difficult to think of psychology as a science in the same sense that physics and chemistry are sciences. They believe that there are aspects of human experience, such as the arts, literature, and religion, that defy scientific analysis. How can the beauty of a Klee lithograph, a Beethoven sonata, a Cartier-Bresson photograph be reduced to cold scientific equations? How can the tender feelings of a first romance, the thrill of driving a sports car at 100 miles per hour, and the agony of a defeated football team be captured in the objective, disinterested fashion required by science?

Some psychologists, known as humanists, would answer these questions in the negative. These humanists, most often clinical and counseling psychologists, claim that to evaluate and test human feelings and experience objectively by traditional scientific methods is impossible. Even tough, "brass-instrument" experimental psychologists concur that the domain of science is limited. We cannot establish or refute the existence of God by scientific means any more than we could test gravity by theological methods. Science operates where it can test hypotheses (see chapter 1). This does not mean that knowledge cannot be gained wherever science fears to tread—that is, by nonscientific means. Many important fields of human endeavor have yet to benefit from extensive scientific analysis—ethics, morals, law, to name but a few.

However, most scientists believe that scientific analysis eventually might be usefully applied to many such areas. Much of contemporary psychology was regarded as the sole property of philosophy at one time. As psychological techniques improved, these aspects of human expertise and behavior moved into the realm of science. And now most psychologists believe that virtually all facets of human experience are fair game for the science of psychology. If testable hypotheses can be made, then scientific psychology can be used. Deriding scientific progress in psychology, as did one U.S. senator who criticized the National Science Foundation for supporting research on romantic love (Elmes, 1988), will not halt efforts to expand psychological knowledge. Although concern for the proper and ethical use of such knowledge is valid and important, ignorance is no solution.

## Hard Science as a Model for Experimental Psychology

Psychologists can be arranged along a continuum according to how well they think physics and chemistry serve as a model for psychology to emulate. The "hard-shelled" psychologists think these older sciences are perfect models, whereas the "soft-shelled" psychologists believe that social sciences must find another model. Because we are experimental psychologists by trade, and because this book is intended as an experimental-psychology text, we tend to sample more from the hard-boiled end of the continuum.

All science has data and theory. What distinguishes among the different sciences, and among the subspecialties within a science like psychology, is the different techniques used. Astronomers do not need Skinner boxes any more than animal-learning psychologists need telescopes. Yet both practice science. A learning theorist's memory drum is not intrinsically superior to a social psychologist's "aggression machine." Even the modern microcomputer of an information-processing psychologist does not guarantee better science, although it may improve the odds. Most of this text is devoted to explaining the techniques needed in psychological research today. Although the hard-shelled psychologist does have more refined techniques, this is in part because of selection of problems that are amenable to sophisticated analysis. As psychology subjects more and more of human experience and behavior to scientific analysis, it is only natural that initial techniques may be crude. At one time this was true of hard-shelled psychology, too. Having a hard shell should not preclude one from having an open mind.

## Psychology and the Real World

Scientists in general, and psychologists in particular, have many reasons for pursuing their profession. We think it rather easy to prove that psychological research does serve humankind (see the Application section in chapter 1). We would like to stress that we do not find service to humankind the only, or necessarily the major, justification for a career as a research psychologist. Many scientists investigate certain problems simply because they find them interesting. We have complete sympathy with a colleague who might state that he or she studies gerbils just because gerbils provoke his or her curiosity. It is true that certain studies are performed on animals because they are unethical or imprac-tical to perform on humans—for example, studies of long-term crowding, pun-ishment, drugs, and so on—but it is equally true that the behavior of animals is interesting in its own right.

As noted in chapter 1, ideas for research come from both theoretical pre-dictions and practical problems, and scientific research is often divided into two categories: basic and applied. **Applied research** aims at solving a specific problem—such as how to cure bedwetting—whereas **basic research** has no immediate practical goal. Basic research establishes a reservoir of data, theo-retical explanations, and concepts that can be tapped by the applied researcher. Without this source, applied research would soon dry up and sputter to a halt, unless applied researchers became of necessity basic researchers. It takes quite a while for a concept developed by basic research to find some useful application in society. Adams (1972) traced five socially important products to discover the impact, if any, of basic research. Although basic research accounted for 70 percent of the significant events, these events occurred twenty to thirty years before the ultimate use of the product. This long time lag obscures the crucial role of basic research so that many persons incorrectly believe that basic research is not very useful to society. Often it is difficult to tell what basic research being done today will have an impact thirty years from now. But this inability to predict does not mean that we should stop doing basic research (Elmes, 1988).

Although the scientific quest for knowledge may be for one purpose only, usually basic and applied interests eventually intermingle in interesting ways, as demonstrated by the various kinds of research done on social loafing. Rin-gelmann's early observations of social loafing in the laboratory were also doc-umented in the workplace (Marriott, 1949). A potentially useful way to improve group productivity then arose from the laboratory work of Latané and his colleagues, who found that individual performance assessment can reduce social loafing.

The division of research into basic and applied categories is common, but a far more important distinction is between good and bad research. The prin-ciples and practices covered in this text apply with equal force to basic and applied research. You can and should use them to evaluate all the psychological research you encounter, whether as a student, a professional psychologist, or an educated person reading the daily newspaper.

**Are Experiments Too Far from Real Life?** Students of psychology typically demand a higher level of relevance in their psychology courses than they expect from other sciences. Students who are not at all dismayed that their course in introductory physics did not enable them to repair their automobile are often disturbed that their course in introductory psychology did not give them a better insight into their own motivations, did not cure their neuroses, and failed to show them how to gain eternal happiness. If you did not find such information in introductory psychology, we doubt that you will find it in this text either. If this seems unfair, read on.

The data that psychologists gather may at first seem unimportant, because an immediate relationship between basic psychological research and pressing social or personal problems may be difficult to establish. Naturally, people then doubt the importance of this research and wonder why the federal government, through various agencies, funds researchers to watch rats press bars or run through mazes.

The difficulty, however, is not with the research but with the expectations as to how "useful" research should be conducted. As noted by Sidman (1960), people expect progress to occur by the establishment of laboratory situations that are analogous to real-life situations: "In order to study psychosis in animals we must learn how to make animals psychotic." This is off the mark. The psychologist tries to understand the underlying *processes* rather than the physical situations that produce these processes. The physical situations in the real world and the laboratory need not be at all similar, provided that the same processes are occurring.

Suppose we would like to know why airplane accidents occur, or more specifically, what the relationship is between airplane accidents and failure of attention on the part of the pilot and/or the air traffic controller. A basic researcher might approach this problem by having college sophomores sit in front of several lights that turn on in rapid succession. The sophomore has to press a key as each light is illuminated. This probably seems somewhat removed from mid-air collisions of aircraft. Yet although the physical situations are quite different, the processes are similar. Pressing a key is an index of attention. Psychologists can overload the human operator by presenting lights faster than he or she can respond. Thus, this simple physical situation in a laboratory allows the psychologist to study failure of attention in a carefully controlled environment. In addition to the obvious safety benefits of studying attention without having to crash airplanes, we will show in later chapters that there are many scientific advantages to the laboratory environment. Because failures of attention are responsible for many kinds of industrial accidents (DeGreene, 1970, chapters 7 and 16), studies of attention by use of lights and buttons can lead to improvements outside the laboratory.

By the same token, establishing similar physical situations does not guarantee similarity of processes. One can easily train a rat to pick up coins in its mouth and bury them in its cage. But this does not necessarily mean that the "miserly" rat and the miserly human who keeps coins under his or her mattress do so because the same psychological processes are controlling their behaviors.

You also should be aware of two important reasons for doing research, the purposes of which (at least initially) may not be directly related to practical affairs (Mook, 1983). One reason that basic research aids understanding is that it often demonstrates what *can* happen. Thus under controlled conditions, it can be determined whether social loafing does occur. Furthermore, the laboratory affords an opportunity to determine the characteristics of social loafing more clearly than does the workplace, where a number of uncontrolled factors, such as salary and job security, could mask or alter the effects of social loafing (see chapter 3).

A second reason for the value of basic research is that the findings from a controlled, laboratory setting may have more force than similar findings obtained in a real-life setting. Showing that the human operator can be overloaded in a relatively nonstressful laboratory task suggests that attentional factors are crucial for performance. Individuals could be even more likely to be overloaded under the stressful conditions of piloting large passenger planes in crowded airspaces.

Of course, if a researcher wants to test a theoretical prediction or apply a laboratory result in an applied setting, then real-life tests will be necessary. Installing a way of assessing individual performance to reduce social loafing in a group manufacturing situation without first testing its applicability in that setting would be foolhardy. The moral, then, is that the researcher needs to be concerned with the goal of the experiments. The researcher or the evaluator of a piece of research should consider well that goal.

## CONCEPT SUMMARY

Good laboratory research
- *examines psychological processes*
- *shows what can happen in a controlled setting*
- *may have more force than real-life research*

One way to summarize the material presented in this chapter is to say that engaging in experimental psychology can be stimulating and enjoyable. The attempt to understand why people and animals behave as they do arises out of curiosity and the search for solutions to basic and applied problems. Although empirical procedures that rely on induction and deduction offer advantages over other methods of fixing belief, the advantages come with a cost. The cost is that theoretical explanations are always tentative because alternative theories lead to the search for new data, and new data provide the bases for modifications of existing theories. Paradoxically, the cost provides the scientific psychologist with a payment by helping to satisfy curiosity, at least temporarily, and by stimulating that curiosity into additional research and theory. Trying to answer questions about ourselves and animals is an exciting challenge. We hope that you are spurred by this challenge and are gratified by the application of sound psychological science to the understanding of behavior.

## SUMMARY

1. Scientific psychology is concerned with the methods and techniques used to explain why people and animals behave as they do. This curiosity may be

satisfied by basic or applied research, which usually go hand in hand to provide understanding.

2. Our beliefs are often established by the method of authority, the method of tenacity, or the a priori method. The scientific method offers advantages over these other methods because it relies on systematic, empirical observation and is self-correcting.

3. Scientists use both inductive and deductive reasoning to arrive at explanations of thought and action.

4. A theory organizes sets of data and generates predictions for new situations in which data have not been obtained.

5. A good theory is parsimonious, precise, and testable.

6. Laboratory research is concerned with the processes that govern behavior and with showing the conditions under which certain psychological processes can be observed.

## Key Concepts

| | |
|---|---|
| a priori method | method of tenacity |
| applied research | organization |
| basic research | parsimony |
| data | precision |
| deduction | prediction |
| diffusion of responsibility | scientific method |
| empirical | self-correcting |
| falsifiability view | social loafing |
| intervening variable | strong inference |
| induction | testability |
| method of authority | theory |

## Exercises

1. Make a list of five statements that might be considered true. Include some controversial statements (for example, men have lower IQs than women), as well as some you are sure are correct. Survey some of your friends by asking if they agree with these statements. Then, ask their justifications for their opinions. Classify their justifications into one of the methods of fixing beliefs discussed in this chapter.

2. Compare and contrast inductive and deductive approaches to science. Clarify your answers by referring to at least one branch of science outside experimental psychology.

3. Discuss social loafing research from the standpoint of strong inference.

4. Is it necessary (or even desirable) for experimental psychologists to justify their research in terms of applied benefits to society?

5. [*Special Exercise.*] In 1983, a researcher studied how three age groups felt about war. One group contained 10-year-olds, a second group consisted of 35-year-olds, and the last group was made up of 60-year-olds. Marked differences in their attitudes about war were observed. There is an important confounding variable in this study. What is it? Speculate on the effects of this confounding with regard to the attitudes of each

age group. (Hint: You might think about this question in terms of the generation gap.)

## Suggested Readings

Further information about the nature of science and scientific psychology may be found in: Kantowitz, B. H., and Roediger, H. L., III, and Elmes, D. G. (1991). *Experimental psychology: Understanding psychological research* (4th ed.). St. Paul: West.

Excellent discussions about the nature and importance of scientific psychology appear in these publications: Broadbent, D. E. (1973). *In defence of empirical psychology.* London: Methuen. Hebb, D. O. (1974). What psychology is about. *American Psychologist, 29,* 71–79. Sidman, M. (1960). *Tactics of scientific research.* New York: Basic Books.

For those of you who are particularly interested in the philosophy of science, we recommend these two books: Kendler, H. H. (1981). *Psychology: A science in conflict.* New York: Oxford. Mayr, E. (1982). *The growth of biological thought.* Cambridge, MA: Belknap Press.

## PSYCHOLOGY IN ACTION
### Intervening Variables and Testability

One way to gauge the value of a theory is to determine its testability. Theories are testable to the extent that the concepts can be manipulated and observed. Hence, connecting intervening variables to independent and dependent variables is crucial for scientific progress. You can assess theories in psychology by how well they define their intervening variables. If you examine a dictionary of psychology such as the one by Chaplin (1968), you can assess a theory. For example, Freud defines *personality* as "the integration of the id, the ego, and the superego." The crux of the definition of the *id* is "that division of the mind, or psyche, which is the seat of the libido. From it (the id) arise the animalistic, chaotic impulses which demand gratification." Are the Freudian notions of *personality* and the *id* formulated as intervening variables? What are the independent variables? What are the dependent variables? Can you generate testable hypotheses from Freud's ideas?

Dollard and Miller (1950) and many other experimentally oriented psychologists believe that Freud's theories do not allow testability. The primary reason is because most Freudian concepts are hard to connect to independent and dependent variables. Dollard and Miller tried to rephrase many of Freud's concepts so that they were intervening variables that could be studied in an objective way.

To assess the scientific value of other theories, you might try examining some other concepts in a dictionary of psychology. *Aggression* and *Sheldon's constitutional theory of personality* are two entries worth exploring for intervening variables.

**Observations are evaluated for**
    construct validity
    external validity
    internal validity

**Descriptive observations include**
    naturalistic observation
    case studies
    surveys

**Relational observations include**
    correlational technique

**Causation is best inferred from**
    experimental observations

# OBSERVATION IN
# PSYCHOLOGICAL RESEARCH

In this chapter we examine observations in psychology. First, we consider the validity or truth of observations, which is evaluated according to whether they have construct validity, external validity, and internal validity. Then, we provide an overview of descriptive and relational observations. Finally, we consider experimental observations from the standpoint of making causal statements about the effects of one variable on changes in another.

Science is an intellectual enterprise that builds cumulatively. From a scientific perspective, we know more about the world today than people have known at any other time in history. On the other hand, literature, art, and most other humanities may be different today than they were in ancient Greece, but we probably cannot say that these disciplines are in better shape or more accurately represent the world.

One primary reason that science cumulates is that scientists strive for the most accurate observation possible of the world. As we have stated, science is self-correcting in that scientists develop theories and hypotheses that allow prediction about what should happen under specified conditions. These ideas are then tested by comparing the predictions to carefully collected observations. When the observations differ drastically from predictions, scientists modify or abandon their theoretical conceptions. Much of the scientific enterprise concerns empirical observation: the collection of data on some particular aspect of the world.

Observers are fallible. Seeing should not be believing—at least not always. Often our perceptions fool us, as we can see by the way we perceive the optical illusions in figure 3–1. We have all seen magicians perform seemingly impossible feats before our eyes, when we knew that we were being tricked by natural means. Such tricks demonstrate that direct perceptions can be inaccurate if we are not careful, and sometimes even if we are.

Scientists, being human, are also subject to errors of observation. Essentially the research techniques employed by scientists—including logic, use of complicated apparatus, controlled conditions, and so on—are there to guard against errors of perception and to ensure that observations reflect the state of nature

**FIGURE 3–1**

(a)

(b)

(c)

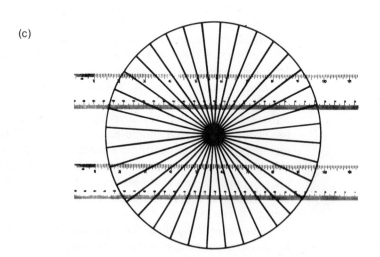

Visual illusions. (a) The Müller-Lyer illusion. The vertical lines are the same length, but appear unequal due to the different directions of the fins in the two cases. (b) The illusion apparently distorts even an objective measuring device, the ruler. But close examination indicates that the ruler is not really distorted and that the lines are of equal length. (c) The rulers now appear bent, due to the influence of the circle. These illusions are maintained even though we "know," as in (b), they cannot be so. Our observations can suffer distortions no matter how careful we are (examples taken from R. L. Gregory, 1970, pp. 80–81).

as accurately as possible. Even with our best methods and most careful techniques of observation, however, we can only approximate this ideal.

In this chapter we first consider the characteristics of sound (valid) observations and examine some of the difficulties associated with making them. Then we outline the major ways in which psychologists make observations.

## VALID OBSERVATIONS

Psychological observations provide scientific understanding by describing behavior (**descriptive observations**), relating two or more behaviors (**relational observations**), and explaining the causes of behavior (**explanation**). When do we know that our descriptions, relationships, and explanations are good? Good observations of any kind are valid. **Validity** in this context refers to the truth of the observations. Because scientific truth changes as new observations are made (see chapter 2), it is probably safest to assert that validity and its converse, invalidity, "refer to the best available approximation to the truth or falsity of propositions" (Cook & Campbell, 1979, p. 37). The validity of descriptions, relationships, and explanations is usually considered in three ways, which we examine in turn: construct validity, external validity, and internal validity.

### *Construct Validity*

In a particular research project, the degree to which the independent and dependent variables accurately reflect or measure what they are intended to measure is called **construct validity** (Cook & Campbell, 1979; Judd, Smith, & Kidder, 1991). Consider the Stroop experiment from chapter 1. Are the three levels of the independent variable used in that experiment valid reflections of reading? Certainly, each task involves reading, so at least for this research project we might safely assume that these are valid ways to test aspects of reading. What about the dependent variable—the time to go through the lists—is it a valid measure of reading? Certainly, how smoothly and quickly one reads is a good indicant of reading. However, there are at least two ways in which our measure may be invalid. One source of invalidity is that some confounding variable could have influenced reading times rather than the independent variable. If you had read the lists out loud as someone was timing you, you might have been somewhat nervous or apprehensive about being evaluated for your reading skill. This could have influenced your reading times in a number of different ways. Your apprehension may have led you to read faster and more accurately than usual so you would "look good." On the other hand, you might have been nervous and not performed as well as when you were not being timed by another person. Such reactivity by research participants is an important source of invalidity, and we discuss ways to control it in chapter 10.

A second threat to construct validity is random error. You or your partner may have misread the timing device, leading to a recording error in one or more of the conditions. This source of invalidity might be important in the Stroop experiment because different modes of timing might have been used by different

## FIGURE 3–2

The composition of a variable could include the construct of interest and two sources of invalidity: confounding variables and error (modified from Judd and others, 1991).

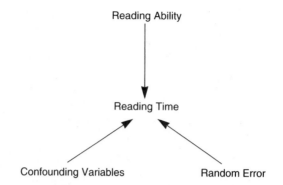

subjects. Thus, the dependent variable might not be a valid measure of reading time, and the experiment would have weak construct validity.

The above leads us to be suspicious about the construct validity of almost any variable that is manipulated and measured in psychological research. The reasons are shown in figure 3–2. A variable could be composed of the construct of interest as well as confounding influences and error (Judd and others, 1991). The extent to which the other sources enter into observations determines the degree of construct validity. So, a prudent researcher tries to minimize construct invalidity by limiting the possibility of confounding and error.

We consider several ways of minimizing construct invalidity throughout the text, two of which are considered here. The first involves operational definitions. An **operational definition** is a recipe for specifying how a construct, such as reading, is produced and measured. The conditions that produce the concept are carefully specified, and the ways in which the concept is to be measured are defined. A concept such as reading, therefore, becomes tied to the independent variables that produce it and the dependent variables that measure it. In this fashion an operational definition is similar to the way in which good theoretical constructs are defined (see the discussion of intervening variables in chapter 2). Operational definitions are an important aspect of research and theorizing, so they are discussed in substantial detail in chapter 10.

Although time was the dependent variable in the Stroop experiment, we need something besides an operational definition to ensure that the behavior is measured accurately. What we need is a protocol. A **protocol** is the specification of how the measurement is to be undertaken. Valid research adheres strictly to a protocol so that the behavior of all subjects is measured precisely, accurately, and the same under all levels of the independent variable.

Providing adequate operational definitions and following protocols do not guarantee construct validity, but they help to minimize invalidity, especially invalidity owing to random error.

## CONCEPT SUMMARY

**Construct validity** refers to the extent to which the variables accurately reflect or measure the behavior of interest

**Operational definitions** and **protocols** help minimize construct invalidity resulting from error

## External Validity

**External validity** refers to the extent to which one can generalize from the research setting and subject population to other settings and populations (Cook & Campbell, 1979). Observations with substantial external validity allow generalization to other situations and subject populations. Externally invalid observations are limited to the original research setting and population of subjects.

A researcher hopes that his or her observations represent a general psychological phenomenon. Thus, a prominent concern is **replication,** whether the observations can be replicated or repeated under different circumstances. In the Stroop experiment done in chapter 1, we would not be interested in those observations if they were true only for college students. We can be confident in the generalizability of the results to other subject populations, because replications of the experiment show that the ordering of the three conditions is the same for adults, high-school students, and college students.

A more serious threat to external validity relates to the experimental setting. The tasks do not seem representative of the kinds of reading that most people do. However, as we noted in chapter 2 and will detail later in chapter 10, the important criterion is not how realistic the tasks are but whether they represent an important psychological process. The general way to determine the generality is to conduct replications that vary the nature of the task and materials. A substantial variety of tasks have been used to induce the kind of conflict seen in our version of the Stroop experiment, which means that our observations have some external validity.

## CONCEPT SUMMARY

**External validity** refers to the extent to which the observations can be generalized to other settings and subject populations

**Replications** help assess the generality of the observations

## Internal Validity

**Internal validity** refers to whether one can make causal statements about the relationship between variables (Cook & Campbell, 1979). When observations are internally valid, the researcher can safely believe that one variable caused changes in another. If the observations are not internally valid, then the researcher is not able to make assertions about whether one variable caused another to change.

In principle, experimental observations permit causal statements. The experimenter varies the independent variable, which may cause changes in the dependent variable. Thus, we can say that a carefully conducted experiment is internally valid. In chapter 1 we discussed the internal validity of the Stroop experiment when we introduced the topic of confounding. We noted that the validity of the experiment was suspect because the levels of the independent variable were confounded with the order in which they were experienced. This means that the results of that experiment may not be internally valid, because something other than the independent variable might have caused the observed changes in the dependent variable. Because scientists often strive to determine what causes what, the bulk of this text concerns how to make internally valid observations.

As a conclusion to this section on validity, we would like to stress what should be obvious from the discussion so far—making valid scientific observations is difficult. Each of the observation procedures that we discuss next can suffer from the three kinds of invalidity, so it is important to be wary of invalidity when conducting your own research and evaluating the research of others. Another source of error in making observations comes from the observer or scientist. The Application section considers some of the psychological factors that can undermine the validity of observations.

# APPLICATION

### Difficulties of Observation

Direct observation may seem a straightforward and simple process: we open our eyes, look hard, and see what is there. But the history of science is replete with examples of phenomena that have eventually turned out to be radically different from the way they were initially perceived. We consider two examples here, one from psychology and one from physics, to show that scientists must be continually vigilant for errors in their own observations.

Ivan P. Pavlov (1849–1936) was a Russian physiologist who won the Nobel Prize for medicine in 1904 for his work on how gastric juices operate during digestion. Pavlov also made important contributions to psychology by identifying and studying classical (or Pavlovian) conditioning. When Pavlov began studying learning in dogs, he and his coworkers discovered they had a problem that had not been apparent when they had previously been concerned only with the digestive system. The difficulty lay in how to describe the behaviors they were observing. Pavlov describes the problem of studying conditioned reflexes:

> But how is this to be studied? Taking the dog when he eats rapidly, snatches something in his mouth, chews for a long time, it seems clear that at such a time the animal strongly desires to eat, and so rushes to the food, seizes it, and falls to eating. He longs to eat. . . . When he eats, you see the work of the muscles alone, striving in every way to seize the food in the mouth, to chew and to swallow it. From all this we can say that he derives pleasure from it. . . . Now when we proceeded to explain and analyze this, we readily adopted this trite point of view. We had to deal with the feelings, wishes, conceptions, etc., of our animal. The results were astounding, extraordinary; I and one of my colleagues came to irreconcilable opinions. We could not agree, could not prove to one another which was right. . . . After this we had to deliberate carefully. It seemed probable we were not on the right track. The more we thought about the matter, the greater grew our conviction that it was necessary to choose another exit. The first steps were very difficult, but along the way of persistent, intense, concentrated thinking I finally reached the firm ground of pure objectivity. We absolutely prohibited ourselves (in the laboratory there was an actual fine imposed) the use of such psychological expressions as the dog guessed, wanted, wished, etc. (Pavlov, reprinted 1963, pp. 263–264).

A second problem is relevant to observation in all types of research. This is the issue of how much our conceptual schemes determine and bias what we "see." Pavlov's statement is eloquent testimony to the difficulty of establishing objective methods that would enable us all to see things in the same way. He had found it initially "astounding" and "extraordinary" that this difficulty existed and was surprised at the elaborate precautions needed to ensure objectivity. Philosophers of science have pointed out that our observations are always influenced by our conceptions of the world—if in no other way, at least by the particular observations we make (see, for example, Hanson, 1958, chapter 2). "Pure objectivity," to use Pavlov's phrase, is quite elusive, if not impossible. Objective and repeatable observation in science is an ideal to be approximated, but we may never be completely confident that we have achieved it. Nevertheless, we must make every possible step toward this ideal, which is what much of the technical paraphernalia of science is designed to help us with.

The problem of observations being unduly influenced by expectations is not, however, automatically overcome by the use of sophisticated equipment, as is evident in an illustration cited by Hyman (1964, p. 38). In 1902, shortly after X rays were discovered, the eminent French physicist Blondlot reported the discovery of "N rays." Other French scientists quickly repeated and confirmed Blondlot's discovery; in 1904, no fewer than 77 publications appeared on the topic. However, the discovery became controversial when American, German, and Italian scientists failed to replicate Blondlot's findings.

The American physicist R. W. Wood, failing to find N rays in his own lab at Johns Hopkins University, visited Blondlot. Blondlot displayed a card to Wood with luminous circles painted on it. Then he turned down the room light, fixed N rays on the card, and pointed out to Wood that the circles increased in luminosity. When Wood said he could see no change, Blondlot argued that this must be because Wood's eyes were too insensitive. Next, Wood asked if he could perform some simple tests, to which Blondlot consented. In one case, Wood moved a lead screen repeatedly between the N rays and the cards, while Blondlot reported the corresponding changes in luminosity of the circles on the card. (The lead shield was to prevent passage of the N rays.) Blondlot was consistently in error, and often reported a change in luminosity when the screen had not been moved. This and other tests clearly indicated that there was no evidence for the existence of N rays, despite their "confirmation" by other French scientists.

After 1909, there were no further publications on N rays. The mistake was too much for Blondlot. He never recovered, and he died in disgrace some years later. We can see from this dramatic example that even with the sophisticated apparatus of physicists, errors of observation are possible and must be guarded against.

Hanson, N. R. (1958). *Patterns of discovery.* Cambridge: Cambridge University Press.
Hyman, R. (1964). *The nature of psychological inquiry.* Englewood Cliffs, N.J.: Prentice-Hall.
Pavlov, I. P. (1963). *Lectures on conditioned reflexes.* New York: International Publishers.

## CONCEPT SUMMARY

**Internal validity** concerns whether one can make causal statements about the relationship between variables

**Confounding** is a major threat to internal validity

# DESCRIPTIVE OBSERVATIONS

The most obvious ways of making observations in psychology have description of behavior as their major purpose. Descriptive observations enumerate what behaviors occur and in what quantity and frequency.

In this chapter we discuss three descriptive methods of gathering psychological data. One such method is **naturalistic observation,** which is the most obvious and, perhaps, the most venerable way of gathering data. Many people, such as bird-watchers, are amateur naturalists, but scientific naturalists, as we will see, are more systematic in their observations. For example, recent work has shown that when the risk of attack by predator hawks is imminent, chickadees give a much higher alarm call than when the risk posed by the predator is not so serious (Ficken, 1990).

An additional classic way of obtaining information is the **case study,** in which detailed information is gathered about a single individual. A recent case study revealed that when Ruth L., age 30, came to therapy, she was showering six or more times daily, washing her hands three times an hour, and completely cleaning her apartment twice daily (Leon, 1990).

Similar to the case study is the **survey,** in which detailed information is gathered from a number of individuals. Colasanto (1989) interviewed people in the San Francisco Bay Area the day following the earthquake that occurred on October 17, 1989. Thirty-seven percent of those people claimed to have been very frightened by the earthquake, and 15 percent of the Bay Area people were not frightened at all.

Another recent survey attempted to determine the sorts of memory problems suffered by elderly Americans (Lovelace and Twohig, 1990). Healthy, older adults with an average age of 68 claim that the most vexing memory problem they have is an inability to remember someone's name. However, most of these respondents report that memory difficulties have little effect on their daily functioning.

Descriptive research plays an important role in psychology. These procedures provide a major part of the database that can lead to subsequent more highly controlled research (Miller, 1977). Description of behavior is a necessary first step in understanding. A familiar example is Harlow's (1958) work on mother love in infant monkeys. Prior to his experiments, Harlow needed to know what behaviors baby monkeys exhibited; he also needed to know some of the things they seemed to like (their soft blankets) and dislike (the wire floor of the cage). With this background information, Harlow could attempt to explain the behavior via experimentation. Thus, we should not view description as somehow secondary or subordinate to experimentation because it lacks control. In the sense just mentioned, description is prior to experimentation. Now we examine the descriptive procedures in more detail.

## *Naturalistic Observations*

One problem facing a person wishing to make naturalistic observations is determining what behaviors to observe. Human observers have a finite capacity to perceive and think about events. Although most of us can walk and chew gum at the same time, most of us cannot attend to and remember twenty different behaviors occurring over short periods of time. Thus, we must set a boundary on the range of behaviors that we plan to observe.

How do we delimit the range of behaviors to be studied? Part of the answer seems straightforward. If we are interested in human nonverbal communication, we observe it. However, this is not necessarily easy to do. In the first place, nonverbal communication is highly complex, which means that observers are faced with the same problem we started out trying to avoid. In the second place, examining nonverbal behavior presupposes that we already know some of the behaviors to describe. Obviously, we do not enter a research project devoid of all knowledge, which is especially the case when we are trying to test certain hypotheses. However, we do not begin description with all the answers. What usually happens is that we begin a series of studies, in which successive projects rely on previous data to refine and delimit the field of inquiry. Let us consider some examples to illustrate how naturalistic observations are conducted.

**Ethology.** Naturalistic research of interest to psychologists is perhaps most prevalent in the area of **ethology,** the study of naturally occurring behavior (often in the wild). Simply observing the behavior of animals or humans allows one to gain a global impression of the characteristics and range of behavior. However, one may soon desire more systematic observation. One way ethologists make more systematic observations is by identifying different categories of experience for the organism under study and then recording the number of times the organism engages in each behavior. These behaviors can be divided into large units such as mating, grooming, sleeping, fighting, eating, and so on, or into much smaller units. For example, an **ethogram** of the various behaviors involved in the courtship pattern of a fish, the orange chromide, is shown in figure 3–3. An ethogram is a relatively complete inventory of the specific behaviors performed by one species of animal. By counting the number of times that any specific behavior occurs, ethologists can begin to get some idea of the significance of the behavior.

This was the way in which Ficken (1990) was able to isolate the types of alarm calls made by chickadees. Obviously, however, Ficken had to be able to record and analyze the checkadees' vocal output. Obtaining accurate records of an animal's behavior in the wild is often difficult. It may be hard to observe an animal continuously in its natural habitat. Researchers cannot remain forever vigilant. The presence of human observers may make the measures reactive. These are only some of the greatest problems. Applying similar techniques to human behavior is even more difficult, for people do not usually appreciate having their every action noted by curious scientists.

Barker and his associates (for example, Barker and Wright, 1951; Barker, 1968) were pioneers in applying methods of naturalistic observation to humans in a number of settings. Let us examine some naturalistic observations of humans.

**Flashing eyebrows.** The famous ethologist of human behavior Eibl-Eibesfeldt (for example, 1970, 1972) has done a substantial amount of field research on human facial expressions. He and his colleagues traveled around the world taking pictures of facial expressions in a variety of contexts. Careful examination of the expressions indicated that many are similar across cultures, and some

**FIGURE 3–3**

a. *Charging:* An accelerated swim of one fish toward another.

b. *Tail Beating:* An emphatic beating of the tail toward another fish.

c. *Quivering:* A rapid, lateral, shivering movement that starts at the head and dies out as it passes posteriorly through the body.

d. *Nipping:* An O-shaped mouth action that cleans out the (presumptive) spawning site.

e. *Skimming:* The actual spawning movement whereby the fish places its ventral surface against the spawning site and meanders along it for a few seconds.

Ethogram showing courtship pattern in orange chromide. An ethogram can be compiled for all behaviors of a species, or for only selected aspects of behavior. (From Drickamer, L. C., and Vesey, S. H. *Animal Behavior: Concepts, Processes, and Methods.* Boston: Willard Grant Press, 1982, p. 28).

are not. In the process of examining facial expressions associated with people greeting each other, Eibl-Eibesfeldt discovered that most humans give a brief eyebrow flash. He went on to examine this phenomenon in detail.

Generally, the eyebrow flash is a brief (one-sixth of a second) raising of the eyebrows, accompanied by a slight smile and a quick nod of the head. The eyebrow flash has been observed in people of many cultures, including Bushmen, Balinese, and Europeans. However, some cultures seem to differ in their uses of the eyebrow flash. The Japanese do not use the flash, because in Japan it is considered suggestive or indecent. Furthermore, Eibl-Eibesfeldt found that the flash occurred in other circumstances, such as in flirting and acknowledging a gift or service (that is, as a kind of thank you), in addition to greeting.

We can see from his work that previous observations suggested additional ones for Eibl-Eibesfeldt, and by delimiting his range of inquiry he was able to garner substantial information about a common human behavior.

**Testing neonates.**  Another example of refinement comes from studies of newborn humans (neonates). What do neonates do and what can we look for in their behavior? Most people think of neonates as being limited in their behavior. However, neonates can do more than eat, sleep, eliminate, and cry. All their senses are operative, and they possess a number of complex reflexes. Brazelton and his associates (for example, Lester and Brazelton, 1982) have spent many years refining a scale to assess the optimal performance of neonates in a variety of behaviors. Initially, the scale assessed reflexes (squeezing, blinking) and a few behaviors. Repeated observations of neonates from a variety of cultures and in a variety of situations led to changes, which, in turn, caused more changes. The resulting Brazelton Neonatal Behavioral Assessment Scale contains measurements of sixteen reflexes and twenty-six behaviors. The reflexes are rated on a three-point scale (low, medium, and high), and the behavioral items, such as responses to a pinprick and hand-to-mouth activity, are rated on nine-point scales.

Earlier observations had suggested that the level of arousal was very important in respect to the appearance and magnitude of certain behaviors, so the current scale indicates when the neonate should be assessed on the various behaviors. For example, responses to a pinprick are assessed when the neonate is asleep or quiet, but not when the neonate is alert or crying. Hand-to-mouth behaviors can be assessed during any state.

Brazelton and his coworkers have been particularly concerned with individual and cultural differences in development, and they have conducted a substantial amount of more controlled research to examine these differences. The controlled research would not have been possible had they not made the exhaustive series of observations that led to the development of the assessment scale.

## The Case Study

Another venerable form of inquiry in psychology is the case study. Freud's psychoanalytic theory arose from his observations and reflections on individual cases. In general, a case study is the intensive investigation of a single case of some sort, whether of a neurotic patient, a spiritual medium, or a group awaiting the end of the world. An interesting case study of this last instance was provided by Festinger, Riecken, and Schachter (1956), who infiltrated a small group of persons who were indeed awaiting the end of the world. The members thought themselves to be in contact with beings from another planet, who had communicated to one member that the destruction of the earth was near. The group was expecting to be rescued by spacecraft before the catastrophe. Festinger and his colleagues were especially interested in the reactions of the group when (if?) the calamity did not occur. They observed that for many of the members of the group, belief in its delusional system actually increased rather than decreased after the predicted date of catastrophe had passed.

The case study is a type of naturalistic observation and is subject to all the disadvantages and the few advantages (to be discussed shortly) of that method. One chief disadvantage is that case studies usually do not allow firm inferences to be made about what causes what. Typically, all one can do is describe the course of events. Often, however, case studies provide implicit comparisons that allow the researcher to make some reasonable guesses as to what causes what. The case study of Ruth L., the compulsive cleaner mentioned earlier, revealed a very stern upbringing that involved an excessive emphasis on cleanliness and neatness. Because the severity of this emphasis on cleanliness was greater than that experienced by most people, the therapist concluded that it was a causal factor in her current compulsion to be neat and clean. This sort of conclusion needs to be tentative, however, because we do not know what kind of adult Ruth L. would have become had she had a more ordinary childhood.

A type of case study that best attempts to minimize the difficulties of making inferences is the **deviant-case analysis.** Here the researcher considers two cases that bear a number of similarities and yet differ in outcome. For example, one twin brother might become schizophrenic and the other not. The researcher attempts to pinpoint, through a careful comparison of the two cases, the factors that are responsible for the difference in outcome. Such comparisons usually cannot be made, because comparable cases that differ in only one factor are rare. Furthermore, any conclusions even from this method cannot really be considered firm or well established, because the researcher can never be certain that he or she has identified the critical causes in the differing outcomes.

These cautions notwithstanding, let us consider a case study recently reported by Butters and Cermak (1986) that illustrates how judicious use of the procedure can provide valuable information. The study is about P.Z., a world-famous scientist who suffered from severe memory loss (amnesia) in 1981 after long-term alcohol abuse. He had extreme difficulty both in remembering new information and in recollecting past events and people. The latter memory deficit was easy to determine, because two years prior to the onset of amnesia, P.Z. had written his autobiography. When he was queried about the names and events mentioned in his autobiography, he showed a drastic memory deficit. P.Z.'s memory for these events was compared with the retention of a similar-aged colleague (the comparison person for deviant-case analysis) who did not have a history of alcohol abuse. The comparison case did not show a memory deficit as serious as P.Z.'s, so Butters and Cermak reasoned that the long-term alcohol abuse was an important causal factor in P.Z.'s amnesia. Furthermore, P.Z.'s memory deficit for new information was very similar to that shown by other people with a history of alcohol abuse. This latter technique of comparing the case's behavior with that of others is essentially an experimental one, and this procedure is emphasized throughout this text.

## Survey Research

Case studies usually involve only a few subjects, and often these individuals are not at all representative of the population at large. P.Z., for example, was both a brilliant scientist and an amnesiac. Often researchers want to obtain information on a large random sample of people in a large geographic area (such as the Bay Area survey mentioned at the beginning of this section), even though the amount of information obtained from any one person is necessarily limited. This technique is little used in most areas of psychology, though it is familiar to most of you through its use in predicting elections and the like. With the precise sampling procedures now available, relatively few people can be queried, and the results will nonetheless generalize well to the population at large.

Because the survey leads to results that are generally descriptive in nature, this method is not particularly popular with psychologists. Nevertheless, clever use of the method may allow contributions to some areas of psychology. The work by Lovelace and Twohig (1990) that was summarized briefly at the outset of this section is a good example. The elderly subjects whom they surveyed reported that they relied very strongly on notes, lists, and other external memory aids to help them remember to do things. Further, the elderly respondents claimed not to rely on various memory "tricks" such as mnemonic devices. The results reported by Lovelace and Twohig agree with other survey data (Moscovitch, 1982), which show that compared with younger people, the elderly are much more likely to make lists and use date books and are less likely to resort to internal memory procedures, such as mnemonic devices. These results are provocative, because they suggest that the elderly are somehow aware that they may have some memory limitations, which they try to minimize by relying on external memory aids. However, more controlled research is necessary before that conclusion can be confirmed.

## Advantages and Disadvantages of Descriptive Observations

As noted earlier, descriptive observation is extremely useful in the early stages of research, when one desires simply to gain some idea as to the breadth and range of the problem of interest (Miller, 1977). It does not, however, allow one to infer how factors may be related. In some cases, there is no way to employ more controlled methods of observation; therefore, only descriptive ones are available. If you want to know how penguins behave in their natural habitat, you simply have to observe them there. Still, for most psychological problems, descriptive observation is useful primarily in defining the problem area and raising interesting questions for more controlled study by other means, especially experimental ones. For example, the case study by Festinger and his colleagues of the group predicting the end of the earth helped lead to Festinger's (1957) cognitive dissonance theory of attitude change, which has been quite important in guiding social psychological research.

The primary problem unique to descriptive observation is that it does not allow us to assess relations among events. An investigator might note that grooming behavior in free-ranging monkeys occurs at certain times, following five different prior conditions (such as eating). If one is interested in finding out which antecedent conditions are necessary to produce grooming, descriptive observation cannot provide an answer, because these antecedent conditions cannot be manipulated. For this, one needs an experiment.

Descriptive observation typically produces data that are deficient in other ways, too. Scientific data should be easy to reproduce by other people using standardized procedures, if these people doubt the observations or are interested in repeating them. Many descriptive methods, such as the case study, do not allow reproducibility; they are thus open to question by other investigators.

Another problem in descriptive approaches is maintaining as strictly as possible a descriptive rather than an interpretive level of observation. In the study of animals, the problem is often one of **anthropomorphizing,** or attributing human characteristics to animals. When you come home and your dog wags its tail and moves about excitedly, it seems perfectly natural to say that it is happy to see you. But this is anthropomorphizing, and if one were engaged in descriptive observation of the scene, it would be inappropriate. Instead, one should record the overt behaviors of the dog with the least possible attribution of underlying motives, such as happiness, sadness, or hunger.

Of course, the case studies of Freud are based entirely on just such interpretations of the facts. Besides being nonreproducible, such cases suffer from the possibility that if we are allowed to (a) select our data from case studies and answers people give to the questions we ask, and then (b) weave these "facts" into a previous conceptual system of our own devising, case studies could probably be used to "prove" any theory. This is not to detract from the creative flair and genius that are evident in Freud's system; he is, however, certainly open to criticism in terms of the evidence on which it is based.

## CONCEPT SUMMARY

Descriptive observations are made by
- *naturalistic observations*
- *case studies*
- *surveys*

Descriptive observations suffer from
- *lack of reproducibility*
- *anthropomorphism*
- *internal invalidity*

## RELATIONAL OBSERVATIONS

Scientists are not long contented with the type of descriptive information that is derived from observational studies. Of much greater interest is how two *variables* are related to one another. The use of correlational techniques permits us to assess and specify the degree of relation between two variables of interest, generally with the hope that given one variable, we can predict the other. The assessment is usually made **ex post facto,** or after the fact. All this means is that the observations of interest are collected and then a **correlation coefficient,** which indicates the degree of relation between the two variables or measures, is computed.

One typical example of the correlational approach is the exploration of the relation between cigarette smoking and lung cancer. Studies in the 1950s and early 1960s consistently found a moderately high positive correlation between cigarette smoking and lung cancer: the greater the number of cigarettes a person smoked, the more likely that person was to have lung cancer. Knowledge of this relation allows predictions to be made. From the knowledge of how much someone smokes, we can predict (though not perfectly) how likely that person is to contract cancer, and vice versa. The Surgeon General's report in 1964, which concluded that smoking was dangerous to health, was based almost entirely on correlational evidence. We shall consider some problems in interpreting correlational evidence; but first, let us consider the properties of the correlation coefficient itself.

## The Correlation Coefficient

There are several different types of correlation coefficients, but almost all have in common the property that they can vary from $-1.00$ through $0.00$ to $+1.00$. Commonly, they will not be one of these three figures, but something in between, such as $+.72$ or $-.39$. The _magnitude_ of the correlation coefficient indicates the degree of relationship (larger numbers reflecting stronger relations), and the _sign_ indicates the direction of the relation, positive or negative. Putting the appropriate sign in front of the correlation coefficient is necessary, because otherwise one cannot know which way the two variables are related, positively or negatively. It is common practice, though, to omit the plus sign before positive correlations, so that a correlation of $.55$ would be interpreted as $+.55$. It is a better practice always to include the sign. An example of a _positive_ correlation is the relation between lung cancer and smoking. As one variable increases, so does the other (though not perfectly, that is, the correlation coefficient is less than $+1.00$). There is also a documented _negative_ correlation between smoking and another variable, namely, grades in college. People who smoke a lot have tended to have lower grades than those who smoke less (Huff, 1954, p. 87).

There are actually several different types of correlation coefficients, and which is used depends on the characteristics of the variables being correlated. We shall consider one commonly used by psychologists: **Pearson's product-moment correlation coefficient**, or **Pearson r**. Because this is only one of several, you should consult a statistics text to determine which is appropriate for your particular case.

Let us imagine that we are one of the many psychologists who devote their careers to the study of human memory. We hit upon a simple, intuitive idea concerning head size and memory: information from the outside world enters the head through the senses and is stored there. An analogy can be made between the head (where information is stored) and other physical vessels, such as boxes, where all kinds of things can be stored. On the basis of such analogical reasoning, which is common in science, we make the following prediction from our knowledge of the properties of physical containers: as head size of a person increases, so should the person's memory. More things can be stored in bigger boxes than in smaller, and similarly more information should be stored in larger heads than in smaller ones.

This "theory" proposes a positive correlation: as head size increases, so should memory. A random sample of the local population could be taken. The persons chosen could be measured on two dimensions: head size and the number of words they can recall from a list of thirty, presented to them once, at the rate of one word every three seconds. Three hypothetical sets of results from ten subjects are presented in table 3–1. For each individual there are two measures, one of head size and the other of number of words recalled. Also, the two types of measures need not be similar in any way to be correlated. They do not have to be on the same scale. Just as one can correlate head size with number of words recalled, one could also correlate I.Q. with street-address number, or any two sets of numbers at all.

The mathematical assessment of correlation coefficients is discussed in appendix A. If you are unfamiliar with this material, you might review box

**TABLE 3–1**   THREE HYPOTHETICAL EXAMPLES OF DATA TAKEN ON HEAD SIZE AND RECALL, REPRESENTING (A) A POSITIVE CORRELATION, (B) A LOW (NEAR-ZERO) CORRELATION, AND (C) A NEGATIVE CORRELATION.

| Subject | (a) Head size (cm.) | Recall (words) | Subject | (b) Head size (cm.) | Recall (words) | Subject | (c) Head size (cm.) | Recall (words) |
|---|---|---|---|---|---|---|---|---|
| 1 | 50.8 | 17 | 1 | 50.8 | 23 | 1 | 50.8 | 12 |
| 2 | 63.5 | 21 | 2 | 63.5 | 12 | 2 | 63.5 | 9 |
| 3 | 45.7 | 16 | 3 | 45.7 | 13 | 3 | 45.7 | 13 |
| 4 | 25.4 | 11 | 4 | 25.4 | 21 | 4 | 25.4 | 23 |
| 5 | 29.2 | 9 | 5 | 29.2 | 9 | 5 | 29.2 | 21 |
| 6 | 49.5 | 15 | 6 | 49.5 | 14 | 6 | 49.5 | 16 |
| 7 | 38.1 | 13 | 7 | 38.1 | 16 | 7 | 38.1 | 14 |
| 8 | 30.5 | 12 | 8 | 30.5 | 15 | 8 | 30.5 | 17 |
| 9 | 35.6 | 14 | 9 | 35.6 | 11 | 9 | 35.6 | 15 |
| 10 | 58.4 | 23 | 10 | 58.4 | 16 | 10 | 58.4 | 11 |
|  | $r = +.93$ |  |  | $r = -.07$ |  |  | $r = -.89$ |  |

A–1, where the mathematical formula for $r$ is presented. Pearson $r$ is calculated for the data presented in (a) column of table 3–1. Working through this example will help you better understand the basis of correlation coefficients. Researchers seldom use the mathematical formula to calculate $r$ by hand. Most researchers now rely on calculators or computers to calculate correlation coefficients for them.

To give you a better idea of the graphical representation of correlations, called **scatter diagrams,** the data in the three panels of table 3–1 are presented in the three panels of figure 3–4, head size is plotted along the horizontal $X$-axis (the abscissa), and number of words recalled is plotted along the vertical $Y$-axis (the ordinate). The high positive correlation between head size and number of words recalled in the (a) panel in table 3–1 is translated into a visual representation that tilts upward to the right, whereas the negative correlation in panel (c) is depicted as sloping downward to the right. Thus you can see how knowing a person's score on one variable helps predict (though not perfectly in these cases) the level of performance on the other. So knowing a person's head size in the hypothetical data in the (a) and (c) panels helps predict recall, and vice versa. This is the primary reason correlations are useful: they specify the strength of relations and allow predictions to be made. This last statement cannot be made about the data in panel (b), where there is essentially a zero correlation. The points are just scattered about, and there is no consistent relation, which is just what a low Pearson $r$ reflects. Even in the cases where the size of the correlation is rather large, it will not be possible to predict perfectly an individual's score on one variable given his or her position on the other. Even with $r = +.75$ between head size and number of words recalled, it is still quite possible for a person with a large head size to recall few words, and vice versa. Unless the correlation is perfect ($+1.00$ or $-1.00$), prediction of one score when given the other will not be perfect, either.

What do you think the real correlation would be between head size and recall for a random sample of the population at large? Although we have not

FIGURE 3–4

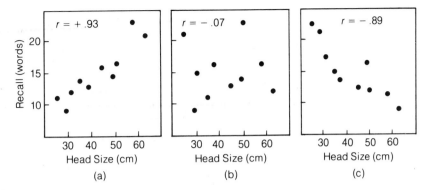

Graphical representation of the data in Table 3–1, showing the characteristic pattern of (a) a high positive correlation, (b) an essentially zero correlation, and (c) a strong negative correlation.

actually done such a study, we think it quite likely that it would be rather large and positive (perhaps +.60 to +.70), in support of the theory of memory storage based on head size. What can we conclude from this? How can correlation coefficients be interpreted? We turn to this issue next.

**Interpreting correlation coefficients.** An important warning is always given in any discussion of correlation: The existence of even a sizable correlation implies nothing about the existence of a causal relationship between the two variables under consideration. On the basis of a correlation alone, one cannot say whether factor *X* causes factor *Y*, factor *Y* causes factor *X*, or some underlying third factor causes both. Let us consider some examples. Suppose we have found a correlation of +.70 between head size and recall of words. This is in general agreement with our theory that larger heads hold more information, but certainly there are other interpretations of this relationship. It could be argued that the high positive correlation between head size and recall is mediated or produced by some third variable underlying both, such as age. We know that people's heads grow as they age and that recall also improves with age. Therefore, age (or one of its correlates) might actually be responsible for the large positive correlation we have found between head size and number of words recalled. In other words, the internal validity of relational research is always suspect.

In correlational studies, we cannot conclude that any one factor produces or causes another, because there are likely to be a number of factors that vary simultaneously with those of interest. In an experiment, we attempt to avoid this problem by directly manipulating one factor while holding all the others constant. If we are successful in holding other factors constant, which is very difficult to do, then the influence of the manipulated factor on whatever we are measuring can be directly attributed to the factor of interest. Recall that when two factors (or more) are varied at the same time, so that we cannot know whether one factor, the other factor, or both operating together produce some effect, we say that the factors are confounded. Confounding is inherent in correlational research and leads to the interpretational difficulties with such research. In the example of the correlation between head size and recall, we cannot say that variations in head size produced or caused differences in recall, because head size was confounded with at least one other factor: age.

In other cases, the relation between two factors may seem to allow a causal interpretation, but again this is not strictly permitted. Some studies have shown a positive correlation between the number of handguns in a geographic area and the number of murders in that area. Proponents of gun control might use this evidence to support the contention that an increased number of guns leads to (causes, produces) more murders, but again this is not the only plausible interpretation. It may be that people in high-crime neighborhoods buy handguns to protect themselves, or that some third factor, such as socioeconomic class, actually mediates both. We can see, therefore, that no conclusion is justified simply on the basis of a moderate or even a high correlation.

Because correlations can be calculated between any two sets of scores, often even very high correlations are accidental and not linked to one another at all. There may be a very high correlation between the number of preachers and the number of pornographic movies produced each year since 1950, with both being on the increase. But it would take an unusual theory to relate these two in a causal manner.

A high degree of correlation is given greater weight in cases in which obvious competing explanations from confounding factors seem less plausible. Most of the early evidence linking cigarette smoking to lung cancer was correlational; yet the conclusion was drawn (over the protests of the cigarette manufacturers) in the 1964 Surgeon General's report that cigarettes were likely to lead to or cause cancer. This eventually led to warnings on cigarette packages and a ban on advertising cigarettes on television, among other things. The correlation was taken as indicative of a causative relationship, probably because competing hypotheses seemed implausible. It seems unlikely, for example, that having lung cancer causes one to smoke more cigarettes (to soothe the lungs?).

More plausible, perhaps, is the possibility that some underlying third variable (such as anxiety) produces the relationship. In fact, Eysenck and Eaves (1981) have recently argued that the correlation between lung cancer and smoking in humans is produced by personality differences. Certain personality types, according to Eysenck and Eaves, are more likely to smoke and also to get lung cancer. Thus they argue that the smoking-cancer correlation does not imply causation. We should mention, though, that the link between cigarette smoking and lung cancer has now been established by experimental studies with non-human animals, typically beagles. Most authorities disagree with the view of Eysenck and Eaves.

As another example of the pitfalls of the correlational approach, consider the negative relation mentioned previously between cigarette smoking and grades. More smoking has been related to poorer grades. But does smoking cause poorer grades? This seems unlikely, and certainly there are ready alternative interpretations. Students with poor grades may be more anxious and thus smoke more, or more sociable students may smoke more and study less, and so on. No firm conclusions on the causal direction of a relation between two variables can be established simply because the variables are correlated, even if the correlation is perfect. As is true for the descriptive methods, the correlational method is very useful for suggesting possible relations and directing further inquiry, but it is not useful for establishing direct causal relationships. The correlational method is superior to descriptive methods, because the degree of relation between two variables can be precisely stated and thus predictions can be made about the (approximate) value of one variable if the value of the other is known.

Remember, the greater the correlation (nearer $+1.00$ or $-1.00$), the better the prediction.

**Low correlations: A caution.** If high correlations cannot be interpreted as evidence for some sort of causal relation, one might think it should at least be possible to rule it out if the correlation is very low, approaching zero. If the correlation between head size and recall had been $-.02$, would this have ruled out our theory that greater head size leads to better recall? Or if the correlation between smoking and lung cancer had been $+.08$, should we have abandoned the idea that they are causally related? The answer: sometimes, under certain conditions. But other factors can cause low or zero correlations and may mask an actual relationship.

One common problem is that of **truncated range.** For a meaningful correlation coefficient to be calculated, there must be rather great differences among the scores in each of the variables of interest; there must be a certain amount of spread or variability in the numbers. If all the head sizes were the same in the panels of table 3–1 and the recall scores varied, the correlation between the two would be zero. (You can work it out yourself using the equation for $r$ in appendix A.) If we looked only at the correlation between head size and recall in college students, it might be quite low, because the differences in head size and recall among college students might not be very great, compared with the population at large. This could happen even though there might be a positive (or negative) correlation between the two variables if head size were sampled over a wider range. The problem of restricted range can produce a low correlation, even when there is an actual correlation present between two variables.

You might think that everyone would recognize the problem of truncated range and avoid it, but it is often subtle. Consider the problem of trying to predict success in college from Scholastic Aptitude Test (SAT) scores at a college with very high admission standards. The scores on the verbal and quantitative subtests can range from 200 to 800, with average (mean) performance of just below 500. Imagine that mean scores at our hypothetical college are 700 on each subtest. The admissions officer at this college computes a correlation between combined SAT scores and freshman grades and finds it to be $+.10$, very small indeed. Her conclusion: SAT scores cannot be used to predict grades in college. The problem, however, is that the only scores considered are ones from a very restricted range, specifically very high ones. People with low scores are not admitted to the college. Obviously, the truncated-range problem is very likely to be a factor here, or in any research situation involving a limited sample of subjects with homogeneous characteristics. If the college had randomly admitted people, and if the correlation had then been determined between SAT scores and grades, it would probably have been much higher. Because psychologists often use homogeneous populations such as college students, the restricted-range problem must be carefully considered in interpreting correlations.

## Complex Correlational Procedures

Does watching violent TV programs cause aggressive behavior? Eron, Huesmann, Lefkowitz, and Walder (1972) measured children's preferences for violent programs and the children's aggressiveness as rated by their peers. For these third-graders, Eron and coworkers found a moderate positive correlation, $r = +.21$, indicating that children who were more aggressive tended to watch more violent TV (and less aggressive children tended to watch less violent programs). How are we to interpret this positive correlation? Can we say that watching violent programs causes aggressiveness? The answer is no. To see why this is the case, all we have to do is to turn our causal statement around and assert that being aggressive causes a preference for violent TV. We have no reasonable way to decide on the direction of causality, based on this one correlation coefficient. As we noted earlier, a valid causal statement cannot be made on the basis of a single correlation.

When we do not know the direction of causality (violent TV causes aggression versus aggressive traits cause a preference for violent programs), there is a strong possibility that some third, confounded variable is the cause of the obtained relation. Because the researchers have not controlled either the programs watched or the initial aggressiveness, they cannot rule out other variables, such as genetic differences in aggressiveness or differences in home life. Causal statements are difficult, if not impossible, to make on the basis of a single correlation coefficient.

The internal validity of correlational research may be enhanced by examining patterns of correlations. One technique is called the **cross-lagged-panel correlation procedure,** and Eron and coworkers used it in a ten-year follow-up study of the same children in the "thirteenth" grade. The results are summarized in figure 3–5. The correlation between a preference for violent TV and aggression was essentially zero ($r = -.05$) in the thirteenth grade. Similarly, they found a negligible relation between preference for violent TV in the third and the thirteenth grade ($r = +.05$). They did obtain a moderate relation between aggressiveness in the two grades ($r = +.38$), indicating that it is a somewhat stable trait. Of more interest are the cross-lagged correlations (the ones along the diagonals of the figure) in assessing the direction of causation. Do aggressive people watch violent TV, or does watching violent TV produce aggressiveness? We can determine which of these two possibilities holds true by examining the diagonal correlations. Essentially no relation exists between aggressiveness in the third grade and watching violent TV in the thirteenth ($r = +.01$). However, a fairly substantial correlation exists between a preference for watching violent TV in the third grade and exhibiting aggressiveness in the thirteenth ($r = +.31$). In fact, the relation is even greater than the one between these two variables in the earlier study, when the subjects were third-graders. Thus the direction seems to be that watching violent TV programs in the third grade may produce aggressiveness later. The underlying assumption is that if one variable causes the other, the first (watching violent TV programs) should be more strongly related to the second (aggressiveness) later in time than when the second (effect) variable is measured at the same time as the first cause. In other words, causes should take some time to produce their effects (see figure 3–5).

Using these cross-lagged-panel correlations and other complex analyses, Eron and colleagues concluded that watching violent TV programs early in life probably causes, in part, aggressive behavior later in life. Recent research by Eron (1982) supports this conclusion (also see Huesmann and others, 1973). Of course, many other factors contribute to aggressiveness; this is just one example of how cross-lagged-panel correlations can aid in arriving at an explanation from correlational research. However, internal validity cannot be as

**FIGURE 3–5**

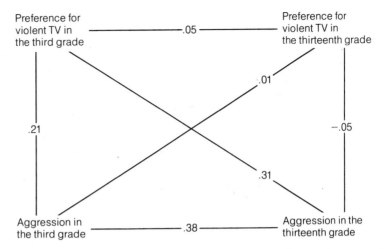

Correlations between a preference for violent television programs and aggression, as rated by peers for 211 males over a ten-year period. The important cross-lagged correlations are on the diagonals. (After Eron, Huesmann, Lefkowitz, and Walder, 1972. Copyright (1972) by the American Psychological Association. Reprinted by permission of the author.)

strong as those that come from experiments, because the variables have not been manipulated by the researcher.

The general strategy of the cross-lagged procedure, then, is to obtain several correlations over time, and then, on the basis of the size and direction of the *rs*, determine what leads to what. The cross-lagged technique is fairly new to psychological research and has the obvious drawback that the research project may be very time consuming. Nevertheless, this method for determining causation from correlational research has been used in several problem areas, for example, to show that a large vocabulary enhances the ability to spell, rather than the other way around, and that air pollution is an important cause of death in large cities, rather than death being a cause of pollution (Cook and Campbell, 1979, chapter 7).

As a general rule, remember that internal validity is always suspect in correlational research because of possible third-variable confounding. Cook and Campbell, as well as others (for example, Rogosa, 1980), have noted that many of the assumptions underlying complex correlational research are questionable. Thus, we have additional reasons to suspect causal statements made on the basis of correlational evidence.

## CONCEPT SUMMARY

In relational research **correlation coefficients** describe the strength and direction of relations, which permit prediction

Correlations have suspect internal validity owing to

- the ***third-variable problem***
- ***truncated range***
- ***unknown direction of causation***

### Experimentation and Internal Validity

We have repeatedly cautioned you about incorrectly concluding that a correlation means causation. Causation is a controversial subject in science and philosophy, and we will now consider some of the issues. Owing to the influence of some philosophers of science, it has become unpopular among contemporary scientists to use the term *cause*, because the philosophical implications become frightfully complicated. Thinking too long about the cause of even a very simple event leads to an infinite regress of causes for that event. For this and other reasons, the term *cause* has dropped out of use in some circles (see Kerlinger, 1986, and the Application section on causation for further discussion).

# APPLICATION

### Causation

If you generate a visual image of something you are trying to remember, you will retain it better than if you simply repeat the information over and over (Bower, 1972). The philosophical implications of *why* imagery enhances remembering can become extremely complicated. Thinking too long about the cause of even a very simple event can lead to an infinite regress of causes for that event. A regressive causal analysis of the effects of imagery might be as follows: Imagery causes better remembering than simple repetition. Why? Because imagery results in more associations than does repetition. Why? Because more protein molecules in the brain become active when imagery is used. Why? Because evolution determined the structure of the human brain. Why? Because . . .

In this book, we use the terms *cause* and *why* because their meanings here are always limited. Experiments can lead to causal inferences because one factor is varied while other factors are held constant, and we can say that the effect was caused by the factor that varied. In the typical psychology experiment, therefore, the immediate causes of an effect are determined. These immediate causes are called the **proximate causes** of an event and are to be distinguished from the **ultimate causes** (Mayr, 1982). Proximate causes derive from the immediate manipulations in an experiment (for example, instructions to the subjects to use imagery or repetition). Ultimate causes are those that are supposed to stop the infinite regress of "why" and "because" as outlined earlier. One kind of ultimate answer to our questions about imagery could be an appeal to evolution. Biologists argue that evolution is the ultimate cause behind all aspects of biology and, thereby, provides the physiological and genetic framework for ultimate causation in psychology (Mayr, 1982). According to such an analysis, imagery instructions would be the proximate cause of differences in retention, and evolutionary forces would be the ultimate cause for the effectiveness of those instructions. There are other possible ultimate causes (for example, a deity), and we could argue that something had to set evolution in motion (perhaps a "big bang"). Because of these possibilities, the distinction between proximate causation and ultimate causation may not be clear or relevant. Therefore, many people prefer asking "Under what conditions does imagery enhance memory?" instead of "Why does imagery enhance memory?" Likewise, instead of saying "Imagery causes better memory" some people prefer to say "Imagery may enhance (is an antecedent condition of, determines, or directly affects) memory." Because we generally will be talking about individual experiments, we will use the latter phrases interchangeably with *cause* and *why* where appropriate.

---

In this book we muddle through, using the term *cause*, because its meaning is always limited; experiments lead to causal inferences because the independent variable is manipulated while all others are, in the ideal case, held constant. Whatever effect on the dependent variable that occurs in such cases has been caused by the factor that varied. Thus, we can say that when the Stroop experiment is conducted in such a way that confounding is minimized, changes in the levels of the independent variable caused changes in the dependent variable.

A more interesting point is that many factors that are experimentally varied are themselves quite complicated sets of independent events, any one of which could be the cause of an experimental effect. Time is a good example of such a variable. If we are interested in the effects of the length of time one studies a persuasive communication on the amount a person's attitude changes toward the communication, we vary the amount of time people spend studying the message. Suppose we find an increase in attitude change with increases in study time, when other factors are held constant. Can we say that time has caused an increase in attitude change? In a sense this is true, but in a more fundamental sense it is not. Presumably, it is some psychological process, acting over time, that causes the attitude change. It is something correlated with time, but not time itself, because time is not a causative agent. If we leave a bicycle outdoors in the rain and it rusts, we do not say that time caused the rust; chemical processes acting over time caused it.

Usually, a manipulated variable is actually composed of a number of complex and interacting parts, any one or set of which may actually cause some effect. For this reason, it is sometimes said that experiments are only controlled correlations, because the variable manipulated is actually composed of a number of confounded parts. This is certainly an accurate characterization in at least some cases; even so we are far ahead of having a simple correlation, because we know the direction of effect. Take the example of how amount of time spent studying a persuasive communication affects attitude change. We could simply give the message to a number of people and let them read it for as long as they desired. We could time this for each person, and then see how much the person's attitude changed. If we found a positive correlation, we would not know whether the time people spent studying the passage caused more attitude change, or whether the more people decided to change their attitudes, the more they studied the passage to make sure they knew the facts. There are other possible reasons for the relationship, too. But in the experiment in which time is varied while other factors are held constant, we can say that more study time leads to (determines, produces, causes) more attitude change.

Experiments allow us to know the direction of the relation. This is their overwhelming advantage to correlations. They also inform us (which a correlation does not) that the causal factor is at least embedded in the independent variable, and not some third outside factor. It is in this sense that they tell us about causes and are internally valid, at least in principle.

## CONCEPT SUMMARY

**Experiments** are internally valid because the causal variables are known and the direction of causation is known

## SUMMARY

1. The validity of observations refers to their approximate truth or falsity.
2. Construct validity concerns the extent to which the dependent and independent variables reflect and measure the variables of interest.
3. External validity refers to whether the results of observations can be generalized to other research settings and populations.
4. Internal validity of observations deals with the possibility of determining whether one variable causes changes in another.
5. The descriptive methods of observation include naturalistic observations, case studies, and surveys. Their primary value is to provide the database that leads to the application of more controlled observation procedures.
6. Relational observations are exemplified by the correlational technique that permits a determination of the strength and direction of relations among variables.
7. The internal validity of the correlational technique is suspect because of third-variable confounding, an unknown direction of causation, and sometimes by a truncated range of scores on one or more of the variables.
8. The cross-lagged-panel correlation procedure can increase the internal validity of the correlational technique by showing the direction of causation.
9. Experimentation allows causal statements in principle, which means that experiments can be internally valid.

### Key Concepts

| | |
|---|---|
| anthropomorphizing | naturalistic observations |
| case study | operational definitions |
| construct validity | Pearson's product-moment correlation coefficient (Pearson *r*) |
| correlation coefficient | |
| cross-lagged-panel correlation procedure | protocols |
| | proximate causes |
| descriptive observations | relational observations |
| deviant-case analysis | replication |
| ethogram | scatter diagrams |
| ethology | surveys |
| explanation | truncated range |
| ex post facto | ultimate causes |
| external validity | validity |
| internal validity | |

## Exercises

1. Discuss the three types of validity, and be sure to show how they relate to a particular research example.

2. [*Special Exercise.*] A psychologist studied the remote memory of college graduates by seeing how many names of old television programs they could correctly recognize. The results indicated that there was no correlation between the subjects' intelligence-test scores and their ability to recognize the names of old programs ($r = +.07$). Assuming that the procedure of memory testing was valid and that the age of the subjects was not a problem, can you think of some problems in this research that would prevent you from making a valid conclusion about the small $r$?

3. An illustration of how Pearson $r$ is calculated for the data in (a) column of table 3–1 is presented in box A-1 of appendix A. Work through this example, and then calculate $r$ values for the data in (b) and (c) columns of table 3–1. Make sure that your $r$ values are the same as those values given at the bottom of table 3–1.

4. The table here shows some fictitious data from a college admissions office. For ten students, we have the scores from the verbal portion of their Scholastic Aptitude Test (SAT) as well as their freshman grade point average (GPA). The GPA is on a four-point scale, where $F = 0, D = 1, C = 2, B = 3,$ and $A = 4$ points. Calculate the correlation coefficient between these two sets of scores. What might you conclude?

| Student | Verbal SAT | Freshman GPA |
|---------|------------|--------------|
| 1 | 471 | 2.00 |
| 2 | 403 | 1.50 |
| 3 | 510 | 2.25 |
| 4 | 485 | 2.00 |
| 5 | 575 | 2.25 |
| 6 | 445 | 1.75 |
| 7 | 400 | 2.50 |
| 8 | 590 | 3.25 |
| 9 | 560 | 2.50 |
| 10 | 555 | 2.75 |

5. [*Special Exercise.*] There are a number of potential methodological problems associated with descriptive research. Some of them are discussed in this chapter. What are these methodological problems and how are they overcome? For a more detailed discussion of these problems and others, see the suggested readings listed below.

## Suggested Readings

An extensive discussion of correlational techniques and methods of observation can be found in Kerlinger, F. N. (1986). *Foundations of behavioral research* (3d ed.). New York: Holt.

An interesting article on the use and development of observational skills is Boice, R. (1983). Observational skills. *Psychological Bulletin, 93,* 3–29.

A detailed discussion of methodological problems and considerations in descriptive research can be found in the following two articles: Woolfolk, A. E. (1981). The eye of the beholder: Methodological considerations when observers assess nonverbal communication. *Journal of Nonverbal Behavior, 5,* 199–204; and Wildman, B. G., & Erickson, M. T. (1977). Methodological problems in behavioral observation. In J. D. Cone and R. P. Hawkins (Eds.), *Behavioral assessment.* New York: Brunner/Mazel.

An extensive discussion of current research relating aggression to watching violent television can be found in Eron, L. D. (1982). Parent-child interaction, television violence, and aggression of children. *American Psychologist, 37,* 197–211.

## PSYCHOLOGY IN ACTION
### Amount of Sleep and Tension Headaches

This project is a variation of a research procedure used by Hicks and Kilcourse (1983). These researchers were interested in the relationship between the number of hours of sleep subjects got and the frequency of tension or migrane headaches the subjects experienced. In a health survey, the researchers asked college students: (1) Estimate the number of hours of sleep you usually get each night, and (2) Do you have tension or migraine headaches often? _____ Sometimes? _____ Never? _____. Hicks and Kilcourse found an inverse relationship between these two variables; that is, people with more headaches slept less than those with fewer headaches. However, the researchers' mode of categorizing the frequency of headaches did not allow them to calculate a product-moment correlation coefficient.

You can modify their second question by asking: "Estimate the number of tension or migraine headaches you have each month." Ask twenty or so of your college acquaintances the modified question and the one concerning the estimated number of hours of sleep. Survey enough people so that you do not have a truncated range on one of your variables. Then calculate the *r* between these two variables.

You can enhance the reliability of your results by combining your data with those of classmates. If you pool your data, make sure that you and the others doing the project are surveying different people. When your data are combined, you may wind up with a large number of subjects, so you will find that MINITAB or some other statistical package will be helpful in calculating *r*.

To anticipate a later Psychology in Action project (chapter 9), you should collect some additional demographic data on your subjects, such as age, sex, and year in school.

Hicks, R. A., & Kilcourse, J. (1983). Habitual sleep duration and the incidence of headaches in college students. *Bulletin of the Psychonomic Society, 21,* 119.

**Scale Properties**
- differences
- magnitudes
- equal intervals
- true zeros

**Scale Type**
- nominal
- ordinal
- interval
- ratio

Measuring sensory thresholds is one of the oldest examples of psychological measurement

Fechner's law [$\Psi$ = K log stimulus] is an ordinal scale of sensory judgments

Stevens' law [$\Psi$ = K(Stimulus)$^n$] is a ratio scale of sensory judgments

# 4

# MEASUREMENT IN PSYCHOLOGICAL RESEARCH

Measurement is one hallmark of science. In this chapter we consider the properties of measurement scales and the types of measurement scales used in psychology. Psychology as a science began when people developed ways of measuring sensory judgments. Thus, we examine how sensitivity is measured and show that it is difficult to measure psychological judgments.

A brief summary of the previous three chapters might go like this: theories and observations result in hypotheses that are testable by empirical observations. The new observations then provide the bases for theoretical development and new testable hypotheses. To complete the background necessary for a detailed examination of research methods, we need to consider the measurement of behavior. According to Boring (1961), the eminent historian of psychology, a science grows and progresses to the extent that it uses measurement. As noted earlier, testable hypotheses imply that the predicted outcomes can be measured. Furthermore, empirical observations in psychology are based on the measurement of dependent variables. Measurement then is an important aspect of scientific psychology.

What is measurement? **Measurement** is a systematic way of assigning numbers or names to objects and their attributes. It is a dictum in psychology that anything that exists, be it alarm calls of chicadees or emotional reactions to earthquakes, exists in some amount. Anything that exists in some amount can be measured. The scientific study of behavior demands that we be able to measure it and its attributes. Otherwise, we will be unable to generate adequate hypotheses and precise theories. In this chapter we first consider the types of measurement scales used by psychologists. Then we examine ways of evaluating measurements and developing measurement scales.

## MEASUREMENT SCALES

When we assign names or numbers to objects and their attributes, we need a measurement scale. When we measure temperature, for example, we usually use either the Fahrenheit scale or the Centigrade scale, and weight can be measured in pounds or kilograms. Measurement scales differ in the information they provide, because different scales, say weight and temperature, result from different measurement operations.

## Properties of Measurement Scales

There are four properties of measurement scales that we need to consider (see McCall, 1990, for additional information). Obviously, all measurement scales require that objects and their attributes have instances that are different from each other. This property, **difference,** means that some temperatures must be hotter (or colder) than others. One detectable difference among people is sex, and we can sort people into two piles: female and male. All measurement scales have this characteristic, but not all have the other properties, which we now discuss.

Some measurement scales can determine the **magnitude** of attributes. This means that the scale can show that one attribute is greater than, less than, or equal to another instance of that attribute. The Mohs' scale determines the hardness of minerals. Diamonds are harder than quartz crystals, and quartz crystals are harder than pieces of mica. A person surveyed about the amount of fear generated by the San Francisco earthquake (none at all, some, or very much) would have his or her magnitude of fear assessed. Using such a survey could reveal that some people were more fearful than others.

Another property of attributes that some scales can determine is whether there are **equal intervals** between magnitudes of the attributes. Both temperature scales have equal intervals, because a one-degree change in temperature is the same magnitude regardless of whether we are considering very hot temperatures or very cold ones. The typical intelligence test assesses magnitudes of intelligence with equal intervals between them. The difference between an intelligence test score, say the familiar IQ measure, of 125 and a score of 120 is believed to represent the same difference that exists between scores of 85 and 90.

A final property of some measurement scales is a **true zero** point on the scale. The true zero is when nothing of the attribute being measured exists. Fahrenheit and Centigrade scales do not have a true zero point. For both scales the zero point does not reflect zero temperature. To detect zero temperature— so-called *absolute zero*—the Kelvin scale must be used.

## Types of Measurement Scales

Psychologists use four types of measurement scales, called nominal, ordinal, interval, and ratio, although other types exist. These scale types are determined by which of the four properties of measurement they possess. The four scale types are listed here according to the increasing informativeness of the scales, with each scale type having the properties of the preceding types in addition to new properties. One thing this means is that data obtained using a ratio scale could be statistically analyzed by methods appropriate to any of the three lesser scales, but statistics appropriate only for a ratio scale would not fit the lesser scales (see the statistical appendixes). A second thing this means is that scales with more properties provide more information.

**Nominal scales.** A **nominal scale** measures just the property of difference and nothing else. A nominal scale merely sorts objects or attributes into different categories. Your ZIP code is a nominal number because it puts you into a particular (geographical) category, but it does not reveal much else about you. Nominal scales are weak ones in the sense that you cannot legitimately perform many mathematical operations on nominal numbers. You might have a use for the average Scholastic Aptitude Test (SAT) score in your class. The SAT scale is considered to have at least interval scale properties (see below). But, what would the average ZIP code of your class tell you? Not much, because the assignment of numbers to geographical area is not based on magnitudes in any obvious way. Likewise, sex is measured at the nominal level, and you cannot average category labels. Even if the category labels were numbers, say male = 1 and female = 2, the assignment of numbers is arbitrary and not based on magnitudes. Thus, statistics such as the arithmetical average (the mean, which is the sum of the scores divided by the number of scores) are inappropriate for nominal numbers. Putting a person into a particular category, such as giving the person a name, merely tells us that the person is different from other people. A nominal number does not assist us in measuring the person's attributes with any depth.

**Ordinal scales.** **Ordinal scales** measure differences in magnitude. An ordinal scale can be achieved by having people rank order a set of objects. You would obtain an ordinal scale if you rank ordered all your friends of the opposite sex according to their attractiveness. The first person in your ranking is the most attractive, the second person on your scale is the next most attractive, and so on. If you try ranking your friends this way, one of the first things you will notice is that the differences between adjacent scale values are not equal for all the people you ranked. The first two people may be nearly equal in attractiveness, but the sixth and seventh people may differ substantially. So, ordinal scales do not have equal intervals, which means that you probably should not add them or perform many other mathematical operations on them. You know from your ranking that the third person is more attractive than the seventh, but you do not know how much more.

**Interval scales.** You can add and subtract numbers from interval scales, because the intervals between adjacent values are equal throughout the scale. **Interval scales** possess the scale properties of difference, order, and equal intervals. A temperature rise of one degree produces the same change from 35° to 36° as it does from 22° to 23°. As noted above many psychologists treat IQ scores as interval level numbers, which means that it is possible to calculate mean IQ scores. It is very difficult to substantiate that IQ differences are equal throughout the scale. Thus, psychologists taking a conservative view would treat IQ scores as ordinal data. If IQ scores are ordinal, then we cannot assume that the difference between a hypothetical IQ score of 120 and 124 represents the same difference that exists between a score of 100 and 104. All we can say if we are conservative is that 124 represents a higher IQ than does 120, and, in turn, 104 is more than 100.

**Ratio scales.**  **Ratio scales** have all four of the properties of measurement scales: difference, magnitude, equal intervals, and a true zero. As such, a ratio scale provides the most information and is usually considered the most powerful form of psychological measurement. Because ratio scales have a true zero, they allow us to determine the ratios of the scale values (hence, the name, ratio scale). Even if IQ were measured at the interval level, it is not sensible to assert that an IQ of 120 is twice that of 60 or half again bigger than an IQ of 80. A typical ratio scale used in psychology is the time it takes someone to complete a task. Zero time truly means no time was spent on the task. Also, four minutes spent on a task bears the same relation to one minute as does twenty minutes to five, because the ratio of the two time periods is 4:1 in both instances.

## Importance of Measurement Scales

Some of the previous discussion of scales may have seemed too abstract to be pertinent to an understanding of behavior. The examples we provided should have indicated that the different scales yield different kinds of information. The more of the four properties (difference, magnitude, equal intervals, and a true zero) possessed by a scale, the more the information provided. You might expect that psychologists should always strive for ratio measurement of behavior, because a ratio scale provides the most information. Unfortunately, deriving a ratio scale for important psychological phenomena is often very difficult. A substantial amount of psychological measurement is at the ordinal and interval level. What does that mean to you? First, as noted above, it will determine the kinds of mathematical and statistical operations that you can use on the numbers. Second, and perhaps more important, it means that when you evaluate the assertions of a researcher, you should be able to identify the measurement scale underlying the assertions. You should recognize that it is invalid to say that "Betty is twice as smart as Tom," unless the measure of smartness is at the ratio level. Furthermore, scale type will also play an important part in your own research. If, for example, you determine that Betty is lazier than Tom but you do not know how much more (an ordinal scale), then you are constrained about what you can say about the differences between Betty and Tom. You are limited further if all you determine is that Tom is witty but Betty is not (a nominal scale). The kinds of conclusions we can draw rests, in part, on the measurement scale. Behavioral data derived from different scales tell us different things.

## CONCEPT SUMMARY

**Measurement scales** can have the properties of difference, magnitude, equal intervals, and a true zero

**Nominal scales** have the property of difference; **ordinal scales** have the properties of difference and magnitude; **interval scales** have the properties of difference, magnitude, and equal intervals; and **ratio scales** have all four scale properties

# RELIABILITY AND VALIDITY OF MEASUREMENT

The different types of scales permit us to make different conclusions. Thus, the validity of our conclusions depends, in part, on whether they are warranted by the type of measurement used. When a psychologist desires a clear answer to a research question, he or she wants the results and conclusions to be both valid and reliable. **Reliability** refers to the consistency of the measures of behavior. Reconsider the research on social loafing that was discussed in chapter 2. Clear answers about the nature of social loafing would be impossible if measures of it were inconsistent. You might suppose that several attempts to measure the same thing would all yield the same numbers, unless of course someone had made an error. In fact, there is always some variability, or differences among scores, in a group of measures, even of the same thing. The amount of variability determines the reliability of the measuring instrument and procedure. Highly variable measures indicate low reliability, and vice versa. The measurement "error" to which psychologists and statisticians often refer is meant to imply not that someone made a mistake, but merely that certain unavoided factors caused unpredictable variability in the data. Psychologists try to reduce this variability, hence increasing the reliability of their measures, by taking their measures under the same conditions. The use of protocols is one way to standardize the conditions of measurement (see chapter 3).

Psychologists often use sophisticated equipment to enhance the reliability of observations and measurements. In particular, the digital computer plays a major role in controlling experimental manipulations and recording dependent variables. For example, suppose you wish to examine how quickly people can respond to pictures that they see for a very short period of time. A properly programmed computer can precisely control the presentation time of the pictures, and it can consistently provide an accurate measure of the response times. One can, for example, program a computer to display a picture for just a few milliseconds (thousandths of a second). If the program sets the display time for ten milliseconds, then that display time will be precisely replicated each time a picture is shown. Also, response times can be measured with millisecond resolution, which is impossible to do with stop watches and difficult with many other kinds of apparatus. It is an understatement to say that the digital computer has markedly increased the reliability and precision of experimental control and measurement.

## *Test Reliability*

The reliability of the results of tests and other descriptive measures of behavior is often checked by taking measures under the same conditions on successive occasions. If identical conditions could be ensured, then variability in measurement would have to be caused by a real change in the measured quantity. If your height is measured on two occasions, with the results 5'8" and 5'10", is this variability owing to error or to a real change in your height? The answer could be either, or both. But the more similar the conditions—shoes worn, posture—the less likely you would be to attribute the difference to error. Also, the closer the two measures were in time, the less likely you would be to attribute the difference to a real change in stature. You have some notion of how quickly stature can change, or of the stability of a person's true stature.

Intelligence and other psychological processes are more difficult to measure than stature, however. It is also more difficult to develop a notion of their stability. Do they vary at all, or do they remain fixed throughout life? If they change markedly, can they do so within a week, a month, a year, or ten years? If something changes, can we determine those factors that produce the change or are the changes the result of unreliable measurement? These are questions that psychologists would like to answer; the answers require measurement. But the alert reader will realize that we have now reasoned ourselves into a logical circle. Let us go around again, and try to get out.

Several measures of the same quantity will not, in general, exactly agree. This variability may be a result either of error or of a real change in the measured quantity. We cannot tell, without some additional assumptions, how much error there is in our measurement. Thus, how can we ask if a psychological process changes? A useful assumption—one that allows the logical circle to be broken— is that the measured quantity is stable over relatively short periods of time. (If a researcher measures your intelligence in the morning and then again in the afternoon under the same conditions, any change can be assumed to be caused by measurement error rather than a real change in intelligence.) With this assumption, a psychologist can estimate measurement error and attempt to improve and specify the reliability of the measuring instrument.

We will examine test reliability in the context of the concept of intelligence, which is not well defined theoretically and is difficult to measure. Some theorists postulate a number of separate mental abilities, perhaps more than a hundred (Guilford, 1967). Others believe that there is one primary mental ability and that although other more specific abilities may be isolated, they are less important. This primary ability has been described as "a capacity for abstract reasoning and problem solving" (Jensen, 1969, p. 19). To test for this ability, collections of problems or tasks are presented to individuals to solve, generally within a specified time period. The score that an individual achieves is then compared with scores obtained by others. Before placing much confidence in an individual's score, however, we need to know how reliable it is. Would the individual achieve about the same score if we were to test him or her again the next day, or a week later? Because we do not believe that the underlying ability changes appreciably over so short a time, we attribute a large change in scores to measurement error, indicating unreliability in our test. This procedure of giving the same test twice in succession over a short time interval is used to determine what is called the **test-retest reliability** of a measure. It is generally expressed as a correlation (see chapter 3) between first and second scores obtained from a large sample of subjects.

A slightly different procedure can be employed to avoid problems such as specific practice effects. This technique involves giving alternate or **parallel forms** of the test on the two testing occasions. Again, if correlations between first and second scores are high, they indicate reliability of the tests. Also, the equivalence of the two forms of the test can be determined in this way.

A third procedure can be used to evaluate reliability with a single test presentation. This technique provides **split-half reliability;** it involves dividing the test items into two arbitrary groups and correlating the scores obtained in the two halves of the test. If these correlations are high, the test reliability is confirmed. In addition, the equivalence of the test items is established. The reliability and validity of the SAT are considered in the Application section.

# APPLICATION

### The Reliability and Validity of the SAT

The College Board Scholastic Aptitude Test (SAT) is one of the most widely used and widely researched tests. Most of you have taken the SAT or a similar test. Is it a good test?

The SAT is a very reliable test. All forms of reliability have been examined, and on all counts the SAT does very well. Generally, reliability is measured by a correlation coefficient (see chapter 3), which tells how two variables relate to each other. A perfectly reliable test, meaning that the two scores are identical at two different times or on alternative forms, would yield a coefficient of + 1.0. The usual finding is that the SAT gives reliability coefficients of + .9 or better. Thus, you need not be concerned about the reliability of the SAT.

What about the validity of the SAT? Validity is usually checked by examining the correlation between SAT scores and grades in the freshman year in college. This type of validity check, using grades as the criterion, is called **predictive validity.** The results here are good but not as dramatic as the reliability results. The typical validity coefficient is around + .35. This means that the SAT is a fair predictor of freshman grades. Usually, the high-school record is combined with SAT scores for predictive purposes, and this yields a much better prediction of freshman grades (a coefficient of better than + .6).

One area the SAT runs into trouble is in predicting the grades of students who score in the middle ranges (combined scores between 900 and 1200 on the verbal and quantitative components). Within this range other factors, such as motivation and emotional stability, seem to play a very important role in college success. Although the SAT is reliable and has fair validity, college success may be related to factors other than high SAT scores, especially the willingness to work hard and the desire to achieve.

Kaplan, R. M. & Saccuzzo, D. P. (1982). *Psychological testing: Principles, applications, and issues.* Monterey, CA: Brooks/Cole.

## *Statistical Reliability and Validity*

Given a set of results, their reliability can be assessed statistically. The methods of inferential statistics (see appendix B) allow the **statistical reliability** of data to be assessed by showing how likely it is to obtain those results by chance. In an experiment, for example, inferential statistics are used to determine whether a difference obtained between conditions results from the operation of the independent variable or from chance factors. If the difference between conditions is great enough so that it would be expected to occur by chance in fewer than one case in twenty, then the researcher rejects the possibility that chance factors produced the result. Instead, the difference is accepted as evidence for a real or statistically significant effect of the independent variable. When the results of the Stroop experiment conducted in chapter 1 are analyzed statistically, we find that the differences are large enough to consider them reliable rather than owing to chance.

## Sampling

Another statistical factor that influences the reliability of measures has to do with the number of observations that are made. When we take measures of behavior, we rarely investigate the entire **population** that we could study (for example, all college students). Rather, we usually select a **sample** to measure, such as volunteer psychology students in our college. Generally speaking, the greater the number of observations in our sample, the more confident we can be that the sample reflects the characteristics of the population. If a sample of persons is asked about preference for candidates in an upcoming election, we can be more confident that the survey results reflect the population of voters if the sample consists of 100,000 people than if it contains only 100.

Most statistical tests are sensitive to the size of the sample. That is, most tests are more likely to detect true effects of independent variables when the number of observations is large than when it is small. When a statistical test can detect effects, it is said to have **power**. The power of most statistical tests is increased by increasing the number of measures.

*How* a sample is determined also can affect the validity of the sample. Because only a sample of an entire population is usually studied in a research project, you need to try to obtain a sample that accurately represents the characteristics of the population. How can you be sure that sophomores taking introductory psychology at your institution are representative of all sophomores in colleges?

Sampling is discussed further in appendix B, and other aspects of representativeness are considered later. For now, we want to emphasize random sampling and its relation to sample size. **Random sampling** means that each member of a particular population has an equal chance of being selected for the sample. Unbiased random selection guarantees in the long run that the sample represents the population. This does not mean that a particular sample will be perfectly representative of the population, and hence a perfectly valid sample of the population; that cannot be guaranteed. What random selection does mean is that you can make a statistical or probabilistic guess that the sample is representative of the population.

You probably believe, intuitively, that large samples are more representative of the population than are small samples. You might expect, for example, that one unusual member of a small sample will distort your results more than if that deviant member was part of a larger sample. You can test this yourself by tossing coins. The more coins you toss (the larger your sample is of all coin tosses), the closer you get to seeing the ideal of 50 percent heads show up (Thompson and Buchanan, 1979).

The value of random selection is related to sample size in an interesting way. Kerlinger (1986) suggests that large sample sizes allow the effects of random selection to work. Very small samples are less likely to be representative of the population because even random selection can yield a limited or biased sample if the sample size is very small. An unusual member of a small random sample can have unfortunate effects even when that individual was selected at random. Thus, a large random sample is likely to yield a more externally valid representation of the population than is a small one. The effect of selecting by chance one unusual individual is diluted in large samples.

Random selection is an ideal that is rarely attained in psychology because it is extremely expensive and time consuming to try to sample from an entire population, such as all college sophomores. Because individuals differ in many ways, we can often assume that the population of possible scores in a research project can vary in a random way (Glenberg, 1988). If that is the case, then it is crucial that participants be assigned to experimental conditions on a random basis. In conducting an experiment on the effects of a brain operation on memory, it is necessary that the operation be the only difference between the operated and unoperated animals. Otherwise, random differences among the subjects could be confounded with the independent variable, and a clear answer to the research question might be unlikely. In this context, *confounding* refers to differences between groups that do not result from the independent variable. Differences attributable to the characteristics of the subjects can be minimized by randomly assigning subjects to conditions. **Random assignment** means that any given subject has an unbiased chance of being in any condition of an experiment. When subjects are assigned randomly, the chances of individual differences confounding the outcome are minimized. Random assignment to conditions helps to increase the internal validity of the research procedure.

## Experimental Reliability

Statistical reliability is an important condition for taking seriously an experimental result, but many researchers prefer to see an experimenter also establish **experimental reliability.** If the experiment is repeated under essentially the same conditions, a replication, will the results be the same as they were before (see chapter 3)? An adage among researchers is that "one replication is worth a thousand *t* tests." (The *t* test is a well-known statistical test used to evaluate the statistical reliability between two conditions.) The gist of the adage is that many researchers are more convinced by replications of the experiment than by inferential statistics applied to the original outcome. Although an outcome may be deemed statistically reliable, the possibility remains that it could have occurred by chance (statistical reliability still allows a 5 percent error rate) or because of some unintentional confounding or error on the part of the experimenter. For example, perhaps smarter subjects happened to be assigned to one condition rather than to another. Although these possibilities might seem unlikely, they do sometimes occur. In some experiments, subjects are randomly assigned to conditions (see above), and then, prior to the main experiment, the various groups are given a pretest to determine whether the groups are actually equivalent (on the average) in ability. Occasionally, pretests of this sort turn up differences, before the independent variable has been introduced (see, for example, Tulving and Pearlstone, 1966). Because such problems can occur even in well-controlled research, researchers encourage replication of experiments, even when inferential statistics indicate that some effect is reliable.

## CONCEPT SUMMARY

**Reliability** refers to the consistency of measures

**Test reliability** is determined by **retesting,** by giving **parallel forms,** or by **split-half** methods

**Statistical reliability** determines whether results are owing to chance

**Random sampling** helps insure the external validity of a sample taken from a population

**Random assignment** to conditions helps insure the internal validity of an experiment

**Experimental reliability** can be assessed by replications

## MEASURING SENSATIONS

In this section we examine a case study of the development of measurement scales in psychology. We do this to illustrate important measurement techniques and to show how difficult it can be to produce a scale that adequately measures psychological judgments. Suppose you wanted to determine whether aspirin alleviated pain. How would you try to do it? You would need to do an experiment; in this experiment, you would measure pain reactions with and without the ingestion of aspirin. This general outline seems straightforward and is the standard way that the effects of analgesics (substances that may reduce pain, such as aspirin) have been tested.

In a large number of experiments, Hardy, Wolff, and Goodell (1952) examined people's reactions to radiant heat presented to their forearms by a piece of equipment similar to a hair dryer, called a *dolorimeter*. A small spot of stimulation was presented at various intensities (usually defined in terms of calories per unit area stimulated, rather than in terms of a temperature scale). The researchers' approach was to determine the intensity of heat necessary for a person to report pain—first without an analgesic such as aspirin, and then when aspirin had been taken prior to the presentation of heat. An increase in the intensity needed to elicit pain after the subjects had taken aspirin would indicate that aspirin had analgesic properties. Indeed, this is what Hardy and associates found. Or, at least, that is what they observed when they used highly experienced subjects (themselves) in the experiment. Much to their surprise, when they tested naive subjects (eighty military recruits, in this case), they found that for more than half of their subjects, the heat intensity required to evoke pain actually went *down* following the ingestion of aspirin.

We discuss the techniques used by Hardy and his associates to measure sensations in this chapter. In chapter 8 we examine an alternative way to measure sensitivity, and in that chapter we consider the unusual results shown by the untrained observers in Hardy's experiments.

Measuring sensations is one of the oldest aspects of psychology and is called psychophysics. **Psychophysics** involves the determination of the psychological reaction to events that lie along a physical dimension. Boring (1950) claims that the introduction of techniques to measure the relation between internal impressions (the "psycho" of psychophysics) and the external world (the "physics") marked the onset of scientific psychology.

Boring marked psychophysics as the beginning of scientific psychology primarily because the scientists using psychophysical techniques were able to formulate the first mathematical laws of psychological phenomena. Although the characteristics of these laws are of interest in and of themselves, their development has other important implications. First, measuring sensations is very difficult, because they are not open to public measurement as is light intensity or the weight of a stone. Second, the internal judgments are not identical to the amount of physical energy influencing the sensory apparatus.

Gustav Fechner formalized the **psychophysical methods,** which measure attributes of the world in terms of their psychological values (1860, republished, 1966). His methods showed that psychological judgments varied in particular ways according to the intensity of the stimulus and according to the particular sensory modality of the stimulus (that is, judgments of visual stimuli differed from judgments of auditory stimuli, which differed from judgments of taste stimuli, and so on). Because these relations held, at least approximately, for many different people, Fechner and other researchers concluded that private, internal judgments had been measured accurately. Just as physicists could measure light intensity, auditory intensity, and weight, so too could psychophysicists measure the corresponding psychological attributes of brightness, loudness, and heaviness.

In the 1800s, the psychophysical methods were used to measure seemingly simple sensations such as brightness, pitch, and so on. At first, this might seem to be an unnecessary enterprise. You may think it is easy to decide how loud a sound is or how painful a stimulus feels. However, it turns out that there is rarely a direct one-to-one relation between physical values and psychological values. If a rock band turned up its amplifiers to produce twice as much energy as it had produced before (a doubling of the physical units), this twofold increase of energy would not result in listeners experiencing a sound twice as loud as before. For a listener to judge the sound to be twice as loud, the energy level would have to be increased roughly ten times. Such discoveries derived from the psychophysical methods have important practical applications. For example, the amplifier or radio dial that you turn to increase volume (that is, the perceived loudness) cannot bear a one-to-one relation between movements of the dial and increases in energy. Rather, the dial has to be calibrated so that its movements increase intensity proportional to increments in loudness. Thus, doubling the volume level on the dial has to increase physical energy about ten times to produce a twofold increase in loudness. Telephones are also designed so that their microphones and amplifiers work in accord with this psychophysical relation between auditory intensity and perceived loudness.

The psychophysical relation between stimulus and judgment depends on the particular sensory modality that is stimulated. Pain judgments in response to increases in electrical intensity of shocks applied to the skin grow much more rapidly than do loudness judgments in response to increases in sound energy.

For one shock to be judged twice as painful as another, the intensity of the shock needs to have been increased by about one-third. We can see, then, that merely measuring changes in physical units does not always help us accurately determine changes in psychological units.

In the following sections we discuss the operational definition of a theoretical construct called a **threshold**. First, we will give the common-language meaning of this term; then, we will see how attempts at increasing the precision of definition have led to rather sophisticated methodological techniques to improve the operational definitions of a threshold.

## Thresholds: Classical Psychophysics

In common language, a threshold is the part of a doorway you step through or over to enter a room. Classical psychophysicists believed that stimuli had to cross such a (hypothetical) barrier to enter the brain or the mind. If a stimulus were strong, it could easily jump over the threshold. A crude analogy that may be helpful is to think of the stimulus as a pole vaulter. The bar corresponds to the threshold. A good jump will put you over the bar (across the threshold), whereas a feeble jump will not. The obvious question, then, is how strong a stimulus is necessary for a signal to cross the threshold. Answering this question was of major concern to classical psychophysicists.

At first, the answer may seem obvious. All we have to do is slowly increase the intensity of a stimulus, such as a tone or a dim light, until the observer responds, "Yes, there it is." Unfortunately, when we try to repeat this process, the point at which an observer suddenly detects the stimulus changes from trial to trial. To deal with this variability, classical psychophysicists developed statistical methods to estimate the best value for the threshold. We will discuss only one of the methods, developed by Fechner, and known as the **method of limits.**

If we performed an experiment using the method of limits to determine the threshold for a tone, results would look like those shown in table 4–1. Each column represents data from one block of trials. The first block starts with a clearly audible tone, to which the observer responds "Yes." The tone intensity is lowered in successive steps until the observer reports "No," thus ending that trial block. The next block of trials starts with an intensity so low that the observer cannot hear the tone and responds "No." On successive trials, the intensity is gradually increased, until the observer reports hearing the tone. This process of altering trial blocks continues until table 4–1 is complete. Each block is started at a different intensity to avoid extra cues that might mislead the observer.

If the observer were a perfect stimulus detector, the point at which responses switched from "Yes" to "No" (or vice versa) would always be the same. This ideal point would be the threshold. Stimuli less intense than this value would never be detected, and stimuli greater than or equal to this ideal threshold would always be detected. Unfortunately, real data from real people do not have this ideal characteristic; instead, they look like the data in table 4–1.

Observers are influenced by their expectations as to when it is time to change their response from "Yes" to "No," or vice versa. For example, if a

| TABLE 4–1 | USING THE METHOD OF LIMITS TO DETERMINE AN ABSOLUTE THRESHOLD |

| Stimulus Intensity | Response | | | | |
|---|---|---|---|---|---|
| | ↓ | | ↓ | | |
| 200 | | | Yes | | |
| 180 | Yes | | Yes | | |
| 160 | Yes | | Yes | | |
| 140 | Yes | Yes | Yes | | |
| 120 | Yes | No | No | Yes | |
| 100 | Yes | No | | No | |
| 80 | No | No | | No | |
| 60 | | No | | No | |
| 40 | | No | | ↑ | |
| 20 | | No | | | |
| | | ↑ | | | Mean |
| Threshold | 90 | 130 | 130 | 110 | 115 |

Note: In the first series of trials, the experimenter starts with a strong stimulus and decreases its intensity until the observer can no longer detect it. The threshold is the mean of the stimulus intensities that yield the first "No" response and the last "Yes" response. In the next series of trials, a weak stimulus is increased in intensity until it is detected. It is customary to start each series at a different stimulus intensity, to make it less likely that the observer's responses will be influenced by the length of a series. Stimuli are in arbitrary units—that is, the intensities ranging from 20 to 200 could represent weight, or anything else that might vary in intensity.

series requires several "Yes" responses before the threshold is reached, some observers may decide that they are giving too many "Yes" responses and prematurely respond "No." Other observers may be very cautious about changing their responses and so may delay too long. Indeed, the same observer at different times may commit both of these kinds of errors. So the threshold is operationally defined as the mean (average) of the points in each trial block at which the observer switches from "Yes" to "No" (or "No" to "Yes"). This is a statistical definition. A threshold defined this way, based on an observer's ability to detect a signal, is called an **absolute threshold,** because the "Yes"-"No" judgments are not based on a comparison of two stimuli, but are absolute judgments about a single stimulus. Hardy and his colleagues used the method of limits to obtain the absolute threshold for pain, using different intensities of heat as the stimuli, rather than tones.

The absolute threshold is a statistical concept, much like the "average taxpayer," so it has other statistical properties in addition to the mean. These will now be illustrated by computing a difference threshold in table 4–2. **Difference thresholds** are based on relative judgments, in which a constant unchanging comparison stimulus is judged relative to a series of changing stimuli. The question being asked by the experimenter is this: "How different must two stimuli be before they can reliably be distinguished?"

The traditional example of a difference threshold requires the observer to lift pairs of weights—one weight always remaining the same—and to judge if the new weight is heavier, lighter, or equal to the standard weight. Several series of ascending and descending trials are given. The upper threshold is the average point at which the observer changes from "Heavier" responses to "Equal" responses. The lower threshold is the point at which "Equal" responses give

**TABLE 4–2   USING THE METHOD OF LIMITS TO DETERMINE A DIFFERENCE THRESHOLD**

| | Comparison Stimulus (grams) | Response | | | | |
|---|---|---|---|---|---|---|
| | | ↓ | | ↓ | | |
| | 350 | | | Heavier | | |
| | 340 | Heavier | | Heavier | | |
| | 330 | Heavier | | Heavier | | |
| | 320 | Heavier | Heavier | Heavier | Heavier | |
| | 310 | Equal | Equal | Heavier | Equal | |
| Standard stimulus | 300 | Equal | Equal | Heavier | Lighter | |
| | 290 | Equal | Lighter | Equal | Lighter | |
| | 280 | Lighter | Lighter | Equal | Lighter | |
| | 270 | | Lighter | | Lighter | |
| | 260 | | Lighter | | | |
| | | | ↑ | | ↑ | Mean |
| Upper Threshold | | 315 | 315 | 295 | 315 | 310 |
| Lower Threshold | | 285 | 295 | 275 | 305 | 290 |

Interval of Uncertainty = 310 − 290 = 20 grams

Note: For descending series, the upper threshold is the mean of the stimuli leading to the last "Heavier" response and the first "Equal" response. The lower threshold is the mean of the stimuli producing the last "Equal" response and the first "Lighter" response. The standard stimulus is always 300 grams. The difference threshold is one-half of the interval of uncertainty (10 grams, in this example).

way to "Lighter" responses. The difference between these two values is called the **interval of uncertainty.** The difference threshold is operationally defined as half the interval of uncertainty. In table 4–2, this equals 10 grams. The mean of upper and lower thresholds is called the **point of subjective equality** (300 grams in table 4–2).

Weber, whose pioneering work in psychophysics preceded Fechner's by about twenty years, discovered some important properties of the difference threshold. One property that Weber determined was that the magnitude of the difference threshold increases with increases in the magnitude of the standard stimulus. This means that if 10 grams is the difference threshold when 300 grams is the standard, the corresponding value for a 600-gram standard stimulus would be a difference threshold of 20 grams. A familiar example will illustrate this psychophysical finding. In a room lit by a single candle, the addition of another lit candle will make the room noticeably brighter. However, in a room illuminated by several intense lamps, adding a single lit candle will not noticeably increase the brightness of the room.

Weber is famous for determining a second property of the difference threshold: *For a particular sensory modality, the size of the difference threshold relative to the standard stimulus is constant.* To return to our earlier example, the ratio of 10 grams to 300 grams is the same as the ratio of 20 grams to 600 grams, 1/30 in this case (the ratio that Weber actually obtained in his experiments). According to Weber's discovery, this means that the difference threshold for a 900-gram standard stimulus should be 30 grams, and it should be 40 grams for a 1,200-gram standard. What should the difference threshold be for a standard stimulus of 50 grams?

TABLE 4–3   USING THE STAIRCASE METHOD TO DETERMINE AN ABSOLUTE
            THRESHOLD

| Stimulus Intensity | Response | | | | |
|---|---|---|---|---|---|
| | ↓ | | | | |
| 180 | Yes | | | | |
| 160 | Yes | | | | |
| 140 | Yes | Yes | | ↓ | Yes |
| 120 | Yes | No | | No | ↑ |
| 100 | Yes | No | | | |
| 80 | No | ↑ | | | |

Threshold = 124

Fechner called relative constancy of the difference threshold **Weber's law.** This law is usually written as $\Delta I/I = K$, where $I$ refers to the magnitude of the standard stimulus, $\Delta I$ is the difference threshold, and $K$ is the symbol for constancy.

Weber's law, or the Weber fraction, as it is sometimes called, varies in size for different senses. For example, it is somewhat larger for brightness than it is for heaviness. A substantial amount of research has shown that Weber's law holds true for greater than 90 percent of the range of standard stimuli tested in a particular sensory modality. It fails to hold for very weak stimuli, such that the Weber fraction for very light standard stimuli is much larger than 1/30, which is what is found in the middle range.

You may think that the method of limits is quite inefficient, because each column contains many successive responses (in table 4–1, either "Yes" or "No") that do not change. A newer version of the method of limits, called the **staircase method** (Cornsweet, 1962), concentrates responses around the threshold. For the first trial, it is similar to the method of limits. However, once an estimate of the threshold is obtained, the staircase method never presents stimuli that are far from this estimate. This is shown in table 4–3. As soon as the threshold estimate is crossed, the direction of stimulus intensity reverses. This improves the efficiency of the method by keeping the stimuli much closer to the threshold than is the case for the method of limits. The threshold is calculated as the mean value of all stimuli presented, starting with the second trial (column 2 in table 4–3).

## CONCEPT SUMMARY

The **psychophysical method** called the **method of limits** attempts to determine **absolute** and **difference thresholds**

We now examine two approaches that have the goal of devising a ratio scale of an internal psychological dimension. The first approach was undertaken by Fechner; he relied on the results of classical psychophysical methods to provide the data for his psychological scale. The second approach we examine is a more modern one, devised by S. S. Stevens.

## Fechner's Law

According to Weber's law, the difference threshold bears a constant relation to the standard stimulus: $\Delta I/I = K$. Fechner assumed that Weber's law was correct, and with two additional assumptions developed his own law of sensation measurement. Fechner first assumed that the absolute threshold indicates the point of zero sensation. Then, he assumed that the **just-noticeable difference (JND),** which is the internal sensation evoked by two stimuli that differ by one difference threshold, is the unit defining the intervals of an internal psychological scale. Because Weber's law was assumed to be accurate, Fechner believed that all JNDs produce equal increments in sensation, as shown in figure 4–1. Each JND step on the psychological scale corresponds to the physical stimulus that is one difference threshold greater than the preceding stimulus. The first unit beyond the zero point corresponds to the physical stimulus that is one JND above the absolute threshold. The next point will be one JND above that, or two JNDs above the absolute threshold.

This process can be continued to build a psychological scale. Once this is done, there is a fixed mathematical relationship between the value of the physical scale corresponding to some point on the psychological scale and the physical value corresponding to the preceding point on the internal psychological scale. To find the physical-scale value that corresponds to a particular psychological value, we first take the physical value of the previous step on the external scale (for example, $X$ in figure 4–1) and multiply it by the Weber fraction. Then we add this product to our original value, so that $Y = X + X$ times the Weber fraction in figure 4–1 (likewise, $Z = Y + Y$ times the Weber fraction). Summing in this fashion yields successive physical values that correspond to successive just-noticeable differences on the internal psychological scale. When

**FIGURE 4–1**

Fechner's law. Equal units on an internal psychological scale correspond to progressively greater units on an external physical scale (the difference thresholds): $\psi = K \log (S)$.

this relationship is expanded and solved mathematically, we find that the psychological-scale value ($\psi$) is proportional to the logarithm of the physical-stimulus value. This equation ($\psi = K \log \text{stimulus}$) is called **Fechner's law.**

According to Fechner's law, all JNDs produce equivalent increments in sensation; therefore, it appears that we have a ratio scale (D'Amato, 1970). The sensation corresponding to six JNDs should be twice the sensation of three JNDs. Two factors we have already discussed should lead you to question whether Fechner has actually devised a ratio scale of sensation. First, Fechner's zero point is arbitrary rather than absolute. The absolute threshold is defined statistically and includes many sensations that do not exceed the decision criterion (see the discussion on thresholds and the discussion of signal detection in chapter 8). Second, we know that Weber's law is only approximately true; this could result in psychological and physical units of varying sizes. There is an additional difficulty with Fechner's formulation. Fechner assumed that each JND was psychologically equal, but if you ask people about the magnitude of the sensory effects produced by stimuli of varying JNDs above threshold, there is poor correspondence between the two (D'Amato, 1970). Thus, Fechner's work is neither a ratio scale nor an interval scale. At best, it is an ordinal scale indicating that sensations are ordered in a particular way with regard to the physical stimuli that produce them.

## Stevens' Power Law

S. S. Stevens (1961) attempted to develop an internal scale of sensation more directly than did Fechner. Fechner used an **indirect scaling** method, in which the psychological scale was built up by putting successive JNDs in a row. The observers did not judge the magnitudes of the JNDs directly, so the psychological-scale values are derived from measures of discrimination; therefore, they are indirect. Stevens used several **direct scaling** techniques, in which the observer responded in psychological-scale units in the first place.

The primary direct scaling procedure used by Stevens was the method of **magnitude estimation,** which requires the observer to state a number that represents his or her sensation of the stimulus intensity. The first stimulus that the experimenter presents is arbitrarily assigned some convenient number, say, 100. Then other stimuli are assigned numbers, depending on how close the perceived intensity is to the first stimulus. For example, the experimenter could present a tone of moderate intensity and tell you it has a value of 100. Then a weaker tone might be presented. So you would give it a lower number, say, 87. These numbers reported by the observer represent perceived psychological values directly. When data are gathered in this way, the equation relating psychological value to physical value differs from the logarithmic relationship of Fechner's law. Instead, the equation obtained by Stevens (1961) is $\psi = K (\text{Stimulus})^n$, where $n$ is an exponent. This equation is called **Stevens' law.**

If we assume that a stimulus of zero intensity always produces zero sensation (that is, there are no false alarms), then we can accept Stevens' law as a ratio psychological scale. With a true zero, and with equal stimulus ratios producing equal sensation ratios (a power relation), we have satisfied the criteria for a ratio scale. If this is the case, then it seems reasonable to accept $\psi = K\,S^n$ as the way in which our internal sensations are related to the external world.

However, Stevens' work and conclusions have not gone without criticism. There is some debate as to what the observer is really reporting in the method of magnitude estimation. One controversy centers on whether observers report the intensity of sensation, as claimed by Stevens, or whether they instead report a learned association based on a correlation with a physical attribute linked to the stimulus—such that, for example, judgments of loudness reflect the experience that softer sounds are farther away from the subject (Warren, 1963).

A related problem has to do with the fact that different people use numbers differently. Some people, for example, always produce very large exponents in the equation of Stevens' law, and it has been found that Stevens' law varies with the range of numbers used by the subjects (Marks, 1974).

A final problem with the magnitude estimation approach is related to operational definitions (see chapter 3). A substantial amount of research has shown that a particular sensory scale, such as brightness or pain, does not have just one psychophysical function that characterizes it. As Marks (1974) notes, you can accurately describe a power function for brightness only if you specify all of the other variables relevant to the perception of brightness—the color and duration of the light, the sensory adaptation of the observer, and so on. Varying these latter factors changes the value of the exponent in Stevens' law. Thus, we must operationally define the psychophysical function we obtain; otherwise, we would present a misleading view of the power function relating sensation to stimulus.

The preceding discussion of thresholds and psychophysical laws should convince you that the development of psychological measurement is very difficult. Nevertheless, procedures such as the method of magnitude estimation have been very valuable in psychology. The range of applicability of such procedures is very broad. For example, the method of magnitude estimation is not limited to developing psychological scales that have an obviously correlated physical dimension. Essay exams are often graded by magnitude estimates. Likewise, a substantial amount of research has examined the measurement of the severity of crimes and legal penalties by using magnitude estimation procedures (Sellin & Wolfgang, 1964; Stevens, 1966).

## CONCEPT SUMMARY

Fechner used the method of limits to determine the psychophysical relation between stimulus and sensation judgment, $\psi = $ **K log stimulus**

Stevens used the method of **magnitude estimation** and determined that the psychophysical relation between stimulus and sensation judgment was $\psi = $ **K (Stimulus)**$^n$

## INTERPRETING TABLES AND FIGURES

Throughout this text, you will have to examine tables and graphical representations of data (usually called figures) to understand many of the points we intend to make and to understand the results of a piece of research. Data often appear in a table or figure, so you need to understand the mechanics of preparing tables and figures so that you can know the important features to look for in them.

## Tables

If you have read the earlier part of this chapter, you already have studied data in a table. In the typical table, such as table 1–4, data and summarized data appear under various headings. Before you look at the data, you should first read the title of the table (the title generally appears immediately under or next to the words Table *n*, where *n* refers to the number of the table). The title of the table should be explicit enough to tell you what sorts of data appear in the table. The title of table 4–1 tells you that it contains information about the absolute threshold. Next, you should examine the headings and subheadings carefully. These will tell you about the conditions or variables that are relevant to the data in the table. For example, in table 4–1 the headings include stimulus intensity, their associated responses, and the threshold intensity. So, you should look for data that show the frequencies of responses and the threshold values. After you have examined the data in a table, you should read any notes that appear at the bottom of the table. The note at the bottom of table 4–1 tells you how to interpret the entries in the table.

## Figures

You have not encountered any figures containing data in this chapter. Some data are shown in figure 4–2. These are the results of an experiment conducted in one of our classes. The experiment concerned conflict resolution, which was tested by having the students read through a series of questions that asked them to choose between two personal characteristics. The characteristics the students chose from were wealth, health, happiness, intelligence, popularity, talent, and attractiveness. Each characteristic was paired with each other one, and the students read through two series of twenty-one questions. One series had questions such as "Which would you rather be, more healthy or more wealthy than you are now?" The other series of questions substituted the word *less* for the word *more* (that is, less healthy or less wealthy). The conflict questions containing the word *more* are called approach-approach conflicts, and the conflict questions with the word *less* in them are called avoidance-avoidance conflicts. The students had to circle the characteristic in each pair that they either wanted more of or less of, and their time to go through each set of questions was measured. In figure 4–2, we see the mean resolution time per conflict scaled on the vertical axis in seconds. The vertical axis is called the **ordinate.** On the horizontal axis, which is called the **abscissa,** we have the two types of conflict. Inside the figure are the results of the experiment. Nearly all figures from any type of psychological research have a scale of the dependent variable (what is measured) on the ordinate. In figures from experiments, the independent variable (what is manipulated) is on the abscissa. In correlational research, another dependent variable is on the abscissa. Be sure to examine the labels on the

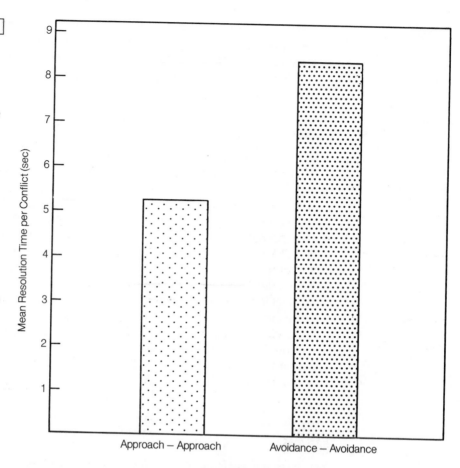

**FIGURE 4–2**

Mean resolution time per conflict in seconds for the approach-approach conflicts and the avoidance-avoidance conflicts. The dependent variable (resolution time) is on the ordinate, or vertical axis, and the independent variable (type of conflict) is on the abscissa, or horizontal axis. Note that the mean resolution time per avoidance-avoidance conflict ($M = 8.46$) is more than three seconds slower than the mean resolution time per approach-approach conflict ($M = 5.25$).

ordinate and abscissa so you know what data are plotted in the figure; then you can examine the data. In figure 4–2 the heights of the bars tell you the mean resolution time per condition, and you can see that it took the students about three seconds longer on average to resolve avoidance-avoidance conflicts than it did to resolve approach-approach conflicts.

Figure 4–2 is a bar graph, and data from an experiment are plotted as bars when the levels of the independent variable are defined at the nominal level. A different way to plot data is shown in figure 4–3. There the data appear as points (circles or triangles) connected by lines (solid or broken). Curves such as these are drawn when the independent variable is measured on a scale other than a nominal scale. In figure 4–3, the abscissa represents the number of steps apart in desirability that two personal traits were for a subject. In the original experiment, students had to choose between all combinations of seven traits: talent, intelligence, wealth, health, happiness, popularity, and attractiveness. The experimenter could have the students rank these traits in importance and then could see if the time to resolve a conflict depended on whether the comparison was between two traits that were close in desirability or between two traits that were very different in desirability. If the traits were ranked in the

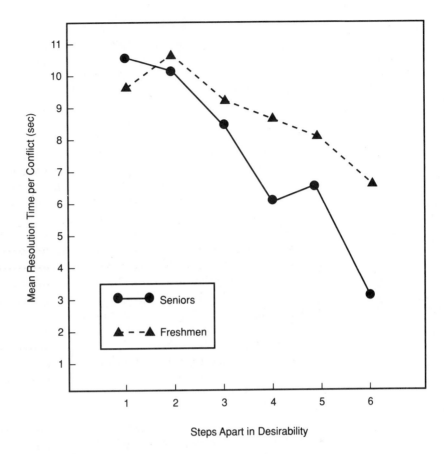

**FIGURE 4–3**

Mean resolution time per conflict (the dependent variable on the ordinate) as a function of the number of steps apart in the desirability of the trait given up in an avoidance-avoidance conflict (the independent variable on the abscissa) for freshmen (triangles with broken lines) and seniors (filled circles and solid lines). Note that the freshmen and seniors do about the same for the first three steps, but that the freshmen have much more difficulty resolving the conflicts for the final three steps. Thus, the two curves diverge (they are not parallel).

order in which they are listed here, we might find that the students had more difficulty choosing between less intelligence or less wealth than choosing between less talent and less attractiveness. (As far as we know, precisely that experiment has not been done. The data shown in figure 4–3 are fictitious.)

The abscissa in figure 4–3 is at the ordinal level, so the data are plotted as points within the figure. A line graph like this is used when the independent variable is ordered along a dimension. This figure has two sets of points, one for freshmen and one for seniors. It is conventional to use different symbols for different curves within a graph, as is done with circles and triangles in figure 4–3. It is also conventional to connect data points with straight lines, unless you actually determine the equation for the curve that could pass through those points. After you have examined the ordinate, abscissa, the parameters within the graph (that is, the labels for the different conditions—in this case, freshmen and seniors), and any legend under the figure, you can then study the data. Two aspects of the fictional data in figure 4–3 are noteworthy. First, freshmen take longer to resolve conflicts than do seniors. Second, freshmen and seniors take about the same amount of time to resolve the difficult conflicts (at steps 1 through 3), but the seniors become progressively faster than the freshmen as they go from step 4 to step 5 to step 6. The second feature means that the curves diverge (they are not parallel), and this divergence is called an

96 *Part I* Bases of Psychological Research

interaction. Interactions are important aspects of experimental data, and later in the text we will spend a considerable amount of time discussing them.

When you are trying to understand the data in a figure, be sure that you pay close attention to the scale of the dependent variable on the ordinate. Sometimes the scale can be misleading: An abbreviated scale with widely spaced numbers will tend to make differences appear more impressive, and a scale with numbers jammed close together will tend to make differences appear smaller. To see how this works, consider the following example.

Suppose that the number of murders in a city increased from 72 to 80 to 91 over three years. The next year, the mayor is running for reelection and is eager to show that the city has been safe for the last three years under her administration. So her campaign workers draw up the graph shown in the left of figure 4–4. By making the scale on the ordinate very long, they create the impression that the murder rate is fairly steady. In the same year, the city police are arguing that they need higher staffing levels. They want to show that the city is becoming more unsafe, so they depict the murder rate as increasing steeply by changing the scale, as in the right-hand graph of figure 4–4.

The facts are shown accurately in both groups. However, the left graph gives the impression that the murder rate is increasing very gradually, hardly worth worrying about. (Hasn't the mayor done a good job leading the city?) The right graph, on the other hand, creates the impression that the murder rate is increasing dramatically. (Don't we need more police?)

These graphing techniques are common. In fact, there are exaggerated scales used in some of the graphs in this book to show patterns of results more clearly. You should always look carefully to see what the scale is in a graph. With experimental data, it is more important to determine whether a difference is statistically reliable than to determine whether the difference appears "large" when graphed.

**FIGURE 4–4**

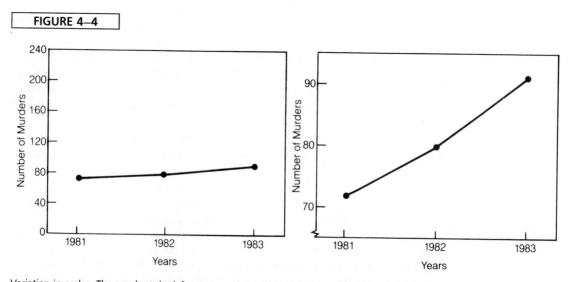

Variation in scales. The graph at the left seems to show the murder rate to be increasing only slightly, whereas the one at the right shows the rate going up dramatically. Yet, both graphs actually show the murder rate accurately—the difference is in the scale on the y-axis. It is important to examine a graph carefully and note the scale of measurement, because scale changes can make small differences look large and vice versa.

## SUMMARY

1. Measurement is a systematic way of assigning numbers or names to objects and their attributes.

2. Measurement scales, such as the familiar scales for temperature and weight can assess four properties: difference, magnitude, equal intervals, and whether there is a true zero.

3. Measurement scales used in psychology differ in how much information they provide. Nominal scales simply measure differences. Ordinal scales measure differences and magnitude. Interval scales add equal intervals to the features of ordinal scales. Ratio scales have all the properties of the other scales and a true zero point.

4. The scale of measurement determines the kinds of statistical treatment that the numbers can receive, and the scale of measurement also determines the kinds of conclusions that can be drawn from the results.

5. The reliability of a measure refers to its consistency. Using standardized conditions (protocols) is an important way to insure the reliability of measurement.

6. The reliability of test results can be shown by test-retest reliability, by split-half reliability, or by using parallel forms of the test.

7. Inferential statistics permit an assessment of statistical reliability by showing whether the results were owing to chance factors.

8. The larger the sample size from a population, the greater is the reliability and the power of the statistical tests.

9. Random samples help to increase the external validity of the sample.

10. Random assignment of subjects to conditions helps to increase the internal validity of an experiment.

11. Experimental reliability is assessed by conducting replications and is often preferred to statistical reliability.

12. Psychophysics studies the measurement of sensations and other psychological judgments. The psychophysical methods, such as the method of limits, were devised by Fechner in the middle of the nineteenth century. Absolute and difference thresholds can be calculated using the method of limits.

13. According to Weber's law, the size of the difference threshold relative to the standard stimulus is constant for a particular sensory modality ($\Delta I/I = K$).

14. Using an indirect scaling method by adding up just-noticeable differences, Fechner held that psychological judgments were related to the physical stimulus logarithmically ($\psi = K \log \text{stimulus}$).

15. Fechner's law leads to an ordinal scale of measurement.

16. Stevens used the method of magnitude estimation, which is a direct scaling method. His law of sensation measurement is a power one, $\psi = K(\text{Stimulus})^n$. This scale is considered to be a ratio one.

17. Understanding tables and figures is crucial for understanding data. The vertical axis of a figure is called the ordinate, on which the dependent

variable is scaled. The horizontal axis of a figure is called the abscissa, and in experiments the independent variable appears on the abscissa.

18. Data can be exaggerated in figures by manipulating the scale on the ordinate. Always examine the scale carefully.

## Key Concepts

| | |
|---|---|
| abscissa | point of subjective equality |
| absolute threshold | population |
| difference | power |
| difference threshold | predictive validity |
| direct scaling | psychophysical methods |
| equal interval | psychophysics |
| experimental reliability | random assignment |
| Fechner's law ($\psi = K \log \text{stimulus}$) | random sampling |
| indirect scaling | ratio scale |
| interval of uncertainty | reliability |
| interval scale | sample |
| just-noticeable difference (JND) | split-half reliability |
| magnitude | staircase method |
| magnitude estimation | statistical reliability |
| measurement | Stevens' law ($\psi = K(\text{Stimulus})^n$) |
| method of limits | test-retest reliability |
| nominal scale | threshold |
| ordinal scale | true zero |
| ordinate | Weber's law ($\Delta I/I = K$) |
| parallel forms | |

## Exercises

1. Discuss the differences between the various types of measurement scales. Indicate the scale properties of each.

2. [*Special Exercise.*] Consider each of the following measures and indicate the type of measurement scale: October 22, 1850; the number of alarm calls by a chickadee in one hour; third place in a beauty contest; having the fifth highest grades in a class of twenty-nine people; and being a sophomore in college.

3. How might the method of limits be used to determine whether *Anacin* or *Motrin* is the better pain reliever?

4. Why is Fechner's psychophysical scale likely to be at the ordinal level of measurement?

5. Why is Stevens' law more informative than Fechner's?

6. [*Special Exercise.*] In an experiment, seven-year-olds and ten-year-olds were given four trials to learn a list of spelling words. On each trial the words were studied individually for 15 seconds apiece. After each of the four study periods, the children wrote down as many words as they could. The mean percentage correctly written down by the ten-year-olds on each trial was: 44 percent, 53 percent, 81 percent, and 90 percent. The corresponding figures for the seven-year-olds were: 27 percent, 33

percent, 56 percent, and 63 percent. Draw a graph illustrating the results of this experiment.

## Suggested Readings

A good general reference for psychophysics is Gescheider, G. A. (1976). *Psychophysics: Method and theory*. Hillsdale, NJ: Erlbaum. Measurement theory is a complex topic. A good introduction can be found in McCall, R. B. (1990). *Fundamental statistics for the behavioral sciences* (5th ed.) San Diego: Harcourt Brace.

# PSYCHOLOGY IN ACTION
## Weber's Law

For this demonstration you will need several empty cardboard milk cartons, a supply of sand, gravel, lead shot, or similar material to partially fill the boxes, and a scale. Fill one of the containers about one-eighth full and add slightly more to another container. Ask a friend to lift them and tell you which weighs more. At first your subject will tell you they are equal in weight. Keep adding material to the heavier container until your subject can tell which is heavier. (Of course, you do not permit your subject to see you filling the heavier container and you randomly place the containers so that the heavier one is not always picked up with the same hand.)

Once the heavier container is determined, it becomes the new standard stimulus. Add material to a new container until it is just noticeably heavier than the standard container. Keep on repeating this procedure until the last container is almost completely filled. Now weigh each of the containers, making careful notes of the differences in weight between adjacent containers. You will find that adding a constant amount of material is not enough to produce a noticeable difference. Imagine that you are holding a three-pound package. You certainly would notice if someone quietly tiptoed up and added another pound. But if you were carrying a 100-pound load, adding another pound would go unobserved. Although *x* amount is sufficient to allow a subject to distinguish between the first two containers, amounts greater than *x* are required before the subject is able to tell apart containers later in the series. If you have done your experiment carefully, you will find that a constant percentage of the weight of a container is required before the next container seems heavier. This percentage is called the Weber fraction. Mathematically, Weber's law can be stated as follows: The difference threshold divided by the stimulus magnitude equals a constant (the Weber fraction). Weber's law does not hold for extreme values of stimulus magnitude. Thus, if you repeated your experiment with barbells or paper clips instead of milk containers, you would not get this result.

The Weber fraction also differs for different individuals and for different tasks. You might try repeating your experiment using lines of different lengths instead of containers of different weight. In this task, your subject would try to determine which of two lines was longer.

The measurement procedure described above is an indirect one because the subjects are required to make judgments about weight or line length according to a small set of categories. How might you undertake the research on line length using the direct-measurement procedure of magnitude estimation?

# EXPERIMENTATION IN PSYCHOLOGY

## BASICS OF EXPERIMEN-TATION
The researcher produces a comparison by letting one or more variables change while holding other variables constant

### Independent Variables
At least two levels of a variable are manipulated to provide a standard of comparison. Interactions may occur when there are two or more independent variables.

### Dependent Variables
Specific behaviors are measured in an experiment.

### Control Variables
In the ideal experiment, all other variables are held constant.

### Experimental Group or Condition
The treatment group or condition that receives the level of interest of the independent variable.

### Control Group or Condition
The group or condition that is untreated or receives a comparison (baseline) level of the independent variable.

CHAPTER

# 5

# BASICS OF EXPERIMENTATION

A tightly designed, well-conducted experiment is the goal of psychologists who attempt to answer the question of why we act as we do. In this chapter we will consider the basic characteristics of a good experiment. The essential ingredient of an experiment is production of a comparison while holding other variables constant.

## EXPERIMENTATION: AN EXAMPLE

Can you name

- A famous theme park in the heart of Copenhagen
- The world's largest single rock in Australia
- The main law court in London
- The actress who starred in *Yentl*
- The actor who played the *Bionic Man*
- The actor who played a Secret Service agent in *The Avengers*

You probably were able to answer some of these questions and were utterly unable to answer others. But there were perhaps some questions where you were not sure of the answer but where you felt you might know the answer. Indeed, the answer might be on the tip of your tongue. [Answers: Tivoli Gardens, Ayers Rock, Old Bailey, Barbra Streisand, Lee Majors, Patrick MacNee.]

The tip-of-the-tongue state has been much studied by experimental psychologists interested in human memory (Brown and McNeill, 1966). It occurs when you have partial knowledge of an answer and the feeling that you could recognize the answer if it were given to you. For example, Brown and McNeill discovered that when people said they were in tip-of-the-tongue states, they could correctly identify the first letter of the answer 57 percent of the time, even though the entire correct answer could not be produced.

What kind of information might help elicit correct answers from people in tip-of-the-tongue states? The answer to this question has important implications for understanding how we encode and store information in memory. Brennen, Baguley, Bright, and Bruce (1990) performed an experiment to discover if a

103

visual picture aided recall in tip-of-the-tongue states. Their first experiment was very simple. They presented a list of fifty questions about television celebrities and noted when their experimental subjects, fifteen college undergraduates, reported they were in a tip-of-the-tongue state. On average, this happened 10.5 times per subject. Of course, some subjects had only a few tip-of-the-tongue states and some had many (the range was four to twenty-two incidences) but on average about 20 percent of the questions produced tip-of-the-tongue states. Once this state occurred, the experimenters either asked the question again or showed a picture of the face of the television personality. Results of this experiment are shown in figure 5–1. Clearly, presenting faces did not help resolve tip-of-the-tongue states any better than merely repeating the question.

One experiment by itself seldom satisfies experimental psychologists, so Brennen et al. performed a second experiment both to expand their findings and to ensure that their initial results could be repeated. In this experiment they doubled the number of subjects to thirty. They also added a new condition where the person's initials were presented. So now there were three experimental conditions: (1) repeat the question, (2) present a picture, and (3) present letter initials. Results of this second experiment are shown in figure 5–2.

These results tell us two important things: First, repeating the questions and presenting a picture were equally effective. This means that the results of the first experiment have been repeated. Second, presenting letter initials was much more effective in resolving tip-of-the-tongue states than either repeating the question or presenting a picture. This result implies that memory information is stored in such a way that only the spelling of a name, and not a visual image, can aid memory retrieval in tip-of-the-tongue states.

## FIGURE 5–1

The results of the first experiment showing the percentage of tip-of-the-tongue states resolved as a function of the two conditions. Adapted from data presented by Brennen and others (1990).

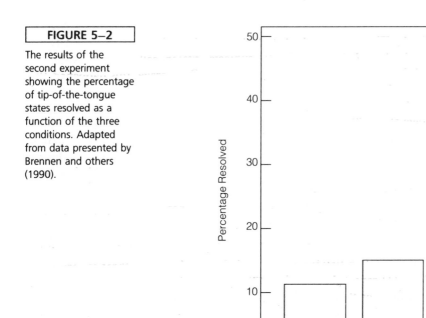

**FIGURE 5–2**

The results of the second experiment showing the percentage of tip-of-the-tongue states resolved as a function of the three conditions. Adapted from data presented by Brennen and others (1990).

This conclusion illustrates how experiments let us find the causes of behavioral events. In the first experiment, similar results for repeating the question and presenting a picture did not allow us to distinguish between these two possible causes of aided memory retrieval. But in the second experiment, presenting letter initials did cause a memory improvement. How do experiments permit us to make such causal statements?

## WHAT IS AN EXPERIMENT?

As discussed in chapter 3, **experiments** are tests designed to arrive at a causal explanation (see Cook and Campbell, 1979). The conditions necessary for arriving at explanations were set forth in the nineteenth century by the philosopher John Stuart Mill (1843/1930). The conditions he outlined provide a good definition of an experiment.

Mill argued that causation can be inferred if some result, $X$, follows an event, $A$, if $A$ and $X$ vary together and if it can be shown that event $A$ produces result $X$. For these conditions to be met, what Mill called the **joint method of agreement and difference** must be used. In the joint method, if $A$ occurs then so will $X$, and if $A$ does not occur, then neither will $X$.

Let us apply this reasoning to the experiment on tip-of-the-tongue states. Here the result $X$ is a correct resolution of the tip-of-the-tongue state. The event $A$ is presenting letter initials. Figure 5–2 showed that event $A$ produced result $X$. Furthermore, if $A$ is absent (for example, the question is repeated but no letter initials are presented) then result $X$ is not produced. This is Mill's joint method of agreement and difference at work.

However, the situation even in this simple experiment is more complicated because event $A$ does not always produce $X$ and the absence of event $A$ does not always fail to produce $X$. In figure 5–2 presenting letter initials does not resolve 100 percent of the tip-of-the-tongue states. Similarly, merely repeating the question does resolve tip-of-the-tongue states a small percentage of the time, and this small percentage is greater than zero. Thus, in practice most experiments do not show causality all the time for every single trial in the experiment. Instead, most experimental psychologists are content if event $A$ produces result $X$ more than some other event $B$. (The question of how much more is answered by statistical analysis explained in appendix B. For now, we ignore how much and only ask if there is any more $X$ produced.)

So a more complete statement of causality is event $A$ (presenting letter initials) produces more resolution of tip-of-the-tongue states ($X$) than event $B$ (repeating the question) or event $C$ (presenting a picture). At first, you might incorrectly conclude that event $A$ causes $X$ a great deal and event $C$ causes only a little bit of $X$. But this would be wrong. Most experiments have within them a baseline condition that evaluates neutral events, such as the passage of time, that are not believed to have causal influence. For some event to exert causal influence on behavior, it must have a greater effect than the neutral baseline event. In this experiment, repeating the question is the neutral baseline event. Any small effect this might produce is not interesting by itself. Instead, this calibrates other events of potentially greater interest. For example, event $C$ (presenting a picture) might be expected (from certain theories of memory) to produce a causal relationship with $X$. If the experimenters had omitted baseline event $B$ (repeating the question) in figure 5–1, they might have mistakenly concluded that event $C$ caused $X$ because more than zero percent of the tip-of-the-tongue states were resolved. But as figure 5–1 showed, event $B$ was as effective as event $C$. Therefore, we conclude that no causal relationship exists between event $C$ and $X$. This lack of a causal relationship inspired the experimenters to perform yet another study (figure 5–2) in which a causal relationship was obtained.

Experiments that fail to reveal any causal relationships are seldom published. Although the lack of a causal relationship where one might be expected due to theoretical reasons is important, it is even more important to show some causal relationship in an experiment. Failure to find any causal relationships could indicate a flaw in the experimental design (perhaps not enough subjects were tested, etc.). Thus, finding at least one causal relation in an experiment gives us some confidence that a failure to exhibit causality with some different event in the same experiment is more likely to be correct rather than to have happened because of some (unknown) deficiencies in the experiment itself.

The hallmark of an experiment is the production of a comparison by controlling the occurrence or nonoccurrence of a variable and observing the outcome. Boring (1954) noted that the concept of **control** in experimentation derives from the joint method of agreement and difference. One way we can view control is in terms of direct manipulation ($A$ occurs or does not occur), which, according to the joint method of agreement and difference, leads to a basis for comparison (hence, the term *control group*, as explained later). Control also suggests that we can eliminate alternative explanations of our results. Usually control in experimentation is thought of in three ways: (1) there is a control condition for purposes of *comparison;* (2) the levels or values of the independent variable can be *produced;* and (3) the experimental setting can be controlled by holding certain aspects *constant* (for example, type of apparatus or method of measurement). These three types of control—comparison, production, and constancy—are crucial to the conduct of an experiment that will yield an explanation of why people and animals behave as they do. In fact, comparison, production, and constancy provide us with a definition of an experiment (see the Concept Summary).

## CONCEPT SUMMARY

An experiment occurs when a particular *comparison* is *produced* while other aspects of the situation are held *constant.*

In summary, producing comparisons, as Brennen and colleagues did, can allow us to rule out the possibility of a mere correlation between variables. Correct use of Mill's procedure can lead to causal statements.

## ADVANTAGES OF EXPERIMENTATION

Let us examine another research problem to illustrate the advantages of experimentation. One characteristic of modern life is that many of us are subjected to changes in atmospheric pressure during air travel. Furthermore, a substantial portion of the world's population lives at elevations between 2,000 and 10,000 feet. What this means is that many people are subjected to mild decompressions in barometric pressure. Are these decompressions hazardous, as are so many other things in the world today (such as pollution, pesticides, and food additives)? This question was the impetus for experiments conducted by Graessle, Ahbel, and Porges (1978). Early research indicated that greatly reduced barometric pressure (as occurs in altitudes greater than 10,000 feet) can retard both fetal and newborn development. Graessle and colleagues wanted to see whether lesser decompressions, more like those experienced during air travel, also affected the development of infants.

To study this problem, the researchers experimented with pregnant rats. The general procedure was to subject the rats to a series of mild decompressions similar to those experienced during air travel (around 6,000 feet), and then compare the growth and behavior of rats born to the mothers that experienced decompression with the growth and behavior of rats born to mothers kept at ground level (728 feet, in this instance).

Now for some particulars of their research. Pregnant rats were randomly divided into two groups: One group received seven daily decompressions for twenty days during pregnancy, and the second group of mothers was kept at ground level. Changes in pressure for the one group (up to a pressure equaling an altitude of 6,000 feet) lasted about twenty minutes. These changes in pressure were gradual, simulating the sorts of changes that occur during air travel.

Following birth, all infant rats were weighed daily and received periodic testing of their ability to grasp a thin wire, turn over (the righting reflex), move on an inclined plane, and climb (pull themselves up a thin wall when suspended by their forepaws).

The *independent variable* (what was varied) was atmospheric pressure, and the *dependent variables* (the things observed and measured) included the weight of the babies and the various behaviors just described. In Brennen's experiments cuing condition was the independent variable, which had two levels in the first study and three levels in the second one. What was the dependent variable? At this point we need to mention a third class of variables, the *control variables*, which the experimenter holds constant. In the decompression experiment, control variables included similar housing and feeding conditions for all rats at all times, identical testing procedures, and the fact that the treated and untreated mothers were of the same strain of rats. Species, age, and persons to be identified were among the control variables in Brennen's work.

Ordinarily we call the group of subjects that receives the independent variable the **experimental group**; the designation for the untreated subjects is the **control group**. (Note that a control group is not the same as a control variable. The meaning of "control group" will become clear momentarily.) In the decompression experiment, the decompressed mother rats and their babies represent the experimental group. The mothers and infants that were kept at ground level as a comparison or baseline group make up the control group. These labels (experimental or control group) make sense in that the control group receives a different treatment, and an examination of this group's behavior serves to indicate changes that would occur in the absence of the independent variable. Thus, the control group *controls* for changes that may occur whether or not any particular variable is introduced into the situation. The experimental group, of course, defines the experiment for us. The experimental group is the one that receives the treatment of interest—decompression, in this case. (Note that we are using Mill's procedure to arrive at an explanation.) Graessle and colleagues found that rats given decompressions before birth began to climb at a later age than the control animals and that the prenatally decompressed rats gained weight more slowly than the controls.

The results of the decompression experiment are intriguing and may have important practical implications. If you were interested in this topic, you might have considered the possibility of doing this experiment with pregnant human beings. The ethics of that tactic would be questionable without knowing in advance the effects of mild decompressions. That is why we do many types of experiments, especially preliminary ones, on animals. An alternative approach to the decompression problem might be to do the research **ex post facto**, which means selecting our subjects after the fact. Thus, we could do a quasi-experiment (see chapter 9). In quasi-experiments the levels of the independent variable are selected rather than manipulated directly by the experimenter. We would find infants whose mothers had flown on airplanes during pregnancy. Then we would compare their development with that of infants whose mothers had remained at ground level during pregnancy. Other than the tedious job of identifying the subjects in the first place (imagine trying to identify human subjects ex post facto for this study), the major drawback to the research done ex post facto is a loss of control. As we will discuss in chapter 9, it is very difficult to hold potentially relevant variables constant after the fact. In particular, we would be hard put to find two groups of subjects whose only difference was that some had flown on planes prenatally and some had not.

We can conclude, therefore, that this animal study about the effects of mild decompression is more ethical, more economical, and better controlled than alternative research procedures. This experiment is not problem free, however. You might find it worthwhile to consider some of the difficulties associated with this experiment. One obvious problem concerns generalizing from rat development to human development.

## CONCEPT SUMMARY

### *Experiment*
A particular comparison is produced while other variables are held constant.
### *Experimental Group*
Receives the important level of the independent variable.
### *Control Group*
Serves as the untreated comparison group or receives a comparison level of the independent variable.

# VARIABLES IN EXPERIMENTATION

Variables are what make experiments run. Effective selection and manipulation of variables make the difference between a good experiment and a poor one. This section covers the three kinds of variables that must be carefully considered before starting an experiment: independent, dependent, and control variables. We conclude by discussing experiments that have more than one independent or dependent variable.

## Independent Variables

**Independent variables** are manipulated by the experimenter. The brightness of a lamp, the loudness of a tone, the number of decompressions given to a rat are all independent variables, because the experimenter determines their amount. Independent variables are selected because an experimenter thinks they will cause changes in behavior. Increasing the intensity of a tone should increase the speed with which people respond to the tone. Increasing the number of decompressions given to a mother rat may change the rate of development of her babies. When a change in the level (amount) of an independent variable causes a change in behavior, we say that the behavior is under control of the independent variable. Failure of an independent variable to control behavior, often called a **null result,** can have more than one interpretation. First, the experimenter may have incorrectly guessed that the independent variable was important, and the null results may be correct. Most scientists will accept this interpretation only reluctantly, and thus the following alternative explanations of null results are common.

The experimenter may not have created a valid manipulation of the independent variable. Let us say you are conducting an experiment on second-grade children and your independent variable is the number of small treats (chocolates, peanuts, or whatever) the children get after each correct response in some task. Some children get only one, whereas others get two. You find no difference in behavior between the two groups. Perhaps if your independent variable had involved a greater range—that is, if it went from one piece of candy to ten pieces of candy—you would have obtained a difference. Your manipulation was not sufficient to reveal any effect of the independent variable. Or perhaps, unknown to you, the class had a birthday party just before the experiment started and your subjects' stomachs were filled with ice cream and birthday cake. In this case, maybe even ten pieces of candy would not have shown any effect. That is why, in studies of animal learning in which food is used as a reward, the animals are deprived of food before the experiment starts. Thus experimenters are careful to produce a strong manipulation of the independent variable. Failure to do so is a common cause of null results. Other common causes of null results are related to dependent and control variables, to which we now turn.

## Dependent Variables

The **dependent variable** is observed and recorded by the experimenter. It depends on the behavior of the subject, which, in turn, is supposed to depend on the independent variable. The time it takes to press a switch, the speed of a worm crawling through a maze, the age when a rat climbs are all dependent variables, because they are observed and recorded by the experimenter.

One criterion for a good dependent variable is reliability (see chapter 4 for a discussion of reliability in testing and measurement). When an experiment is repeated exactly—same subject, same levels of independent variable, and so on—the dependent variable should yield about the same score as it did previously. Unreliability can occur if there is some deficit in the way we measure the dependent variable. Let us say we want to measure the weight in grams of a candle before and after it has been lit for fifteen minutes. We use a scale that has a spring which moves a pointer. The spring contracts when it is cold and expands when it is hot. As long as our weight measurements are taken at constant temperatures, they will be reliable. But if temperature varies while objects are being weighed, the same object will yield different readings. Our dependent variable is then unreliable. Generally, we want our measuring devices to be consistent, just as it is crucial for the observer to be consistent (as in following a protocol, see chapter 3).

Null results can often be caused by deficits in the dependent variable even if it is reliable. The most common cause is a restricted or limited range of the dependent variable so that it gets "stuck" at the top or bottom of its scale.

Imagine you are teaching a rather uncoordinated friend how to bowl for the first time. You know from introductory psychology that reward improves performance, so you offer to buy your friend a beer every time he or she gets a strike. Your friend gets all gutter balls so you drink the beer yourself. Thus you can no longer offer a reward, which means that the unrewarded performance should decrease. But because it is impossible to do any worse than all gutter balls, you cannot observe any decrement. Your friend is already at the bottom of the scale. This is called a **floor effect.** The opposite problem, that of getting 100 percent correct, is called a **ceiling effect.** Ceiling and floor effects prevent the influence of an independent variable from being accurately reflected in a dependent variable (these effects are discussed in detail later).

A final source of null results is one associated with inferential statistics. The results of a statistical test (see appendix B) may fail to reject the hypothesis that the experimental and control groups do not differ when, in fact, they do. This failure to reject the null hypothesis when it should be rejected is called a **type 2 error.** The likelihood of committing a type 2 error increases as we lower the level of statistical significance, but the likelihood can be decreased by increasing the power (sensitivity) of the experiment (see appendix B).

## Control Variables

A **control variable** is a potential independent variable that is held constant during an experiment. It does not vary, because it is controlled by the experimenter. For any one experiment, there are more desirable control variables than can ever be controlled in practice. In even a relatively simple experiment (for example, requiring people to memorize three-letter syllables), many variables should be controlled. Time of day (diurnal cycle) changes a person's efficiency, and ideally this should be controlled. Temperature could be important because your subject might fall asleep if the testing room were too warm. The time that has elapsed since a person's last meal might also affect memory performance. Intelligence is also related. The list could go on. An experimenter tries to control as many salient variables as possible, hoping that the effect of uncontrolled factors will be small relative to the effect of the independent variable. The smaller the size of the effect produced by the independent variable, the more important it is to carefully control other extraneous factors. Holding a variable constant is not the only way to remove extraneous variation. Design techniques, which we shall discuss in the next chapter, also control extraneous variables. However, holding a variable constant is the most direct experimental technique for controlling extraneous factors, and so we shall limit our definition of control variables to this technique. Null results often occur in an experiment because there is insufficient control of these other factors—that is, they have been left to vary unsystematically. This is especially true in studies outside of laboratories where the ability to hold control variables constant is greatly decreased. Remember, we call these unintended effects **confoundings,** because their influence confounds (or confuses) the proper interpretation of the results. An example of a confounded experiment is presented in the Application section.

# APPLICATION

### Confounded Experiments in Advertising

A major value of a tightly controlled experiment is that the results are unambiguous: You can be confident that the independent variable led to changes in the dependent variable. Your conclusion about the effectiveness of the independent variable depends on minimal effects of extraneous factors—confounding variables. An advertising campaign presented an incorrect conclusion because the intended independent variable (Pepsi versus Coke) was confounded with another variable.

In the advertisement, people were asked to choose between the two cola drinks. In one series Pepsi was in a cup labeled *S* and Coke in a cup marked *L*. Most people chose the drink in the *S* cup (Pepsi), so the conclusion was that cola drinkers prefer Pepsi. Is this a legitimate conclusion?

An experiment by Woolfolk, Castellan, and Brooks (1983) calls the advertising results into question. These authors reasoned that the labels on the cups may have had some influence on the choices made by the people in the advertisement. This supposition is based on the knowledge that labeling of various kinds can have a strong effect on consumer behavior. As a first step in their research, Woolfolk and her associates determined that college students like the letter *S* better than the letter *L*. Then the researchers had other students choose between the colas presented in cups labeled *L* and *S*. In this experiment, unlike in the advertisement, the letters were the only independent variable, because the type of cola in the cups was held constant. For half the subjects, both cups contained Pepsi; and for the other half, both cups contained Coke. Regardless of the type of cola in the cups, the students preferred cola *S* to cola *L* in 85 percent of the cases. Thus, it is possible that the conclusion in the advertisement was confounded by the preference for certain letters and did not result just from the preference for different colas. Let the viewer beware!

Woolfolk, M. E., Castellan, W., & Brooks, C. I. (1983). Pepsi versus Coke: Labels, not tastes, prevail. *Psychological Reports, 52*, 185–186.

## CONCEPT SUMMARY

- *Independent* variable is *manipulated*
- *Dependent* variable is *observed*
- *Control* variable is held *constant*

## Name the Variables

Because independent, dependent, and control variables are so important, we have included some examples here for you to check your understanding of these terms. For each situation, name the three kinds of variables. Answers are provided at the end of this section.

1. An automobile manufacturer wants to know how bright brake lights should be, in order to minimize the time required for the driver of a following car to realize that the car in front is stopping. An experiment is conducted to answer this. Name the variables.

2. A pigeon is trained to peck a key if a green light is illuminated but not if a red light is on. Correct pecks get rewarded by access to grain. Name the variables.

3. A therapist tries to improve a patient's self-image. Every time the patient says something positive about himself or herself, the therapist rewards this by nodding, smiling, and being extra attentive. Name the variables.

4. A social psychologist does an experiment to discover if men or women give lower ratings of discomfort when they are one of six people crowded into a telephone booth. Name the variables.

## Answers

1. Independent (manipulated) variable — Intensity (brightness) of brake light.

   Dependent (observed) variable — Time from onset of brake light until depression of brake pedal by following driver.

   Control (constant) variables — Color of brake light, shape of brake pedal, force needed to depress brake pedal, external illumination, and so on.

2. Independent variable — Color of light (red or green).

   Dependent variable — Number of key pecks.

   Control variables — Hours of food deprivation, size of key, intensity of red and green lights, and so on.

3. Independent variable — Actually, this is not an experiment because there is only one level of the independent variable. To make this an experiment, we need another level (say, rewarding positive statements about the patient's mother-in-law). Then the independent variable would be kind of statement rewarded.

   Dependent variable — Number (or frequency) of positive statements about self.

   Control variables — None. This is a poor experiment.

4. Independent variable — Sex of the participant. Note: This is not a true independent variable, because the experimenter did not manipulate it. This is a quasi-experiment.

Dependent variable          Rating of discomfort.

Control variables           Size of telephone booth, number of persons (six) crowded into the booth, and so on.

## More Than One Independent Variable

It is unusual in a psychology journal to find an experiment in which only one independent (manipulated) variable was used. The typical experiment manipulates from two to four independent variables simultaneously. There are several advantages to this procedure. First, conducting one experiment with, say, three independent variables is often more efficient than conducting three separate experiments. Second, experimental control is often better, because with a single experiment some control variables—for example, time of day, temperature, and humidity—are more likely to be held constant than would be the case with three separate experiments. Third, and most important, results generalized across several independent variables—that is, shown to be valid in several situations—are more valuable than data that have yet to be generalized. Fourth, just as it is important to establish generality of results across different types of experimental subjects and settings, we also need to discover whether some result is valid across levels of independent variables.

Let us say we wish to find out which of two rewards facilitates learning geometry by high-school students. The first reward is an outright cash payment for problems correctly solved, and the second is early dismissal from class— that is, each correct solution entitles the student to leave class five minutes early. Assume that the results of this hypothetical experiment showed early dismissal to be better. Before we make early dismissal a universal rule in high school, we should first establish its generality by comparing the two kinds of reward in other classes, such as history and biology. Here, subject matter of the class would be a second independent variable. It would be better to put these two variables into a single experiment than to conduct two successive experiments. This would avoid problems of control, such as one class being tested the week of the big football game (when no reward would improve learning) and the other class being tested the week after the game was won (when students felt better about learning).

When the effects produced by one independent variable are not the same across the levels of a second independent variable, we have an **interaction**. The search for interactions is a major reason for using more than one independent variable per experiment. This can be best demonstrated by example.

Piliavin, Piliavin, and Rodin (1975) were interested in discovering under what conditions a bystander would help someone in an emergency. The emergency was faked on a New York City subway car (the F train, appropriately enough). A white male carrying a cane stumbled and fell to the floor. Would other passengers aid this "victim"?

The experiment had two independent variables. In half of the trials, victims had an ugly red birthmark placed on their face with theatrical makeup. The presence or absence of this birthmark was the first independent variable. An observer wearing a white medical jacket (identifying him as a physician or a medical intern) was present in half the trials. The same observer was present without the white jacket for the other trials. So, the presence or absence of the supposed physician was the second independent variable. The combination of the two independent variables yields four conditions: (1) birthmark and intern; (2) birthmark and no intern; (3) no birthmark and intern; (4) no birthmark and no intern. The dependent variable was the percentage of trials in which passengers came to the aid of the victim by either touching the victim or asking him if he needed help.

Results of this experiment are shown in figure 5–3, with each independent variable plotted alone. People were more willing to help victims who lacked an ugly birthmark. They were also more willing to help when no medical intern was present.

Figure 5–4 shows, however, that this interpretation of the results can be misleading. If, as figure 5–3 implies, both independent variables have their own unique effect, the results should look like the two parallel lines plotted in figure 5–5. Instead, the lines in figure 5–4 are not parallel, which indicates an interaction between the two independent variables. The percentage of trials in which help was given depends on the levels of each independent variable. If the victim had no birthmark, then the presence or absence of an intern had little effect on helping. But when the victim had a birthmark, passengers were far less willing to help when an intern was present.

Now let us imagine that this experiment had been performed in two separate parts. In the first part, only the birthmark was varied. The experimenter would not have known that the presence of an intern would have reduced helping. In

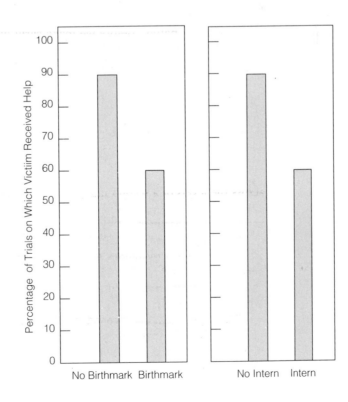

**FIGURE 5–3**

Effects on helping of two independent variables. Each variable is plotted separately. (Data from Piliavin et al., 1975. Copyright 1975 by the American Psychological Association. Adapted by permission of the author.)

Effects of two independent variables on helping behavior. (Data from Piliavin et al., 1975. Copyright 1975 by the American Psychological Association. Adapted by permission of the author.)

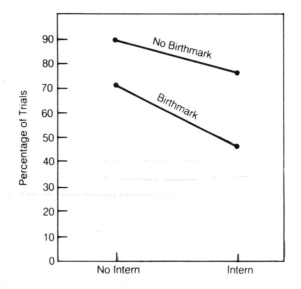

the second part, only the presence of the intern was varied. Results would have been quite different, depending on whether the victim had a birthmark. You can see that by doing the experiment in two parts, we would have lost a great deal of information.

Figure 5–4, which contains the actual results, shows an interaction. The effects of one independent variable depend on the level of the other independent variable. The least amount of help was given when the victim had a birthmark and the intern was present. Although figure 5–4 should technically be drawn as a set of bar graphs, like figure 5–3, it is instead drawn with lines to emphasize the interaction. In a line graph it is easy to visualize an interaction when lines are not parallel.

In summary, an interaction occurs when the effects of one independent variable are determined by the levels of other independent variables. When

Fictitious data showing no interaction between the two independent variables.

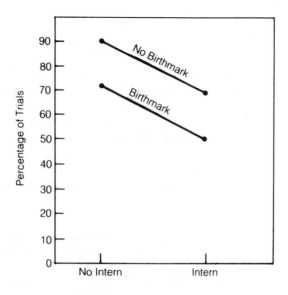

interactions are present, we do not discuss the effects of each independent variable separately. Because the effects of one variable depend on the levels of the other variables, we are forced to discuss interacting variables together. Interactions are an extremely important topic, so they will receive additional discussion in chapter 7.

## More Than One Dependent Variable

The dependent (observed) variable is used as an index of behavior. The experimenter must decide which aspects of behavior are relevant to the experiment at hand. Some variables are traditional, but this does not mean they are the only, or even the best, index of behavior. Take, for example, the behavior of a rat pressing a bar or a pigeon pecking a key. The most common dependent variable is the number of presses or pecks observed. But the force with which a key is pecked can also lead to interesting findings (see Notterman and Mintz, 1965), as can the latency or time to respond. Researchers can usually come up with several dependent variables that may be appropriate. Let us say we wish to study the legibility of the typeface that you are now reading. We cannot observe legibility, of course. What dependent variables might we observe? Here are some that have been used in the past: retention of meaningful information after reading text, time needed to read a fixed number of words, number of errors in recognizing single letters, speed in transcribing or retyping text, heart rate during reading, and muscular tension during reading. This list is far from complete.

Reasons of economy argue for obtaining as many dependent measures at the same time as is feasible. Nevertheless, the typical experiment uses only one or at most two dependent variables simultaneously. This is unfortunate because, just as the generality of an experiment is expanded by having more than one independent variable, it is also expanded by having several dependent variables.

## CONCEPT SUMMARY

VARIABLES IN EXPERIMENTS

| Type | Operation | Example |
|---|---|---|
| • Independent variables | At least two levels of a variable are manipulated | Cue type; decompression |
| • Dependent variables | Particular behaviors are measured | Percentage resolved; infant growth and movement |
| • Control variables | Other variables are held constant | Strain of animals; general test environment |

Multiple independent and dependent variables are important. An interaction occurs when the effects of one independent variable depend on the level of another independent variable.

One reason for not using several measures is that the results may be hard to interpret. Sometimes it may not be possible to determine whether the dependent variables are measuring the same thing or different things. Another reason more dependent variables are not used is that it is statistically difficult to analyze several dependent variables at once. Modern computer techniques make the calculations feasible, but many experimental psychologists have not been well trained in these multivariate statistical procedures and thus hesitate to use them. Although separate analyses could be conducted for each dependent variable, this loses information in much the same way that separate analysis of independent variables ignores interactions. Because multivariate analysis is complex, we will not discuss it here. Nevertheless, you should be aware that it is often advantageous to use more than one dependent variable in an experiment.

## SUMMARY

1. The joint method of agreement and difference permits causal explanation by showing that result $X$ occurs when event $A$ occurs, and that result $X$ does not occur when event $A$ does not occur.

2. An experiment can be defined as the production of a particular comparison while other aspects of the situation are held constant. Thus, comparison, production, and constancy are the hallmarks of control in experimentation.

3. Independent variables are those manipulated by the experimenter. It is important to select appropriate levels of the independent variable to avoid null results.

4. The dependent variable is the behavior observed and recorded by the experimenter. A reliable dependent variable is consistent. You need to guard against the possibility of ceiling and floor effects on your dependent variable by making sure that it does not have a restricted range of values.

5. A control variable is a potential independent variable that is held constant during an experiment. It is controlled to minimize confounding.

6. Using more than one independent variable is important in ensuring general results. When the effects produced by one independent variable are not the same across the levels of a second independent variable, we have an interaction.

7. Obtaining measures on more than one dependent variable can provide important information and increase the generality of the results of the experiment.

### Key Concepts

| | |
|---|---|
| ceiling effect | ex post facto |
| confounding | floor effect |
| control | independent variable |
| control group | interaction |
| control variable | joint method of agreement and difference |
| dependent variable | |
| experiment | null results |
| experimental group | type 2 error |

## Exercises

1. [*Special Exercise.*] An experimenter examined the effects of LSD on complex learning of rats. One group of rats was given a very small dose of LSD, so small a dose that it was unlikely to have any behavioral effects. A second group was given a large dose. Then, both groups ran through a complex maze several times. The dependent variable was the number of errors the rats made before obtaining the food reward at the end of the maze. The large-dose group made 4.5 times as many errors as the small-dose group, and the experimenter concluded that LSD can negatively affect complex learning. Comment on the levels of the independent variable that were used. What other dependent variables could be recorded? Comment on the conclusion by the experimenter.

2. Define what an experiment entails. Your definition should include mention of independent, dependent, and control variables.

3. Design an experiment to determine the effect of sex of the person to be identified on tip-of-the-tongue states. Specify the levels of your independent variable, describe your dependent variable, and note important control variables.

## Suggested Readings

Numerous experiments on a variety of topics can be found in Elmes, D. G. (1978). *Readings in experimental psychology.* Chicago: Rand McNally.

## PSYCHOLOGY IN ACTION
### Preference for Cola Drinks

A good follow-up to the findings of Woolfolk and associates (1983) that were discussed in the Application section would be to do the taste-test experiment appropriately. Perform the experiment with unmarked cups (or at least cups that do not have markings that are visible to your subjects). You will need some small paper cups and a supply of beverages (say, Pepsi and Coke, or perhaps Sprite and 7-Up). Allow each person to taste a small amount of each beverage and then indicate his or her preference. Make sure that your subjects do not know the brand names of your drinks (and, of course, make sure they do not see you pouring the drinks into the cups). A rating-scale procedure or a magnitude-estimation procedure (see chapter 4) could be used as an alternative dependent variable. If you use one of these dependent variables, you will probably want to have your subjects make judgments about each drink separately along some dimension (say, a goodness-of-taste dimension).

One thing you should try to do in this experiment is to make sure that half your subjects taste Coke first, then Pepsi, and that the other half of your subjects taste the beverages in the reverse order. This reversal of order is called **counterbalancing** and is used to guard against the possibility that the order of tasting the drinks has an effect on the dependent variable. Counterbalancing is discussed in chapter 6.

## EXPERIMENTAL DESIGN

Variables should be arranged to maximize internal validity

### Between-Subjects Design

In the simplest case, the experimental group receives the independent variable and the control group does not.

To minimize the confounding of subject characteristics with group membership, randomly assign participants to conditions or match their characteristics between groups.

### Within-Subjects Design

Each participant receives all levels of the independent variable.

To minimize confounding caused by carryover effects, the order of testing each level of the independent variable must be counterbalanced or randomized.

# 6

# EXPERIMENTAL DESIGN

A carefully designed experiment will permit valid conclusions to be drawn about the effects of the independent variable on the dependent variable. In this chapter, we consider how to design experiments with a between-subjects configuration, where independent groups of subjects receive the different levels of the independent variable. We also consider a within-subjects configuration, in which all subjects receive all levels of the independent variable. A threat to validity for the between-subjects case has to do with the initial equality of the subjects in the different groups. In within-subjects experiments, the effects of one treatment may carry over to another, which could confound the effect of the independent variable.

# INTERNAL VALIDITY IN EXPERIMENTS

In a properly conducted experiment, the situation is controlled so that changes in dependent variables result solely from changes in independent variables. In a good experiment, we can make valid causal statements about the results. A valid observation, as noted in chapter 3, is one that is sound or genuine because it reveals a true effect. A properly designed experiment can have valid results, and experiments that lead to valid results are said to be **internally valid** (see Cook and Campbell, 1979). By means of control (such as the joint method of agreement and disagreement), the researcher rules out inadvertent confounding, and the results reflect the effects of the intended variables. As discussed in chapter 5, Brennen et al. (1990) were able to assert that presenting letter initials was more effective in resolving tip-of-the-tongue states than presenting pictures. Their experiment was designed to maximize effects of presenting pictures and to minimize the effects of extraneous variables, which means their work was internally valid.

Experiments are internally valid in principle. Internal validity does not occur automatically, but rather through a careful selection of variables and an adequate experimental design. Underwood has noted that there is one basic principle of research design: "design the experiment so that the effects of the independent variables can be evaluated unambiguously" (1957, p. 86). In this chapter, we will discuss features of experimental design that help provide internal validity. To illustrate how experimental design is related to validity, we will first consider two situations in which design flaws could prevent valid causal statements.

## Executive Monkeys

The topic of stress-induced ulcers, especially among high-powered executives, is a common one in the popular press. Early laboratory experiments by Brady (1958) and his colleagues (Brady, Porter, Conrad, and Mason, 1958) demonstrated the development of stress ulcers in "executive" monkeys. Brady initially tested monkeys to see whether they could learn to respond quickly by pressing a button to avoid electric shock. Monkeys that responded at a high rate during this test were allowed to be executives in a second phase of the experiment. In the second part of the experiment, an executive monkey and a "coworker" received strong electric shocks periodically over long periods of time (usually a four-hour session). This was considered to be a highly stressful work situation for the monkeys. The executive monkeys could press a button that would postpone the shock. In this avoidance task, the coworker of the executive received a shock every time the executive received one, but the coworker did not have any control over the occurrence of the shocks. The executive had control over the presentation of the shocks by being able to avoid them. If the executive did not press the button often enough, both he and his helpless coworker would get shocked. Brady found that the executives developed severe gastrointestinal ulcers and died, whereas the helpless coworkers did not develop any obvious disorders. This finding led Brady, along with many other psychologists, to conclude that the stress of management could produce ulcers under controlled conditions.

Brady's conclusion was considered to be a valid one for quite some time. But then a number of laboratory reports began to appear that seemed to indicate greater production of stress ulcers in helpless animals than in those who had control over electric shock (for example, Weiss, 1968). Were the earlier findings the result of poor design, or were the later results a fluke? Subsequent work by Weiss (1971) confirmed the fact that helpless animals were indeed more affected than those who had control, and his work suggested why the original studies about executive monkeys were flawed and, thereby, invalid. Weiss noted that Brady's executives responded at a high rate at the beginning of the experiment. Then Weiss demonstrated that animals which respond at high rates in a stressful avoidance task are likely to get ulcers, regardless of whether they are helpless or in control. Because the tendency to respond at high rates was confounded with the independent variable (helplessness or executive control) in Brady's work, some psychologists made the invalid conclusion that control under stressful situations leads to ulcers. The critical design flaw underlying the invalid conclusion was assignment of the highly responsive monkeys to the executive condition. Later we will consider some general rules for ensuring that the characteristics of the subjects do not have a confounding influence on the effects of the independent variable. Without such rules it would be difficult, if not impossible, to have an internally valid experiment.

## Experiments with LSD

Lysergic acid diethylamide (LSD) is a hallucinogenic substance that was a popular and dangerous drug used to induce a "high" in the drug culture of the late 1960s and early 1970s. Because LSD was so popular and also seemed to produce some of the symptoms associated with schizophrenia, a severe mental disorder, psychologists tried to determine the effects of LSD on behavior in the controlled environment of the laboratory.

Laboratory research on the effects of LSD began in the early 1960s, and some of those studies provide useful lessons in designing internally valid experiments. We shall examine an early study by Jarrard (1963) that illustrates an experimental design in which each subject receives all levels of the independent variables (several different-sized doses of LSD, in this case). This type of design is called a **within-subjects design** and differs from the **between-subjects design** used by Weiss, in which different subjects received the various levels of the independent variable (the animals were ether helpless or executives, but not both).

Jarrard wanted to determine the effects of several different doses of LSD on well-established behavior. Initially, he trained rats to press a lever to obtain a food reward. When the behavior of the rats stabilized and they were performing well, Jarrard began testing the effects of LSD on the rate of lever pressing. His experiment involved six levels of the independent variable. The baseline or control amount of LSD was zero—the rats were injected with a saltwater solution that matched the salinity of their body fluids. The remaining five doses of LSD represented a proportion of each rat's body weight and were .05, .10, .20, .40, and .80 milligrams of LSD per kilogram of body weight. The general procedure involved placing the rats in the lever box immediately after injection for a two-hour test period. Several days separated each test of the injections.

At this point we need to consider several problems that could prevent Jarrard from having an internally valid experiment. Suppose Jarrard tested all his animals in the same order, going from the control dose to the largest dose. Such a design could lead to problems, because the susceptibility to LSD could change across successive administrations. The rats could become more tolerant of LSD (less affected by it), or they could become sensitized (more affected by it). In either case, tolerance or sensitization, the effects of later doses of LSD would be influenced by the rats' having received the earlier doses. This confounding effect also could occur if testing began with the largest dose and ended with the smallest.

Because Jarrard did not know whether LSD had long-term carryover effects such as tolerance and sensitization, he needed to find a way to administer doses so he could determine the effects of a particular dose independent of the other doses. He chose to counterbalance the order of doses across subjects. **Counterbalancing** means offsetting some contrary influence. The possible confounding effect of carry-over from one dose to another was counterbalanced by having each dose appear equally often at each ordinal position in the test sequence. For example, one subject might have received the following sequence: control, .05, .40, .10, .80, .20. Another subject might have received .40, control, .10, .20, .05, .80. The remaining four rats would then receive different orders of treatments so that for all six rats, each dose was tested first, second, third, fourth, fifth, and sixth. This procedure should balance across doses any tolerance or sensitization that could occur as a result of repeated administration of LSD. On the average, each condition occurs at each ordinal position.

Jarrard found that the pressing of a lever for food was slightly enhanced by the two smallest doses of LSD and severely impaired by the two largest doses, compared with the effects of the saltwater injection (the control condition). These are internally valid results because they are not confounded by carryover effects caused by repeated testing of the independent variable. A major topic of this chapter is prevention of carryover effects in within-subjects designs.

# EXPERIMENTAL DESIGN

The work of Weiss and Jarrard that we have just discussed illustrates the purpose of good experimental design: to minimize extraneous or uncontrolled variation in order to increase the likelihood that an experiment will produce internally valid results. Here we will cover some common techniques used to improve the design of experiments. This discussion should provide you with an understanding of the aims of the psychologist designing a particular experiment.

The first design decision an experimenter must make is how to assign subjects to the various levels of independent variables. The two main possibilities are (1) to assign only some subjects to each level, as Weiss did, or (2) to assign each subject to every level, as Jarrard did. As mentioned earlier, the first possibility is called a between-subjects design and the second a within-subjects design. Let us reconsider Weiss's study from the standpoint of the two types of design and pretend that we are going to repeat his work. The two main conditions in that experiment were the executive condition, in which the animals had control over the shocks, and the helpless condition, in which the animals received shocks regardless of what they did. Let us assume that we have ten rats available for our study. A between-subjects design and a within-subjects design for the experiment are illustrated in table 6–1. The between-subjects design calls for you to divide your subjects in half (into two groups of five rats each), with one group receiving the executive treatment and the other the helpless treatment. (The proper method for assigning subjects to each group will be discussed shortly.) The within-subjects design has all ten rats tested with both levels of the independent variable; that is, each rat is tested in the executive condition and in the helpless condition. (The proper method to determine the order in which each subject gets these two treatments will also be discussed later.) Before reading on, consider which design you would use and provide reasons. The factors involved in this sort of decision are considered below.

## Between-Subjects Designs

The between-subjects design is conservative (safe) because there is no chance of one treatment contaminating the other—the same subject never receives both treatments. However, the between-subjects design must contend with the possibility that the subjects in the two groups are different enough to influence the effects of the treatments. Any between-subjects experiment has the potential for being confounded because of differences among the subjects in the two groups. For example, the results of Brady's experiment were confounded by putting the highly responsive animals in the executive condition.

**TABLE 6–1  BETWEEN-SUBJECTS AND WITHIN-SUBJECTS DESIGNS FOR WEISS' EXPERIMENT, WITH TEN RATS AS THE SUBJECTS (NUMBERED 1 TO 10)**

**Between-Subjects Design**

| Individual subjects | Independent Variable | | |
|---|---|---|---|
| | **Executive Group** | **Helpless Group** | |
| | 1 | 6 | Half of the subjects are in |
| | 2 | 7 | the executive group and |
| | 3 | 8 | half are in the helpless |
| | 4 | 9 | group. |
| | 5 | 10 | |

**Within-Subjects Design**

| Individual subjects | Independent Variable | | |
|---|---|---|---|
| | **Executive Condition** | **Helpless Condition** | |
| | 1 | 1 | All subjects receive both the |
| | 2 | 2 | executive and the helpless |
| | 3 | 3 | treatments. |
| | 4 | 4 | |
| | 5 | 5 | |
| | . | . | |
| | . | . | |
| | . | . | |
| | 10 | 10 | |

**Randomization and matching.** In any between-subjects experiment, the researcher must somehow guarantee that as few differences as possible exist among the subjects in the various treatment groups. Clearly, if we took the five animals most susceptible to stomach ulcers and put them into the executive group, and we put the five least susceptible into the helpless condition, we might arrive at results that mask the true effects; we would have an internally *invalid* experiment. This is exactly what happened in the original executive-monkey experiment, because we now know that highly responsive animals are likely to ulcerate under stress. To prevent this kind of outcome, the experimenter tries to have groups that are equivalent at the beginning of the experiment.

One possible technique to use is called **matching,** in which important subject characteristics are matched in the various treatment conditions. In this experiment, one way to match subjects would be to administer a pretest to the animals to determine their response rates. Then subjects that had equal or very similar rates of response could be paired up. Unlike the procedure Brady used to assign subjects, this procedure calls for one member of each pair being randomly assigned to one group and the other member being assigned to the second group. One difficulty with matching is that an experimenter cannot match for everything. Indeed, the experimenter may not know what characteristics should be matched. Even though matched on some characteristics, the groups may differ on some other potentially relevant dimension. Thus, matching is done on the basis of the most likely confounding variables. Even so, matching on one variable could cause a mismatch on another.

In addition to the problems mentioned, another difficulty—**subject attrition**—can make matching an ineffective way to try to equate groups. Subject attrition means that one or more of the subjects in an experiment do not complete participation, or their behavior changes for reasons other than the independent variable. Attrition can occur for any number of reasons. For example, a subject might get sick and fail to continue. An animal subject might die or perform so poorly that the data are uninterpretable. A human subject in the experiment might refuse to continue to participate. In a long-term experiment, the subjects might mature, which means that their characteristics change during the course of the experiment. If we carefully match our subjects across conditions in order to equate our groups, then subject attrition in one group will make our groups unequal and our matching will have been in vain. This may be true even if just one subject is lost from a particular group.

If group characteristics are determined by an unbiased procedure (random assignment), attrition will have a less detrimental effect. However, attrition can still pose problems with both the reliability and the validity of our observations. If some form of attrition is likely, matching should not be used.

**Randomization** is a more common technique to ensure the formation of equivalent groups of subjects (see chapter 4). One way to form two groups by randomization would be to assign arbitrary numbers to the subjects and then pull numbered slips of paper out of a hat or some other container. Similarly, when we are ready to assign a particular subject to a condition, we could throw a die, with even throws being assigned to one group and odd throws to the other. If we do not have any dice, a table of random numbers could be used to generate odd and even digits.

A table of random numbers is provided in table C–7 in the appendix. Random-number tables are very easy to use. To generate odd and even numbers, select a row of numbers in the table. Proceed across the row, noting whether each number is odd or even. If you reach the end of a row, simply select a different row of numbers and continue the procedure.

Each of these methods of randomization ignores the characteristics of the subjects and leads to a random, unbiased assignment to conditions. Randomization means that each subject has an equal and unbiased opportunity to be in any of the conditions of the experiment. Randomization is how Weiss improved the design of the executive-monkey experiment. However, randomization does not guarantee that your groups will always be equal. By chance, more of the highly responsive animals might be assigned to one of the groups. The odds of this rare occurrence can be calculated by the methods of statistics. This is one reason experimental design and statistics are often treated as the same topic. However, experimental design has to do with the logic of arranging experiments, whereas statistics deals with calculating odds, probabilities, and other mathematical quantities. Although perfect matching may be preferable to randomization, in some cases we may not be sure about the basis of matching so that randomization is the preferred assignment procedure.

## CONCEPT SUMMARY

BETWEEN-SUBJECTS DESIGN

Separate groups of subjects receive different levels of the independent variable.

To control for individual differences

- *randomly assign subjects to conditions, or*
- *match subject characteristics in each group*

## Within-Subjects Designs

Many experimental psychologists prefer the within-subjects design to the between-subjects design. The within-subjects design is generally more efficient, because each subject is compared with himself or herself in the different experimental conditions. In our experiment, this means that any differences resulting from the executive and helpless treatments would not be caused by differences between the animals in the two conditions (as could be true of the between-subjects design), because all subjects receive all treatments.

As indicated in the earlier discussion of Jarrard's LSD experiment, the efficient within-subjects design brings with it the serious risk of **carryover effects** from one treatment to the next, which could result in an invalid experiment. That is, the effects of one treatment may carry over to another condition. These are particularly serious if the conditions affect each other (or carry over) in different ways (e.g., the experimental condition affects the control differently than the control condition affects the experimental condition). Imagine that ten rats first underwent the helpless condition and then were placed in the executive condition in Brady's experiment with executive monkeys. As a result of their earlier experience with being helpless, the animals may react poorly to the executive condition, where they now have control over the shocks. This would destroy any true differences between the two levels of the independent variable. Any within-subjects experiment has the danger that experience in an early part of the experiment might change behavior in a later part of the experiment, because the effects of one treatment might carry over to the other treatment. This can be caused even by routine factors, such as practice or fatigue. How do we reduce this source of invalidity?

**Randomization.** One way to minimize carryover among treatments is to randomly determine the order of their application. A random order can be established by using a table of random numbers or by writing the treatments on slips of paper and drawing them out of a hat. The logic is the same as that just described for assigning subjects to conditions in between-subjects designs. However, although randomization produces equivalent treatment orders in the long run, it is less likely to be suitable when there is only a small number of treatments. In most experiments, the number of subjects exceeds the number of treatments, so randomization is a good technique for assigning subjects to conditions but not for determining the order of treatments.

**Counterbalancing.** As mentioned earlier, Jarrard used a technique called counterbalancing to balance the order of treatments across stages of his experiment. By balancing the effects of order of treatments across subjects, Jarrard was able to minimize carryover effects. In counterbalancing, each treatment occurs in each time period of the experiment. This means that every treatment has the same chance of being influenced by confounding variables. In other words, we *counter* the effects of potential confounding variables by *balancing* them over the periods when the treatments are administered.

Complete counterbalancing requires that all possible treatment orders are used. In the executive-monkey experiment this is easy, because there are only two orders of treatments: helpless then executive, executive then helpless. An example of such counterbalancing is presented in the Application section.

# APPLICATION

### Counterbalancing in the Wild

Saari and Latham (1982) wanted to determine the effect of payment schedule on the performance and attitudes of beaver trappers in southwestern Washington. The trappers worked for a forest-products company and were paid an hourly wage during the course of the following experiment.

After a baseline measure of trapping performance under the hourly payment scheme, two incentive conditions were introduced in a within-subjects design. When trappers were under a continuous reinforcement schedule, they received an additional dollar for each beaver that was trapped. When the trappers were under a variable ratio schedule of four, they received four dollars when they brought in a beaver, if they correctly predicted twice whether the roll of a die would yield an odd or an even number (by chance alone, the trapper could pick the correct solution one out of four times). Thus, in one condition there was always a one-dollar payment, whereas in the other the payment was on the average given once every four times. Counterbalancing of the order of treatments was accomplished in the following way: The trappers were randomly split into two groups, and then the groups alternated weekly stints under either the continuous or the variable payment schedule. The alternating schedule continued for the entire trapping season.

Saari and Latham found that the number of beavers trapped increased under both payment schedules, but the increase was much larger under the variable ratio schedule than under the continuous one. Furthermore, they found that the trappers preferred the ratio schedule to the continuous schedule.

These results are very similar to those found when rats or pigeons are put under variable ratio schedules of reinforcement. Generally, behavior is more persistent under variable schedules of reinforcement than under continuous ones.

Saari, L. M., & Latham, G. P. (1982). Employee reactions to continuous and variable ratio enforcement schedules involving a monetary incentive. *Journal of Applied Psychology, 67,* 506–508.

As the numbers of conditions increase, the numbers of orders get larger. Three treatments have six different orders, four treatments have twenty-four different orders, five conditions have one hundred and twenty different orders, and so on. So, as the levels of the independent variable increase, complete counterbalancing soon becomes impractical. Instead, experimenters must settle for incomplete counterbalancing, in which each treatment occurs equally often in each portion of the experiment. In other words, condition A occurs first, second, and third equally often, as do conditions B and C. This arrangement is called a **Latin-square design.**

Figure 6–1 shows a 4 × 4 Latin square, which contains four treatments (A, B, C, and D). The columns of the square represent the sequence of these treatments, and the rows represent subjects being tested in the experiment. For example, subject 1 receives treatment A first, then treatment B, followed by treatments C and D. Other subjects receive these four treatments in a different sequence, or order, as we usually name this independent variable. Because a Latin square must always have equal numbers of rows and columns, the experimenter must use at least the same number of subjects as there are treatments. So figure 6–1 requires at least four subjects for the experiment. However, it is usually desirable to have more subjects than treatments for statistical reasons. This means that in practice the experimenter must obtain a number of subjects that is some multiple of the number of treatments in the Latin square. For the

**FIGURE 6–1**

A Latin square for counterbalancing the order of four treatments. Letters represent treatments. Thus, the first subject receives treatment *A* first, *B* second, and then *C* followed by *D.* Note that each treatment occurs only once in each row and each column.

| | Order | | | |
|---|---|---|---|---|
| | 1st | 2nd | 3rd | 4th |
| 1 | A | B | C | D |
| 2 | B | C | D | A |
| 3 | C | D | A | B |
| 4 | D | A | B | C |

Subject Number

square shown in figure 6–1, an experimenter could use 8, 12, or 16 subjects, because these numbers can be divided by four leaving no remainder.

What sequence of treatments should be used for these additional subjects? The experimenter has two choices. First, the same Latin square can be used over and over again. For example, using the square from figure 6–1, subject 5 would receive the same order as subject 1, subject 6 the same as subject 2, subject 7 the same as subject 3, and subject 8 the same as subject 4. When this procedure is used, good statistical practice requires the experimenter to compute a test for square uniqueness. If this test turns out to be statistically significant, it means that the partial counterbalancing of treatments was not successful and calls the results of the experiment into question. This is the danger of using a Latin square as opposed to complete counterbalancing. If the experimenter is unfortunate enough to select a particular Latin square that contains treatment sequences that somehow are related to effects of the treatments, the assumption that incomplete counterbalancing is sufficient fails. Fortunately, the statistical test for square uniqueness allows the experimenter to determine the success of this assumption. If the test is not significant, then the partial counterbalancing was successful, allowing the experimenter to avoid the expense of complete counterbalancing.

The second choice for testing additional subjects uses different Latin squares for each successive group of subjects. So, referring again to a 4 × 4 design, subjects 5 through 8 would get their own Latin square, which would have a different arrangement than figure 6–1. The advantage of this procedure is that as more Latin squares are used within an experiment, the chances of partial counterbalancing failing are decreased. So this is a reasonable choice when enough subjects are tested to allow using several different Latin squares. However, the disadvantage of this procedure is that it is not possible to calculate a statistic for square uniqueness. If the assumption of partial counterbalancing being adequate is wrong, the experimenter will never know because there is no appropriate statistical test.

Figure 6–2 shows a special kind of Latin square in which each treatment precedes and follows every other treatment equally often. This is called a **balanced Latin square**. Although many experimenters believe it offers better opportunities for successful partial counterbalancing than do normal Latin squares, there is no statistical test to prove this. Even so, when it costs nothing extra to use a balanced Latin square, this should be done, because it cannot hurt the experiment and might help. Such is the case for Latin squares with even numbers of treatments. A single balanced Latin square is impossible when there is

| FIGURE 6–2 |
| --- |

Balanced Latin square. Note that each treatment preceeds and follows every other treatment.

|  | Order | | | |
| --- | --- | --- | --- | --- |
| Subject Number | 1st | 2nd | 3rd | 4th |
| 1 | A | B | C | D |
| 2 | B | D | A | C |
| 3 | C | A | D | B |
| 4 | D | C | B | A |

an odd number of treatments. Although one can deal with this problem by adding an extra Latin square that is a mirror image of the first square, adding or subtracting a treatment to ensure that the number of treatments is even when using a Latin square may be easier.

g is useful not only for assigning treatment orders, but also order of testing when there is more than one dependent ry concern is to balance any potential carryover effects for To illustrate, let us reconsider the decompression study r 5. In that study, baby rats received several tests so that ald determine whether prenatal decompression had affected e is reason to believe that the infant rats' performance on nbing, could influence their behavior on another test, such n though the different measures are not independent var- ense, the order in which they are administered may affect )ne test might make the infant rats tired or could, conceiv- muscle tone. If we have two measures, *A* and *B*, we can palance the order of assessment across subjects so that the t be balanced.

omplete counterbalancing is the safest technique for within- al designs. When the number of treatments is small, com- ing is always preferred to Latin squares. However, with reatments, complete counterbalancing is often not practical. nter must assume the risk of using partial or incomplete ith a Latin square. A statistical test for square uniqueness of this textbook, but see Kirk, 1982, or other advanced ivailable to determine if incomplete counterbalancing was s not successful, the experiment must be repeated using a lare or perhaps avoiding a within-subjects design entirely. lares and within-subjects designs are very efficient, they are all experiments.

## CONCEPT SUMMARY

WITHIN-SUBJECTS DESIGN
All subjects receive all levels of the independent variable. To try to minimize carryover effects
• *randomize the order of treatments, or*
• *counterbalance the order of treatments*

## CONTROL CONDITIONS

Most experiments contain some *control group* (between-subjects design) or **control condition** (within-subjects design). In its simplest form, the control group is the group that does not receive the levels of interest of the independent variable. It is misleading to say that the control group does not receive the independent variable, because independent variables must by definition have at least two levels, one of which may be the control level. For example, say we are interested in analyzing the effect of noise on studying. Using a between-subjects design, we would expose one group of subjects to loud noise for half an hour while they were studying; this is the level of interest of the independent variable. A control group would study the same material for half an hour, but in a quiet setting. Then we would test both groups on the material. Any difference in test performance between the two groups would be attributed to the effect of noise.

In the experiment just described, the control group did not receive any treatment (no noise was introduced). This is not always the case. As you will recall from chapter 5, we described a study on decompression in which the control condition was ground-level pressure at 728 feet. Another control condition could have been sea level (zero altitude). In another part of the country, 1,000 feet might have been the appropriate control altitude. The important characteristic of a control condition is that it provides a **baseline** against which some variable of the experiment can be compared. Sometimes the best baseline is no particular treatment, but many times the best baseline requires some activity. This problem occurs sometimes in memory research.

Let us say that a group of subjects is required to learn two different lists of words (table 6–2); the experimenter is interested in how learning one list interferes with learning the other. The experimental group (receiving the level of interest of the independent variable) first learns list A, then learns list B, and then is tested again on list A. The experimenter would like to show that learning list B interferes with learning list A. But before any conclusion of this sort can be reached, a comparison control condition is required. Merely comparing the results of the final test of list A with the results of the first test is insufficient, because subjects might do less well on the last list-A test simply because they are tired, or do better because of extra practice. If a control condition with no treatment were used, a control group would learn list A, then would sit around for the time it takes the experimental group to learn list B, and then would be tested again on list A. But this would be a poor control condition because subjects might practice or rehearse list A while they are sitting around. Practicing would improve their final performance on the last list-A test and incorrectly make the experimental group look as if learning list B interfered with learning list A more than it really did. A proper baseline condition would occupy the control group during the time the experimental group was learning list B. Perhaps these subjects would be instructed to do arithmetic or some other busywork that would prevent rehearsal. An example of such an experimental design is shown in table 6–2. Another example is the baseline condition used by Jarrard in the LSD study. He used a placebo injection of saline instead of no injection at all. The reason for this injection baseline is that the injection itself could have disrupted the behavior of the rats. Without this comparison, there may have been an inappropriate assessment of the effects of LSD.

Sometimes the control condition is contained implicitly within the experiment. Suppose we want to study learning in rats, and our independent variable is the number of food pellets (one or five) we give the rats when they make the correct response. No experimenter would bother to include a control group or condition with zero pellets, because no learning could occur under this odd circumstance. The control condition is implicit, in that five pellets can be

| TABLE 6–2 | EXAMPLES OF EXPERIMENTAL AND CONTROL GROUPS FOR LIST LEARNING | | |
|---|---|---|---|
| | **First Period** | **Second Period** | **Third Period** |
| Experimental group | Learn list A | Learn list B | Test list A |
| Control group | Learn list A | Do arithmetic | Test list A |

compared with one, and vice versa. The experimenter might well be as interested in the effects of a single pellet as in five, so we probably would not explicitly call the one-pellet level a control condition. But it does provide a baseline for comparison—and so, for that matter, does the five-pellet condition, because the one-pellet results can be compared with it.

### Mixed Designs

Experiments need not be exclusively of within-subjects design or between-subjects design. It is often convenient and prudent to have some independent variables treated as between-subjects and others as within-subjects in the same experiment (assuming the experiment has more than one independent variable, of course). If one variable seems likely to cause transfer or carryover effects (for example, administering a drug), it can be made a between-subjects variable while the rest of the variables are within-subjects. This compromise design is not as efficient as a pure within-subjects design, but it often is safer. Mixed designs are described in more detail in the next chapter.

## CHOOSING AN EXPERIMENTAL DESIGN

We have noted that the between-subjects design precludes carryover effects from one treatment to another, and that the within-subjects design does not confound subjects with conditions. Furthermore, we have suggested that the within-subjects design is usually more efficient than the between-subjects design, so obtaining repeated observations from the same subjects may be preferable to using independent groups. In this section, we will consider some rules of thumb for selecting an experimental design, regardless of the particular research topic. At the end of this section, there are several experimental problems for which you are to choose a design.

### Carryover Effects

If your independent variable is likely to have a permanent effect on the subject and would prevent subsequent unconfounded testing, then a between-subjects design should be used. What sorts of independent variables would operate in this way? Independent variables that permanently alter the state or development of the subject would certainly have carryover effects. These might include effects of prenatal compression, prenatal nutrition, nearly all kinds of physiological damage (brain lesions, some drugs, toxic chemicals, and so on), most time-dependent variables (the effect of persuasion on later consumer behavior or the effects of a particular reading technique on second-grade achievement), and any other variable whose effects are likely to be irreversible. Most subject variables (sex, age, ethnic group, and so on) require a between-subjects design, but these variables are not true independent variables. The special problems associated with research involving subject variables is examined in chapter 9.

If you are interested in changes of behavior over time, such as improvements in learning, changes of strategy in a particular task, or optimal performance on a task, then you will want to use some variant of a within-subjects design. You either will need to expose your subjects to repeated measures (for example, you might place rats in a maze twice each day for a month), or you will need to give each subject several treatments over time. In effect, you are looking for a carryover effect, which is really what a great deal of learning research is all about.

## Individual Differences

You might think it trivial of us to say that people differ from each other. However, **individual differences** among subjects are not a trivial problem when it comes to designing a good experiment. If your subject pool contains individuals who are markedly different from each other or if you expect that large individual differences in behavior are likely to show up in your experiment, you may be better off using a within-subjects design rather than a between-subjects design. The within-subjects design automatically takes care of differences among your subjects. As long as you counterbalance appropriately (and carryover effects are not a problem), you can control for these individual differences in a within-subjects design.

A case in point is testing the effectiveness of drugs. Drug manufacturers know that people and animals differ in their sensitivity to drugs, which is one of the reasons Jarrard used a within-subjects design to test the effects of LSD. Once the drug is marketed, many different types of people will be taking the drugs. Therefore, it is imperative that many different types of people be tested and that several drugs be tested on the same person. Within-subjects administration of several levels of a drug compared with a placebo will also control for individual differences that may appear on the behavioral or attitudinal task used to assess drug effects. For example, a within-subjects design is important when studying the effects of a drug on pain tolerance, because we know ahead of time that there are tremendous individual differences in reaction to pain in the absence of any externally administered substance.

Obviously, if a drug is likely to have long-term effects, a between-subjects design must be used. Another reason that many clinical tests of drug effectiveness use between-subjects designs is that subjects with certain diseases are selected. The experimental group of subjects is given the drug, and a control group with the same disease is given a placebo or another drug. If one of the drugs is effective, then for humanitarian reasons all patients in the study receive it after the experimental comparison is completed.

Many research problems pose a particular dilemma: You must balance carryover effects against the possible contaminating effects of large individual differences. There is no easy solution to this problem. Sometimes the easiest way is to do the study one way (for example, within-subjects) and then do it the other way (between-subjects). Although such a tactic may seem inefficient, in the long run it will add to the generality of the results.

## Design Problems

For each of the following problems, decide on a within- or between-subjects design. If you think the situation warrants it, set up your experiment with both types of design. For practice, you should indicate the independent, dependent, and control variables. If you choose a within-subjects design, specify the counterbalancing procedures, and if you use a between-subjects design, indicate how subjects will be assigned to conditions. Regardless of your design, indicate your reasons for selecting either the within- or between-subjects configuration.

1. A researcher wants to see which is easier to learn: hard-to-pronounce syllables (such as WMH, JBT, SJK) or easy- to-pronounce syllables (such as LEJ, NAM, HEK). Two lists, containing either twenty pronounceable syllables or twenty hard-to-pronounce syllables, will be prepared. Each element in a list will be shown for two seconds. At the end of the series, the subjects will try to write down the syllables from memory.

2. A cleanser manufacturer is interested in the effects of package color on the sales of Scrubbo super cleanser. Cartons of Scrubbo that are identical except for the background color of the label (maroon, pink, or aqua) will be prepared. Sales will be monitored for the next four months.

3. A child psychologist wants to determine the effects of cloth versus paper diapers on toilet training. Day-old infants will be used to begin the project. The age at which diapers are no longer needed (to the nearest week) will be determined.

4. A researcher wants to determine whether rats learn a complex maze more quickly when practice is spaced (spread out in time) rather than massed. The effects of massing practice trials (one trial every ten seconds) will be compared with the effects of distributing practice trials (one every ten minutes). The number of trials the rats need to learn the maze perfectly will be counted.

5. The Burpo beer company is test marketing flavored light beers. It wants to see whether consumers prefer strawberry-, licorice-, or avocado-flavored Burpo. Several bottles of each flavor will be made. Consumers will fill out a questionnaire on how much they like the flavor, body, and aroma of the various flavors.

## CONCEPT SUMMARY

SUMMARY OF CONTROL TECHNIQUES FOR BETWEEN- AND WITHIN-SUBJECTS DESIGNS

| *To Control for* | *Between-Subjects Design* | *Within-Subjects Design* |
|---|---|---|
| Individual differences (sex, age, I.Q.) | Randomized assignment—unbiased assignment of subjects to groups | Individual differences automatically controlled |
| | Matched assignment Hold variable constant across groups (test only females) Equate variables across groups (use equal numbers of right-handed and left-handed subjects) | |
| Situational differences (time of day the data are collected, room temperature) | Randomize the effects of these variables Hold constant or equate these variables | Same as between-subjects |
| Carryover effects (order of testing, assignment of materials) | Usually carryover effects do not occur, if they do, use same techniques as in within-subjects | Randomized order Complete counterbalancing Incomplete counterbalancing (Latin-square designs) |

## SUMMARY

1. Experiments with well-chosen variables and clean designs permit accurate conclusions to be drawn from the results. Such experiments are said to have internal validity.

2. In a between-subjects design, different subjects are assigned to the different levels of the independent variable.

3. In a within-subjects design, each subject receives all levels of the independent variable.

4. With a between-subjects design, there is no chance for the effects of one treatment to contaminate the effects of another. However, the differences

between the people in the different groups may confound the effects of the independent variable.

5. The within-subjects design is more efficient than the between-subjects design, and we do not have to be concerned about differences between subjects contaminating the results. However, we do have to worry about the carryover of one treatment to another.

6. To ensure that the individual differences between subjects in various groups are not confounding a between-subjects experiment, we should assign the subjects to conditions on a random basis. Alternatively, the subjects' characteristics can be matched across groups.

7. By varying the order of presenting the treatments, we can minimize the carryover effects in the within-subjects design. The order can be randomized or completely counterbalanced. When there is a large number of treatments or levels of the independent variable, we can achieve incomplete counterbalancing by using a balanced Latin square.

8. A control group or control condition provides a baseline against which some variable of an experiment can be compared.

9. If the independent variable is likely to have a permanent effect on the subject and would prevent subsequent unconfounded testing, then a between-subjects design should be used.

10. If large individual differences in thought or behavior are likely to occur, a within-subjects design may be preferable to a between-subjects design.

## Key Concepts

| | |
|---|---|
| balanced Latin square | internal validity |
| baseline | Latin-square design |
| between-subjects design | matching |
| carryover effects | randomization |
| control condition | subject attrition |
| counterbalancing | within-subjects design |
| individual differences | |

## Exercises

1. [*Special Exercise.*] What is wrong with the following experimental design? To study how the creation of mental images affects retention, an experimenter used a within-subjects design. A long list of unrelated words was presented to the subjects, with each word being presented one at a time. Half the words were printed in black ink and the other half in red ink. The subjects were told to create a vivid mental image of the red words and to simply say the black words over and over to themselves until the next word was shown. After all the words were presented, the subjects had to write down as many of the words as they could, in any order they wished.

2. [*Special Exercise.*] Find the problem in this between-subjects experiment. An experimenter wanted to determine how a monetary payment affected attitude change. The

first twenty-two subjects to appear at the laboratory were offered fifteen dollars if they agreed to publicly endorse an unpopular candidate. The next twenty-two subjects to appear at the laboratory were offered one dollar is they agreed to endorse the same candidate. The percentage of people who agreed to the request in each group was the dependent variable.

## Suggested Readings

A complete discussion of the advantages and disadvantages of between- and within-subjects designs can be found in Kerlinger, F. N. (1986). *Foundations of behavioral research*. New York: Holt, Rinehart & Winston.

For a discussion of subtle biases that can occur with the use of within-subjects designs, see the following article: Poulton, E. C. (1982). Influential companions: Effects of one strategy on another in the within-subjects designs of cognitive psychology. *Psychological Bulletin, 91*, 673–690.

An interesting historical perspective of the use of control conditions in the design of experiments can be found in Boring, E. (1954). The nature and history of experimental control. *American Journal of Psychology, 67*, 573–589.

# PSYCHOLOGY IN ACTION
## The Stroop Effect

An interesting within-subjects experiment is a follow-up to the one in which you participated in chapter 1. That experiment used a within-subjects design, and the three conditions were reading digits, naming the number of pluses, and naming the number of digits, where the name of the digits was incongruent with the number of digits (for example, you read "3 3," and you were to say "2"). Your follow-up could include a fourth condition in which the name of a digit and its quantity were congruent (for example, 4 4 4 4). You could use the three series from the original experiment and devise your own congruent fourth series. There are thirty-two items in a series, and the numbers (or quantities) 1 through 4 are counterbalanced in the sequence via a Latin square. You will need a stopwatch or clock to determine the time it takes to read through each series.

To design this experiment appropriately, set up a counterbalancing scheme to determine the order in which a subject receives each condition. A balanced Latin square is the best way to do this, so that across subjects each condition occurs first, second, third, and fourth equally often, and each treatment precedes and follows every other treatment equally often (see figure 6–2).

Additional information on reading and naming can be found in chapter 11 under the heading "Stroop Effect." This effect is named after a scientist named Stroop who first used conflicting reading and naming stimuli to study these processes (Stroop, 1935). In its use of conflicting and congruent quantities of digits, your follow-up experiment is similar to one done by Windes (1968), who used a between-subjects design. Your experiment is also similar to one done by Hintzman and associates (1972), who, using a within-subjects design, printed names of colors in congruent or incongruent ink colors, and then asked the subjects to name the ink color.

You might want to combine your results with those of your classmates. Each member of the class could test four subjects. Each set of four subjects would complete a single balanced Latin square used to determine the order of conditions. Your interest should focus on the differences among the three naming conditions: neutral (+ +), incongruent (3 3), and congruent (2 2). If your results follow those of Hintzman, and coworkers, you should find that the congruent is faster than the neutral, which serves as the control condition, and the incongruent is slower than the neutral.

Hintzman, D. L., Carre, F. A., Eskridge, V. L., Owens, A. M., Shaff, S. S., & Sparks, M. E. (1972). "Stroop" effect: Input or output phenomenon? *Journal of Experimental Psychology, 95,* 458–459.
Windes, J. D. (1968). Reaction time for numerical coding and naming of numerals. *Journal of Experimental Psychology, 78,* 318–322.

# COMPLEX EXPERIMENTATION
Interactions between independent variables

## Between-Subjects Experiments

| Description | Features | Problems |
|---|---|---|
| 2 × 2 factorial design: 2 independent variables, each with 2 levels yielding 4 independent groups | 2 main effects and an interaction of the 2 variables | Confounding of subjects with groups |

## Within-Subjects Experiments

| Description | Features | Problems |
|---|---|---|
| 2 × 2 within factorial design (treatments × treatments × subjects); each subject receives each level of each independent variable (4 treatments in a 2 × 2) | More efficient than between designs; each subject is its own control; main effects and interactions can be determined | Confounding via carryover effects must be minimized—counterbalance or randomize; use several observations in each condition to increase reliability |

## Mixed Designs

| Description | Features | Problems |
|---|---|---|
| A combination of independent variables manipulated both between and within subjects; each subject receives each level of the within-subjects variable, and separate groups are determined by the levels (and types) of between-subjects variables | Has virtues of the above; very good for looking at interaction of practice (trials) with another independent variable | All controls above must be considered, but carryover is usually a variable, so its effects are measured. |

# COMPLEX EXPERIMENTATION

■
■
■
■      This chapter discusses the design and interpretation of experiments that have more
■      than one independent variable. Such multifactor experiments emphasize the in-
■      teraction betwen independent variables. Multifactor experiments can be viewed as
■      extensions of one-variable experiments. Some designs vary the independent vari-
■      ables between subjects and others vary them within subjects. It is also possible to
■      have a mixture of a between-subjects and within-subjects manipulation of the
■      independent variables. We will consider all three of these possibilities here.
■

## FACTORIAL DESIGNS

Why perform complex experiments? Later we will see that increased control
in quasi-experiments comes about by including both subject variables and true
(externally manipulated) independent variables in the study. However, increased control is not the primary reason for conducting laboratory experiments
with more than one independent variable. Rather, the major reason has to do
with the complexity of thought and behavior. Limiting experimental analysis
to a one-at-a-time variable manipulation cannot mirror the numerous, inter-
twined forces that influence people outside the laboratory. Therefore, multifactor experiments are likely to have better ecological validity than single-factor
experiments. The topic of ecological validity—whether an experiment has external as opposed to internal validity—will be discussed later. We can increase
the generality of our results by doing experiments that attempt to match the
complexity of forces that combine to influence our thought and behavior. In
addition, complex causal statements can be made, which should increase internal
validity.

Does this mean that what we have said before about analysis is invalid?
No. In any research problem, the basic factors need to be determined before
we can make more complex observations. In much the same way that naturalistic
observation and correlational studies often precede basic experimentation, simple experiments often provide the groundwork for more complex ones. Scientific
maturity occurs gradually. The database grows slowly, and the theories gradually develop. We begin with description and prediction, and we end with

explanation. Explanation itself goes through a developmental process—from simple experiments to complex ones.

## A 2 × 2 Experiment in Social Psychology: The Sleeper Effect

An extremely common finding in memory research is that information fades over time. When new information is presented you can easily remember it immediately. But as time passes, your ability to recall this information decreases. However, there is an interesting finding in social psychology in which the passage of time improves the effect of a persuasive message. This interesting quirk is called the **sleeper effect.** Imagine that you have just watched a television commercial for a new food product: Bulimia diet pizza. You can indicate how persuasive this message was by rating how likely you are to run to your local grocery store and purchase this new food. Let us pretend that, on a scale of one to ten, your rating was five. If you are asked to rate this food again at a later time, and you give a rating that is higher than five, you have just demonstrated the sleeper effect: The impact of the persuasive message has increased over time.

To obtain the sleeper effect, the persuasive message must be accompanied by a **discounting cue.** This is a message that causes you to distrust the accuracy or credibility of a persuasive message. For example, imagine that you have just read a one-page rave review of a new sports car manufactured by General Motors. If you were then told that the review came from the pages of *Car and Driver* magazine, your reaction would be different than if you were told that the review was written by the General Motors press department. *Car and Driver* would be a confirming cue that improves your belief in the message, whereas the General Motors press department would be regarded as a biased source of information. The sleeper effect is most likely to be obtained when the cue—a discounting cue—casts a doubt on the source of the message.

Although many explanations of the sleeper effect have been offered, those that focus on the role of memory have been the most popular (Pratkanis, Greenwald, Leippe, & Baumgardner, 1988). One such explanation is called the dissociation hypothesis. At the time of presentation, the persuasive message and the discounting cue are strongly attached. Thus, they tend to cancel one another out, and little opinion change occurs. After time has passed, the link between the message and the cue gets weaker. In particular, while the message is remembered, the discounting cue is forgotten. The discounting cue is not retrieved because the link between message and cue has weakened over time. This causes a net positive change in opinion, resulting in the sleeper effect.

To explain the logic behind a 2 × 2 experimental design, we shall consider a portion of recent results on the sleeper effect reported by Pratkanis and coworkers (1988). In a **2 × 2 factorial design,** there are two independent variables, each with two levels, or values. The word *factorial* indicates that all possible combinations of all levels of each independent variable are examined. Thus as shown in figure 7–1(a) a 2 × 2 factorial design contains four combinations of conditions: {1A}, {1B}, {2A},{2B}. In the Pratkanis experiment, two independent variables were (1) whether the discounting cue was presented before or after the persuasive message, and (2) the length of the delay (either 0

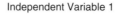

**FIGURE 7-1**

(a) The four treatment combinations in a 2 × 2 factorial design, in which separate groups of subjects receive each combination. (b) The 2 × 2 factorial design of the experiment by Pratkanis and coworkers (1988).

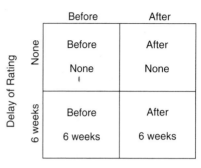

(a) The four treatment combinations in a 2 x 2 factorial design, in which separate groups of subjects receive each combination.

(b) The 2 x 2 factorial design of the experiment by Pratkanis and coworkers (1988).

or 6 weeks) between the message and the opinion rating. Thus, there were four combinations of interest: {before-none}, {after-none}, {before-6 weeks}, {after-6 weeks}. The design of the experiment is shown in figure 7–1(b).

Figure 7–2 shows the effects of cue presentation on the opinion rating. The line is almost flat, indicating little effect. On the basis of figure 7–2, we

**FIGURE 7-2**

Effects of cue presentation on the sleeper effect. Adapted from Pratkanis and coworkers (1988). (Copyright 1988 by the American Psychological Association. Reprinted by permission of the author.)

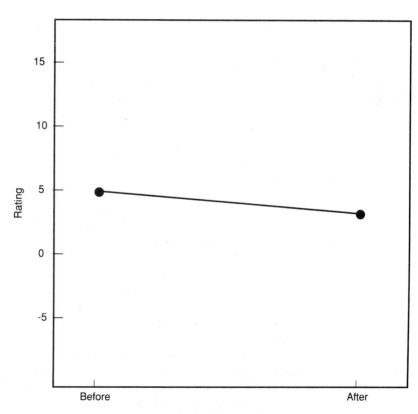

would conclude that cue presentation does not alter the sleeper effect. The effect of a single independent variable in a factorial experiment is called a **main effect**. Figure 7–2 shows that the main effect of cue presentation is almost zero because there is almost no difference between the ratings for level A (before) and for level B (after) for cue presentation.

Now look at figure 7–3, which shows the effects of delay on the opinion rating. Here there is a main effect. The rating is higher, indicating greater persuasion, at the six-week delay. This result is, of course, the sleeper effect. However, based only on figures 7–2 and 7–3, which show only main effects, we would conclude that the sleeper effect and effects of cue presentation are unrelated. Although the experiment reveals a sleeper effect, it appears that the effect has othing to do with whether the discounting cue comes before or after the persuasive message.

However, this conclusion is wrong. Figure 7–4 shows results for all four combinations in the 2 × 2 factorial design. The interpretation of results here is quite different. When the cue comes before the message, there is no sleeper effect. When the cue comes after the message, there is a large sleeper effect. So, contrary to the wrong conclusion drawn from figures 7–2 and 7–3, the timing of the discounting cue is absolutely crucial. An accurate interpretation of these reults requires knowledge of all four combinations of independent

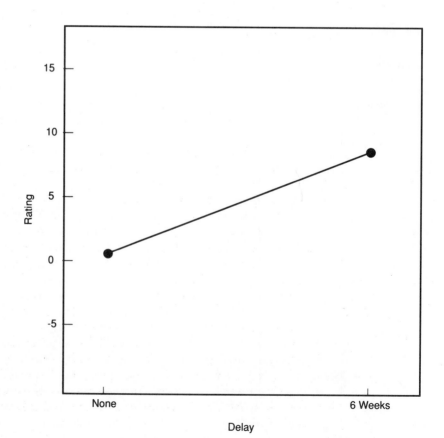

| FIGURE 7–3 |

Effects of delay on the sleeper effect. Adapted from Pratkanis and coworkers (1988). (Copyright 1988 by the American Psychological Association. Reprinted by permission of the author.)

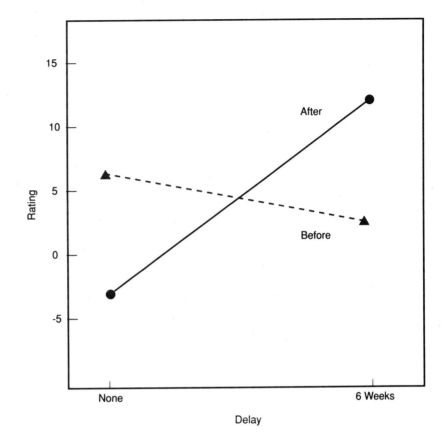

**FIGURE 7–4**

The interaction of delay and cue presentation and their influence on the sleeper effect. Adapted from Pratkanis et al. (1988). (Copyright 1988 by the American Psychological Association. Reprinted by permission of the author.)

variables. This outcome is called an **interaction.** An interaction occurs when the effects of one independent variable depend on the level of another independent variable. In figure 7–4 the effects of delay depend on the presentation of the discounting cue. Thus, there is an interaction between delay and presentation.

According to Pratkanis and colleagues, the results of figure 7–4 cast doubt on the dissociation explanation of the sleeper effect because the dissociation explanation predicts a sleeper effect regardless of when the cue is presented. A better explanation is called *differential decay.* It states that the impact of the cue decays more rapidly than that of the message (Pratkanis et al., 1988). Presenting the cue before the message eliminates the sleeper effect by weakening the persuasive impact of the message. However, as is the case with most critical experiments, a firm believer in the dissociation explanation might also adopt this latter explanation and argue that postulating a second factor—persuasive impact to explain the lack of a sleeper effect—applies equally to the dissociation hypothesis. Although Pratkanis and coworkers offer other arguments for differential decay, especially those that relate the sleeper effect to other findings in memory research, it is clear that more research is required to pin down this interesting quirk. In the words of Pratkanis and colleagues: "Long live the sleeper effect."

## CONCEPT SUMMARY

INTERACTIONS
In multifactor experiments, an interaction occurs when the effects of one independent variable depend on the level of other independent variables.

### *Patterns of Interaction*

Main effects are statistically independent of interaction effects. This means that
knowing the amount and direction of main effects provides no information
about possible interaction effects. In this section we discuss three sets of artificial
data that all have identical main effects. However, the patterns of interaction
are quite different.

Table 7–1 shows that the main effect of independent variable 1 is 20 units
and the main effect of independent variable 2 is 60 units. These main effects
hold for all the examples in this section.

Table 7–2 shows a 2 × 2 factorial combination with no interaction between
independent variables 1 and 2. Once a value has been selected for one particular
cell of the 2 × 2 matrix, all of the other cell values are determined by the main
effects. Let us take cell A1 to illustrate this point. It has an arbitrary value of
20 units. To find the value for cell B1, we add the main effect of independent
variable 1: 20 + 20 = 40, the value for cell B1. To find the value for cell A2,
we add the main effect of independent variable 2: 20 + 60 = 80. We now have
three of the four cells filled in. There are two possible ways to calculate the
value for cell B2. First, one could add the main effect of independent variable
1 to cell A2: 20 (main effect) + 80 (value in cell A2) = 100. Second, we could
add the main effect of independent variable 2 to cell B1: 60 (main effect) +
40 (value in cell 1) = 100. We get the same result (100) either way. Thus,

| TABLE 7–1 | MAIN EFFECTS | | | | |

| Independent Variable 1 | | | Independent Variable 2 | | |
|:---:|:---:|:---:|:---:|:---:|:---:|
| A | B | B − A | 1 | 2 | 2 − 1 |
| 50 | 70 | 20 | 30 | 90 | 60 |

**TABLE 7–2   ADDITIVITY (NO INTERACTION)**

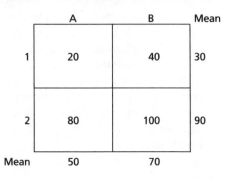

|  | A | B | Mean |
|:---:|:---:|:---:|:---:|
| 1 | 20 | 40 | 30 |
| 2 | 80 | 100 | 90 |
| Mean | 50 | 70 | |

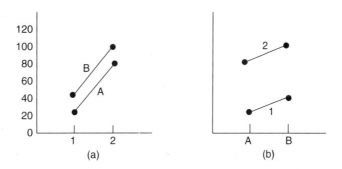

FIGURE 7–5

Additivity.

results are additive, and additivity is another term that means no interaction has occurred between independent variables.

These results are plotted in figure 7–5. In figure 7–5(a), independent variable 2 is plotted on the *x*-axis, and two different lines are drawn for the two levels of idependent variable 1. In figure 7–5(b), independent variable 1 has been plotted on the *x*-axis. Both ways of drawing figure 7–5 are correct. In both graphs, the two lines are parallel. This is a clear visual indication of additivity. When there is no interaction between two variables, they appear as parallel lines when graphed.

Table 7–3 contains a 2 × 2 matrix with an interaction between independent variables 1 and 2. If we tried to construct the cell values by adding the main effects as we did the table 7–2, the answer we would get would be wrong. (Try this for yourself.) When an interaction is plotted (figure 7–6), lines do not appear parallel. Although figures 7–5 and 7–6 represent identical main effects, the two graphs look quite different.

TABLE 7–3    INTERACTION

|        | A   | B   | Mean |
|--------|-----|-----|------|
| 1      | 30  | 30  | 30   |
| 2      | 70  | 110 | 90   |
| Mean   | 50  | 70  |      |

FIGURE 7–6

Interaction.

TABLE 7–4    CROSS-OVER INTERACTION

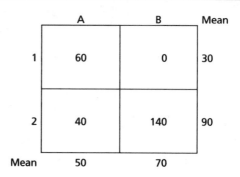

|   | A | B | Mean |
|---|---|---|------|
| 1 | 60 | 0 | 30 |
| 2 | 40 | 140 | 90 |
| Mean | 50 | 70 | |

FIGURE 7–7

Crossover Interaction.

 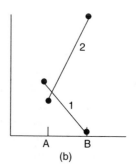

Table 7–4 represents a very important kind of interaction, called a **crossover interaction.** When it is plotted (figure 7–7), the two lines actually cross over one another. Crossover interactions are the most convincing form of interaction because they cannot be explained by problems in measuring and scaling the dependent variable (see chapter 4 for mathematical properties of different kinds of measurement scales). Again, table 7–4 has exactly the same main effects as tables 7–3 and 7–2. But figure 7–7 looks quite different from figures 7–6 and 7–5.

The moral of this section should be very clear. Patterns of interaction must be carefully considered before one tries to interpret any main effects in an experiment that has more than one independent variable.

## Control in Between-Subjects Factorial Designs

In a between-subjects design, each combination of independent variables is administered to a separate group of subjects. We want to make sure that the characteristics of the subjects are not confounded with group membership. In the ideal case, we would randomly select our subjects and then randomly assign them to our conditions. We are usually unable to have total random selection of our subjects because we do not have the procedures available to select, in an unbiased fashion, from *all* rats or *all* college students. It is therefore essential that we assign our subjects to conditions in a way that minimizes the possibility of confounding subject traits with our manipulations. When there are many groups in a factorial design, unbiased assignment is crucial. (Recall that chapter 6 outlines ways to randomly assign subjects.)

Another way to make unbiased assignments of subjects to groups is to use a balanced Latin square to determine group membership. The way to use this counterbalancing technique for subject assignment in a $2 \times 2$ design is as follows: Label the four groups (for example A, B, C, and D) and then make a balanced square for those symbols. Use the order of conditions in the rows of the resulting Latin square to determine assignment. The first subject to appear in the laboratory is assigned to condition A, the second to B, the third to D, and the fourth to C. Then use the next row to assign the next four subjects, and so on until all subjects are tested. You may have to construct many squares or use the same square repeatedly if you have more subjects than cells in your square. The purpose of this procedure is the same as random assignment to conditions: to make sure there is little relation between the subject's characteristics and assignment to a particular group. One advantage of the Latin-square technique is that in a large experiment that takes a long time to conduct, the order in which the treatments are conducted is known well in advance and also balanced across time. Thus, any historical factors that might be confounded here are balanced across groups.

In general, randomization, counterbalancing, and other control techniques help prevent potential confounding variables from interacting with the independent variables. In your design, you should try to reduce the possibility of such unwanted interactions. There are no hard-and-fast rules for choosing a control technique. The ones used are often chosen pragmatically. The particular control procedure you use is up to you: Make sure that you minimize confoundings and that you use controls that are easy to implement.

We limited the discussion of between-subjects designs to what is often called a **random-groups design,** which refers to unbiased assignment of subjects to conditions. An alternative method of assignment is matching (see chapter 6). In a **matched-groups design,** the experimenter tries to reduce the variability of observations between groups resulting from subject differences by matching the subjects on other variables. Thus, in the sleeper-effect experiment we just described, subjects could be matched on the basis of IQ before randomly assigning them to conditions. (Each subgroup of matched subjects is randomly assigned to the groups.) In our earlier discussions, we pointed out the difficulty of matching on relevant variables. Some subject variables, such as sex and age, can be matched across groups, or they can serve as quasi-independent variables. If matching is going to be difficult, you might want to use a complex within-subjects design, which we will discuss next.

## CONCEPT SUMMARY

FACTORIAL DESIGNS
All possible combinations of each level of each independent variable are examined. For example, a 3 × 3 case having independent variable A with levels A1, A2, and A3 and independent variable B with levels B1, B2, and B3 yields nine groups:

- *A1B1*
- *A2B1*
- *A3B1*
- *A1B2*
- *A2B2*
- *A3B2*
- *A1B3*
- *A2B3*
- *A3B3*

# COMPLEX WITHIN-SUBJECTS DESIGNS

The within-subjects design is often used instead of a between-subjects design, because within-subjects manipulation is more economical (requires fewer subjects) and automatically controls for individual differences. Of course, if permanent carryover effects are likely, a within-subjects design may be inappropriate.

Using a within-subjects design can result in a substantial reduction in the number of subjects needed for testing. However, the reduced number of subjects may require that you increase the number of observations per subject in each condition to ensure that your data are reliable. We should obtain numerous samples of a subject's behavior (just as is done in small-*n* experiments: see chapter 8). By doing so, we reduce the likelihood that some extraneous factor has influenced the results. For instance, in many learning, memory, perception, and reaction-time experiments, events occur rapidly, placing great demands on the subject. If the subject coughs or blinks at an inappropriate time, we may incorrectly underestimate performance on that trial.

Thus, whereas in a between-subjects design we test a large number of subjects, in a within-subjects design we obtain several observations on a small number of subjects. Even with numerous observations per subject, the within-subjects design is usually more efficient than the between-subjects one.

## A Complex Within-Subjects Experiment

Do you like to solve puzzles? Many people do. One kind of popular puzzle is the anagram, which consists of a word in which the letters have been rearranged. The solver tries to recreate the word from the anagram. Psychologists have examined many of the factors involved in anagram solution, because these puzzles seem to represent a relatively simple sort of problem-solving task. (Many psychologists probably study anagram solution because they like to solve them themselves.) One important variable in anagram solution is the frequency of the solution word. The higher the frequency of the word in written English, the easier people can solve an anagram of the word (Mayzner and Tresselt, 1966). One hypothesis suggests that the effects of solution-word frequency occur because people generate words as they are attempting to solve anagrams, and they are more likely to generate high-frequency words than low-frequency ones.

Dewing and Hetherington (1974) noted that the imagery of a word is associated with ease of learning and remembering. They predicted that if high noun imagery (a word such as *chair*) leads to greater availability than does low noun imagery (a word such as *truth*), then anagrams whose solution words have high imagery should be easier to solve than those whose solution words have low imagery. It should be easier to solve AHICR than URTTH. The researchers also wanted to determine the effects of hints on the ease with which subjects solved the anagrams. They presented a structural hint (the first and last letter of the solution word), a semantic hint (the title of the category to which the solution word belonged), or no hint. They hypothesized that if availability is important, the structural hint would help more when there were low-imagery solution words than when there were high ones because the structural hint would delimit the number of possible solutions. However, if the subjects did not generate low-frequency words as solutions to the anagram, then semantic clues would not help them solve low-imagery anagrams. Therefore, Dewing and Hetherington examined the effects of two independent variables on anagram solution: the imagery value of the solution word (high versus low) and the type of hint (none, structural, or semantic).

If this were a between-subjects experiment, we would call this a $2 \times 3$ factorial design. However, Dewing and Hetherington used a within-subjects design in which all levels of each independent variable were experienced by all subjects and thus we have what is usually called a **treatments × treatments × subjects design.** This designation derives from the type of statistical analysis associated with the design (see appendix B). Because in this experiment all combinations of variables were tested (as in a between-subjects design), within-subjects factorial is a good shorthand label. In this experiment, there were six conditions ($2 \times 3$), representing all combinations of the levels of each independent variable: Anagrams with low-imagery solution words were solved with three different hints, and anagrams with high-imagery solution words were solved with the same three types of hint. Dewing and Hetherington chose to use a within-subjects design rather than a between-subjects one because individuals differ markedly in their ability to solve anagrams. By using a within-subjects design, the researchers were assured that each subject served as his or her own comparison across conditions, which eliminated individual differences as a confounding factor in the experiment.

Before considering the results of this experiment, let us examine some additional details of the procedure. Every subject had to solve two anagrams under each of the six ($2 \times 3$) conditions. The high- and low-imagery words were chosen carefully: They were all five-letter nouns, they were all of about the same frequency of occurrence in written English, and different anagrams were developed for each word and administered to different subgroups of subjects. The time taken to solve each anagram was the dependent variable.

The results of the experiment by Dewing and Hetherington are shown in figure 7–8. As is true of a multifactor between-subjects design, you need to examine the results for both main effects and interactions. When there are two independent variables, you need to look for two main effects and one interaction. Note in figure 7–8 that much faster solution times occurred for the high-imagery solution words than for the low-imagery ones. Note also the striking effects of the hints: Performance was much slower when no hint was given. The lines of the functions are not parallel, so you should expect an interaction. The effects

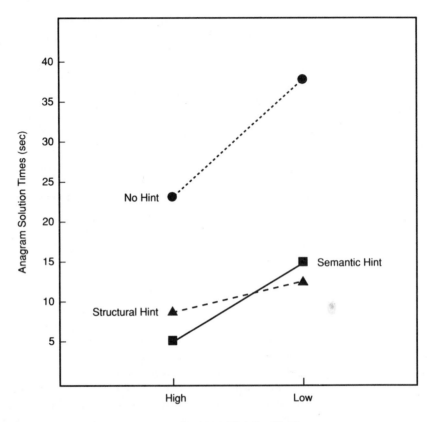

of the hints depended on the imagery value of the solution word. For the high-imagery words, the semantic clue aided solution more than the structural hint did, but for the low-imagery words, the opposite was the case. Statistical analyses by Dewing and Hetherington confirmed that both main effects were reliable, and there was a statistically significant interaction.

The role of imagery in a practical setting is discussed in the following Application section.

# APPLICATION

### Improving the Learning of Foreign-Language Vocabulary

Many laboratory experiments indicate that imagery and the type of rehearsal can improve retention. Do these kinds of results also occur in more practical situations?

Atkinson (1975) indicates that certain kinds of rehearsal techniques can dramatically improve the learning and retention of foreign-language vocabulary. One procedure that has been successful is called the keyword method. We will outline how this method is appropriate for learning Russian vocabulary, although it has worked in the learning of other languages as well. The keyword method splits vocabulary learning into two parts. In the first part, the subject associates a spoken foreign word with the keyword. This is easily done because the keyword sounds very much like the foreign word. In the second part, the subject tries to form a mental image of the keyword and the English translation interacting in some way. So, first the foreign word is connected to the keyword and then the keyword is connected to the English translation.

In Russian, the word *dym* (as spelled in our alphabet) sounds similar to the English word *dim* and means smoke. If we use the English word *dim* as the keyword, *dim* and *dym* are first linked together. Then we might form a mental image of a dim picture that has been clouded by smoke. In Atkinson's experiments, subjects hear the foreign words and are given the keyword and the English translation. The subjects provide their own mental image linking the keyword to the translation.

Learning is much faster with the keyword technique than without it—control subjects take about one-third longer to learn the same number of translations as do similar subjects who use keywords. Tests of retention up to about six weeks later indicate that the subjects using keywords recall about 65 percent more than the controls. Use of memory techniques in many situations can lead to superior retention.

Atkinson, R. C. (1975). Mnemotechnics and second-language learning. *American Psychologist, 30,* 821–828.

## Control in Complex Within-Subjects Designs

When a complex within-subjects design is used, you need to be concerned about carryover effects just as you do when only one independent variable is varied within subjects. Furthermore, you need to guard against many kinds of confounding that can occur in any multifactor experiment.

How did Dewing and Hetherington avoid the possibility of carryover effects from one treatment to another? They needed to be sure that having solved one type of anagram with a specific hint (say, a high-imagery solution word with a structural hint) did not influence the ability to solve another type of anagram with a different clue. Another potential carryover they had to consider was practice, because each subject had two tries on each type of anagram, and the subjects might have gotten better at solving anagrams during the course of the experiment. Dewing and Hetherington minimized carryover effects by having a different random order of the twelve anagrams for each subject. Presumably, the cards on which the anagrams and hints were written were shuffled before testing began. Thus, each condition had an unbiased chance of being tested in any of the twelve test orders, and each condition had an unbiased chance of being preceded and followed by every other condition. Because there are seventy-two subjects, Dewing and Hetherington had seventy-two random orders of presenting the twelve conditions, and it is unlikely that any inadvertent carryover occurred to confound the results.

The use of a random order should guard against both types of carryover (effects from condition-to-condition, and practice effects). However, Dewing and Hetherington did not have to worry much about differential practice effects, because earlier research had shown that practice effects are minimal unless the subjects receive several weeks of practice. Nevertheless, it would have been dangerous for them to have confounded conditions with order of testing. A small amount of confounding could occur, and here is no reason to tempt fate.

Two alternative procedures for controlling carryover in the anagram experiment are **block randomization** and counterbalancing (see chapter 6). The major difference between block randomization and complete randomization is that the order of treatments is randomized twice in the block-randomization technique. Each of the six conditions appears once in a random order in the first six trials, and then each treatment is tested again in a random order in the second block of six trials. One advantage of block randomization over complete randomization is that the blocking procedure guarantees that every condition will be tested before a particular condition is tested again. Across test trials, therefore, block randomization is less likely than complete randomization to confound test order and condition. Typically, block randomization is determined for each subject, just as a different random order was determined for each subject by Dewing and Hetherington.

Counterbalancing could minimize carryover effects as well. One way to counterbalance would be to generate 6 × 6 balanced Latin squares for the six treatments and assign two rows to each subject to determine the order of presenting the conditions. An advantage of this procedure over randomization (either blocked or complete) is that balanced Latin squares ensure that each treatment precedes and follows every other treatment equally often. A disadvantage might be that the researchers would have to test subjects in multiples of six to be sure that all sequences in the Latin squares were administered.

Some additional aspects of the design used by Dewing and Hetherington are noteworthy. Because the high-imagery and low-imagery solution words came from different semantic categories, Dewing and Hetherington wanted to be sure that the semantic hints they used were not better for one class of solution word than the other. Prior to conducting the anagram experiment, they conducted pilot work (see chapter 1) in which they had ten other subjects rate the degree of association (on a five-point scale) between each solution word and its semantic clue. The raters, who did not know the purpose of the anagram experiment, determined that the degree of association between semantic hints and solution words was about the same for the high- and low-imagery words. Alternatively, Dewing and Hetherington could have attempted to find high- and low-imagery words that belonged to the same semantic categories so that the same semantic clue could be given to each. This would have been difficult, because it is hard to conceive of a low-imagery piece of furniture to pair with the high-imagery word *chair*. Other matches for high- and low-imagery words are also unlikely.

Another variable that could have been controlled but was not, is the spelling of the solution words. The high- and low-imagery solution words had different first and last letters, and this may be an important confounding. However, finding words with the same first and last letters that differed only in imagery would be difficult. One thing Dewing and Hetherington did to account for different spellings was to consider the frequency with which successive letter pairs in the solution word occurred in the English language. This is known as bigram frequency. Earlier research had noted that the bigram frequency of the solution word interacted with the bigram frequency of the anagram. Solution times were fastest for anagrams whose bigram frequency matched the bigram frequency of the solution word. This was true for both high and low bigram frequencies. In Dewing and Hetherington's experiment, solution-word bigram frequency was similar for the high- and low-imagery words, and, as noted previously, the experimenters used three different anagrams for each solution word.

Finally, we should note that Dewing and Hetherington completely counterbalanced clue conditions across the three anagrams generated for a particular word. In other words, the three sets of anagrams were combined factorially with the three hint conditions. In the nine lists of anagrams generated by this $3 \times 3$ combination, each of the treatment conditions was assigned to each anagram. This procedure probably was effective in eliminating a confounding of materials with conditions, which means that a particular anagram could not account for the differential effect of the hints.

## CONCEPT SUMMARY

### COMPLEX WITHIN-SUBJECTS DESIGNS

Every subject receives all combinations of each level of the independent variables.

For example, Dewing and Hetherington's (1974) experiment had the following conditions: an independent variable for solution-word imagery (high imagery or low imagery) and an independent variable for type of hint (semantic, structural, or none). A factorial combination of the $2 \times 3$ conditions yields high, semantic; high, structural; high, none; low, semantic; low, structural; and low, none.

# MIXED DESIGNS

There are advantages and disadvantages to both pure within- and pure between-subjects designs, so it is not surprising that many researchers use **mixed designs**. Mixed designs have one or more between-subjects independent variables and one or more within-subjects conditions. Mixed designs are very common in learning and physiological research, in which the interest is in the effects of some variable over time or practice. Usually the variable of primary interest has strong carryover effects (such as brain damage), so it is manipulated between subjects. Practice or time is necessarily a within-subjects variable in this case, because the same organism is repeatedly measured. You will sometimes see within-subjects designs, especially those involving large numbers of practice trials, called **repeated-measures design**. The experimenter using this kind of mixed design is often interested in an interaction between the two variables. Does behavior under the different levels of the between-subjects factor differ across trials (or whatever the within-subjects factor may be)?

To illustrate a mixed design, we will consider an experiment dealing with a classic problem in the psychology of learning: the partial-reinforcement effect. We will examine only one aspect of this phenomenon; namely, behavior is usually more persistent following intermittent presentation of reinforcement than after continuous presentation. This means that when a reinforcement is withheld, responding persists longer if partial reinforcement has been used than if continuous reinforcement has been presented. One way to study this phenomenon is to reinforce some animals in a maze on every trial and to reinforce others less than 100 percent of the time. After the animals have learned, we withdraw all reinforcement and see how long the behavior of running the maze lasts, or, in the jargon of learning, how long it takes the behavior to extinguish.

The simplest sort of maze is the straight alley, which is composed of a start box in which the animal is placed, an alley through which the animal runs when the start-box door is opened, and the goal box where the animal is reinforced. The reinforcement is generally food, and usually the animal has been deprived of food prior to the experiment. The dependent variable is the running speed, or the time it takes the animal to run the straight-alley maze. Often the animal's speed in each section of the runway is measured, and we determine a speed for leaving the start box, for traversing the alley, and for approaching the goal. Learning is indicated by the fact that after a number of trials, the rat's speed increases (the latency decreases). At first the rat dawdles along, but on later trials it goes through the maze quickly.

Suppose we now wanted to ask a straightforward question about learning in this situation: How is learning affected by the amount of reinforcement? Intuitively you might expect learning to increase as the amount of reinforcement increases. You should realize that this depends on how the "amount of rein- forcement" and "learning" are defined. We could vary the amount of rein- forcement by varying the percentage of trials on which subjects receive reward, or by varying the magnitude of reward after each trial. We could also measure learning in at least two ways—one might be running speed, the other resistance to extinction. The latter measure is found by seeing how long after training an animal will continue running a maze when it no longer receives reinforcement. Let us confine our interest to varying the percentage of rewarded trials. The experiment that is needed to answer our question has now become more man- ageable. We vary the percentage of trials on which the animals receive a reward for running the maze (the independent variable), and we measure the time it takes the animals to run the maze and their resistance to extinction (or running speeds during extinction training).

If subjects are rewarded only on some percentage of trials and we want to see how this affects extinction of maze running, should we use a within-subjects or a between-subjects design? If we use a within-subjects design, we would need fewer subjects and the variability within conditions would be less. How- ever, in using a within-subjects design we would have to be concerned with the effects of one training schedule on the others used. Once an animal has learned a task under one reinforcement schedule, the animal will not approach the task as though it were new when the task is relearned under a new schedule of reinforcement, even if there has been extinction of the response after it was first learned. (Extinction does not eliminate the memory of the training; it simply stops the animals from responding.) Because of the danger of such carryover effects from one condition to another in this situation, it would probably be better to use a between-subjects design. Weinstock (1958) conducted an ex- periment in which the percentage of trials on which subjects received reinforce- ment was varied between subjects. Weinstock was interested in the effects of reward percentage on changes in behavior across trials, so part of his experiment included repeated measures within subjects. Thus, the complete design is a mixed one: Trials is the within-subjects variable, and percentage of reward the between-subjects variable.

Weinstock tested female rats under six conditions of reinforcement in a simple maze. The rats were tested after twenty-two hours of water deprivation, and access to water in the goal box was the reinforcer. Each rat was given only one trial a day. If more than one trial a day had been given, then rats that had received water on the early trials would have been less motivated to run on later trials than rats that had not received water on the early trials. Having rats run only one trial per day at a constant twenty-two hours of water deprivation eliminated this problem, but it made the experiment quite lengthy and onerous for the experimenter. It took Weinstock about half a year, testing rats eight hours a day, to complete this experiment.

For the first twelve trials, all rats received continuous reinforcement (CRF) and were rewarded with water after each trial. On trials 13 to 108, the subjects were tested on one of six reinforcement schedules in a between-subjects design. It is easiest to think of these ninety-six trials as being composed of eight blocks of twelve trials, with the partial-reinforcement schedule as the number of reinforced and nonreinforced trials in each block of twelve. One group of subjects received continuous reinforcement (twelve reinforced and zero nonreinforced, or 12–0), and five other groups received partial reinforcement. One group received ten reinforced and two nonreinforced trials in each block of twelve; other groups can be labeled 8–4, 6–6, 4–8, and 2–10, according to the number of reinforced and nonreinforced trials in a block of twelve. It was randomly determined within a block of twelve trials which trials would be reinforced and which not for each condition. After ninety-six trials under one of these six schedules of reinforcement, all rats were given sixty more trials during which they received no reinforcement. Thus these are extinction trials. Weinstock's experiment is outlined in table 7–5.

The extinction running speeds from Weinstock's experiment are shown in figure 7–9. Running speeds during extinction declined with increases in the percentage of trials for which the subjects received reward during acquisition. The continuously reinforced subjects ran the slowest during extinction, and the groups that received the fewest rewarded trials ran the fastest. Thus, learning produced by partial-reinforcement schedules does not extinguish as rapidly as learning produced by continuous-reinforcement schedules. This result is called the partial-reinforcement extinction effect.

The results in figure 7–9 show an interaction. The effects of one variable depend on the level of the other. Performance decreases in extinction (across nonreinforced trials), but it extinguishes more rapidly in some conditions (group 12–0) than in others (group 2–10). In general, when one of the variables in a mixed design involves repeated measures, one of the things to look for is an

---

**TABLE 7–5** AN OUTLINE OF WEINSTOCK'S (1958) EXPERIMENT ON THE EFFECTS OF PARTIAL REINFORCEMENT ON MAZE RUNNING SPEED.

| | Days | | | |
|---|---|---|---|---|
| 1–7 | 8–19<br>Trials 1–12 | 20–115<br>Trials 13–108 | RF–NRF[a] | 116–176<br>Trials 109–169 |
| All rats were handled 6–8 minutes per day. | All rats received continuous reinforcement for 12 trials. | Rats received reinforcement according to six schedules of reinforcement for 96 trials in blocks of 12 trials. | 12–0<br>10–2<br>8–4<br>6–6<br>4–8<br>2–10 | All rats received nonreinforced (or extinction) trials. |

[a]The number of trials in each block of 12 trials for which subjects received reinforcement (RF) or nonreinforcement (NRF).

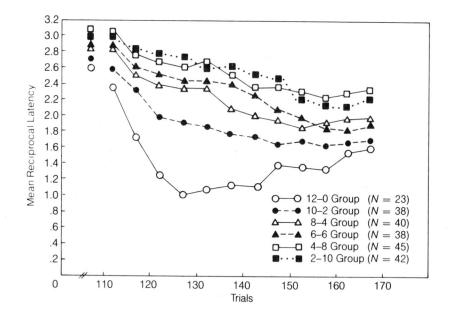

Mean reciprocal latency (speed) of maze running as a function of trials (in blocks of five, with one trial occurring each day) during extinction in Weinstock's experiment. The less reinforcement the rats received during acquisition (the fewer trials on which they were reinforced), the greater their speed during extinction, or the more slowly the behavior extinguished. This is the partial-reinforcement extinction effect. (Copyright 1958 by the American Psychological Association.)

interaction indicating a differential effect of the between-subjects variable over trials.

In most mixed designs, the control procedures we have already discussed will be applicable. Obviously, when trials or practice is an independent variable, you will have carryover effects. In that instance, you need to observe or measure these effects rather than eliminate them, as would be the case when trials or practice simply covaries with the independent variable under investigation.

## SUMMARY

1. Multifactor experiments have more than one independent variable, and these variables may have more than two levels.

2. When more than two independent variables are varied, we have a factorial design in which all possible combinations of the levels of the independent variables are examined. In a 2 × 2 factorial design, there are four combinations of levels of independent variables.

3. The primary reason for using multifactor designs is to look for interactions. An interaction is when the effects of one independent variable depend on the level of other independent variables.

4. When there are two independent variables, there are two main effects (one associated with each variable), and there can be an interaction.

5. Treatments × treatments × subjects is the designation usually given to factorial designs in which the variables are manipulated within subjects.

6. The control procedures used in multifactor experiments can be complicated, but they are similar in principle to the procedures (randomization, coun-

terbalancing, and so on) used in experiments that have just one independent variable.

7. The within-subjects design is sometimes called a repeated-measures design when trials or practice is the variable of interest.

8. In a mixed design, one or more variables are varied between subjects and one or more variables are varied within subjects.

## Key Concepts

| | |
|---|---|
| block randomization | mixed designs |
| crossover interaction | random-groups design |
| discounting cue | repeated-measures designs |
| interaction | sleeper effect |
| main effects | treatments × treatments × subjects design |
| matched-groups design | 2 × 2 factorial design |

## Exercises

1. Discuss the advantages of using complex within-subjects designs as opposed to complex between-subjects designs.

2. [*Special Exercise.*] A researcher varied the size (large or small) of the food reinforcement that was given to rats in a straight-alley maze. The time it took the rats to run down the alley was the dependent variable, and the mean time in seconds for each block of ten trials was as follows:

| | Block 1 | Block 2 | Block 3 | Block 4 |
|---|---|---|---|---|
| Large reward | 38 | 30 | 20 | 15 |
| Small reward | 52 | 32 | 16 | 12 |

The experimenter concluded that because the overall time was slower in the small-reward group, large rewards lead to more rapid learning. What other conclusions can be drawn from the data in the table? Draw a figure showing these results.

3. [*Special Exercise.*] An experimenter is interested in studying the effects of practice on retention. If a within-subjects design is used and the independent variables are types of rehearsal (rote and elaborative) and number of presentations (1, 2, 3, and 4), indicate how the words to be remembered could be counterbalanced over the four different numbers of presentations. What are some additional confoundings that must be eliminated?

## Suggested Readings

Several complex experiments are reprinted in Elmes, D. G. (1978). *Readings in experimental psychology*. Chicago: Rand McNally. See especially articles 14 and 25.

# PSYCHOLOGY IN ACTION
## Distraction and Difficulty in Letter Detection

Detection of various kinds of targets (for example, planes on a radar screen) usually deteriorates when the observer is distracted or is under stress of some sort (Broadbent, 1971). The purpose of this experiment is to see whether distraction interacts with the difficulty of the detection task.

The subject's task will be to read through a newspaper article at a rapid rate, crossing out certain letters as he or she is reading. Half of the detection periods will occur in a quiet setting and the other half will take place where moderately loud music is playing. Thus you will need a newspaper and a radio (or some other source of music).

The difficulty of the task will be determined by the particular letters that the subjects are to cross out. Half the time the subjects should cancel out all the *u*'s they can find, and on the rest of the trials they should cancel out all the *f*s. The letter *f* was chosen because people generally make a substantial number of errors when they try to detect *f* (Read, 1983). This occurs because the letter *f* is often pronounced as a *v* (as in the word *of*), and people usually do not cancel out those *f*s. The letter *u* was chosen because it occurs with about the same frequency as the letter *f*, and only occasionally is it pronounced in an unusual fashion (as a *w* in words beginning with a *q*, which means you might want to select newspaper passages that do not contain the letter *q*).

You should probably use a within-subjects design in this experiment, so you will have to figure out some sort of counterbalancing scheme (see chapter 6) for the four conditions: detecting the letter *u* in a quiet setting, detecting the letter *f* in a quiet setting, detecting the letter *u* with music playing, and detecting the letter *f* with music playing.

Subjects should be tested in each condition once. Allow each subject to read for thirty seconds. After testing, you can calculate the error rate by dividing the number of correct detections (*f* or *u*) by the total number of *f*s or *u*'s in the passage. (Be sure that you detect all the *f*s when you are scoring the data.) You should combine your results with those of other students to increase the stability of your data.

Look for an interaction in your results. Usually, the most difficult detection task is the one most affected by the distraction.

Broadbent, D. E. (1971). *Decision and stress.* New York: Academic Press.
Read, J. D. (1983). Detection of Fs in a single statement: The role of phonetic recoding. *Memory & Cognition, 11*, 390–399.

| **SMALL-*N* EXPERIMENTATION** Numerous observations on small numbers of subjects | **Psychophysical Problems** |
|---|---|
| | *Sensitivity and decision criteria:* |
| | signal-detection methods |
| | ROC curves |
| | |
| | **Operant-Conditioning Designs** |
| | *Reversal design* (ABA) |
| | |
| | **Clinical Psychology** |
| | *Multiple Personality Disorder* |

# 8

# SMALL-*N* EXPERIMENTATION

In this chapter, we will examine slightly different ways of applying Mill's **joint method of agreement and difference.** Small-*n* designs present levels of the independent variable numerous times to a small number of subjects. Such experiments are common in psychophysical, clinical, and operant-conditioning research.

The control-group (between-subjects) and control-condition (within-subjects) designs discussed in the previous three chapters represent the major types of experimentation in psychology. In the past, however, studies of behavior usually involved experiments on single subjects or a small number of subjects. Fechner, the first psychophysicist (see chapter 4), studied himself and a relative in his pioneering work of the 1850s. Later in the 1880s, the first laboratory experiments on memory examined the retention of a single subject, Hermann Ebbinghaus, the man who devised and conducted the experiments. Even Pavlov, the pioneer in the study of classical conditioning, focused his attention on a small number of dogs.

Today, these **small-*n* designs** (*small* refers to the number of subjects) are used in many areas of psychological research, as well as in many areas of applied psychology. Rather than having a few observations on large groups of subjects, small-*n* experiments entail a substantial number of observations on a small number of subjects. During the course of an experiment, various levels of the independent variable(s) are introduced, and the resulting changes in behavior are measured. Because small numbers of subjects take part in small-*n* experiments, economy and control usually are imposed through the use of variants of the within-subjects procedures. Thus, each subject typically receives each level of the independent variables several times. Versions of between-subjects designs also have been used.

Some small-*n* experiments require special control procedures, which we will consider here. Our treatment will focus on three substantive areas of psychology—psychophysics, operant conditioning, and clinical psychology—which best represent modern uses of small-*n* experiments. We will have to detail some of the specific content and theories associated with these three fields. Psychophysics, operant conditioning, and clinical psychology all have broad general concerns, however, so you should not be misled into thinking that the use of small-*n* experiments is limited to these areas. Small-*n* experiments are powerful tools for determining why people and animals act as they do.

## PSYCHOPHYSICAL EXPERIMENTS

Psychophysics, you will remember from chapter 4, refers to the branch of psychology that attempts to relate psychological judgment to the characteristics of physical stimuli. In the typical psychophysical experiment, a small number of subjects may make a number of judgments about a large number of stimuli. Very often a subject will be required to rate or otherwise judge the same event several times. This was the case with the Hardy et al. (1952) experiment that studied the effects of aspirin on the threshold for pain.

In using the method of limits and its variants, classical psychophysicists, like Hardy and his colleagues, assumed that they were measuring a person's sensitivity. Any momentary differences in willingness to respond were supposed to be eliminated by obtaining substantial numbers of observations from highly trained observers. Thus, they believed that pure measures of sensitivity were obtained. About twenty years ago, a new method was devised to measure sensitivity. This procedure, which was derived from the **theory of signal detection,** became the dominant psychophysical method. Signal-detection theory assumes that response bias is always present, and the method provides an estimate of this bias instead of trying to average it out as in the method of limits. In an exciting contradiction to earlier work, signal-detection theory denies the very concept of a threshold.

### *No Thresholds: The Theory of Signal Detection*

According to signal-detection theory, two basic internal processes control our detection of signals. Arrival of a signal or stimulus at a receptor creates a (hypothetical) **sensory impression** that on the average depends on the intensity of the signal. However, this impression is not sufficient to cause a Yes response even for strong signals. Instead, a subsequent **decision process** evaluates the magnitude of this sensory impression. Both sensory and decision processes must be involved for an observer to report sensing a signal. We will consider an everyday example of these two processes.

Any decision you make depends on the costs and benefits associated with it. Imagine that a friend has set up a blind date for you. The costs of accepting the blind date (a wasted evening) are probably less than the possible benefits (an enjoyable evening now and more enjoyment in the future), which means many of us would accept a blind date even though we know nothing about the person we will be dating. Because we lack information about the stimulus (the person who is our date), a Yes response is based mostly on our decision about costs and benefits. Now imagine a situation in which the costs are high: accepting or offering a proposal of marriage. Those of us who eagerly accept blind dates would not get married if we were offered only the information needed for us to decide whether to go on a blind date. The costs of an unsatisfactory marriage are much greater than those of a miserable blind date. In terms of decision theory, we are conservative decision makers when considering marriage but liberal decision makers when considering a blind date. This decision bias does not depend on the characteristics of the stimulus; indeed the same stimulus (person) could be involved in both instances, but only on the costs and benefits of our decision.

We have just presented a situation in which decision processes played a primary role. Let us now consider how sensory information enters into signal detection. The sensory process transmits a value to the decision process. If this value is high, the decision process is more likely to yield a Yes response, once costs and benefits are evaluated. If the sensory value is low, the decision process is more likely to yield a No response, even if costs and benefits favor a Yes decision. How does the sensory process find a value to send?

Signal-detection theory assumes that **noise,** a random disturbance that can be confused with signals, is always present in the human observer. (A typical auditory signal-detection experiment will have, in addition to signals, white noise—a hissing sound you can hear by turning your television to an unoccupied channel.) Imagine sitting in a soundproof booth and wearing headphones. On each trial you must decide whether you heard a faint tone combined with white noise or only the white noise by itself. Signal-detection theory assumes that any stimulus, even noise, produces an **internal distribution** of sensory impressions. The sensory impression on each trial provides only one point, and the distributions develop from the many sensory impressions that occur during an experiment (see the discussion of distributions in appendix A). Sensory impressions cannot be directly observed, so the distributions for stimulus trials and for noise trials are hypothetical. The sensory impression arising when only noise occurs will tend to be small, so over many trials a (hypothetical) distribution with a small mean will be established. When a signal and noise occur, the sensory impression will tend to be larger, so a distribution with a greater mean will be formed over many trials.

Therefore, during an experiment two distributions will develop—one for noise only and one for signal plus noise. Two hypothetical distributions of sensory impression are shown in figure 8–1. Because the two distributions overlap in the middle, some values of sensory impression are ambiguous; they could have occurred as a result of noise or the signal. Ambiguity would be minimized if the two distributions were very far apart. But even in the laboratory, life is usually not that simple because the decision process needs to be considered. A **criterion,** shown as a vertical line in figure 8–1, must be set to determine whether a response will be Yes or No. The decision process sets the position of the criterion. If costs and benefits favor a liberal decision policy, the criterion will be set far to the left so that most responses will be Yes. If a conservative policy is used, the criterion moves to the right, which will yield mostly No responses. In either case, some errors will be made.

Correctly detecting a signal when it is presented is called a **hit.** Incorrectly responding Yes when only noise is presented is called a **false alarm.** With a liberal decision strategy (criterion set to the left), hits will be high, but because there are numerous Yes responses, the number of false alarms will also be high. (Imagine someone who said Yes on every trial. The hit rate would be 100

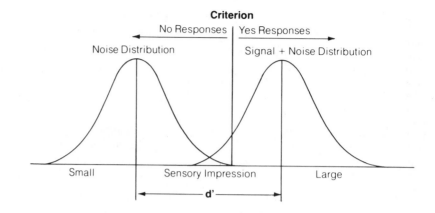

Hypothetical distributions along a sensory continuum. Once a particular sensory impression occurs, the criterion determines whether a Yes or No response will be made. Large impressions to the right of the criterion lead to Yes responses, and small impressions to the left lead to No responses. The distance between the means of the two distributions is called *d'*.

percent and so would the false-alarm rate.) With a conservative decision strategy, false alarms will be low but so will hits. (If someone said No on every trial, the false-alarm rate would be zero percent, as would the hit rate.) If we plot hits as a function of false alarms, as the decision criterion moves from conservative to liberal we get the representation depicted in figure 8–2. The curve in this figure is called a **receiver-operating-characteristic** (or ROC) function. Both hits and false alarms are infrequent (conservative criterion) at the lower left of the curve. As the criterion becomes more liberal, hits and false alarms become more likely, and the ROC curve moves upward to the right. The slope of the ROC curve tells us the criterion. Flat slopes reveal a liberal decision criterion (generally, the upper right of the curve) and steep slopes a conservative criterion—generally, the lower left of the curve. (The slope of curves like ROC functions is determined by the slope of a line that is drawn tangent to a particular point on the function and intersects one of the axes of the graph.) The distance from the diagonal tells us how far apart the noise and signal-plus-noise distributions of figure 8–1 lie. When they are far apart, indicating a more discernible signal, the ROC curve moves upward to the left, away from the diagonal. When the signal is less detectable and the two distributions are closer together, the ROC curve moves closer to the diagonal. Thus, the ROC function tells us about both the sensory process (distance between signal-plus-noise and noise-only distributions) and the decision process (slope). Because an experimental condition generates only a single point on the ROC curve, many conditions are needed to alter the hit and false-alarm rates. Usually, hit and false-alarm rates are manipulated by altering the payoff associated with them. (If a hit were worth two dollars and a false alarm penalized you fifty cents, would you be more liberal or more conservative than if a hit were valued at fifty cents and a false alarm penalized you two dollars?) Another way of manipulating the rate of hits and false alarms is to vary how often the signal occurs. If, over a series of trials, a signal occurred 90 percent of the time, you would be more likely to say Yes on any trial than when the signal occurred very infrequently on the previous trials.

By now you may be wondering what all this has to do with thresholds. Nowhere does the ROC curve have a label that reads "threshold." Whether an

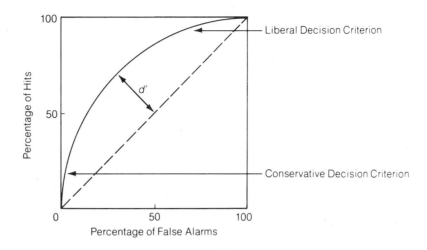

FIGURE 8–2

A receiver-operating-characteristic function. The distance from the diagonal to the center of the curve is proportional to *d'*. The diagonal represents chance performance; the observer guesses about the presence or absence of a signal. Thus, the percentage of hits equals the percentage of false alarms along this "guessing" diagonal.

observer will respond Yes or No depends on the sensory impression and the decision criterion. Signal intensity may be held constant, but because there are varying payoffs for hits and false alarms, you can generate an ROC curve showing **d'** (sensitivity) and the slope of the curve at various points. There is no operational definition of a threshold. Instead, two quantities are operationally defined. The sensitivity of the observer is called *d'* and is defined as the distance between signal and noise distributions in figure 8–1, or as the maximum distance between the ROC curve and the diagonal in figure 8–2. The criterion of the decision processes is often called **beta** and is the slope of the ROC function at the point of interest, for example, a hit rate of 55 percent. Together these two quantities determine what a classical psychophysicist would call a threshold.

A major advantage of signal-detection methods over a classical procedure such as the method of limits is the ability to measure both sensitivity and response bias. In many areas of applied psychology, being able to assess these two perceptual processes is very important. Let us consider just one example.

Most people do not like pain, so anything that decreases pain is of interest. Many reports from China have indicated that the insertion of needles into parts of the body can reduce pain; the procedure is called acupuncture. A reasonable question to ask is whether the reduction in pain after acupuncture treatment results from a lowering of sensitivity to pain or from a higher, more conservative criterion for reporting the presence of pain. Clark and Yang (1974) tried to determine how acupuncture works on the perception of pain.

In Clark and Yang's experiment, observers had one arm treated with acupuncture needles, and one arm untreated. On signal trials, each arm was then stimulated with intensely painful radiant heat. The acupuncture worked: The perception of pain in the acupunctured arm was lower than in the untreated arm. A signal-detection analysis revealed that *d'* (sensitivity to pain) was about the same in the two arms. However, acupuncture did raise the criterion for making a pain response. This means that the control of pain by acupuncture did not result from changes in sensitivity, but rather from changes in response bias. Acupuncture worked to reduce the perception of pain and, therefore, should be a useful clinical tool for managing pain. The way it did so (by influencing response bias) may tell us something about how acupuncture works in general. Thus, this work is an advance over that of Hardy et al (1952), because it specifies a mechanism (beta) for understanding pain perception.

To recapitulate, psychophysical procedures, both classical and modern, obtain substantial numbers of observations from a small number of subjects. Typical independent variables include stimulus intensity, stimulus frequency, and response payoff. Several levels of these variables are presented many times, and changes in behavior, such as detection or hits and false alarms, are observed.

Psychophysical procedures have many important practical and theoretical uses. As indicated by the work of Clark and Yang on acupuncture, and as shown in the Application section that follows, psychophysical techniques have been used successfully in many applied settings. An understanding of the methodological principles underlying accurate psychological measurement is a crucial tool for the psychologist who desires to determine why people and animals behave as they do.

# APPLICATION

### Interpreting a Chest Radiograph

Radiologists are physicians who interpret x-ray examinations. They must find patterns of abnormality within radiographs. Swensson (1980) showed that this kind of visual search behavior can be illuminated by the theory of signal detection.

The target (signal) that the radiologist seeks is some pathological feature within the x-ray radiograph. Because normal x-ray patterns contain portions that may appear similar to actual pathologies (noise), this is not an easy decision for the physician to make. Failure to detect an abnormality, for example, the start of a breast cancer tumor, could literally condemn a patient to death. But, incorrectly deciding that a tumor is present also has the cost of subjecting the patient to expensive, uncomfortable, and sometimes risky medical procedures. So the radiologist must perform an important and difficult signal-detection task.

Eight radiologists interpreted x-ray films that might contain certain chest abnormalities. In the free-search task, the physicians reported any abnormalities they observed. In the focused-search task, the search was limited to specific areas of each radiograph. In the nonsearch task, the physicians evaluated all 129 test features (signals and noise) specified by the precise location of the feature and its alleged abnormality. Results showed that radiologists did much better (higher d′) in the search tasks. There was no difference between free search and focused search.

These results have two important implications. First, the signal-detection model works well at explaining the behavior of physicians reading x-ray films. Thus, this powerful tool can help improve the interpretation of radiographs. Second, the better performance for search tasks means that physicians can and should avoid the exhaustive evaluation of every pattern feature that might represent an abnormality.

Swensson, R. G. (1980). A two-stage detection model applied to skilled visual search by radiologists. *Perception & Psychophysics, 27,* 11–16.

## CONCEPT SUMMARY

PSYCHOPHYSICS PROBLEMS AND SOLUTIONS

| *Problem* | *Solution* |
|---|---|
| *Determining sensitivity* | *Measure criterion and sensitivity via signal-detection methods* |

# OPERANT-CONDITIONING EXPERIMENTS

The work of Skinner (1938) and his associates (Sidman, 1960) is classified as small-*n* because most of the experiments involve the conditioning of a small number of subjects under a number of tightly controlled conditions. The general approach has been dubbed the *experimental analysis of behavior,* and a journal, *Journal of the Experimental Analysis of Behavior,* is devoted to such small-*n* experimentation. In operant-conditioning experiments, the argument for using few subjects does not have to do with economy, as it does in psychophysical research. Proponents of this approach argue that by very carefully controlling the experimental setting and by taking numerous and continuous measures of the dependent variable, powerful control can be obtained and valid conclusions can be reached. In contrast to standard experimental procedures in which conclusions are based on average performance of large numbers of subjects randomly assigned to conditions, this small-*n* approach relies on a detailed examination of the behavior of a small number of organisms.

## The Reversal Design

The logic behind the **reversal design** is straightforward: First obtain a baseline measure of the subject's behavior, then see how that behavior changes when an independent variable is introduced, and finally reverse the conditions back to the original and measure the behavior again under this second baseline. In its basic form, this design is labeled the *ABA design,* where A and B refer to the different phases of the experiment. Use of an AB design without a second A phase does not allow an experimenter to make definite statements about the effects of the variable introduced during the B phase. If there is a change in the dependent variable when the treatment is administered in the B phase, the experimenter cannot conclusively establish that it is owing to the independent variable, because there is a lack of control comparisons (we are not using a form of Mill's joint method of agreement and difference). The change in the dependent variable might have occurred anyway, without the treatment variable being applied, as a result of confounding from some uncontrolled variable the experimenter might not have observed. In the AB design there is always a time confounding with the introduction of B following A. The third phase in the ABA design, the reintroduction of a baseline, serves to rule out the effects of confounding by returning the conditions of the experiment to their original, baseline level, with the independent variable no longer applied. If behavior in the second A phase returns to its baseline level, an experimenter can conclude that it was the independent variable that affected the change during the B phase. The only time this generalization does not apply is when a secondary variable, not detected by the experimenter, happens to be perfectly correlated with the independent variable. Such situations are unlikely.

The results of an applied reversal design are shown in figure 8–3. In this interesting experiment, Hart, Allen, Buell, Harris, and Wolf (1964) wanted to decrease the excessive crying of Bill, a nursery school student. During the A phases, the nursery school teacher simply counted the number of Bill's crying episodes and tried to comfort him. During the B phases, the teacher attempted to decrease crying by extinguishing it. The teacher ignored his crying episodes and rewarded Bill with attention every time he responded to minor calamities (such as falls or pushes) in a more mature way. Usually the teacher paid attention to Bill's crying in the A phases. Leaving Bill in an A phase (crying excessively) would be counter to the purpose of the experiment, so a second B phase was instituted to reduce crying. As shown in figure 8–3, the number of crying episodes decreased markedly in the first B phase, which completes the AB phase of the design. But we cannot be certain that the combination of extinction and reward of appropriate behavior was responsible for Bill's improved behavior. Perhaps he was getting along better with his classmates, his parents were treating him better at home, or there was some other factor that improved his disposition. Thus, the A phase was reintroduced; that is, Bill was again reinforced via attention for crying. As shown in the third panel of figure 8–3, it took only four days to reestablish the baseline level of crying, which led the experimenters to conclude that reward (paying attention to appropriate behavior) and extinction (ignoring crying) were responsible for the termination of crying in the first B phase. Because the second B phase also resulted in the extinction of crying, the reward hypothesis is supported.

The reversal design is commonly used in applied settings (as in the case of Bill), and it is also frequently used in basic experiments. Boe and Winokur (1978) used a reversal design to study what controls a person's choice of words

---

**FIGURE 8–3**

The number of crying episodes exhibited by Bill, a nursery school student, during the four phases of an ABAB experiment initiated to control his crying problem. (After Hart et al., 1964, from Wolf and Risley, 1971. Reprinted by permission of the author and publisher.)

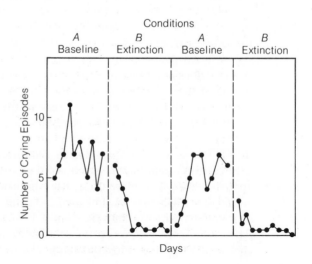

in conversations. The subject's task was to orally answer three questions during each of three sessions that occurred at weekly intervals. The questions contained target words that the experimenters thought the subjects would echo in the course of answering each question. The first and last sessions (the A phases) had the following target words: *changes, feel, society, employment, wages,* and *training.* The target words in the questions of the B phase were synonyms of those used in the A phases: *effects, believe, culture, hiring, salaries,* and *preparation.* All of the questions were about the women's liberation movement, and Boe and Winokur expected that answers concerned with job payment would include *wages* in the A phases and *salaries* in the B phase if the subjects were echoing the wording of the questions. The results followed expectation: More B words were emitted during the B phase than during the A phases, and vice versa for the A words. Use of the ABA design allows us to conclude that the specific content of the questions exerted some control over the content of the answers. Use of the AB design would not have permitted that conclusion.

## Extensions of the Reversal Design

As in the standard within-subjects experiments, small-*n* experiments often include carryover effects that prohibit using the reversal design. If the treatment introduced in the B phase has long-term effects on the dependent variable, then reversal is impractical. Furthermore, the experimenter may want to obtain several samples of the subjects' behavior under the same independent variable or under several independent variables. There are a number of ways to solve these problems, but we will consider just one.

Rose (1978) used what could be called an ACABCBCB design, where A phases refer to baseline conditions, and B and C phases include different independent variables. Rose was interested in the effects of artificial food coloring on hyperactivity in children. Two hyperactive eight-year-old girls were subjects. They had been on a strict diet, the K-P diet (Feingold, 1975), which does not allow foods containing artificial flavors and colors and foods containing natural salicylates (many fruits and meats). On the basis of uncontrolled case studies (AB designs), Feingold reported that the K-P diet reduced hyperactivity.

Rose's A phase was the behavior of the two girls under the ordinary K-P diet. The B phase was another type of baseline. It involved the introduction of an oatmeal cookie that contained no artificial coloring. The C phase included the independent variable of interest: oatmeal cookies containing an artificial yellow dye. This artificial color was chosen because it is commonly used in the manufacture of foods, and it had the additional benefit that it did not change the taste or appearance of the cookies. (When asked to sort the cookies on the basis of color, judges were unable to do so systematically with regard to the presence of the dye.) The subjects, their parents, and the observers were blind to when the children ate the dye-laced cookie. Various aspects of the two girls' behavior were recorded during school by several different observers.

All measures are in agreement for both subjects, so we show in figure 8–4 the percentage of time one of the girls was out of her seat (that is, when she was overactive). Hyperactivity occurred only in the C phase, when the child had ingested a cookie with artificial coloring in it. There was no placebo effect

**FIGURE 8–4**

Percentage of time out of seat during baseline (A), placebo cookie (B), and artificially colored cookie (C) phases. Asterisk indicates a C phase resulting from a violation of the diet, but one that was inadvertent, not experimentally introduced. (After Rose, 1978, in *Journal of Applied Behavior Analysis,* vol. 11, p. 444. Copyright 1978 by the Society for the Experimental Analysis of Behavior, Inc. Reprinted by permission of the publisher and author.)

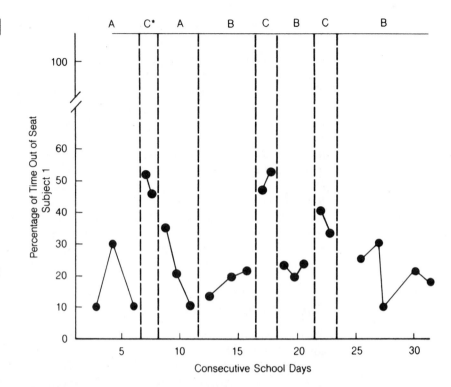

(B phase), because the behavior during the A and B phases is essentially the same. Thus, Rose concluded that artificial colors can lead to hyperactivity in some children.

## CONCEPT SUMMARY

SMALL-*N* DESIGNS IN OPERANT-CONDITIONING RESEARCH

### *Reversal Design (ABA or ABAB)*

Interspersed between baseline periods (*A*) are independent-variable phases (*B*). If the behavior reverses to baseline levels, we assume that the independent variable caused the changes that occurred during the B periods.

### *Extensions of the Reversal Design*

More than one independent variable is used, and there are numerous baseline periods.

## CLINICAL PSYCHOLOGY

### *Multiple Personality Disorder*

Someone suffering from multiple personality disorder has several distinct personalities, each of which claims to have no direct awareness of the others.

Furthermore, each personality cannot remember events that occur to the other personalities, although it can remember events that happened to it. Thus, memory dysfunction is a crucial part of the multiple personality syndrome.

Nissen and her colleagues (Nissen et al., 1988) were able to study a patient with multiple personality disorder. Their research strategy focused on a variety of memory tests that would allow them to determine to what extent one personality had access to the knowledge of other personalities. Because this research is based on a single subject ($n = 1$), it is an example of the **case study,** which always is classified as a small-*n* experiment, even though a survey of patients with multiple personality disorder found a mean of thirteen different personalities per patient (Putnam et al., 1986).

The patient they studied was a 45-year-old right-handed Caucasian woman who had been divorced five times. She has shown twenty-two different personalities ranging in age from 5 to 45 years. Three personalities are male, and three are left-handed. Testing focused on eight personalities.

The general experimental procedure was to present information to one personality, and after a retention interval of 5 to 10 minutes, have the patient's psychiatrist request a change of personality. The new personality would be given a task that ordinarily would be sensitive to the prior information.

Results showed that there were some tasks in which one personality was influenced by knowledge presented to another personality and other tasks in which it was not. Simple and clear tasks did show influence. For example, one such task used four-alternative forced-choice recognition. Alice was shown fifty-four photographs from old high-school yearbooks and asked to rate them (i.e., sad, happy, or neutral). Bonnie was then shown a different set of fifty-four photographs and also asked to rate them. Bonnie then received the four-alternative forced-choice recognition test in which four faces were presented and Bonnie had to indicate or guess which face seemed most familiar. When the alternatives included one face previously shown to Bonnie, she selected that face 52 percent of the time. When the alternatives included a face that Alice, but not Bonnie, had seen before, Bonnie selected that face 42 percent of the time. This is higher than the 25 percent that would be expected by chance if Bonnie had been uninfluenced by what Alice saw. When the alternatives included one face that Alice had seen and also one that Bonnie had seen, Bonnie selected the face she had seen 33 percent of the time. On the remaining trials, given that Bonnie did not select the face she had seen, she selected the face that Alice had seen 63 percent of the time, again indicating her selection had been influenced by what Alice saw.

A more ambiguous task, repetition priming of stem completion, did not show such influence. Alice saw twenty-four words and judged how pleasant each one was. Bonnie then received a list of forty-eight three-letter word stems and had to complete them. Each stem had ten possible correct answers. Half of the word stems could be completed to make a word Alice had seen. Bonnie did not exceed the level of chance (10 percent) in creating such words. Thus there was no influence from words seen by Alice. When this procedure was repeated for Bonnie five days later, there was an influence from words that had been previously presented to Bonnie. So this ruled out the possibility that Bonnie by herself would not show the repetition effect. The authors interpreted this finding to imply that ambiguous stimuli are more likely to have personality-specific interpretations and so would not show influence from one personality to another.

This is an interesting study because it combined two different methodologies in psychology that are seldom used together. The case study is most often used in clinical psychology, whereas studies of memory most often involve many subjects. This experiment reminds us that it is possible to be creative by combining different techniques within a single experiment.

## CONCEPT SUMMARY

SMALL-*N* DESIGNS IN CLINICAL PSYCHOLOGY
### *Multiple Personality Disorder*
The case study is a small-*n* design often used in clinical psychology.

## SUMMARY

1. Small-*n* experiments, in contrast to most control-group and control-condition designs, involve numerous observations on small numbers of subjects.

2. The theory of signal detection assumes that perception is composed of a sensory impression, which is then evaluated by a decision process.

3. Signal-detection experiments involve some trials that have a signal embedded in noise, and other trials that have noise only. The observer's tasks is to respond Yes on signal-plus-noise trials.

4. According to signal-detection theory, hypothetical internal distributions of sensory impressions develop across a series of trials. The difference between the means of the noise distribution and the signal-plus-distribution represents signal strength ($d'$), and a decision criterion set within these distributions determines whether a response is Yes or No.

5. A hit occurs when a subject correctly detects a signal that is presented. A false alarm occurs when the subjects incorrectly report a signal when only noise is presented.

6. A plot of hits against false alarms yields a receiver-operating-characteristic (ROC) function.

7. Flat slopes on the ROC function indicate a liberal decision criterion leading to numerous hits and false alarms. Steep slopes show a conservative criterion with fewer hits and fewer false alarms. The criterion measured this way is often called beta. The distance of the ROC curve from the "guessing" diagonal is a measure of sensitivity ($d'$), which varies with signal strength.

8. Hit and false-alarm rates are varied by the payoff associated with each kind of response and by the probability of signal-plus-noise trials.

9. Signal-detection methods are useful in determining whether a particular perception is influenced by sensitivity or the decision criterion.

10. Operant-conditioning experiments in the tradition of Skinner use small-*n* designs, on the assumption that valid conclusions can be reached by making large numbers of observations on a few subjects in a carefully controlled experimental setting.

11. The reversal design (ABA design) is a common within-subjects design that involves independent-variable periods (B phases) interspersed among baseline periods (A phases).

12. The case study is a common small-*n* design used in clinical psychology.

## Key Concepts

| | |
|---|---|
| beta | internal distribution |
| case study | noise |
| criterion | receiver-operating-characteristic (ROC) |
| *d'* | |
| decision process | reversal design (ABA) |
| false alarm | sensory impression |
| hit | small-*n* designs |
| | theory of signal detection |

## Exercises

1. Relate the presentation of signals in the signal-detection method to the occurrence of the independent variable in the reversal design used in operant conditioning.

2. Discuss the differences between the method of limits and signal-detection methods. How might each be used to test whether a placebo pill (a pill that is inert, such as a sugar pill) alters sensitivity to pain.

3. Discuss the logic underlying the use of the reversal design and extensions of it. How do these relate to Mill's joint method of agreement and difference?

## Suggested Readings

A good, general reference for psychophysics is Gescheider, G. A. (1976). *Psychophysics: Method and theory*. Hillsdale, NJ: Erlbaum.

You will find that the following book discusses both the design of small-*n* experiments and the application of behavior modification techniques to your own problems: Williams, R. D., & Long, J. D. (1979). *Toward a self-managed life style* (2d ed.). Boston: Houghton-Mifflin.

An interesting source of clinical case studies is the work of Oliver Sacks. One of his most intriguing books is: Sacks, O. (1985). *The man who mistook his wife for a hat and other clinical tales*. New York: Summit.

# PSYCHOLOGY IN ACTION
## Can You Put Yourself on a Better Schedule of Reinforcement?

All of us have habits we would like to break, and other habits we would like to develop. Smoking, drinking, nail-biting, watching too much television, and not studying enough are some of the bad habits that college students often say they would like to alter. Failure to control these behaviors is often blamed on laziness or a defective personality. However, a behavioral analysis of such problems suggests a simple alternative to these interpretations: bad habits are being reinforced, and to change them we must alter the schedule of reinforcement by which we live. If all these bad habits are learned, then they can be altered by learning, too. The general aim is to alter the reinforcements in our lives so that they occur after desirable behavior and not after undesirable behavior.

Suppose you are in danger of flunking out of school because you study too little and, being addicted to the movies, you attend them too often. You know you have a problem, but you are in a rut and you do not know how to get out. What can you do to modify your behavior?

The first step is to set a goal for yourself. It is not enough to say that you want to study more; you must have a concrete, measurable goal. Say you decide to study six hours a day outside of class. Your second step would be to institute some means of carefully monitoring your study behavior. How much do you already study, on the average? You should carry a notebook and record every studying episode as it occurs each day, and then total these episodes at the end of the day. You can also get a weekly average. Say you discover at the end of a week that you are averaging fifty-nine minutes of studying per day; obviously you are a long way from your target of six hours a day.

The next step is to set yourself a realistic goal in your first attempt. It might be too much of a shock to your system to go directly from one to six hours of studying per day; worse, you might give up early on, deciding it is impossible. So let us assume that you plan to increase your studying to two hours a day at first. But how? You should analyze the situation and see what activities prevent you from studying. The main deterrent is your going to the movies, but surely other activities also intrude. You might set up an activity schedule to monitor your behavior, as shown in the table on page 177.

You should then try to change your environment so that it is more conducive to study. Try to avoid those friends who might encourage you to go to the movies. Do not avoid them entirely, of course, but plan to spend more time at the place where you study. Analyze your study area—are there many distractions? (These might include roommates, magazines, radios, and televisions.) If there are many distractions, abandon your room as a place of study and find a quiet hideaway where only you and your books will be present. Studies have shown that if you can associate a particular place exclusively with study behavior and then force yourself to go to this place, you can increase studying dramatically. Finally—and this is one of the most important steps—you must figure out a reward for yourself for successfully studying the allotted amount of time. For example, you could promise yourself that if you have studied two hours each day during the first week, you can go to the movies

| Time | Monday | Tuesday | Wednesday | Thursday | Friday | Saturday | Sunday |
|------|--------|---------|-----------|----------|--------|----------|--------|
| 7:00 | | | | | | | |
| 8:00 | | | | | | | |
| 9:00 | | | | | | | |
| 10:00 | | | | | | | |
| 11:00 | | | | | | | |
| 12:00 | | | | | | | |
| 1:00 | | | | | | | |
| 2:00 | | | | | | | |
| 3:00 | | | | | | | |
| 4:00 | | | | | | | |
| 5:00 | | | | | | | |
| 6:00 | | | | | | | |
| 7:00 | | | | | | | |
| 8:00 | | | | | | | |
| 9:00 | | | | | | | |
| 10:00 | | | | | | | |
| 11:00 | | | | | | | |

with your friends. Thus one of the main reinforcers in your life—going to the movies—is made contingent on other behavior. In essence, you are reinforcing yourself for studying.

During the next week, try studying three hours a day, continuing to carefully monitor your time and study habits. In each successive week, increase your amount of study per day, until you reach your goal in a few weeks. Technically, you are *shaping* study behavior in yourself by reinforcing successive approximations to the target behavior, just as animals are taught complicated tricks by being reinforced for gradual approximations to them. If you can keep the reinforcement contingencies in place, you will have dramatically changed your behavior.

The case we have used here may not apply directly to your situation, but in all likelihood you have habits you would like to break or change. You can do so by applying the rules specified here: Set a concrete target goal and by reinforcing yourself for each step taken, gradually alter your behavior to approximate that goal. R. D. Williams and J. D. Long have written a book, *Toward a Self-Managed Life Style,* that explores the possibility of changing many areas of our lives by effectively reinforcing positive behavior and not rewarding negative behavior. Besides methods for improving study habits, they discuss behavioral self-management programs for losing weight, increasing exercise, managing time, controlling smoking and drinking, and becoming more assertive.

| **QUASI-EXPERIMENTATION**<br>Increasing internal validity when the variables are selected, not manipulated | *Sources of invalidity in quasi-experiments*<br>   history<br>   maturation<br>   selection bias<br>   mortality<br>   delayed effects<br>   regression artifacts |
|---|---|
| | *How does one make valid causal statements in* |
| | **Case Studies?** — Use *deviant-case analysis* (a nonequivalent control group); examine several dependent variables |
| | **Interrupted Time Series?** — Use *nonequivalent control group;* study several dependent variables; search for additional natural treatments |
| | **Subject-Variable Research?** — Use matching on potentially relevant characteristics; beware of regression artifacts |
| | **Developmental Research (Age)?** — Use *cross-sequential design* to minimize generation and time-of-test confoundings; include *true independent variable* and look for interactions |

# QUASI-EXPERIMENTATION

In this chapter, we consider research that includes independent variables that are selected rather than manipulated by the researcher. Many experiments done in the field, and laboratory experiments that have subject variables as the independent variables, use manipulations that occur naturally and either are selected by the investigator for subsequent observation or are actually investigated ex post facto. These natural treatments represent a form of correlation (they are, in essence, dependent variables), which poses many difficult control and interpretive problems.

## INTERNAL VALIDITY IN QUASI-EXPERIMENTS

**Quasi-experiments** refer to experimental situations in which the experimenter does not directly manipulate variables as in a typical laboratory experiment. In a quasi-experiment, some or all of the variables are selected, which means that they are not under direct control of the experimenter. Either the effects of natural "treatments" (such as disasters) are observed, or particular subject variables (such as age, sex, weight) are of interest. In either case, we must be wary of internal validity, because the experimenter does not manipulate the variables. In other words, the joint method of agreement and difference is not under direct control. Quasi-experiments have the advantage of being intrinsically interesting, and they also allow researchers to examine variables that would be unethical to manipulate directly. In this chapter, we will consider the pitfalls of quasi-experiments and how to minimize those problems.

### Natural Treatments

Ex post facto analyses of the effects of some naturally occurring event, such as a disaster or a change in school curricula, are usually interesting and important but are often difficult to interpret in a causal fashion. Most quasi-experiments involving naturally occurring treatments have a structure that is similar to some of the small-$n$ experiments ($ABA$) discussed in chapter 8. We might, for example, have records of third-grade achievement before and after (the $A$ phases) the introduction of a new method for teaching reading (the $B$ phase). Note carefully: This example does not represent a true reversal design, because there is not a removal of the treatment to allow a return to the original baseline. In fact, most quasi-experiments of the general form **observation-treatment-observation** cannot be true reversal designs for two reasons: (1) the treatment is not under the experimenter's control; and (2) most natural treatments, such as curriculum revision, are likely to have long-term carryover effects. We must be concerned not only with carryover effects, but also with the changes in the subjects themselves. If we examine the effects of a new reading program on third-grade achievement, one thing that is confounded with the introduction of our treatment is a change in the age of our subjects. Although age itself does not cause anything, many important changes correlate with age: more experience in school, better test taking, improved linguistic skills, better social adjustment, biological maturation, and the like. These changes, which are called **maturation,** nearly always can confound the results of research concerned with natural treatments. Furthermore in a classroom setting, numerous outside influences could affect the results. Because the researcher does not have direct control over the setting, the subjects are not insulated from numerous possible distractions as they are in a true experiment. This source of confounding is called **history** by Cook and Campbell (1979).

Thus, two particular threats to internal validity with naturally occurring treatments are the history of the subject and any changes in the subject that occur over time. Either or both of these factors could vary directly, inversely, or not at all with the intended treatment. In addition, the effects of history and change could interact in several different ways. Ways to minimize these difficulties (for example, matching) generally involve more active participation on the part of the experimenter. One thing that could be done in ex post facto analysis of the effects of reading techniques is to find a control-group third-grade class that did not have this new technique imposed on it, which would result in a quasi-experimental design similar to the one shown in table 9–1. This looks like an ordinary experimental design, but remember—we have no direct control over the situation, and, as we shall soon see, by adding a matched control group we have incurred additional threats to internal validity. This type of design is sometimes called a **nonequivalent control group** design because random assignment to conditions is not used, and matching is attempted after the fact. Because the subjects are not randomly assigned to groups, we have the possible problem of **selection bias.** As discussed in chapters 4 and 6, random assignment to conditions generally equates the subject characteristics in the

---

**TABLE 9–1    A HYPOTHETICAL QUASI-EXPERIMENTAL DESIGN FOR EXAMINING CURRICULA CHANGES ON THIRD-GRADE ACHIEVEMENT SCORES.**

Time ————————————————————————————————————————→

| | | | |
|---|---|---|---|
| *Experimental Third Grade* | Observe Achievement ——→ | Change Reading Method ——→ | Observe Achievement |
| *Control Third Grade* | Observe Achievement ——→ | (no change) ——→ | Observe Achievement |

Note: The third-grade classes are assumed to be very similar, differing only in terms of the imposed curriculum change. There was not random assignment to the two groups, and usually the control group is determined ex post facto. Thus, this design includes a nonequivalent control group.

various conditions of the experiment. With natural treatments, on the other hand, we select our subjects, not assign them, and we have no guarantee that our selection will be as unbiased as randomization in a true experiment.

We will now consider two quasi-experimental designs that appear in the psychological literature: the one-shot case study and the interrupted-time-series design.

## One-Shot Case Studies

We can view the **one-shot case study** in the following way: We have a long-term treatment on an individual and after the fact we obtain some measurements of that individual's thought and action. If we use the same notation that we used for the reversal design, we can all this an *AB* design (where *A* is the history and *B* is the current behavior). Treatments occur and then we observe their effects. Note that the treatments do not allow baseline observations. Viewing the one-shot case study as an *AB* design immediately points to the threat to internal validity: There is no baseline or control condition.

Deviant-case analysis is one way to obtain a control group in case-study research. In deviant-case analysis (see chapter 3), we take an individual as similar as possible to our case except for a crucial missing treatment (a drunkard for a father, a disabling illness, and so forth) and determine how the individuals are different from each other. The similar individual is a nonequivalent control, not a true control. Reconsider the case of P.Z. that was discussed in chapter 3. P.Z. was an elderly, world-famous scientist who suffered from a severe memory loss. P.Z. had a history of alcohol abuse (Butters & Cermak, 1986). Deviant-case analysis was used to determine whether the memory deficit could be attributed to the alcohol abuse. A similar-aged colleague of P.Z. was tested for the retention of facts and names that should have been familiar to him and to P.Z. The colleague is the companion person for the deviant-case analysis. Whereas P.Z. showed a severe retention loss, the colleague did not. Because the comparison case had not abused alcohol, Butters and Cermak concluded that alcohol was the causal factor in the memory loss.

In this deviant-case analysis, the quasi-independent variable—alcohol abuse—was selected, not manipulated. Further, the comparison case is a nonequivalent control, because the case also was selected and not randomly assigned to the "control" condition. These threats to internal validity make it difficult to come to firm causal conclusions. The best that the researcher can hope for is to probe for suspected causal factors as carefully as possible. The comparison case permits the tentative conclusion that simply being old or being a scientist do not by themselves result in severe memory deficits. Additional comparisons showed that P.Z.'s inability to remember new information was similar to that exhibited by other alcoholics (also a nonequivalent control group). Alcohol abuse is the prime suspect remaining.

In a sense, therefore, interpreting a case history is similar to doing detective work. The typical case study involves a large number of dependent variables. Thus, the researcher who wishes to make causal statements on the basis of a case study has to look for important clues and then interpret the meaning of those clues in the context of all the other observations. Be careful how you interpret this discussion. As a laboratory research design, the one-shot case study with only one or two dependent variables would be sloppy and internally invalid. It is simply a terrible experimental design. However, in the typical case study, in which a great deal of information is available, causal "detective" work is often more reasonable and more likely to lead to internally valid conclusions. The researcher gains control by increasing the number and complexity of the observations. Remember too that case studies often involve retrospective reports, which means that the life-history "facts" may be forgotten or distorted. A cautious investigator might tentatively accept the reports as internally valid.

Case studies are a major source of descriptive data for clinical psychology. As we have just seen, deriving causal conclusions from them is very difficult. Can case studies be used for prediction? This issue is addressed in the Application section.

# APPLICATION

### Predicting Behavior from Case Studies

Case studies provide substantial information about an individual, and clinical psychologists often rely on them to determine the causes of current behavior. However, such an endeavor may be difficult, and valid causal statements from case studies may be impossible. Are case studies good for predicting future behavior? You know that prediction on the basis of correlations can be successful. Can the information from a case study be used in the same way?

Given that you are a psychology major taking a college-level course in research methods, can we predict that you will be a research psychologist? Based just on your case, our prediction is likely to be inaccurate. If we examine the case histories of some psychologists, it is easy for us to see that prediction can be poor.

John B. Watson (1878–1958), founder of the school of behaviorism in psychology and pioneer in the field of learning, was a philosophy major as an undergraduate. After he was forced out of academic psychology because of an adulterous affair with a graduate student, he became an executive in a large advertising agency.

Probably none of his classmates or teachers would have predicted that B. F. Skinner would become an influential and famous psychologist. Skinner was an English major as an undergraduate, and after graduation he spent some time leading a bohemian life as an aspiring writer of fiction.

As a more contemporary example, consider Gordon H. Bower, the distinguished investigator of learning and memory. Bower, who wanted to be a psychiatrist, attended college on a baseball scholarship. He had received offers of professional baseball contracts, but a fortunate experience in an experimental psychology course and a desire to avoid the military draft led him to choose experimental psychology over baseball.

Each of these vignettes indicates that accurate predictions from case studies can be difficult. This difficulty is very obvious in the field of criminal law, where it is often necessary to predict whether convicted felons will continue their criminal behavior or be law-abiding citizens following their release. There is considerable controversy in psychology and psychiatry concerning attempts to predict the future actions of a dangerous criminal, such as a murderer or a rapist. Accurate predictions about rapists and murderers are crucial, but difficult. Usually only a weak probabilistic statement can be made: "The chances are that this criminal will not rape again." Most people do not consider this a strong enough prediction. To generate more accurate predictions, we need more detailed information than a simple case study can provide. At the very least, a substantial number of correlations among various kinds of behavior patterns must be made before reasonable predictions are possible. An important area of research awaits you.

## Interrupted-Time-Series Design

The **interrupted-time-series design** is often encountered in quasi-experimental research, and it represents the logical extension of the general observation-treatment-observation design (see table 9–1). In the simplest time-series design, we have a single experimental group for which we have multiple observations before and after a naturally occurring treatment. Instead of examining just one or two third-grade classes, we could observe third-grade classes over several years. Or we could follow the achievement of the pupils across their entire school career. We need to know when the time series is interrupted by some treatment. Then we compare observations before and after the treatment to see whether it had any effect. Suppose we had records of public-school achievement for a city that added fluoride to its water one year. We would plot achievement against time and look for changes in achievement subsequent to fluoridation.

Such a hypothetical time-series analysis is shown in figure 9–1. What we look for in a time-series analysis are changes following interruption by the

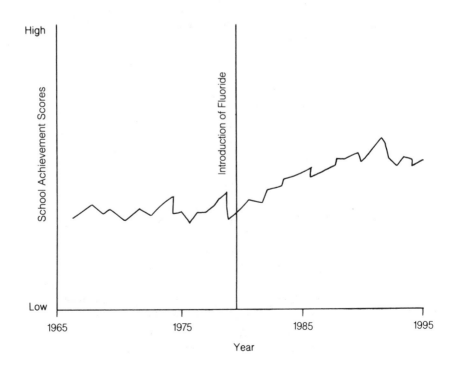

**FIGURE 9–1**

A hypothetical example of a time-series analysis of the effects of fluoride on school achievement scores.

treatment. Note the rather dramatic increase in achievement following the introduction of fluoride. Can we assert that fluoride causes better achievement? No—for the same reason that we have difficulty interpreting a single correlation coefficient. Possibly, fluoride had an indirect effect, which means that some confounding factor is the principal cause. Perhaps fluoride reduced absenteeism resulting from dental appointments, and it was the reduced absences that permitted higher achievement. The possibility of such indirect effects makes it difficult for researchers to arrive at internally valid conclusions.

In our example, we could examine the absence rate before and after the introduction of fluoride. This could be done by plotting absence rate as well as achievement over time. Or we could try to find a control group that was similar to our experimental group but was untreated with fluoride. Finding a satisfactory control group might be difficult (imagine trying to find a town that differed from yours on only one dimension). Furthermore, such a control group would be nonequivalent and would leave us open to the problems of matching. Of course, our control group would have to have an absence rate similar to that of the experimental group, but it would still be nonequivalent because random assignment was not used.

Although a no-treatment control is often desirable, there are other things to look for in a time-series analysis that may be helpful (back to the detective's clues). We can use several dependent variables, such as absenteeism and the number of extracurricular activities, but we also can examine other treatments in much the same way that a case study is combed for additional hints. Time series often involve a long time period, so the researcher has to rely on the availability of complete and accurate records. In our example, we would need to have detailed records of every student, the administration, and the faculty in order to make internally valid statements. Without these records, we could not rule out plausible alternative explanations.

Even with the records, there may be difficulties. The innumerable other changes that can take place mean that confounding is always a threat to internal validity. Over a thirty-year period, performance in school could change for several reasons, and these natural treatments could operate independently or they could interact. Teachers and administrators change, curriculum changes, and economic changes occur, which could all lead to internal invalidity. A major source of confounding in a long-term time series is what is called **mortality.** Pupils graduate and move away, or they may die. Such changes in the group of subjects would lead to a special form of selection bias (Cook and Campbell, 1979), because the same subjects would not be studied before and after the introduction of the treatment.

The difficulties of the interrupted-time-series design are magnified when the effect of the treatment is delayed or masked by other variables (Cook and Campbell, 1979). The effects of fluoride are unlikely to be immediate. Fluoride reduces dental problems, such as cavities. If absenteeism changes because of a reduction in cavities, then we might have additional interpretive problems. Cavities take time to develop, and fluoride does not eliminate cavities once they have taken hold. Thus, the effects of fluoride might be delayed, and we would not be in a position to interpret what caused the changes in achievement. Furthermore, the effects of fluoride could be masked by the intrusion of some variable that counteracts its effects, such as a bubble-gum factory moving to town.

These cautions notwithstanding, the interrupted-time-series design is very useful, especially in applied research. A good example of a time-series analysis is a study by McSweeny (1978) who showed that the introduction of a small fee for directory assistance (the "Information" operator) dramatically reduced the number of directory-assistance calls. Because most such calls were for numbers and addresses that were published, the telephone company wanted to eliminate these nonessential calls to keep the lines open for essential assistance. The number of daily calls in Cincinnati dropped by about 70,000 following the introduction of the 20-cent fee, showing that the strategy was an effective one.

Phillips used time-series analyses to investigate some of the psychological reasons leading to death. In an extensive and interesting series of papers, Phillips examined some of the causes of natural death (1972), the precipitants of suicide (1977, 1978), and the causes of homicides (1983). His general strategy involves determining the number of deaths before and after a particular event. Thus, death rate is the dependent variable, and the quasi-independent variable is the event that interrupts the time span over which Phillips makes his observations. Let us examine how he used an interrupted-time-series analysis to investigate the effects of mass-media violence on homicide rates in the United States.

Phillips began his study of the effects of media violence on homicides by carefully examining the literature on television violence and aggression (see the discussion in chapter 3 about the work by Eron and associates). From this literature, he concluded that aggression was most likely to occur following a story in which violence appeared to be (1) justified, (2) exciting, (3) real, and (4) rewarded. A natural violent event that fits these characteristics is a heavyweight-boxing match. Using an interrupted-time-series analysis, Phillips determined the number of homicides that occurred before and after boxing matches that received wide media presentation over the period 1973–1978.

Phillips found a remarkable 12.4 percent increase in homicide rates following the publicized boxing matches. He also found that this increase could not be attributed to extraneous variables such as the season of the year or the day of the week. If there is a causal relationship here, how did Phillips determine the aspects of prize fighting that lead to increase in homicides? Phillips became a detective. First, he determined that boxing matches do not simply precipitate a homicide that would have occurred in the absence of the match. He arrived at this conclusion by showing that the number of homicides did not go down before boxing matches, which they would have to do if the homicide rate is roughly constant over time and is merely pushed into reality by the match. Second, Phillips ruled out the possibility that the homicide rate increased because boxing matches are associated with gambling. He found that other major sporting events usually associated with gambling, such as the Super Bowl and the World Series, do not lead to an increase in the homicide rate.

Phillips concluded that the relationship between boxing and homicide rate is probably a result of modeling; that is, social learning processes that induce people to model or imitate others seem to account for the increase in homicides following the major prize fights. Phillip's reasoning went like this: If imitation or modeling is important, then the victims of homicides should be similar to the victim in the boxing match. This means that if a young white male loses a boxing match, for example, then the murders of young white males should increase, but the murders of young black males should not. Phillips found substantial evidence to support his modeling idea: The increase in homicide rate following a boxing match mostly includes murders of people who are very similar to the losers of the match.

Phillip's use of the interrupted-time-series analysis has been a valuable way to determine the effects of media violence on homicide rate. His use of detective work in trying to arrive at a causal analysis of his findings is a good lesson in probing for answers and rejecting alternative explanations.

## CONCEPT SUMMARY

INCREASING INTERNAL VALIDITY
In case studies, use
- *deviant-case analysis*
- *nonequivalent control*
- *multiple dependent variables*

In interrupted-time-series studies, use
- *nonequivalent control*
- *multiple dependent variables*

**(Beware of confounding caused by lack of control)**

## DESIGNS EMPLOYING SUBJECT VARIABLES

Much research in psychology is concerned with differences in the way various groups of people behave. A **subject variable** is some measurable characteristic of people. Examples are numerous and include intelligence (IQ), weight, anxiety, sex, age, need for achievement, attractiveness, race, ability to recall dreams, as well as many types of pathological conditions (schizophrenia, alcoholism, brain damage, and so on). Subject variables are often used in psychological research, but their use demands special consideration because investigation or selection of them is made after the fact. Thus, because the subject variables are not manipulated directly, designs using subject variables represent one more type of quasi-experimental research.

In experiments, an investigator has control over manipulation of the independent variable; it can be manipulated while all else is held constant. If we are interested in the effect of pornographic movies on physiological arousal and later sexual excitement, we can take two statistically equivalent groups of people (or the same people at different times), show them a movie with pornographic scenes included or omitted (while we hold other variables constant), and measure their responses. We can then be confident (but never certain) that the difference between the movies produced any observed differential effect in arousal. The case is very different with subject variables, though. An experimenter cannot manipulate a subject variable while holding other factors constant; he or she can only select subjects who already have the characteristic to some degree, and then compare them on the behavior of interest. If the subjects in the different groups (say, high, medium, and low IQ) differ on the behavior, we cannot conclude that the subject-variable difference produced or is responsible for the difference in behavior. The reason is that other factors may vary with the subject variable and thus be confounded with it. So if high-IQ subjects perform some task better than low-IQ subjects, we cannot say that IQ produced or caused the difference, because the different groups of subjects are likely to vary on other relevant dimensions such as motivation, education, and the like. When subject variables are investigated, we cannot safely attribute differences in behavior to them, as we can with true experimental variables. Such designs, then, essentially produce correlations between variables, and we should be wary of the same types of confounding that occur in correlational research. We can say that the variables are related, but we cannot say that one variable produced or caused the effect in the other variable.

This is a very important point, so let us consider an example. Suppose an investigator is interested in the intellectual functioning of people suffering from schizophrenia. People diagnosed as belonging to this group are given numerous tests meant to measure various mental abilities. The researcher also gives these tests to another group of people, so-called normals, as a control measure. He or she discovers that schizophrenics do especially poorly (relative to normals) in tests involving semantic aspects of language, such as understanding the meaning of words or comprehending prose passages. The investigator concludes that the schizophrenics perform these tests more poorly *because* they are schizophrenics and that their inability to use language well in communication is a likely contributing cause of schizophrenia.

Studies like this are common in some areas of psychology. Conclusions similar to those just mentioned are often drawn, but they are completely unjustifiable. Both conclusions are based on correlations, and other factors could well be the critical ones. Schizophrenics may do more poorly than normals for any number of reasons. They may not be as intelligent, as motivated, as educated, or as wise at taking tests. Possibly, the fact that they have been institutionalized for a long time with resulting poverty of social and intellectual intercourse accounts for the differences. We cannot conclude that the reason the two groups differ on verbal tests is schizophrenia or its absence in the two groups. Even if we could, it would certainly not imply the other conclusion, that language problems are involved in causing schizophrenia. Again, all we would have is a correlation between these two variables, with no idea of whether or how the two are causally related.

Use of subject variables is very common in all psychological research, but it is absolutely crucial in areas such as clinical and developmental psychology, so the problems with making inferences from such research should be carefully considered. A primary variable in developmental psychology is age, a subject variable, which means that much research in this field is correlational in nature. In general, the problem of individual differences among subjects in psychology is often ignored, though there are often appeals to consider the problem as crucial (for example, Underwood, 1975). Let us look at some ways to make more sound inferences from experiments that use subject variables.

## Matching

The basic problem in the investigation of subject variables, and in other quasi-experimental research, is that whatever differences are observed in behavior may be caused by other confounded variables. One way to try to avoid this problem is by **matching** subjects on the other relevant variables. In the comparison of schizophrenics and normals we noted that the two groups were also likely to differ on other characteristics, such as IQ, education, motivation, institutionalization, medication, and perhaps even age. Rather than simply comparing the schizophrenics with normals, we might try to compare them with another group more closely matched on these other dimensions so that the main difference between the groups is in the presence or absence of schizophrenia. For example, we might use a group of neurotics who, on the average, are similar to the schizophrenics in terms of age, IQ, length of time institutionalized, sex, and some measure of motivation. When the two groups have been matched on all these characteristics, then we can more confidently attribute any difference in performance between them to the factor of interest, namely, schizophrenia. By matching, we attempt to introduce the crucial characteristic of experimentation—being able to hold extraneous factors constant to avoid confoundings—into what is essentially a correlational observation. Our goal is to be able to infer that the variable of interest (schizophrenia) produced the observed effect.

There are several rather serious problems associated with matching. For one thing, matching often requires a great deal of effort because some of the relevant variables may be difficult to measure. Even when we go to the trouble of taking the needed additional measures, we may still be unable to match the groups, especially if few subjects are involved before matching is attempted (for example, research on an unusual type of brain damage or other medical disorder). Even when matching is successful, it often greatly reduces the size of the sample on which the observations are made. Thus, we then are less confident that our observations are reliable (stable and repeatable).

Matching is often difficult because crucial differences among subjects may have subtle effects. In addition, the effects of one difference may interact with another. Thus, *interactions* among matched variables may confound the results. To illustrate these difficulties, let us reconsider some of the work done by Brazelton and associates on neonatal behavior mentioned in chapter 3 (Lester and Brazelton, 1982).

Brazelton's primary interest is in cultural differences in neonatal behavior as measured by the Brazelton Neonatal Behavioral Assessment Scale. The general strategy is to compare neonates from various cultures and ethnic groups with neonates from the United States. In these quasi-experiments, culture or ethnic group, which is a subject variable, is the quasi-independent variable. Attempts are usually made to match the neonates from different cultures along various dimensions such as birth weight, birth length, and obstetrical risk (including whether the mother received medication during birth, whether the baby was premature, and so on). Lester and Brazelton show that there is a synergistic relationship among these factors. **Synergism** in a medical context means that the combined effects of two or more variables are not additive—the combined effect is greater than the sum of the individual components—which means that the variables interact. The way in which neonatal characteristics and obstetrical risk interact is as follows. Studies have shown that the behavior (as measured by the Brazelton scale) of slightly underweight infants is more strongly influenced (negatively) by small amounts of medication taken by the mother than is the behavior of neonates who are closer to the average in weight. So it is very difficult to match subjects appropriately because low

FIGURE 9–2

Hypothetical changes in IQ scores resulting from regression to the mean. The high-scoring and low-scoring subgroups regressed toward the mean of the entire group when they were retested.

birth weight interacts with medication, which has effects on the behavior of the children. Even though the neonates are carefully selected, the synergistic relation between the matched variables can influence the results. This is an especially difficult problem in Brazelton's work, because much of his research has examined neonates from impoverished cultures, where birth weight is low and obstetrical risk is very high. Generally, you should remember that matched variables are rarely under direct control, which means that the possibility of confounding is always present.

Another problem with matching involves the introduction of the dreaded **regression artifact**. This is discussed in chapter 11, but we will explain it briefly here. Under certain conditions in many types of measurements a statistical phenomenon known as **regression to the mean** occurs. The mean of a group of scores is what most people think of as the average—the total of all observations divided by the number of observations. For example, mean intelligence in a sample of sixty people is the sum of all their intelligence-test scores divided by 60 (see appendix A). Generally, if people who received extreme scores (that is, very high or very low) on some characteristic are retested, their second scores will be closer to the mean of the entire group than were their original scores.

Extreme scores are likely owing to measurement error. If the error is random and normally distributed (see appendix A), then subsequent measures will have smaller errors—they will be less extreme. Consider an example. We give 200 people a standard test of mathematical reasoning for which there are two equivalent forms, or two versions of the test that are equivalent. The average (mean) score on the test is 60 of 100 possible points. We take the fifteen people who score highest and the fifteen who score lowest. The means of these groups are 95 and 30, respectively. Then we test them again on the other form of the test. We might find that the means of the two groups are 87 and 35. On the second test, the scores of the two extreme groups regressed toward the mean; the high-scoring group scored more poorly, whereas the low-scoring group had somewhat better scores. This sequence of events is illustrated in figure 9–2. In the high-scoring group, some people whose true scores are somewhat lower than the scores they received were simply lucky on the first test and scored higher than they should have. When retested, these subjects tended to score lower, nearer their true score. The situation is reversed for the low-scoring group.

This regression toward the mean is always observed when there is a less-than-perfect correlation between the two measures. The more extreme the selection of scores, the greater the regression toward the mean. It also occurs in all types of measurement situations. If abnormally tall or short parents have a child, its adult height will probably be closer to the population mean than to the height of the parents. As with most statistical phenomena, regression to the mean is true of groups of observations and is probabilistic (that is, it may not occur every time). For example, in the second test of mathematical reasoning, a few individual subjects may score higher or lower than before, but the group tendency will be toward the mean. In any event, if we had selected subjects on the basis of their reasoning scores and then matched them in two groups, subsequent differences may have been caused by some treatment or may have been the result of regression to the mean. If we do not have the true scores, and if we do not use random assignment, then regression to the mean may be a confounding factor leading to changes in behavior.

Ex post facto research and quasi-experiments with subject variables are conducted often to evaluate educational programs, so those who practice such research need to be aware of the many thorny problems associated with it. Without matching, an investigator may not be able to say much about the results. Matching helps alleviate the problem of confoundings in some cases, but then the possibility of regression artifacts arises. And many researchers seem unaware of this problem.

When matching is a practical possibility, and when regression artifacts are evaluated, we can be somewhat more confident of conclusions from our results. But we still have only a correlation, albeit a very carefully controlled one. Matching is useful, but it is not a cure-all. In our example involving schizophrenics, if the schizophrenics perform worse than the new matched control group of neurotics, can we then conclude that schizophrenia *produces* inferiority in language usage? No, we cannot. There could be something else, some other difference between the two groups. We can never be sure that we matched on the relevant variables. Perhaps neurotics are superior in their use of language!

## CONCEPT SUMMARY

MATCHING
Be alert for
- *synergism*
- *regression artifacts*

### Age as a Variable

One subject variable, age, deserves its own discussion for two reasons. In the first place, developmental psychology is a popular and important part of scientific psychology. In the second place, age as a variable poses very difficult confoundings that have generated some interesting and powerful research designs.

Suppose we are interested in determining the effects of age on the ability to use two types of learning strategies. One type of strategy might improve recall (Tversky and Teiffer, 1976), because when our subjects use this strategy correctly they will be able to associate one thing with another. In remembering the names of simple objects (for example, *knife, tree,* and *cat*), subjects recall one object which helps them recall another object (for example, recalling *cat* reminds them of *tree,* because cats climb trees and trees make them think of *knife,* because they carve their initials in a tree with a knife). We will call this the recall strategy. The other strategy might help your subjects recognize things (as in a multiple-choice test). In this recognize strategy, subjects look for minute differences among objects so that they can later specify which of several similar objects was actually shown to them.

We decide to see how children of different ages utilize these two strategies. How are we going to design our project? The most straightforward (and most likely) design is the **cross-sectional method.** Using this method, we would select children of different ages (for example, ages 5, 8, and 12) and then randomly assign half of each age group to one of the strategy conditions. Or we could use the more time-consuming **longitudinal method.** Here, we would test a subject when he or she was 5, then at 8, and then again at age 12. In the cross-sectional method, we figuratively cut through the age dimension, and in the longitudinal method we follow a particular individual along the age dimension. These two developmental methods are quite often used in studies in which age is a variable, yet they both contain serious confoundings that could make the internal validity of the research highly suspect.

What are some of these serious confoundings? Before we can discuss them, we need to discuss age itself. Age is a subject variable, so it cannot be considered a true independent variable. Age is a dimension; in particular, it is a time dimension along which we can study behavior. Some developmental psychologists have suggested that we consider age as a dependent variable because it is a variable that varies with other subject characteristics from birth to death (Wohwill, 1970).

In any event, we cannot directly vary age, so we must be wary of any concomitant variables associated with it. Different research designs have different confoundings. In the cross-sectional method, age is confounded with the generation of birth. Not only is one of the authors of this textbook twenty-two years older than his son, he and his son also differ in terms of the generations in which they were born, and generation itself is a complex variable. In this sense the generation gap is real—someone born in 1942 is not just twenty-two years older than someone born in 1964. The older person was born into a different world populated by different people who had different attitudes and education than the counterparts (what the developmental psychologists call cohorts) of the younger person.

When we use the longitudinal method, we follow a particular individual who will maintain the same cohorts. With this method, therefore, we do not have to worry about the generation/age confounding. However, the longitudinal method confounds age with time of treatment or testing. If you test the memory of a child at age 5 and then at age 12, not only is the person seven years older on the second test, but the world has changed in the interim. Using the longitudinal method, we might find that college students' attitudes about energy conservation in 1991 have changed since the subjects were 5 years old in 1977. Is the change in attitude owing to a change in age or to a change in the world?

Figure 9–3 shows some research designs that can be used when age is a variable. The **time-lag design** (the design indicated along the diagonal) aims at determining the effects of time of testing while holding age constant (only 19-year-olds are tested in this example). As is true of the cross-sectional design, the time-lag design confounds cohorts of the subjects with the target variable.

Schaie (1977) has outlined many sophisticated designs to overcome the confoundings we have just described. One of these designs is illustrated in figure 9–3. The **cross-sequential design,** indicated by the central box, involves testing two or more age groups at two or more time periods. This design includes

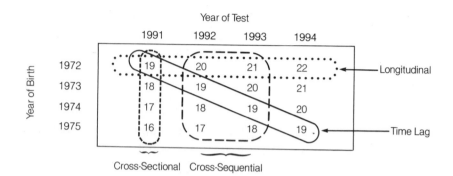

**FIGURE 9–3**

Some quasi-
experimental designs
used when age is a
variable at the time of
testing.

features of the other three designs we have mentioned. Subjects of different ages are tested at the same time as in the cross-sectional method; an individual is tested successively as in the longitudinal method; and different subjects of the same age are tested at different times as in the time-lag design. In the cross-sequential design, therefore, the researcher can determine the effects of most of the potential confoundings. Consider just one example from figure 9–3— the 20-year-old who was born in 1972. The effects of age are tested both longitudinally and sectionally (a 20-year-old is compared with subjects of different ages in 1992 and that 20-year-old is tested again in 1993). If the effects of age are the same in both of these comparisons, then we can rule out cohorts and time of testing as important confoundings.

The cross-sequential design is cumbersome. Many subjects have to be tested over a period of time, which may make a research project impractical. Therefore, this design is not used as often as it probably should be. Most developmental researchers use the more manageable cross-sectional design.

A typical cross-sectional experiment has age as a quasi-independent variable as well as another true independent variable. In the Tversky and Teiffer (1976) study outlined earlier, three age groups were tested on their ability to use the recall strategy and the recognize strategy. The recall strategy improved retention at all ages (5, 8, and 12), but the recognize strategy proved beneficial only to the oldest children. Such results are an example of an **interaction** (see chapter 7), which means that the effects of one variable are dependent on the level of the other variable—the effects of type of strategy depended on the age of the subjects.

The tactic of using age and a true independent variable in developmental research means that the researcher expects an interaction. Whatever variables are confounded with age (in the Tversky and Teiffer study, age was confounded with grade in school in addition to the usual confoundings associated with a cross-sectional design) might be differentially affected by a true independent variable. The clever psychologist tries to pinpoint what components of age determine thought and behavior, and the search for particular interactions may help. The purpose of both the cross-sequential design and the search for interactions is to enhance the internal validity of developmental research. Age is a complex variable, and we must simplify it in order to have a valid analysis.

A final way that the internal validity of research with subject variables can be enhanced is to use construct validity as a mode of converging operation (see chapter 11). Instead of searching for interactions to try to tease apart the true effects of a subject variable from those effects owing to variables that are correlated with it, we could coordinate the results with a particular theory. Highly refined theories of personality and child development use this technique. For example, Piaget developed a comprehensive theory of child development that makes particular predictions about the kinds of behavior exhibited by children at different stages of cognitive development (Piaget and Inhelder, 1969). Although these stages are partially associated with chronological age, they are presumed to be a function of maturation and experience. Thus, the stage of development, as shown in certain kinds of behaviors, and not age, is viewed as the causal factor. Piaget's theory specifies how and when these stages will occur, so that age-related behavioral differences should fit into the network of the theory. When the predicted changes do occur (that is, when they agree with Piaget's theory), we say that there is construct validity for the theory. The theory permits one to rule out the effects of a correlated variable (age in this case) and converge on an explanation of why certain behaviors are observed.

## CONCEPT SUMMARY

THREATS TO INTERNAL VALIDITY IN QUASI-EXPERIMENTAL RESEARCH WITH SOME SOLUTIONS

| *Research Procedure* | *Threat to Internal Validity* | *Ways to Enhance Internal Validity* |
|---|---|---|
| Case studies | Source of causation; baseline "condition" maturation; history; selection bias | Deviant-case analysis (a nonequivalent control); detective work |
| Interrupted time series | Changes in subjects and environment; delayed effects | Nonequivalent control group; detective work |
| Subject variables | Dimensions on which to match; regression artifacts | Matching; include true independent variable and seek interactions |
| Age as a variable | Confoundings with: time of testing, generation of birth | Cross-sequential design; include a true independent variable and seek an interaction; converging operations |

## SUMMARY

1. In research that is internally valid, straightforward statements can be made about cause and effect. In quasi-experimental research, in which there is no direct control over the independent variables (they are examined after the fact), causal statements may not be possible because of confoundings.

2. Quasi-experiments have one or more ex post facto components: either naturally occurring variables or subject variables (or both).

3. When there are natural treatments, problems such as history, maturation, selection bias, and nonequivalent control groups may confound the results.

4. One-shot case studies and the interrupted-time-series design are two quasi-experimental procedures with low internal validity. The researcher must be a good detective to determine the causal agents in these procedures, because mortality and delayed effects are threats to internal validity.

5. Likewise, the researcher needs to be a good detective when he or she tries to handle subject variables by matching subjects on the basis of particular characteristics. Just what characteristics are to be matched often poses a difficult problem, and those characteristics may regress toward the mean in many instances, and interactions among the matched variables may occur.

6. Age as a subject variable provides many real threats to internal validity because it is confounded with numerous other factors.

7. Using the cross-sequential design and looking for interactions of age with true independent variables are two ways to enhance the internal validity of developmental research.

## Key Concepts

| | |
|---|---|
| cross-sectional method | observation-treatment-observation |
| cross-sequential design | one-shot case study |
| history | quasi-experiment |
| interaction | regression artifact |
| interrupted-time-series design | regression to the mean |
| longitudinal method | selection bias |
| matching | subject variable |
| maturation | synergism |
| mortality | time-lag design |
| nonequivalent control group | |

## Exercises

1. [*Special Exercise.*] A considerable amount of evidence indicates there is an inverse relationship between birth order and intelligence (Zajonc and Marcus, 1975). Birth order refers to the order in which children enter the family unit (first born, second born, and so on). Intelligence tends to be lower for later-born children than for the earlier ones. List as many factors as you can that might be confounded with birth order. How might you determine which of these factors is important in influencing intelligence? In other words, how do we enhance internal validity when birth order is the variable? What quasi-experiments can be done?

2. The *Journal of Applied Psychology* often reports studies that used an interrupted-time-series design. Examine several recent issues and note, in particular, any control conditions that are included.

3. Age as a variable in geriatric research (the study of old age) is often more difficult to analyze than in child development studies. Why?

4. Discuss the ways in which mortality, selection bias, history, and maturation can threaten the internal validity of quasi-experiments.

## Suggested Readings

Donald T. Campbell has written a great deal about quasi-experimental research. The best place to begin is with the first book listed here. More detail is presented in the second one. Campbell, D. T., & Stanley, J. C. (1963). *Experimental and quasi-experimental designs for research.* Chicago: Rand McNally. Cook, T. D. and Campbell, D. T. (1979). *Quasi-experimentation: Design and analysis issues for field settings.* Chicago: Rand McNally.

## PSYCHOLOGY IN ACTION
### A Quasi-Experiment

Try these quasi-experiments as a follow-up to the correlational research described in the Psychology in Action section for chapter 3. The project there dealt with the relationship between amount of sleep and tension or migraine headaches.

If you recorded demographic data (age, sex, year in school) for each of your subjects in the sleep/headache research, you can do a quasi-experiment using one of your demographic variables to define your independent variable. For example, you could compare the number of headaches reported by men and women. Another quasi-experiment could examine the amount of sleep obtained by freshmen, sophomores, juniors, and seniors. There are other possibilities, which we will allow you to figure out.

Although these quasi-experiments may look like ordinary between-subjects experiments, do not forget that you have not manipulated an independent variable—your groups here are determined by selection, not manipulation. Thus, you need to be cautious about making causal statements.

# TACTICAL
# ASPECTS OF RESEARCH

| **THREATS TO VALIDITY** | **Questions to Answer** |
|---|---|
| Reactions of participants, researcher bias, and problems in communication | *How will the participants in my project react?* Is my naturalistic observation unobtrusive? Can I assess normal and motivated forgetting in my case study by corroborating evidence? Is my test able to counteract the problem of response styles? Does my experimental plan contain "blinding" or other procedures to ensure that the subjects react appropriately to the independent variable? |
| | *How will I, the researcher, influence the results of my project?* Will my personal characteristics influence the behavior or the subjects? Have I defined a research plan that permits me to treat all participants the same (except for deliberate variation)? Do I have to be blind to certain aspects of the research in order to be unbiased? Am I aware of my own biases and preconceptions? Am I an objective researcher? |
| | *Do other scientists understand what I am investigating?* Are my terms operationally defined? |
| | *Does my project represent an externally valid attempt to determine why people think and act as they do?* Are my subjects representative? Have I selected meaningful variables to examine and vary? Is the setting I plan to use ecologically valid? |

# GUARDING AGAINST THREATS TO VALIDITY

Conducting a good research project is difficult because there are numerous problems awaiting you. The purpose of this chapter is to forewarn you about many of these difficulties, most of which have to be confronted before all the details of your research plan have been determined. Other pitfalls can influence how you interpret the *results* of research; these will be examined in a later chapter. In this chapter we will discuss (1) how the researcher and subject react to being involved in research; (2) how to ensure accurate communication among scientists; and (3) how to try to determine the validity of your research procedure. Good research requires careful planning and cautious interpretation. In this chapter, we are concerned with the various problems that can arise during the course of your research. In our discussion, we review relevant concepts covered in previous chapters, and we introduce a number of new terms and ideas. All of the ideas presented here, both old and new, are potential obstacles to good research. By bringing these different issues together under a single heading, we hope to increase your awareness of the variety of problems you face in doing psychological research. We also suggest how you can avoid many of these pitfalls through careful planning.

## PITFALLS RESULTING FROM REACTIONS OF PARTICIPANTS

In many areas of psychological research, we can view the reactions of the participants not only in terms of the project itself, but also in terms of everyday social interaction. Suppose you are responding to a survey that asks you to estimate the number of times a day you think about sex. Go ahead and make a guess. Now, suppose you are asked the same question in a personal interview. Would your answer in the interview be the same as the one given in the survey? You might be reluctant to say "I think about sex at least fifteen times a day." On the other hand, writing "15" in response to a question on an anonymous survey might not bother you at all. In general, ordinary social interaction may put demands on a research participant that changes the way he or she reacts.

Weber and Cook (1972) used the phrase **subject roles** to highlight the important social and psychological factors that occur in research and may influence the results. As used here, *role* refers to how the participants perceive the research setting and how they then react to it. Because the perceived role may determine how the subjects respond, unnatural responding, **reactivity,** could occur and confound the results. We will consider several examples of reactivity and some possible solutions.

The term **demand characteristics** was at one time the standard way to refer to subject reactivity. The phrase was coined by Orne (1962) to highlight the pressure put on people participating in research. Orne emphasized the obedience of the subject to the researcher's demands. We believe that reactivity is a more general term to describe the roles that subjects may adopt than is the phrase *demand characteristics.*

## Reactivity in Descriptive Research

**Naturalistic observation.** There are two general ways to guard against the participants' reactions ruining observations: (1) we can make unobtrusive observations, or (2) we can take unobtrusive measures (Webb, Campbell, Schwartz, and Sechrist, 1981).

First we will consider **unobtrusive observations.** Imagine that you are walking down a street in your hometown. Occasionally you greet a friend (perhaps with a handshake, perhaps with an eyebrow flash). As your walk continues, a man with a large camera approaches and proceeds to take moving pictures of you every time you greet one of your friends. How are you likely to react to this attention? Quite likely, your mode of greeting people would change dramatically. (Have you ever noticed how spectators behave at sporting events when they know the television camera is on them?) Eibl-Eibesfeldt guarded against participant reactivity in his research by using a camera with a special sideways lens (his work is also discussed in chapter 3). This lens permitted him to aim the camera 90 degrees from the subject; presumably, the subject would think that Eibl-Eibesfeldt was photographing something else. Thus, the subject would not react abnormally to the presence of the observer and his camera; instead, the subject would act naturally, which is what Eibl-Eibesfeldt intended. The special camera lens allowed the researcher to observe without intruding on the subject, which means that Eibl-Eibesfeldt used an unobtrusive observation technique.

In general, unobtrusive observations of subjects are likely to reveal more natural behavior than if the subjects are aware of being observed. In studying animals, researchers use unobtrusive observations whenever possible so that the behavior of interest will not be affected by the observer's presence.

Sometimes, however, either the subjects themselves, the terrain, or some other aspect of the project demands close contact. In these situations, **participant observation** often provides a solution. For example, Fossey (1972) spent a great amount of time observing the mountain gorilla. The mountain gorilla lives in central Africa, and its habitat is threatened by human beings who are moving into that area. The mountain gorilla's natural habitat is in the mountainous rain forest, which makes long-range unobtrusive spying out of the question. Fossey was particularly concerned with the free-ranging behavior of the gorillas, so she decided to become a participant observer. This was difficult, because the gorillas are not tame. She had to mimic the gorillas so that they would become accustomed to her presence. She mimicked aspects of the animal's behavior, such as eating, grooming, and making weird gorillalike vocalizations. As she said, "one feels like a fool thumping one's chest rhythmically or sitting about pretending to munch on a stalk of wild celery as though it were the most delectable morsel in the world. But the gorillas have responded favorably" (p. 211). It took several months for Fossey to gain the confidence of the gorillas, and she continued to live with and study the gorillas until her death in 1986. How would you like to act like a gorilla for ten or fifteen years?

**Unobtrusive measures,** in contrast to unobtrusive observations, are usually indirect observations of behavior. Unobtrusive measures are indirect because it is the result of behavior, not the behavior itself, that is being studied. Thus, instead of measuring behavior directly, we examine it after the fact by looking at what the behavior accomplished. Instead of observing a student's studying activities, we examine his or her transcript. Instead of living with the gorillas, we look at their effect on the environment. Obviously, unobtrusive measures are not suitable for all questions being investigated (an unobtrusive measure of an eyebrow flash might be difficult), but for some these measures are not merely good, they are the only ones that are feasible. Consider the question of graffiti in public restrooms. Who does it? What does the graffiti usually concern? A number of serious ethical questions (ethics are discussed in chapter 12) would be raised if a researcher stood around in restrooms observing the patrons. However, the graffiti topics can be examined and can provide substantial information. Kinsey, Pomeroy, and Martin (1953) discovered that graffiti in men's restrooms was more erotic than graffiti in women's restrooms. Furthermore, they found more graffiti in men's rooms than in women's rooms.

Using unobtrusive measures is akin to a hunter following animal tracks or a police officer examining clues such as fingerprints. Tracks and clues are left behind and often allow us to infer things about the behavior that caused them. Recently, a popular psychological and anthropological unobtrusive measure has been to examine the garbage and other refuse that people discard. From the characteristics of the discarded objects, the observer attempts to understand some aspect of the behavior behind that refuse (for example, a discarded liquor bottle or love letter that has been thrown away could reveal information about behavior).

**Case Studies.** Case studies are individual histories, which means that much of the evidence in these studies is **retrospective** in nature. In other words, it comes from looking back into the past. Looking backward often causes problems. One difficulty is that the evidence may be inaccurate as a result of ordinary forgetting. We may not remember what our thoughts and actions were in nursery school because what has happened since then interferes with our memory of early events. Another difficulty with case studies is that participant reactivity may lead to **motivated forgetting.** Motivated forgetting refers to the active way in which humans reconstruct their past experiences. People may distort their memories to match their current beliefs. For instance, a politician who has changed views on a controversial issue such as the death penalty may recall the former stance as having been much more moderate than it really was. Similarly, people may inflate their memory for positive events. A powerful example of this type of positive distortion can be seen in the memory of John Dean during the Watergate scandal in the early 1970s. Appearing before a congressional committee, Dean described personal conversations between President Nixon and himself. In these descriptions, he generally overestimated his role in the conversation, and he tended to exaggerate any praise bestowed on him by the president (Neisser, 1981). We know that John Dean's recollections were distorted because audiotapes of these same conversations have since been compared with the congressional testimony. The example of John Dean illustrates that an effective method for dealing with motivated forgetting is to obtain corroborating evidence from other sources. Unfortunately, such evidence may be difficult to obtain, and if other people serve as additional sources, then their memories are subject to the same problems.

**Surveys, interviews, and tests.**  To the extent that other forms of descriptive research rely on retrospective reports, they face the same reactivity problems (i.e., both ordinary and motivated forgetting) as case studies. However, many of the responses on tests and surveys are not retrospective, and we instead face problems resulting from **response styles** or *response sets*. Different people may have habitual ways of answering questions. These habits may result from how they view themselves or from the expectations of the researcher and society (more on this later). In general, there are three kinds of response styles: yea-saying or **response acquiescence,** nay-saying or **response deviation,** and **social desirability.** College-bound high-school graduates tend to respond no to the question "Do you use marijuana daily?" Does this answer reflect the true behavior of these people, or does the answer reflect the habitual tendency to say no (response deviation)? Or the answer could be a socially desirable one because marijuana is a controlled substance and many authorities frown upon its use. The high-school graduates not heading for college tended to answer yes to this question twice as often as the college-bound (Bachman and Johnston, 1979). Is this answer a true one, or does the answer simply indicate that these people are likely to acquiesce and say yes regardless of what the question is? Based on the answer to this one question, we cannot determine whether the answer is a true one or the result of a particular response style.

Edwards (1953, 1957) has developed an interesting solution to the response-style problem, at least for certain kinds of descriptive research. In particular, Edwards suggested the use of a **forced-choice test** in which participants must choose between two alternatives of equal social desirability in a personality test. On Edward's test, called the Personal Preference Schedule, the respondent has to select one of two activities or indicate which of two thoughts or feelings better reflects the characteristics of the respondent. For example, the respondent might have to choose between playing tennis or water skiing. Although equal in social desirability, the two alternatives are hypothesized to be associated with different personality characteristics. Here, water skiing may be the more typical choice of extraverted individuals. The forced-choice technique decreases the influence of social desirability as well as eliminating the possibility of response acquiescence or response deviation.

Associated with the problem of response styles is one more difficult to cope with, the **volunteer problem.** Volunteer subjects differ in a number of ways from potential participants who do not volunteer (Rosnow and Rosenthal, 1970). Volunteers tend to be more intelligent, better educated, more cooperative, better adjusted, and in greater need of social approval than nonvolunteers. These characteristics of volunteers could strongly influence participant reaction. The volunteer problem might also limit the generalizability of results in an experiment.

What the volunteer problem means in terms of your own research is that you have to be careful in sampling from the population of participants available to you. If your test or survey is boring and requires that the respondent go to extreme lengths to be cooperative (trudging through a blizzard at 11:00 P.M. to the psychology building), then the answers you get may be based on a biased sample of opinion (this is an example of selection bias; see chapter 9). The problem is also serious, as Rosnow and Rosenthal point out, in opinion surveys that rely on volunteer mailings or phone-ins. What are we to make of the results of a magazine survey that relies on voluntary compliance of the readers? Or, how about the radio survey that solicits calls from its listeners? In both cases we do not know anything about the people who did not respond, nor do we know anything about the people who do not read that magazine or listen to that station. We can find out about the nonrespondents by expending a great deal of time and effort. Usually, this effort is not made.

There are three possible solutions to the nonrespondent problem, although none of these solutions are completely satisfactory. First, you can get a **random sample** of the entire population that is available to you. This means that every potential respondent has an equal chance of being questioned. Of course, this assumes that all subjects in the population will participate if questioned. Second, you could give the nonrespondents some kind of extra incentive to participate in your project. They could be offered money or be given detailed information about the research project. The extra inducements might bias the results of the research, however, by treating some subjects differently from others prior to participation in the project. Third, you could replicate your research with additional samples of subjects. Although your project may again be plagued with the same volunteer problem, this would be a good solution if the problems associated with volunteers and nonrespondents were not likely to recur in your replication.

## Correlational Research

As mentioned in chapter 3 many of the subject reactivity problems found in descriptive research are also applicable to correlational research because test results and survey data often provide the bases for correlations. In fact, demands on participants might be magnified in correlational research that involves two measures that are taken at the same time. Participants do not usually react passively to the inquiries of the researcher. Instead, they often try to figure out what is going on and respond according to their perceptions of the project and in ways that will make themselves look good to the researcher (Weber and Cook, 1972). For example, suppose you surveyed a college population about their sexual and religious attitudes. At the same time, you also asked them about their use of drugs. Most college students could figure out at least some of the purposes of the project, and as a consequence, their responses to the two sets of questions asked together might differ from their responses to either set asked alone.

## Experimentation

The problem of subject reactivity is not restricted to descriptive and correlational research. Research involving experimental procedures (see chapter 5) faces similar difficulties with reactivity. In fact, just telling someone that he or she is in a psychology experiment may cause reactivity problems. To illustrate, walk up to a stranger and say, "Please do me a favor by doing ten push-ups." Repeat your request to several others. Then, repeat the procedure, but this time say, "I'm doing a psychology experiment. Please do me a favor by doing ten push-ups." The odds are that you will get very little compliance from the first group of people and very few refusals from the second group. People sometimes will do things in the name of science and experimentation that they will not ordinarily do (Orne, 1962). In other words, experiments may not only examine behavior, they may produce it! Reactivity can be an important source of contamination in experimental data.

Orne (1962, 1969) noted that subjects entering an experiment have some general notions of what to expect and are usually trying to figure out the specific purpose of the experiment. They are likely to believe that reasonable care will be taken for their well-being and that whatever the experimenter asks them to do will serve a useful purpose. Because many psychological experiments would provide uninteresting results if the true purpose were known, elaborate deceptions are often used to mask the goal of the experiment. But, as Orne points out, these might sometimes be rather transparent. At any rate, the general problem exists as to how the subject's expectations affect or determine her or his behavior in an experiment. Orne notes:

> Insofar as the subject cares about the outcome, his perception of his role and of the hypothesis being tested will become a significant determinant of his behavior. The cues which govern his behavior—which communicate what is expected of him and what the experimenter hopes to find—can therefore be crucial variables. Some time ago I proposed that these cues be called "*demand characteristics* of an experiment." . . . They include the scuttlebutt about the experiment, its setting, implicit and explicit instructions, the person of the experimenter, subtle cues provided by him, and, of particular importance, the experimental procedure (Orne, 1969, p. 146, italics added).

Participant reaction may limit the generality of the results of an experiment because, if the results are produced by just the participants' perception of the experimental situation, they will not generalize to other situations. Frequently, when people know they are being observed, their behavior is greatly affected. One famous case of this is the **Hawthorne effect,** named after the Western Electric Company plant at which an experiment was conducted on factors affecting worker productivity (Homans, 1965). Six average women workers participated in a longitudinal study of factors affecting the rate at which they assembled telephone relays. First, the baseline rate of producing relays was measured. Then the women were placed in a special test room, and, after a period of adjustment to their new circumstances, they experienced a number of changes in their daily routine that were supposed to affect productivity. During one period of the study, rest pauses were inserted into their schedule, and later the frequency of pauses was increased. During another period, their method of payment was changed, and during yet another, a light lunch was provided, and so on. The experiment lasted for more than a year and the results were quite surprising. With few exceptions, no matter what changes were made—whether there were many or few rest periods, whether the workday was made longer or shorter, and so on—the women tended to produce more and more telephone relays. Although the reason for this change is difficult to determine (because a number of variables were confounded), the fact that the women knew they were in an experiment, felt the special attention, and wanted to cooperate are likely candidates. The workers knew that the experimenters expected the changes in the working conditions to affect them, so they did. The women kept working harder and harder. (For a different interpretation, see Parsons, 1974).

Because the changes in behavior apparently resulted from the fact that the workers were in an experiment and not because of the independent variables that were manipulated, we can say that the Hawthorne effect represents one kind of reactivity. Orne argues that to some extent experiments with humans always have this feature built in. The subject is an active participant interested in what is happening and is usually eager to help. Orne and his associates have done a great deal of research on demand characteristics in experimentation. Some of the most interesting studies deal with reactivity in hypnosis research.

Investigators have asked subjects under hypnosis to do all sorts of things, often with notable success. One apparently well-established finding is that subjects under hypnosis can be led to perform various antisocial and destructive acts, such as throwing acid in someone's face and handling venomous snakes (Rowland, 1939; Young, 1952). Orne and Evans (1965) suspected that this might have been owing more to the demand characteristics of the situation than to the effects of hypnosis. They asked subjects to perform a series of dangerous acts such as grasping a venomous snake, taking a coin from fuming acid, and throwing nitric acid in the experimenter's face. There were several treatment conditions: (1) subjects who were under deep hypnosis, (2) subjects who were told to simulate being hypnotized, (3) awake control subjects who were not asked to simulate hypnosis but who were pressed by the experimenter to comply with the requests, (4) awake control subjects who were not pressed to comply, and (5) people who were asked to perform the task without being made part of an experiment. The experimenter did not know which condition the subjects were in, so as to minimize bias. The results are summarized in table 10–1. As would be expected, people not in the experimental setting refused to carry out

TABLE 10–1 PERCENTAGE OF SUBJECTS WHO PERFORMED DANGEROUS TASKS IN RESPONSE TO REQUESTS BY THE EXPERIMENTER (ADAPTED FROM ORNE & EVANS, 1965. COPYRIGHT 1965 BY THE AMERICAN PSYCHOLOGICAL ASSOCIATION. ADAPTED BY PERMISSION OF THE AUTHOR.)

| Subject Group | Grasp Venomous Snake | Take Coin from Acid | Throw Acid at Experimenter |
|---|---|---|---|
| Real hypnosis | 83 | 83 | 83 |
| Simulating hypnosis | 100 | 100 | 100 |
| Waking control— pressure to comply | 50 | 83 | 83 |
| Waking control— without pressure to comply | 50 | 17 | 17 |
| Nonexperimental | 0 | 0 | 0 |

the antisocial tasks, but as other investigators had reported, a high percentage of hypnotized subjects did carry out the tasks as instructed. However, *all* simulating control subjects also performed the tasks and even the nonsimulating controls, if pressed to comply, performed them to a large extent, which demonstrates the power of the experimental situation. Thus, hypnosis is not necessarily responsible for subjects performing the antisocial acts. Rather, reactivity to the experimental situation, including the setting, the instructions, and the way subjects think they are supposed to behave while under hypnosis, is sufficient to produce the antisocial acts. Perhaps people can be induced to perform antisocial acts under deep hypnosis, but current studies do not offer reliable evidence to support this idea.

# APPLICATION

### Witness Reactivity

Research cited in this chapter indicates that some aspects of hypnotic behavior in the laboratory result from reactivity; that is, people under hypnosis may simply act as if they were hypnotized. When hypnosis is used for practical purposes, the resulting changes in behavior may also occur because of reactivity.

Suppose you are the victim of a mugging. You were roughed up by the perpetrator and were very distraught afterward. You were so upset that you had some difficulty remembering the particulars of the crime, and you were vague about the physical characteristics of the mugger. Police hypnotize you to refresh your memory and you report many details that you did not recall before. Furthermore, you are very confident that one of the members of a lineup is the mugger.

Did the hypnosis enhance your memory? There are several reasons why a positive answer may not be justifiable. First, we do not have a control condition for purposes of comparison. Was the independent variable hypnosis, or was it some other variable such as additional attempts at recall? Second, a review of the laboratory research concerned with hypnotic enhancement of memory indicates that hypnosis does not necessarily lead to better retention (Smith, 1983).

Another research report adds additional cautions to the use of hypnosis as a method of enhancing memory. Sanders and Simmons (1983) had people view a videotape of a person having his pocket picked. Later, the viewers attempted to pick the criminal out of a videotaped lineup and answer some questions about the crime. Half the viewers were tested under ordinary waking conditions, and the other half were hypnotized prior to testing.

Simmons and Sanders found that the hypnotized subjects were less accurate at identifying the pickpocket than were the controls, and the hypnotized subjects were less accurate in answering questions about the crime. The reason the hypnotized people exhibited inaccurate memory was that they were swayed by misleading aspects of the task. For example, in picking a person out of the lineup, they were very likely to choose someone who was wearing clothes similar to those of the criminal, even though the person did not look like the criminal. Furthermore, the hypnotized subjects were just as confident in the correctness of their identifications when they were wrong as when they were correct. Thus, it appears that hypnotized subjects are highly susceptible to misleading information, which could have serious consequences in a real crime.

Current court rulings are in line with the research evidence. In contrast to several years ago, now many states have very stringent guidelines for the use of hypnosis as a possible memory enhancer. Most states do not allow testimony based on hypnotic enhancement. Rather, those states rely on the Frye rule (*Frye* v. *United States,* 1923). This rule of law asserts that scientific procedures will be acceptable in court to the extent that they are generally accepted by the relevant scientific discipline. Attempting to enhance memory by means of hypnosis does not appear to be an acceptable scientific procedure.

*Frye* v. *United States,* 293 F. 1013 (D.C. Cir. 1923).
Sanders, G. S., & Simmons, W. L. (1983). Use of hypnosis to enhance eyewitness accuracy: Does it work? *Journal of Applied Psychology, 68,* 70–77.
Smith, M. C. (1983). Hypnotic memory enhancement: Does it work? *Psychological Bulletin, 94,* 387–407.

Weber and Cook (1972) described various social roles that could influence behavior in a laboratory setting. These roles are similar to the response styles we discussed. Subjects might adopt a **good-subject role** in accordance with the theory of demand characteristics put forth by Orne. A subject acting in a good-subject manner will do anything necessary to validate the experimental hypothesis. The **faithful-subject role** is one in which the participant attempts to be honest and faithful, even if he or she has some idea about the experimental hypothesis. The participant who exhibits a **negativistic-subject role** will attempt to sabotage or otherwise mess up the experiment (Masling, 1966, has called this the "screw you effect").

In an extensive review of the literature, Weber and Cook did not find much evidence that these roles played a significant part in the confounding of laboratory experiments. However, they did find some evidence for the importance of a fourth role—the **apprehensive-subject role** (also see Rosenberg, 1969). The apprehensive subject feels uncomfortable about being evaluated in an experiment, and because of this **evaluation apprehension** the participant tries to respond in a socially desirable way. Weber and Cook summarized a number of studies that point to evaluation apprehension as an important potential confounding in experiments. Unfortunately, predicting exactly what kinds of behaviors will be elicited by evaluation apprehension is very difficult. For example, Weber and Cook report that in conformity studies, subjects who have some idea about the purpose of the experiment tend to conform less than unaware subjects (because of apprehension, the aware subjects do not want to appear to be "sheep"). On the other hand, in learning studies in which better performance signifies a "better" subject, aware participants often perform better than unaware ones. Thus, it is hard to predict what changes in behavior may occur as a result of apprehension.

Countering the effects of reactivity in experimentation is often very difficult. Unobtrusive measures and observations may not work in a laboratory setting because most people know they are in an experiment. Consequently, many psychologists do their experiments in a natural setting. This **field research** is similar to naturalistic observation, except field experiments have a real or ex post facto independent variable. Going into the field, where people may be unaware that they are in an experiment, poses additional problems: Loss of control that is characteristic of laboratory experiments may exist, and unobtrusive measures may violate some of the ethical standards of research. Furthermore, as we will discuss in more detail later, field studies are not necessarily more externally valid than laboratory experiments. Dipboye and Flanagan (1979) found that field studies in industrial and organizational psychology generally involve a narrow range of subjects, settings, and dependent variables.

One way to insert unobtrusive measures into laboratory experiments is to use **deception.** Deception can push reactivity in a particular direction so that the subject will respond naturally to the true independent variable. In a famous example of deception by Milgram (1963), participants were led to believe that they were giving shocks to a "learner" in order to improve the rate of learning. In fact, the shock apparatus was fake and the learner just pretended to receive severe shocks. From the point of view of the participants, they willingly caused pain and suffering to another person. Many people regard this sort of deception as unethical (see chapter 12).

Another way a researcher can try to control reactivity is to omit information about the experiment. For example, let us say that half of the participants in a memory experiment receive special instructions on how to learn and remember. The other half of the participants do not receive these instructions; this group serves as a baseline for "natural memorizing." The experimenter might not tell the participants in the control condition that other participants were treated differently. Despite its usefulness, omitting information about the experiment can present ethical problems, particularly when the information is relevant to an individual's decision about whether to participate in the experiment. For instance, participants in a study on anxiety may not be told that the experimental procedure is likely to make them feel uneasy and nervous. Alerting them of possible reactions might induce those very reactions; however, withholding this information is deceptive. Deception by omission may be warranted in some circumstances; however, when it is used, we must be careful to maintain the dignity of the person being studied.

When we withhold some pertinent information from the participant, we say we are running a **blind experiment.** A good example is a study by Carver, Coleman, and Glass (1976), who examined the suppression of fatigue by Type A and Type B men. Type A's are aggressive people who really strive to win in competitive situations, and they are supposed to be prone to coronary heart disease (Wright, 1988). Type B's are less aggressive and competitive, and they are less likely to have heart problems. Types A's and B's were put on an exercise treadmill to see how long they would exercise relative to their maximum capacity. Carver and associates also got subjective estimates of fatigue from the participants. During the course of the experiment, the researchers made every attempt to remove any hint of competition—both against the clock and against other people's performance on the treadmill. In fact, the subjects were told they would be removed from the treadmill after a predetermined time. In actuality, the time on the treadmill was determined by the participant, who indicated when he had had enough. Confronting the Type A's with evidence of competition might have enhanced their competitive drive, and the experimenters wanted the A's to become fatigued in the absence of any apparent competition. So, making the subject blind to the nature of the experiment seemed important. In this instance, the deception does not seem unethical. Carver and coworkers found that the Type A's worked longer on the treadmill than B's. Despite the extra effort, the A's reported less fatigue than the B's.

Another way to control reactivity is to conduct a **simulated experiment,** as Orne and Evans (1965) did in their hypnosis study. As mentioned earlier, they used people who simulated being hypnotized as well as people who were hypnotized. The logic here is straightforward. The demands of the situation are assumed to be the same for participants in both the experimental condition and the simulating control condition. If the experimental manipulation (hypnosis) is truly effective, then the behavior of the experimental group should differ reliably from that of the simulating group. Another approach to simulating an experiment is to tell simulating participants what the independent variable is and ask them what they would do in the experimental situation (Richman, Mitchell, and Reznick, 1979). If the results of the simulated experiment are highly similar to the results owing to the independent variable in the actual experiment, we can conclude that there are likely to be important reactivity factors contaminating the effects of the independent variable.

## CONCEPT SUMMARY

### SUBJECT REACTIVITY: PITFALLS AND THEIR SOLUTIONS

| Research Procedure | Pitfall | Possible Solution |
|---|---|---|
| Observation | Reactivity | Unobtrusive measures and observations |
| Case study | Motivated forgetting | Corroborating evidence |
| Surveys, tests, and correlation | Response styles | Forced-choice responding |
| | Volunteer problem | Random sample, extra incentives, replications |
| Experimentation | Reactivity (Hawthorne effect) | Deception ("blind") |
| | | Simulated experiments |

## RESEARCHER BIAS

While you are carefully watching your subjects to make sure there are no disruptive reactivity effects in your project, you should be spying on someone else—yourself. Barber (1976) makes a distinction between the investigator, the person responsible for designing, analyzing, and interpreting research, and the experimenter, the person actually conducting the study. He has presented an extensive and valuable discussion of ten investigator and experimenter effects. You are likely to be both investigator and experimenter in your research, so we combine our discussion of these problems under one heading—**researcher bias.**

The researcher, just like the subject, is fallible. Thus, we need to know where and when the researcher can have detrimental effects on the outcome of an experiment. Pitfalls associated with the researcher can occur either deliberately or inadvertently. We hope that there are few deliberate effects, because they can be very costly.

### Deliberate Researcher Bias

When scientists engage in research, they expend substantial time and effort, and their prestige and career advancement often depend on the success of their research. Under these pressures, some scientists are not completely honest in their treatment of their experiments and their data. Instances of deliberate falsification can range from "fudging" or "cooking" data—results are manipulated so as to make them look better—to "forging" data—observations are reported that were never in fact made (Kohn, 1986).

A frequently cited example of fudging is the case of Sir Cyril Burt. He was a well-respected psychologist who studied the role of heredity in intelligence. He published several papers reporting data collected on identical twins, some reared together, others reared apart. The data were collected in the period 1913–1932. In three papers, he reported a correlation in IQ scores of .944 for twins reared together and of .771 for twins reared apart. Although the correlations were identical for the three papers, each reported an appreciably different number of subjects. That the correlations would remain unchanged despite the addition of new subjects is extremely improbable. This evidence, along with a number of other suspicious facts, has led some scientists and historians to conclude that Burt's data were not completely honest (Kohn, 1986; Broad and Wade, 1982).

There are a number of examples of forging data. A famous case is that of the "Piltdown Man" discovered in England in 1912. The Piltdown Man consisted of a skull of humanoid appearance and an apelike jawbone; it was proclaimed as the "missing link" between apes and humans. The finding was widely, although not universally, accepted for fifty-seven years until suspicious scientists used a variety of dating methods to show that the jaw was of modern origin whereas the skull was substantially older. The jaw was actually shown to be identical to that of an orangutan. Piltdown Man was a hoax, and although there are a number of theories as to who perpetrated the hoax, the evidence is inconclusive.

Deliberate researcher bias can be more subtle than forging or even fudging data. A researcher can choose not to report results that are incompatible with a personal theory or even with his or her political or social beliefs. Similarly, a biased scientist may design projects such that negative or ideologically bad results are unlikely.

How do we detect deliberate researcher bias? Science is self-correcting; the truth will win out. When an important finding is published, the scientific community takes it seriously and pursues the implications of the reported data. When other scientists try to repeat the fraudulent experiment, they will fail to get the reported results, and such failures will eventually lead scientists to conclude that the findings were not real. Thus, the repetition of experiments is important to detecting scientific fraud (Barber, 1976). It may take many failed repetitions and years of effort, however, before the entire scientific community agrees that the fraudulent results should be discarded, a fact that illustrates the serious consequences of scientific fraud.

## Inadvertent Researcher Bias

Inadvertent effects are probably more widespread and harder to detect than deliberate researcher bias. Just how often they occur is difficult to determine because many parts of the research process may be inadvertently contaminated. A scientist's political beliefs, for example, could result in an incomplete survey that assesses some attitudes and not others. This does not necessarily indicate deliberate bias, but may merely represent the fallibility of the scientist. The scientist can think about only a limited number of things at a time, so the research designs will partially reflect his or her own preferences. A famous example of faulty research design is the case of Samuel G. Morton, a well-known physician and scientist in the early and middle 1800s. He collected over one thousand human skulls of people belonging to different races. He believed that skull volume was indicative of intelligence; hence, he used his collection of skulls to examine intelligence differences among races, reporting that Caucasians were the most intelligent, blacks were least intelligent, and Native Americans were in between, a conclusion in perfect agreement with the prejudices of the time. It was not until 1978 that Stephen Jay Gould, a Harvard paleontologist, concluded, from the very data reported by Morton, that there were no differences at all among races. Gould showed that Morton had chosen his skulls in line with his expectations: For one group of blacks, he used an all-female sample whereas for the comparison group of whites he used an all-male sample, ignoring the fact that male skulls tend to be larger than female skulls (Broad and Wade, 1982). One aspect of the Morton affair that should be kept in mind is that the scientific community of that time accepted his research as scientifically valid; only under the scrutiny of contemporary scientists with different social beliefs was the biased design exposed. Thus, the questions asked by a researcher and the methods he or she uses to answer those questions may be the result of the researcher's preconceptions about the problem. There are two solutions to this dilemma: (1) Researchers should be aware of their own underlying preconceptions (these preexisting notions are what philosophers of science call "paradigms"; Kuhn, 1962); and (2) many scientists should undertake a variety of attacks on a problem.

Another source of researcher bias derives from treating participants in a project differently over and above any *planned* differences in treatment. A substantial amount of evidence indicates that how the researcher treats the subjects can have a profound effect on the results of the experiment (Barber, 1976). What measures can be taken to prevent a researcher from inadvertently influencing the outcome? Suppose you were the researcher in the study by Carver, Coleman, and Glass (1976) about fatigue suppression in Type A's and Type B's. You know ahead of time that half your subjects (the A's) might be prone to coronary heart disease. You record the exercise time on the treadmill as the subjects are working at or beyond their maximum oxygen consumption.

Would you treat Type A's and Type B's differently? Would subtle body movements or the tone of your voice clue the Type A's to take it easy so they do not overstress their hearts? (This is unlikely, because the Type A's were young—they supposedly had the *potential* for coronary problems later in life.)

There are two ways to minimize this type of researcher bias. In the first place, the researcher must conduct the project as uniformly as possible for all participants (see chapter 3). The only differences in treatment should be those that are introduced deliberately—independent variables, different questions in a survey, different observing times, and so on. Type A's must be treated exactly like Type B's. This was done by Carver and coworkers, who even went so far as to eliminate the data on a subject who was acquainted with one of the data collectors.

A second way to minimize inadvertent differential treatment is to make the researcher *blind* with respect to potentially important attributes of the participants or the task. The experimenters in the study by Carver and associates did not know whether a subject was a Type A or a Type B, which diminished the chances of treating the Type A's differently on the treadmill. When subjects' behaviors are recorded in some way for later analysis, the people who score the recorded behavior often are blind to the treatment administered to a particular subject. In this instance, being blind to the treatment condition increases the likelihood that the scorer of the results will be objective and not be biased by his or her expectations of what the results should be. The tactic of making the researcher blind is the other side of the coin of making the subjects blind to aspects of the task. If both the subject and the researcher are blind, we have what is called a **double-blind design.**

Double-blind designs are common in medical experiments that test the effectiveness of drugs. The experimental group is given the drug, and the control group is given a placebo substance. A **placebo** (the word is derived from a Latin word meaning "I shall please") is a pharmacologically inert substance (a "sugar pill") given to control subjects to deceive them. The controls, along with the experimental group, assume they are receiving a real drug, so the expectations are the same for the two groups. Not only are the placebo subjects blind, but so is the researcher. The researcher does not know who is receiving the placebo and who is getting the real drug. In the typical drug experiment, the substances have code numbers that cannot be deciphered by the person administering the drugs. However, someone knows who received the placebo and who received the drug. These precautions decrease the possibility of the control subjects being treated differently than the experimental subjects (apart from the drug, of course).

The personal attributes of a researcher may bias the actions of the participants. The age, sex, race, and authority of the researcher may determine how the subjects react. For example, a subject in an interview is more likely to report sexual thoughts when the interviewer is of the same sex (Walters, Shurley, and Parsons, 1962). This kind of problem is solved if there is more than one researcher and each one follows the research protocol exactly. In your own research, you may not be able to enlist assistance from others. Therefore, you should try to treat each subject identically.

Strict adherence to procedure is important to minimize inadvertent researcher bias. This advice is particularly true when considering how data is recorded. Barber (1976) discusses several studies which show that data recording errors do occur and tend to bias the results in the direction desired by the experimenter. Hence, in every condition for every subject, we must record data in the same way. This means that before the project is begun, we must define exactly what constitutes an acceptable datum.

Another potential researcher bias occurs in research with animals. When working with animals, a researcher must guard against **anthropomorphizing** (see chapter 3). This refers to the tendency to attribute human characteristics, especially thoughts and feelings, to animals. Anthropomorphism is sometimes obvious, as in "The dog loved and respected its master," and sometimes not so obvious, as in "The rat was hungry so it ate a lot." A similar problem arises in describing the thoughts and feelings of people belonging to technologically primitive cultures. An observer might attribute standard Western thought to such groups, as in "Their love of individual liberty conflicted with the socialist ideology of the tribal council." All of these examples are actually theoretical statements that may not be warranted on the basis of the data. How do we define "love" in a dog? Does it mean the dog wagged its tail or came when it was called? What is hunger for a rat? These sorts of issues are examined in the next section.

## CONCEPT SUMMARY

CONTROLLING RESEARCHER EFFECTS

### *Deliberate Effects*

- *Objectivity*
- *Direct replications*

### *Inadvertent Effects*

- *Uniform treatment*
- *Double-blind design*

## RELIABILITY OF COMMUNICATION

We have discussed pitfalls in the research process resulting from participant bias and experimenter bias. Assuming that you have effectively dealt with problems in these areas, another pitfall awaits you in conveying the results of your research to other scientists.

No serious discussion, scientific or otherwise, can progress very far unless the participants agree to define the terms they are using. Imagine that you and your date are having a friendly argument about who is the best athlete of the year. How do you define athlete? You both would agree about such common sports as tennis, swimming, and gymnastics. But what about more esoteric sports such as frisbee throwing, hang gliding, and hopping cross-country on a pogo stick? Should practitioners of these activities be considered for your athlete-of-the-year award? Until this question of definition is answered, your discussion may just go around in circles.

Similar problems can arise in scientific discussions. Let us imagine that scientists in psychophysical laboratories in West Lafayette, Indiana, and Clayton Corners, Arkansas, are studying tail-flicking responses of the horseshoe crab to flashes of light. One laboratory finds that crabs give tremendous tail flicks, whereas the other lab finds that crabs hardly move their tails at all. The scientists are very concerned and they exchange terse letters and autographed pictures of their respective crabs. Eventually they discover the reason for the discrepancy. They were each defining the flash of light differently (their flashes were of different durations), even though the brightness of the two flashes was similar. When they adjusted their flashes to be the same, both labs obtained the same results. This example is a little farfetched since, as we all know, crabs cannot autograph their pictures. Furthermore, all good psychologists know the importance of defining the stimulus exactly, so this confusion would probably not have occurred in the first place. But this example does show what *could* happen if scientists were not very careful about defining their terms.

Although social conversation and scientific discourse both require definitions, the requirements for scientific definition are more stringent. Terms that are perfectly adequate for ordinary conversation are usually too vague for scientific purposes. When you state that someone has a pleasant personality, other people have a good idea of what you mean. But when a psychologist uses the term *personality* in a technical sense, a great deal of precision is necessary. This important distinction between technical usage and common usage occurs frequently in psychology. It is all too easy to slip and use technical language imprecisely, especially in psychology. Words such as *information, anxiety,* and *threshold* have broad everyday meanings, but they must be precisely limited when they are used in a technical sense. The most common way of providing such technical meaning is by using an **operational definition,** which we discussed in chapter 3.

An operational definition is a formula for building a construct in a way that other scientists can duplicate. "Take the eye of a newt, the leg of a frog, three oyster shells, and shake twice" is an operational definition, although we may not know what is being defined. This recipe can be duplicated and so meets the major criterion for an operational definition. You can tell from this example that an operational definition does not have to make any sense, as long as it is clear and can be copied. In general terms, something is operationally defined when the procedures or operations used to produce and measure it are clearly specified. For instance, we might operationally define a construct called *centigrams* as the product of your height in centimeters and your weight in grams. Any scientist can easily determine the centigram score, so this is an operational definition. Of course, it probably could not be used for any important scientific purpose, but the potential utility of an operational definition is a separate issue from its clarity.

The major virtue of operational definitions is that they help prevent us from confusing technical concepts with their equivalents in common language. Let us look at an experiment where participants were faced with two rows of ten lights and one row of ten buttons (Morin and Grant, 1954), as shown in figure 10–1. A stimulus lamp went on, and a correct button press would extinguish it and present the next stimulus lamp, and so forth. This task would be simple if each light were connected to the button directly underneath it. However, lights and buttons were haphazardly joined. This was why the top row of feedback lights was used. Pressing any button lit up a feedback light showing which stimulus light (that is, the one directly below the feedback light) was controlled by that button. After several days of practice, the experimenters tested participants to see whether they had learned the light-button relation-

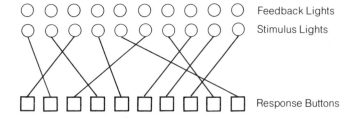

**FIGURE 10–1**

A schematic diagram of the apparatus used by Morin and Grant (1954). Stimulus lights and response buttons are not linked in any obvious relationship. For example, pressing the leftmost response button does not control the leftmost light, but instead turns off the third light from the left.

Feedback Lights

Stimulus Lights

Response Buttons

ships. All participants could correctly draw a diagram linking lights and buttons, so the experimenters disconnected the feedback lights. The time taken to press the buttons went up dramatically. A similar effect occurs when we learn to operate a typewriter. It does not take long to be able to diagram the relationship between keys and letters. But even though we know where each letter is on the keyboard, we need a fair amount of practice before we can type equally well with our eyes opened or closed. This seems like a contradiction. On the one hand, the ability to draw the diagram correctly is evidence that the light-button relationships were learned. On the other hand, the increase in time is evidence that the relationships were not learned.

This apparent contradiction stems from using the term *learning* in its common-language sense. Technically, learning can never be observed directly. Instead, it is inferred from a change in behavior—that is, we need to measure a behavior at least twice before we can state that learning occurred. In the light-button experiment, learning was measured in two ways. One measure of learning was the decrease in time needed to press the buttons with succeeding days of practice. This measure was taken when the feedback lights were connected. It is not very surprising that when conditions were changd by removing the feedback lights, the participants performed differently (needed more time). The other measure of learning—the ability to accurately draw a diagram—assumes that no one could have drawn the diagram before the experiment began, because participants would have had no experience with the arbitrary connections between lights and buttons. Thus, there was no need to measure drawing ability twice, and it was measured only after participants had been exposed to the experiment. Because the participants were able to draw an accurate diagram, learning could be inferred. Note that the operational definitions of learning are quite different. The first uses time as a measure, and the second uses ability to draw a diagram. These definitions differ, and we should not think it odd that the results of the two different measures of learning also differ. The confusion arises from the common-language habit of calling both of these measures indices of learning. They have separate operational definitions, so we could call them by different names, for example, learning (time) and learning (drawing). Thus, measurement of any process that must be inferred rather than directly observed should be tied to an operational definition.

The way in which terms are operationally defined is illustrated in table 10–2. In this example, the concept, learning, is defined by the operation used to produce it (practice on the button-pressing task) and the operations used to measure it (drawing a diagram versus time to perform the task). Because learning

| TABLE 10–2 | OPERATIONAL DEFINITIONS OF LEARNING IN THE MORIN AND GRANT EXPERIMENT | |
|---|---|---|
| **Operation Producing Concept** | **Concept Defined** | **Measurements** |
| Button-pressing practice | Learning | Time to perform |
| Button-pressing practice | Learning | Drawing accuracy |

Note: Practice, the antecedent condition, produces learning, which is reflected in the behaviors that were measured (the dependent variables). Because antecedent conditions are rarely manipuated directly in nonexperimental research (such as tests, surveys, and naturalistic observation), we usually have to guess at or infer the conditions that produced what we are studying.

was examined in an experimental situation, we can specify both the causes of learning (changes in the independent variable) and the results of those causes (changes in the dependent variables). If we simply measured or assessed learning by means of observation or test (or survey), we could define our concept only in terms of dependent variables. The additional operational specification that results from experimental manipulation indicates another advantage of experimentation over other forms of research. When independent variables are varied, both "sides" of a concept can be tied to the operations that are performed. When there are no independent variables, the operations that produced the concept under investigation may be indeterminate.

The problem with having a few dozen varieties of learning, each with its own operational definition, is that so many definitions can make it difficult for us to get any kind of theoretical integration. Considerable economy or parsimony exists when we have to discuss just one kind of learning. Psychology, like any science, strives for general concepts that unify data. Thus, undue preoccupation with operational definitions might seem to be pushing us in the wrong direction. In fact, some philosophers of science have suggested abandoning operational definitions entirely. Such a drastic solution seems too risky to us: It would lead to difficulties as in the earlier example of the light flashes and the horseshoe crabs. A better solution is to seek operational definitions that come to a focus on common theoretical constructs. This notion is referred to as converging operations. It is a concept of some importance and will be discussed at length in chapter 11.

When we link our operational terms, we make them valid. In other words, our concepts become useful, reasonable explanations, not just clear, reliable ones. In a very real sense, then, the goal of scientific psychology is to provide valid explanations for why we behave as we do.

## EXTERNAL VALIDITY OF THE RESEARCH PROCEDURE

Another area in which problems arise in the design of a research project concerns its relation to what is often termed the "real world." We might ask whether our research has anything to do with why people and animals think and act as they do. Have we selected an object of study that is representative? Is our research setting one that will yield a valid answer to our fundamental question? In sum, is our research externally valid?

We alluded to some of these issues in chapters 2 and 3. Several problems associated with external validity must be dealt with before a project is begun.

In this section, we will detail the problems of subject representativeness, variable representativeness, and setting representativeness. We will also present some ways in which these problems can be handled.

## Subject Representativeness

Basic research in psychology draws a large number of its participants from two populations: white rats and college students. Rats and other animals are often used because the scientist can control the heredity and environment of animals more easily (and more ethically) than that of humans. Also rats and college students are readily available to most researchers. The justifications for using rats and college students are control, convenience, and ethics. The question remains: Are these organisms representative? Are data from these organisms pertinent to general statements about psychological processes? In other words, is there **subject representativeness?**

Limiting your observations to these populations may present some problems. A major difficulty is **reversibility** (Uttal, 1978). In mathematics, reversibility refers to an attempt to determine the problem or equation from a solution. Consider the answer 7. Can we figure out what led to 7? Not without more information. The answer 7 could have come from *4 + 3 = ?, 377 − 370 = ?, $\sqrt{49}$ = ?, How many days are in a week?*, or any of an infinite number of other possibilities. The answer 7 is not reversible. Thus, given the answer 7 twice, there is no way to know whether the 7s arose from the same equation or different equations. Reversibility poses a similar problem in research. Just because a particular behavior is observed both in a rat and in a human, it does not follow that the underlying processes (the mathematical equation) are the same in both instances. For example, if we damaged a rat brain in order to understand how the human brain works, we have to assume that the brain processes in both species are the same (have the same equation). Physiological psychologists assume that the solution (the rat's behavior) is unique to a particular equation (the rat's brain) and that the equation is the same for rats and humans. Thus, by reversing the solution (damaging the rat's brain to eliminate a particular behavior), we arrive at the problem (what aspect of the brain controlled that behavior). In other words, damaging the rat's brain should lead us to understand how its brain controlled particular behaviors, and because we assume equivalence between the brain of a rat and the brain of a human, we further our understanding of human brain functioning.

The difficulty, of course, is the assumption of equivalence between rats and humans. The problem remains even if one ignores physiology and tries to generalize across species at the purely behavioral level. There is still the assumption of equivalence in whatever mechanism is hypothesized to account for the behavior. Harlow summarized the dilemma this way: "Basically the problems of generalization of behavior between species are simple—one cannot generalize, but one must. If the competent do not wish to generalize, the incompetent will fill the field" (Harlow, Gluck, and Suomi, 1972, p. 716).

Despite the difficulties it poses, generalizing across species can lead to spectacular successes. In the nineteenth century, Mendel, a Czechoslovakian monk, determined the basics of genetics by studying garden peas. More recently, the discovery of neurotransmitters in the brain that function like opiate drugs was based on work concerned with neural transmission in the reproductive organs of rats. If we view the results of animal research as a model or analogy, then we recognize that our cross-species generalizations are always tentative. We may have to perform many tests on many species before we can make strong conclusions.

The difficulties we have just examined also pertain to research that uses college students as subjects. How representative are the results obtained from such studies? The answer to this question is vague; it depends on the purposes of the research and the boldness of the investigator. If we are concerned with processes that are likely to be shared by all humans, such as basic sensory processes or simple forms of learning and retention, we can be fairly sure that our data on college students will be representative of human beings in general.

A difficulty arises, however, when we are interested in complex psychological processes. Language, problem solving, and sophisticated memorizing strategies require that the subject possess characteristics that may not be common to everyone. We cannot limit our psychology to normal human adults living in Western cultures. Young children, Ibos living in Africa, and individuals with hearing impairments are likely to possess abilities different from those of the typical college student. Imagery may enhance memory in college students (Atkinson, 1975; Bower, 1972), but its success for young children has limits (Tversky and Teiffer, 1976), and cross-cultural differences in the use of imagery exist as well (Cole, Gay, Glick, and Sharp, 1971).

Because of the limits in generalizability from easily available populations, it is sometimes necessary to seek out participants from special populations. For instance, if we are interested in whether the incidence of depression found in young people is the same for elderly people, we must find a population of elderly individuals willing to participate in our study. Despite the convenience of the white rat and the college student, these populations alone cannot meet all research needs.

The moral here is that we should be careful in generalizing on the basis of a single sample of participants from a subset of the population at large. If we are too bold ("Imagery always aids memory, no matter who uses it."), we run the risk of being wrong. Again, if we view the college student as a model for psychological processes in the same way that we view the white rat as a model, we will recognize that some of our conclusions must be tentative. This is particularly true when basic research findings are used for applied purposes. The generalization should be tried out on the target population before a particular policy or practice is implemented. Time and effort would be wasted if, on the basis of Bower's (1972) work with college students, imagery training were instituted in a nursery school.

## Variable Representativeness

We want our results to generalize across different subject populations. In the same way, we want our results to have **variable representativeness**—the ability to generalize across different experimental manipulations. For example, if a researcher were interested in whether background noise hurts reading comprehension, he or she might compare music to silence. If it were shown that noise and music both hurt comprehension relative to silence, the researcher would have an interesting finding; however, it would be premature to assume that the results would generalize for any kind of background noise. The results may have been unique to the kind of music chosen or to the particular volume at which the music was played. Likewise, the results may have been different if random environmental noises had been used instead of music. Further experimentation would be necessary to determine the generality of the effect of background noise. By using a wide range of independent variables to address a particular question, we can also get a better idea of how the variables we have chosen relate to the situation in the real world which we are trying to address.

## Setting Representativeness

Perhaps the major issue associated with representativeness has to do with the setting. **Setting representativeness,** often called **ecological validity,** can be a serious problem in experimentation, where, by definition and through the imposition of control, the experimental setting is an artificial one. Neisser (1976, 1978, 1982), for example, questions the ecological validity of laboratory experiments, particularly those involving cognition and memory. He argues that psychologists have avoided studying natural memory in natural settings, which means that "the orthodox psychology of memory has very little to show for a hundred years of effort, perhaps because it has always avoided the interesting issues" (1982, p. 3). Neisser is correct in his concern for ecological validity, but, as we shall see, he is incorrect in his indictment.

When considering the problem of ecological validity, we need to distinguish between **realism** and **generalizability** (Berkowitz and Donnerstein, 1982). Realism refers to whether the experimental setting bears a resemblance to the real world. Do the experiments involving rats learning in Skinner boxes resemble any learning situation in the real world? The answer, of course, probably not. However, the critical question has to do with the importance of this mundane realism. As was true of the problem of subject representativeness, our concern with ecological validity should be with its relation to psychological processes. If we can demonstrate that the processes exhibited by rats in artificial settings are similar to the processes occurring in the real world, then we can say that realism is not a crucial threat to external validity. Thus it follows that the ability of an experimental result to generalize to other situations is more important than its superficial resemblance to the real world. Various tests try to determine whether the processes observed in the laboratory are also the processes involved in settings representative to the real world. In the next chapter, we will consider some other aspects of generalization, but for now we will examine some direct tests of generalizability.

The strategy used to test the generalizability of experimental results is to repeat the observations in a natural setting—a field study. Obviously, studying memory in a classroom or decision making in a courtroom is less controlled than the corresponding laboratory study. This is why laboratory experiments are conducted—to provide an internally valid causal statement about a psychological process. If we are going to try to generalize our results beyond the laboratory, we may need to conduct a less well controlled field experiment.

Before considering such tests of generalization, we should note that field studies do not necessarily permit broad generalization. As pointed out earlier, Dipboye and Flanagan (1979) found that a narrow range of subjects, settings, and variables had been used in field studies done in industrial and organizational psychology. The tests should be varied and not just "natural."

Many applied psychologists have questioned the external validity of laboratory studies on decision making. A substantial amount of laboratory work has examined how people integrate many sources of information to arrive at a decision, and there are many sophisticated mathematical theories describing information integration (Anderson, 1981). Levin, Louviere, and Schepanski (1983) conducted a number of direct tests of the external validity of results from laboratory studies involving decision making, and they found excellent correspondence between the laboratory and the real world. They discovered that the choice of transportation to get to work, as well as choice of shopping location, are almost perfectly predicted by models derived from laboratory studies of decision making. They also report that several other behaviors in the real world coincide with results from strictly controlled experiments. These behaviors include gambling decisions, jury decisions, and occupational choices. Thus, laboratory studies of decision making may be contrived and artificial, but they also predict behavior in the real world.

What about Neisser's (1978) criticism of laboratory work in memory? Encouraged by Neisser's critique of memory, some memory researchers have abandoned their laboratories and have begun to conduct their research in real-world settings. Their experiments often lack the strict experimental control of laboratory research, but adherents to what is called the "Everyday Memory movement" argue that what they lack in control is more than made up by increased ecological validity. Banaji and Crowder (1989) responded strongly to Neisser's criticisms (and to the Everyday Memory movement in general), arguing that he ignored the distinction between realism and generalizability. Hence, Banaji and Crowder point out that results derived from laboratory experiments may or may not generalize to a variety of situations, but they also point out that results derived from everyday memory experiments, despite their surface realism, still may or may not generalize to other situations. Because surface realism does not guarantee an increase in generalizability, Banaji and Crowder question whether the loss of experimental control is worth the increased (surface) realism of the everyday memory experiments.

Banaji and Crowder's (1989) article has stirred up considerable controversy among memory researchers. In fact, a recent issue of *American Psychologist* (January 1991, Volume 46) includes nine articles (pp. 16–49) discussing the various aspects of this debate. In contrast to the stereotype of the cold, objective scientist, some of the authors exhibit a great deal of emotion in addressing this topic. We recommend that you read some of these articles. Although the debate is specifically addressed to the study of human memory, the issues raised regarding ecological validity are quite general, and the same arguments would apply to almost any area of psychology.

In summary, surface realism in an experimental setting does not guarantee ecological validity. In fact, an experiment can be ecologically valid with little or no surface realism. Nevertheless, some researchers argue that experiments with surface realism are more likely to lead to results with high generalizability, but this argument remains controversial. In any case, it is generalizability rather than surface realism that determines whether an experimental procedure is ecologically valid.

## CONCEPT SUMMARY

Your choice of
- **subjects**
- **variables**
- **setting**

may all distort the underlying psychological processes.

Generalization can be enhanced by using
- **different subjects**
- **different variables**
- **different settings**

## SUMMARY

1. Because research is a social endeavor, how your participants react to you and the setting can influence the outcome of your research.

2. In descriptive research, motivated forgetting may distort the results.

3. The particular response style exhibited by a participant (response acquiescence, response deviation, and social desirability) can contaminate the results of tests, surveys, and interviews. A forced-choice test can minimize the effects of these response styles.

4. Volunteer subjects differ in their characteristics from the population in general. Thus, a project may have invalid results if these characteristics are likely to mask the effects of an independent variable or alter performance on a test.

5. The demands of an experiment may lead a subject to adopt a particular role: the faithful-subject role, the good-subject role, the negativistic-subject role, or the apprehensive-subject role.

6. Evaluation apprehension is likely to be common in experiments, leading subjects to perform in ways that will make them look good to the experimenter.

7. Reactivity in experiments may be countered by deception, which means that the participants are misled as to certain aspects of the experiment. Simulated experiments also may be useful.

8. Deliberate researcher bias, such as faking data, is controlled by replicating the work of others and by the self-correcting nature of science.

9. Inadvertent researcher bias is controlled by strict adherence to research procedures for all subjects and by double-blind experiments.

10. Operational definitions of concepts, in which the operations needed to produce and measure a concept are clearly specified, are essential for reliable scientific communication.

11. Invalid conclusions may be drawn from research if the subjects, variables, or settings distort the underlying psychological processes in question.

12. Because experiments are well controlled, and therefore artificial, the ecological validity of experiments is often called into question. The crucial problem is not realism, but whether the experimental results generalize to other settings, which they often do.

13. Many field studies (experiments done in natural settings) show that the results of laboratory studies do generalize to the real world.

## Key Concepts

| | |
|---|---|
| anthropomorphizing | random sample |
| apprehensive-subject role | reactivity |
| blind experiment | realism |
| deception | researcher bias |
| demand characteristics | response acquiescence |
| double-blind design | response deviation |
| ecological validity | response styles or sets |
| evaluation apprehension | retrospective |
| faithful-subject role | reversibility |
| field research | setting representativeness |
| forced-choice tests | simulated experiment |
| generalizability | social desirability |
| good-subject role | subject representativeness |
| Hawthorne effect | subject roles |
| motivated forgetting | unobtrusive measures |
| negativistic-subject role | unobtrusive observations |
| operational definition | variable representativeness |
| participant observation | volunteer problem |
| placebo | |

## Exercises

1. [*Special Exercise.*] Design problem. Two men, about to be promoted to assembly-line foremen, were sent by their company to the California Redlands Area School for Supervisors (CRASS) to learn how to be good supervisors. Because the classes at CRASS were oversubscribed, one of the men took a course in Behavioral Administration Development (BAD), and the other took a course in Workers Organizational Reeducation Studies and Training (WORST). On returning to their home office, the men were put in charge of two different shifts of the same assembly line. After two months, the productivity of each shift was determined, and the job satisfaction of

the male and female workers was assessed. Productivity under the BAD foreman was about the same as that under the WORST foreman. Furthermore, job satisfaction was only slightly better on the WORST shift than on the BAD shift. The company president decided that the similarity in performance by the BAD and WORST shifts indicated that the CRASS programs were a waste of time and that in the future no new foremen would be sent there. Why might the conclusion of the president be wrong? What pitfalls exist in this training program?

2. Which of the following words does not belong with the others? *Hunger, anxiety, learning, response, motivation.* Why?

3. You want to do a laboratory experiment on the effects of various mnemonic devices on the learning and retention of textbook material. How would you determine the ecological validity of your task?

4. Specify how the volunteer problem could confound the results of an experiment.

5. Discuss the issue of subject representativeness. How is subject representativeness a threat to the external validity of an experiment?

## Suggested Readings

Robert Rosenthal has written extensively on subject and experimenter reactivity in research. Although some of his research concerning inadvertent experimenter effects may be overstated (see Barber, 1976), all of his works are valuable.

You will find T. X. Barber's little book, *Pitfalls in human research: Ten pivotal points,* (1976), New York: Pergamon, to be an excellent source of information about investigator and experimenter bias. Barber also details many solutions to these problems.

Parsons has suggested that most of the Hawthorne effect can be attributed to operant conditioning (that is, the rewards and feedback provided the assembly-line workers). You might find the article interesting: Parsons, H. M. (1974). What happened at Hawthorne? *Science, 183:* 922–931.

# PSYCHOLOGY IN ACTION
**The Power of Being in an Experiment**

As we discussed earlier, people often do things when they are in an experiment that they would not do under other circumstances. You can demonstrate this by performing a simple experiment with your friends. Find ten friends and randomly assign each to either the experimental or the control condition so that there are five people in each group. The independent variable for the two groups is the statement you make at the beginning of the experiment. Say to the experimental subjects: "I would like you to do some things for me as part of a psychology experiment for one of my courses." Say to the control group, "I would like you to do me a favor." Then tell each friend that you have a request; you would like him or her to do five jumping jacks, six sit-ups, four push-ups, and to make a paper airplane as fast as possible. You should have a watch available to time each person. In addition, you should try to elicit comments from the subjects regarding what they thought of the task.

Of course, the small number of subjects in the experiment makes it difficult for you to draw any strong conclusions (you might want to combine your data with that of other classmates). In any event, you will probably make one interesting discovery—the friends you asked to help you with a psychology experiment were probably much more cooperative. They probably did more of the activities, did them faster, and asked fewer questions. People in the control group probably thought you had been studying too hard.

This demonstration shows that psychology experiments do not just provide neutral surveys of behavior; they also can create or alter the behaviors that are studied. When people know they are being observed in an experiment, they may react differently. An even more powerful way of showing this would be to repeat the experiment with strangers, rather than friends, as your subjects. The reactions of the people in the control group are likely to be very interesting. To anticipate the kinds of behaviors you might witness, imagine that a stranger came up to you and said, "Do me a favor—do five jumping jacks, six sit-ups, . . ." What behavior would that experiment produce in you?

| **INTERPRETING THE RESULTS OF RESEARCH**<br>How to assess whether the research is both reliable and valid | **Questions to Answer**<br><br>*Is there a scale-attenuation problem?* Are there ceiling or floor effects?<br><br>*Is a regression artifact present?* Do the data provide a "true" measure of the behavior?<br><br>*Are the experimental results reliable?* Has the experiment been replicated directly? Have conceptual or systematic replications been undertaken?<br><br>*Have the results and concepts been validated by converging operations?* Do the results of several converging observations eliminate alternative explanations of the results? |

# INTERPRETING THE RESULTS OF RESEARCH

After you have collected and analyzed your data, you are in a position to interpret them. This chapter will help you understand some of the pitfalls that impede correct interpretation of your data. We will consider problems associated with the interpretation of both specific results and results from a connected series of studies. Your data, even if collected and statistically analyzed correctly, may be difficult to interpret if performance is extremely good or extremely bad (the scale-attenuation problem). Often, your subject's true score or performance differs from the data you have collected, which means that a regression artifact has occurred. Have you obtained reliable results—would you find the same effect if the research were replicated? Are your data valid—do several results converge on an understanding of a concept? Solutions to these problems are suggested.

## INTERPRETING SPECIFIC RESULTS

### *The Problem of Scale Attenuation*

The first topic we consider here is important but is often overlooked in psychological research. The general problem is how to interpret performance on some dependent variable in an experiment when performance exceeds the limitations of the measurement scale. When performance is at the upper limit of the scale, we say we have a **ceiling effect.** An example of a ceiling effect might be a math test which is so easy that nearly everyone in the class gets all of the problems correct. When performance is at the bottom of the scale, we say we have a **floor effect.** An example of a floor effect might be another math test which is so difficult that no one in the class gets any of the problems correct. Collectively, ceiling and floor effects are known as **scale-attenuation effects.**

To best illustrate scale-attenuation effects, we will use an example of a physical rather than a psychological scale. The advantage of a physical scale is that its accuracy can be objectively determined. We will therefore look at how ceiling effects can make the measurement of a physical characteristic, namely weight, problematic. We will then show how scale attenuation can hinder the interpretation of psychological measures.

Suppose two obese men decided to make a bet as to who can lose the greatest amount of weight in a certain amount of time. One man looked much heavier than the other, but neither was sure what he actually weighed, because they both made a point of avoiding scales. The scale they decided to use for the bet was a common bathroom scale that runs from 0 to 300 pounds. On the day they were to begin their weight-loss programs, each man weighed himself while the other watched and, to their great surprise, both men weighed in at exactly the same value, 300 pounds. So despite their different sizes, the men decided that they were beginning their bet at equal weights.

The problem here is one of ceiling effects in the scale of measurement. The weight range of the bathroom scale did not go high enough to record the actual weight of these men. Suppose that one really weighed 300 and the other 350, if their weights had been measured on a scale that had a greater range. After six months on the weight-loss program, let us further suppose, each man actually lost 100 pounds. They reweighed themselves at this point and discovered that one now weighed 200 pounds and the other 250. Because they thought they had both started at the same weight (300), they reached the erroneous conclusion that the person who presently weighed 200 had won the bet (see figure 11–1).

Unfortunately, scale-attenuation effects in research may not be as obvious as the ceiling effect in our contrived example. However, scale attenuation can lead to highly erroneous conclusions, so it is important that you know what to look for in your own research and in the work of others. You should not only

**FIGURE 11–1**

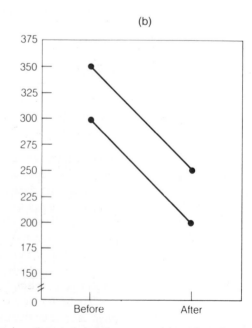

The left panel (a) illustrates the situation as the obese men believed it to be—they started at the same weight and one lost twice as much as the other. The right panel (b) reveals the actual case, with the ceiling effect in the scale of measurement removed. In fact, both men lost 100 pounds. Scale attenuation (ceiling and floor effects) can hide actual differences that may exist between conditions in an experiment.

be wary of the scale used to measure behavior, but also consider the task imposed on the subjects participating in the project. For example, suppose you devised a memory experiment that involved recalling phone numbers. The people in your experiment had to study a typical seven-digit phone number for one minute and then had to dial that number on a telephone. You would probably discover that all of your subjects did fine; in fact, they all remembered the numbers perfectly. What does that tell you? If a task is too easy (or too difficult), differences in behavior will not appear. Whenever you examine research results, you should ask yourself: Are the limits on performance I observe legitimate ones, or are they imposed by the measurement scale or the task used to assess behavior?

**The eyes have it: Scarborough's experiment.** Let us consider the results of an experiment that contains a scale-attenuation problem. Scarborough (1972) was interested in the question of modality differences in retention. Do we remember information better if it comes through our eyes or through our ears? Is information better remembered if it is presented to both the ears and the eyes simultaneously than it if is presented to only one or the other? These questions have both theoretical and practical importance. When you look up a phone number and need to remember it while you cross the room to the telephone, is it sufficient to simply read the number silently to yourself as you usually do, or would it be better for you to also read the number aloud so that information enters both your ears and your eyes?

In Scarborough's experiment, all subjects received thirty-six consonant trigrams (for example, *JBT*) presented for .7 second. There were three groups of six subjects; the method by which the trigrams were presented differed for each group. One group saw the trigrams (visual-only condition); another group heard the trigrams (auditory only); and a third group both saw and heard the trigrams (visual plus auditory). Three between-subjects conditions (visual only, auditory only, visual plus auditory) were combined with six within-subjects conditions (retention intervals of 0, 3, 6, 9, 12, or 18 seconds) in the experiment. The retention interval is the delay between trigram presentation and attempted recall.

The results of Scarborough's experiment are reproduced in figure 11–2, where the percentage of times a trigram was correctly reported is plotted as a function of retention interval. It is apparent from this figure (and Scarborough's statistics offer support) that subjects who received only visual presentation of the trigrams generally recalled them a greater percentage of the time than subjects who received only auditory presentation. Furthermore, receiving the information in both modalities simultaneously did not produce any better recall than receiving the information only visually; the percentage correct at each retention interval is roughly the same for visual-only and visual-plus-auditory subjects. So far so good. But what else can we conclude from figure 11–2? Can we conclude anything about the rates of forgetting information that is presented auditorily and visually? Is the rate of forgetting the same or different in the two cases? Did you ask yourself about the source of limitation on performance?

Scarborough was quite careful on this score. Although the auditory-only and visual-only functions appear to diverge increasingly as the retention interval becomes longer, Scarborough did not draw the conclusion that the rate of

FIGURE 11–2

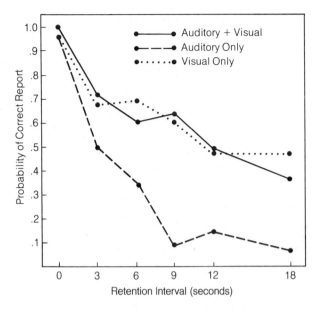

The probability of correctly recalling a stimulus trigram as a function of the three presentation conditions and the duration of the counting task. Notice that (a) visual presentation is generally superior to auditory presentation, and (b) simultaneous auditory and visual presentation is no better than visual-only presentation. (Scarborough, 1972. Copyright 1972 by the American Psychological Association. Reprinted by permission of the author.)

forgetting is greater for information presented through the ears than through the eyes. However, consider what Massaro (1975) has to say about this experiment:

> The figure shows that the curves intercept the $Y$ ordinate at roughly the same point and diverge significantly. The intercept value at zero sec. provides a measure of the original perception and storage of the stimuli, since it measures how much information the subject has immediately after the presentation of the stimuli, when no forgetting has taken place. The rate of forgetting can be determined from the slopes of the forgetting functions. According to this analysis, Figure [11–2] shows that the items presented auditorily are forgotten much faster than the items presented visually. (pp. 530–531)

Unfortunately, this conclusion must be called into question. We have the same problem the obese men had: Our scale at the ceiling is not sensitive enough. Performance at the zero-second retention interval is very nearly perfect in all conditions. When performance is perfect, it is impossible to tell whether there are any real differences among conditions because of scale attenuation, in this case a ceiling effect. If the scale of the dependent measure were really long enough, it might show differences between auditory and visual presentation even at the zero-second retention interval. So Massaro's conclusion that the rate of forgetting is greater for auditory than for visual presentation cannot be accepted on the basis of the argument we just quoted, because the assumption of equivalent performance at the zero-second retention interval may not be correct. There is no better way for us to know the rate of forgetting in the two conditions than there is for the obese men to know the rate of weight loss in judging who won their bet. In neither case can we assume equivalent initial scores before the measurement of loss begins.

**Possible solution.** How can we avoid misinterpretation after the data are collected? (We might have considered using an additional dependent variable, such as time to respond, but the experiment had been completed. Response, or more commonly, reaction time, might have spread out the scale by showing faster times for better-learned trigrams.)

One way to avoid this problem in Scarborough's experiment is to ignore the data points at the zero-second retention interval and ask whether the rate of forgetting is greater between three and eighteen seconds for auditory than for visual presentation. We can do this by computing an interaction between presentation and retention interval over the range of three to eighteen seconds. However, by simply inspecting figure 11–2, we get some idea as to whether the auditory-only and visual-only points are diverging increasingly. We see that they are diverging increasingly between three and nine seconds, but after that the difference between them remains constant. However, this lack of an increasingly larger difference over the last three points may be caused by a floor effect in the auditory-only condition because performance is so poor, especially on the last point (only 7 or 8 percent correct). We must be very careful in interpreting data when ceiling or floor effects exist. A prudent investigator would hesitate to draw any conclusion from the data in figure 11–2 about rates of forgetting, which is just what Scarborough did. But we should also note that over the retention intervals where there are neither ceiling nor floor effects (3, 6, and 9 seconds), forgetting seems to be greater with auditory than with visual presentation.

Unfortunately, there are no hard-and-fast rules for avoiding scale-attenuation problems. Researchers usually try to design their experiments to avoid extremes in performance, and they often test small groups of pilot subjects (see chapter 1 for a discussion of pilot work). If these subjects perform near the ceiling or floor of the scale, then revision of the experimental task often will be necessary. For example, if performance in a memory experiment is too good (remember the hypothetical telephone-number experiment described at the beginning of the chapter), the amount of material being given can be increased so as to lower performance. Similarly, if the task is so hard that people barely remember anything, the task can be made easier by reducing the amount of material, presenting it more slowly, and so on. The careful investigator will usually make the effort to test pilot subjects before launching into an experiment that may turn out later to have been flawed by ceiling or floor effects. As noted in chapter 1, the testing of pilot subjects also permits the researcher to learn about other problems in the design or procedure of the experiment.

## CONCEPT SUMMARY

BEWARE OF CEILING AND FLOOR EFFECTS
Conduct pilot work to determine scale sensitivity and task difficulty.

## Regression Artifacts

A serious problem in many areas of research is known as statistical **regression to the mean,** or the **regression artifact.** The word *artifact* in this context refers to an unwanted effect that occurs during an investigation (thus, it is a synonym for confounding factor), and *regression* means to go back to the mean or true score (this problem was outlined in chapter 9—now we will consider it in detail).

You can best appreciate this unwanted phenomenon by allowing yourself to become a victim of it. Try the following exercise, proceeding through the steps as given:

1. Roll six dice on a table in front of you.
2. Place the three dice showing the lowest numbers on the left, and the three dice showing the highest numbers on the right. In case of ties, randomly assign the dice to the two groups.
3. Compute and record the mean number-per-die for each group of three dice.
4. Raise both hands over your head and loudly proclaim, "Improve, in the name of science."
5. Roll the three low-scoring dice and compute a new mean number-per-die for the low group.
6. Roll the three high-scoring dice and compute a new mean number-per-die for the high group.
7. Compare the pre- and posttreatment scores for both groups of dice. Combine your data with that of your classmates, if possible.

On the average, this experiment will produce an increase in the performance of the low group and a decrease in the performance of the high group. You might be tempted to conclude that invoking the name of science has a beneficial effect on underachieving dice, but that overachieving dice require more individual attention to maintain their outstanding performance. Such conclusions, however, fail to consider the effects of regression to the mean. This regression artifact reflects the tendency of many types of measures to yield values close to their mean. You know that the roll of a fair die can yield values from 1 to 6, but that the average value from many rolls will be about 3.5. The likelihood of the average of three dice being close to 3.5 is higher than the likelihood of this average being close to 1 or 6. Thus, when you select three dice that give you a low average and then you roll them again, they will tend to yield a higher average value (a value closer to the mean of 3.5). In the same way, the three dice in the high group should yield a lower value when rolled again.

What does all this have to do with psychological research? By now you are well aware of the fact that accurate measurement lies at the heart of assessing the effects of a variable. Whenever there is a measurement error, such as the regression artifact, there is also the possibility of wrongly concluding that some sort of change has occurred or has failed to occur. Although this statement may appear less than profound to you, a number of psychological studies have been faulted for failing to take adequate account of its truth.

Quasi-experimental designs (see chapter 9), like the dice exercise, are particularly susceptible to bias because of the regression artifact. In such studies, you will remember, subjects are not assigned to treatment and control groups on a random basis, but on the basis of some factor or factors not under experimental control, such as IQ scores or SAT scores. Whenever subjects are assigned to groups because of particularly high or particularly low test scores, regression artifacts are a danger. In a group chosen for low values on some measure, regression to the mean might inflate the apparent effect of some treatment (e.g., "Improve, in the name of science."). Conversely, when a group is chosen for high values on some measure, the effects of a treatment might be masked by the group's tendency to score closer to the mean (and hence lower) on a second test.

The reason regression to the mean often occurs is that all psychological measures are subject to a certain amount of unreliability, or measurement error. Without measurement error, no regression artifact is possible. For instance, if you were to measure the height of each of your classmates to the nearest foot and then measure the shortest and tallest of them again, you would be unlikely to observe any regression to the mean because such gross physical measurements are nearly perfect. With any measure that is not perfectly reliable, however, the group of subjects obtaining the highest scores contains not only those who really belong in the highest category, but also others who are placed in this category owing to chance errors of measurement. On a retest, the chance measurement errors that inflated some of the scores are unlikely to be as large; therefore, the observed score will not be as high. The regression artifact does not imply that the true score of the subject has changed. Regression to the mean merely implies that the initial measurement contained error. To illustrate this point more clearly, an example of regression to the mean with a physical scale might be useful. Imagine that you measured the weight of each of your classmates on an unreliable bathroom scale: On any given weighing, it could err by as much as twenty-five pounds in either direction. As a consequence, some people of average weight were recorded as being very heavy, others as being very light. If you were to weigh everyone again on the same scale, it is unlikely that the average people who weighed in at the extreme ends of the scale would get the same erroneous readings a second time. The second weighing of the high and low weight people would therefore show regression to the mean; however, no one would claim that there was any actual change in weight.

**Regression in compensatory education.** The importance of regression artifacts in quasi-experimental studies of education has been the subject of much debate. One influential study of the effects of the Head Start program of the 1960s (Cicirelli et al., 1969) received particular attention. In this study, called the Westinghouse-Ohio study, children completing their Head Start experience were randomly selected for evaluation. A control population of children from the same area who had been eligible for the program but had not attended was then defined. Control children were selected at random to be matched with experimental children on the basis of sex, racial or ethnic group membership, and kindergarten attendance. After the final selection of experimental and control subjects was made, additional measures of socioeconomic status, demographic status, and attitude were compiled and compared in the two groups. Differences were reported to be slight. Measures of experimental (Head Start) and control (no Head Start) children's academic achievement and potential were then computed and compared. The general conclusion from this large study was that Head Start was not effective in removing the effects of poverty and social disadvantage.

Other psychologists (Campbell and Erlebacher, 1970a) were quick to criticize this study on several grounds. First, they pointed out that the results of the study were undoubtedly caused partially by regression artifacts. Worse, the magnitude of the artifacts could not be estimated, casting doubt over the entire set of findings.

What is the basic problem? Can you see why the matching of subjects may not have been effective? Cicirelli and coworkers laudably tried to match the sample of disadvantaged children who had been in the Head Start program with others from the same area who had not been in the program. Differences that show up later between the two groups should result from the program. Right? Not necessarily. That conclusion is correct only if the two samples came from the same underlying population distributions, which is unlikely.

What is more likely is that the two populations differed, with the disadvantaged treatment (Head Start) children coming from a population that was poorer in ability than the control (no Head Start) children. The treatment children were usually preselected to be from a disadvantaged background: That is why they were included in the program. The control subjects, on the other hand, who were not in the program, were likely to be from a different population that was greater in ability (a nonequivalent control group). The basic problem was that subjects were not randomly assigned to conditions, so the researchers tried to match control subjects with experimental subjects. To match samples from these different populations, the experimenters had to select children *above* the population mean for the disadvantaged treatment group and *below* the population mean for the control group. But when this was done, the regression artifact was introduced. When each group was retested, the subjects' performance tended to regress to the mean of the group; in other words, the disadvantage group tended to perform worse on the retest and the control group tended to perform better.

Regression to the mean can occur in the absence of any treatment being given and despite matching. Because in the Head Start study we already expected a difference between groups (favoring the control), regression to the mean makes it difficult to evaluate the outcome of the study. Cicirelli and coworkers found no difference between the groups. Given that the treatment (Head Start) group was probably worse to begin with, does this mean the group actually improved because of Head Start?

It is impossible to answer this question, because in the Westinghouse-Ohio evaluation of Head Start the direction or magnitude of regression artifacts could not be assessed. In the preceding paragraph, we made reasonable assumptions concerning regression artifacts in this type of study. Strictly speaking, however, we cannot conclude that Head Start had no effect. In fact, we cannot draw any conclusion on the basis of that study, because we do not know how regression artifacts affected the results.

In general, then, regression artifacts of a difficult-to-estimate magnitude are highly probable in this type of study, a fact acknowledged by most researchers. Why, then, would such studies be conducted, particularly when important political, economic, and social decisions will be based on their results? This question was raised both by Campbell and Erlebacher (1970a, b) and by Cicirelli and his supporters (Cicirelli, 1970; Evans and Schiller, 1970). Their answers were quite different, and they represent the type of issue that frequently confronts scientists but which science can never resolve. Campbell and Erlebacher (1970a) proposed that bad information was worse than no information at all; that if properly controlled experiments could not be performed, then no data should be gathered. On the other side of the issue, Evans and Schiller replied, "This position fails to understand that every program *will* be evaluated by the most arbitrary, anecdotal, partisan, and subjective means" (p. 220). Campbell and Erlebacher concurred but stated that "we judge it fundamentally misleading to lend the prestige of science to any report in a situation where no scientific evaluation is possible" (1970b, p. 224). As a final solution, they proposed that a commission "composed of experts who are not yet partisans in this controversy" be convened to decide the matter.

**Possible solutions.**  We may not be able to decide this issue on strictly rational grounds, but we can all agree that a research study should be conducted according to the best scientific procedures available. After the fact, of course, we are not able to interpret the results of a quasi-experimental study in which there are substantial and unknown regression artifacts. The question becomes: How could the Westinghouse-Ohio study have been properly conducted? The best way would have been to randomly assign participants to either the no-treatment or treatment conditions. There is no substitute for random assignment in eliminating confounding factors (that is, there is no substitute for doing a true experiment). However, it seems unfair to give half the children who seek the help of a remedial program no training whatsoever. Of course, there is no guarantee at the outset that the program will be beneficial to them; that is what the study is designed to discover. The same issue arises in medical research when a control group with a disease is given a placebo rather than a treatment drug. The argument could be made in both cases that in the long run more people will be aided by careful research into the effectiveness of treatments than may be harmed because treatment is withheld. Unfortunately, the issue is not quite that simple. In the case of medical research, for example, preliminary testing of an antiencephalitis drug showed that 72 percent of the patients receiving the drug survived the disease and led normal lives, but only 30 percent of the control group, which received placebos, survived (Katz, 1979). Is such a toll necessary for effective research design in drug development? Again, the issue is difficult to resolve solely on rational or scientific grounds.

There are other solutions to the regression problem (in the Westinghouse-Ohio study) besides random assignment. One is to randomly assign all the children to different groups and put them in different programs to pit the effectiveness of the programs against one another. The difficulty here is that we do not have a no-treatment baseline, and if the programs turn out to be equally effective, we would not know whether any of them were better than no program at all.

## CONCEPT SUMMARY

**Regression artifacts** mask true behavior in quasi-experiments and matching studies.

Use random assignment to treatments whenever possible.

# INTERPRETING PATTERNS OF RESEARCH

The problems of scale attenuation and regression artifacts focus on the results of a particular piece of research. The topics we want to examine now are concerned with interpreting patterns of research. No single observation can stand alone for long. When we are confronted with the results of psychological research, we must always ask whether they are reliable and valid. In chapters 3 and 4 we discussed the reliability and validity of data. Here we will expand on some of that discussion so you can grasp the importance of determining whether a particular result displays regularity and whether a particular datum fits with other, related observations.

## Reliability and Replication

Suppose we have been hired to assess presidential preferences in the United States. Our job is to find out who the people seem to prefer for president in the upcoming election. After we develop a survey, we take a random sample of the people in the United States. What sorts of things will make us confident of our results? First, we can be more confident that the results accurately reflect the attitudes of the population if our sample consists of 100,000 people rather than only 100. Second, we should expect a second random sample to yield a similar result (assuming that one of the major candidates has not committed a gross moral or legal transgression during the time between the two surveys). Large numbers of observations and a repeatable result are two key factors to ensure reliability. We should always try to maximize the number of observations and devise our research in a way that allows us to determine whether our results are consistent over time.

**Test reliability.** In chapter 3, we discussed the ways in which **test reliability** is assessed. Remember that a reliable test is one that yields consistent results. If a test is inconsistent because it is poorly designed (and not because of changes in the person taking the test), we will be unable to determine whether the test is measuring what it is supposed to measure. Thus, an unreliable test is also one that is invalid. The same is true of experiments, which we will discuss next.

**Experimental reliability: Replication.** The basic issue regarding reliability of experimental results is simply this: If an experiment were repeated, would the results be the same as those found the first time? Obviously, repeatability is a crucial topic in psychological research, for an experimental outcome may be worthless if we cannot have reasonable certainty that the results are reliable. Because we usually are unable to conduct the same study twice using the same subjects (with the possible exception of some small-$n$ work), we usually repeat an experiment with a different sample of subjects. If the results of the two experiments are similar, we can be confident that we have demonstrated reliability.

Many psychologists find **experimental reliability** more convincing than statistical reliability, because a statistically reliable finding in a single experiment may be the result of a set of accidental circumstances that favor one condition over another. We emphasize that the results of any particular experiment are to be viewed against the background of others on the same issue. If a phenomenon is not repeatable, we are likely to find out rather quickly. **Replication,** a synonym for *copy* or *reproduction,* is the term usually used to describe experimental reliability. We will now consider an example of replication in the context of a series of famous experiments conducted by Luchins (1942).

**Luchins's Einstellung (set) experiments.** Abraham S. Luchins (1942) was interested in the following: "Several problems, all solvable by one somewhat complex procedure, are presented in succession. If afterwards a similar task is given which can be solved by a more direct and simpler method, will the individual be blinded to this more direct possibility?" Subjects may develop a particular approach to a class of similar problems. After the problems are changed so that this set (as in mind set) is no longer the most efficient method of solution, will people hang on to the set, or will they recognize the more direct method? The German word for *set* is **Einstellung;** our everyday problem solving frequently involves an Einstellung: We try our habitual ways of attacking a particular problem even though we may have more efficient procedures readily available to us.

Luchins usually used the water-jar problem in his experiments. People were given two or three jars of water of varying capacity and were supposed to figure out how to obtain a required amount of water by performing arithmetic operations on the volumes the jars would hold. For example, if jar A holds 6 gallons, jar B holds 15 gallons, and jar C holds 2 gallons, how can you obtain exactly 7 gallons? In this example, you could fill jar B (15), then fill jars A (6) and C (2) from the contents of B, leaving 7 gallons in B. The basic eleven problems appear in table 11–1. To become familiar with the Einstellung effect, solve all eleven problems in order before you continue reading.

In Luchins's first study, the first problem served as an illustration of the task. The appropriate solution is to take the larger jar (29) and subtract the smaller jar (3) three times to get the desired amount (20). Subjects next solved problems 2 through 6, which may be considered set-establishing problems

| TABLE 11–1 | THE WATER-JAR PROBLEMS LUCHINS USED IN HIS EINSTELLUNG EXPERIMENTS | | | |
|---|---|---|---|---|
| | Given the Following Empty Jars as Measures | | | Obtain the Required Amount of Water |
| Problem | A | B | C | |
| 1 | 29 | 3 | | 20 |
| 2 | 21 | 127 | 3 | 100 |
| 3 | 14 | 163 | 25 | 99 |
| 4 | 18 | 43 | 10 | 5 |
| 5 | 9 | 42 | 6 | 21 |
| 6 | 20 | 59 | 4 | 31 |
| 7 | 23 | 49 | 3 | 20 |
| 8 | 15 | 39 | 3 | 18 |
| 9 | 28 | 76 | 3 | 25 |
| 10 | 18 | 48 | 4 | 22 |
| 11 | 14 | 36 | 8 | 6 |

because they all are most easily solved by the same method of solution. In each case, the solution is to take the largest jar (always the middle one), subtract the first jar once, and finally subtract the last jar twice. If we label the jars $A$, $B$, and $C$ from left to right, then the set the subjects developed for problems 2 through 6 can be represented as $B - A - 2C$.

Besides the experimental or Einstellung group, there were two others. One group, a control of sorts, began with problems 7 and 8 so that the experimenter could see how the group would solve them with no induced set solution. Another group was treated in the same manner as the Einstellung group, except that before problem 7 each subject wrote "Don't be blind" on the response sheet. Luchins had the subjects write this phrase so that they would be cautious and not be foolish when they solved subsequent problems. Thus, the primary dependent variable was the number of subjects using the Einstellung solution ($B - A - 2C$) on problems 7 and 8, even though problems 7 and 8 had much more efficient and direct solutions ($A - C$ for 7 and $A + C$ for 8). The results were that none of the control subjects used the inefficient solution in solving problems 7 and 8, 81 percent of the Einstellung subjects used the inefficient solution on 7 and 8, and the "Don't be blind" warning reduced the use of the Einstellung solution to about 55 percent. Furthermore, after doing problem 9, which cannot be solved via the set-inducing method, 63 percent of the Einstellung subjects continued with the old solution on problems 10 and 11, whereas only 30 percent of the "Don't be blind" subjects reverted to the set solution.

How reliable are the results from this experiment? Luchins's work was published before the use of statistical tests was common in psychological research, so statistical tests to establish reliability were not performed. However, such tests were largely unnecessary in this case, because Luchins provided us with evidence that his results could be replicated in other experiments. Many experiments are included in the original report, and the results are in general agreement with the Einstellung results just outlined. Altogether, Luchins tested more than 9,000 subjects in his original studies. As noted previously, experimental reliability or replication is an exceptionally convincing way to demonstrate the reliability of a phenomenon—the Einstellung effect is a reliable one.

There are three types of replications: direct, systematic, and conceptual. **Direct replication** is simply repeating an experiment as closely as possible with as few changes as possible in the method. Luchins replicated his original experiment several times with only slight changes in the subject population tested; such experiments constitute cases of direct replication.

In a **systematic replication,** all sorts of factors are changed that the investigator considers irrelevant to the phenomenon of interest. If the phenomenon is not illusory, it will survive these changes. So, for example, in a systematic replication of Luchins's experiments, we might vary the nature of the problems so that the set involves a different rule (or several different rules), vary the instructions, vary the type of subjects used, and so on. The Einstellung effect should be robust across all of these manipulations. If it is not, then we have found that variables previously thought to be irrelevant are actually important, and this is crucial knowledge.

In a **conceptual replication,** we attempt to replicate a phenomenon or concept in an entirely different way. In the language of chapter 10, we simply use a different operational definition of the concept. Luchins examined other tasks besides the water-jar problem to establish the Einstellung phenomenon in diverse situations. He used series of geometry problems, words hidden in letters, and paper mazes. Although the operational definitions of a problem and of a solution changed from experiment to experiment, in each case, subjects solved several problems that had a unique solution before they came to the critical problems that could be solved either by the Einstellung solution or by a much more simple and direct solution. Just as in the water-jar experiments, subjects usually used the old, circuitous solution and ignored the more efficient solution. These experiments constitute conceptual replications of the concept of Einstellung.

You should note the following carefully: The problem of reliability of results is interwoven with the problem of generality and validity. As we progress from direct to systematic to conceptual replication, we show not only reliability, but also increasing validity. Are we studying something that ties in with or is related to our knowledge of other psychological phenomena in a reasonable way? A conceptual replication is closely related to converging operations, which are procedures that validate a hypothetical construct used to explain behavior by eliminating alternative explanations.

# APPLICATION

### A Failure to Replicate

A variety of behavior-modification techniques (see chapter 8) have been very successful in treating certain kinds of psychological disorders, including phobias and anxiety, among others. However, these techniques have been spectacularly unsuccessful in treating smoking and overeating behaviors. Current estimates indicate that only 10 to 20 percent of the people treated for smoking or obesity maintain the benefits of behavior therapy (Schachter, 1982). In other words, about 80 to 90 percent of the smokers return to smoking after the therapy, and about the same percentage of obese people gain weight after therapy.

Why is there such a dramatic failure to replicate the success seen with other disorders? The standard interpretation is that smoking and overeating are addictions, which means that these habits are more difficult to break than other unfortunate habits, such as snake phobias. Recently, Schachter has argued that this interpretation is misleading. Schachter interviewed a substantial number of people in two areas of New York state. These people, who represented a broad cross-section of the population, were asked a number of health-related questions. What Schachter found was surprising. The success rate for smokers who had tried to quit was nearly 64 percent, and the average length of time they had refrained from smoking was about seven years. The corresponding figures for the obese people who had tried to lose weight were 63 percent and more than eleven years of successful weight reduction. These results are markedly different from the low success rates observed for smokers and overeaters after they had completed formal therapy. Why?

There are at least two reasons Schachter found higher success rates. First, people in the general population are likely to have tried to quit smoking or lose weight several times; in contrast, the therapy results generally refer to one stint in therapy. Thus, the repeated attempts at self-therapy may have increased the number of successful outcomes. Second, those who seek professional help might do so because they have been very unsuccessful in treating themselves. For whatever reason, those who undergo therapy may have a particularly tenacious problem, which would bias against successful results.

Schachter offers his findings as encouragement to those who have tried to lose weight or quit smoking and have failed. "If at first you don't succeed, try, try again."

Schachter, S. (1982). Don't sell habit-breakers short. *Psychology Today, 16,* 27–33.

## CONCEPT SUMMARY

To ensure experimental reliability, conduct
- **direct replications,** in which as little as possible is changed
- **systematic replications,** in which many things are varied to determine which variables are truly relevant
- **conceptual replications,** in which the same question is asked using different variables in order to demonstrate generality

### Converging Operations

Suppose that Luchins had conducted just the one experiment outlined in table 11–1. What sorts of conclusions could he have drawn from his results (assume, too, that he directly replicated the study so that he knew his results were reliable)? Can he legitimately conclude that Einstellung caused the results? Without additional independent evidence, he could have said that the results were owing to a "water-jar effect" or "$B - A - 2C$ effect" rather than an Einstellung effect. This is because each of these concepts was part of the one experiment, and each is a reasonable cause of the results. By doing systematic and conceptual replications, Luchins ruled out the alternative hypotheses of effects limited to particular variables and made the concept of Einstellung a reasonable explanation of the rigidity seen in many problem-solving situations.

In other words, the results of experiments that had different rules and different problems converged on the Einstellung hypothesis by systematically eliminating alternative hypotheses. **Converging operations,** then, are a set of two or more operations that eliminate alternative concepts that might explain a set of experimental results. The importance of converging operations in psychological research was initially emphasized in a landmark paper by Garner, Hake, and Eriksen (1956). They noted that converging operations are necessary to validate operationally defined concepts (see chapter 10) as well as experimental results. When an abstract concept, Einstellung, for example, is limited to one operational definition, the meaning of the concept is effectively limited to a description of the operations involved. When the concept can be operationally defined in several different ways, however, it can have meaning beyond its operations. Thus, Einstellung refers to a blindness to an easy solution to a problem as a result of prior experience with similar problems having more difficult solutions. The meaning of the term transcends its operational definitions and has construct validity (see chapter 3). Because converging operations are crucial to an understanding of psychological research and psychological theorizing, we will consider two more examples of converging operations at work.

**Stroop effect: Input or output?**  Before the discussion continues, we want you to try a simple experiment. All you need are some index cards, colored markers, and a watch with a second hand or, even better, a stopwatch. Take sixteen index cards and, using your markers, write the name of the color in its color—that is, with green marker write "green," and so on. If you have eight markers, repeat each color twice. If you only have four markers, repeat each color four times. Take another sixteen index cards and write color names that do not correspond to the ink—that is, with a green marker write "red," and so on. Your stimuli are now complete. Pick one of your two decks, and for each card, name the color of the ink. Time how long it takes you to go through all sixteen cards. Do the same for the other deck. Did you go faster using the deck that had compatible color names and inks?

You probably found that you responded more slowly when ink colors and color names were mismatched than when they were compatible. Furthermore, you probably noticed that you made mistakes, stuttered, and hesitated when the color names and inks were in the incompatible condition. A variation of this frustrating experiment was first done by Stroop (1935); the **Stroop effect** refers to the increase in time required to name the ink color when the ink and color names do not match. This is the same kind of experiment in which you participated in chapter 1, where the mismatch was between the quantity of the digits and the names of those digits.

The Stroop effect is a highly reliable one; the question is, what causes the Stroop effect? One possibility is that it results from the input or perceptual aspects of the task. Stroop and others found that reading is usually faster than naming; therefore, the perceptual argument is that reading color words inhibits the perception of the ink color. An alternative hypothesis is that output (the subject's responses) is affected, not perception. The output notion goes like this: After the subject has perceived both the ink color and the color word, there is response competition when two different color names are elicited—one by the ink and another by the word. On the basis of Stroop's original work, we have no way of deciding between these two hypotheses. Which is important: the perceptual system or the response system?

A simple but clever experiment was conducted by Egeth, Blecker, and Kamlet (1969) to answer this question by using converging operations. Three important conditions from one of their studies are shown in figure 11–3. The control or baseline condition is shown at the top of the figure (neutral condition). Subjects saw two colored patches with a neutral symbol (XXXX) embedded in them. These patches were either the same color or different colors. An important factor in this study is that instead of responding with color names, the subjects responded SAME when the color of the two patches matched and DIFFERENT when the colors of the two patches were different.

| FIGURE 11–3 | | | | |
|---|---|---|---|---|

|  | Response | Symbols in Colors | | Color of Patches |
|---|---|---|---|---|
| Neutral Condition | Same | XXXX | XXXX | Both patches red |
|  | Different | XXXX | XXXX | One patch red, one blue |
| Perceptual Inhibition Condition | Same | RED | RED | Both patches red |
|  | Different | RED | RED | One patch red, one blue |
| Response Competition Condition | Same | SAME | SAME | Both patches red |
|  | Different | SAME | SAME | One patch red, one blue |

An outline of some of the conditions in the work by Egeth, Blecker, and Kamlet (1969). In all three conditions, subjects responded SAME when there was agreement among the stimuli and DIFFERENT when there was a mismatch. Subjects saw two colored patches on each trial and responded on the basis of the colors. The neutral condition served as a control by having neutral symbols (XXXX) embedded in colored patches. Color names were in the patches in the perceptual inhibition condition—the color names should inhibit the perception of the colors. SAME or DIFFERENT appeared in the patches in the response competition condition—reading the response SAME in different colored patches should inhibit the correct response of DIFFERENT. The Stroop effect occurred in the response competition condition but not in the perceptual inhibition condition.

The crucial conditions of the experiment are illustrated in the next rows of figure 11–3. As in the baseline condition, the subject responded SAME or DIFFERENT on the basis of the colors of the two patches. In the perceptual inhibition condition, color names appeared in the colored patches, and on a given trial the same color name appeared in both boxes. Both colored patches could be the same and match the color name (a SAME trial), or the colored patches could be different, with only one patch matching the names (a DIFFERENT trial). Response competition arises when several responses struggle to be executed (Kantowitz, 1974). For example, at a stoplight a red signal calls for a driver to step on the brake with her foot. A green light calls for stepping on the accelerator pedal. If only one signal lamp occurs, there is no response competition. But if the traffic light is defective so that both red and green signals are illuminated, there will be response competition between brake and accelerator pedals because prior learning has strengthened the connections between (1) red traffic lights and brake pedals, and (2) green traffic lights and accelerator pedals.

In the perceptual inhibition condition there is no prior learning to connect color names and the responses SAME or DIFFERENT. Thus, there should be no response competition in this condition. Should responding in this condition be slower than the neutral condition, this result could not be explained by response competition. Therefore, any Stroop effect obtained in the perceptual inhibition condition must result from perceptual inhibition rather than response competition. However, the results obtained by Egeth and his associates were that response times were equal for the perceptual inhibition condition and for the neutral (control) condition. This means that no Stroop effect was obtained. The perceptual similarity between the colors of the patches and the color names failed to produce any Stroop effect. Although this outcome suggests that perceptual factors are not an important cause of Stroop interference, converging operations are needed to bolster this conclusion.

So far so good. We seem to have eliminated one alternative as an explanation of the Stroop effect. Now for a converging operation that will bring back the Stroop effect and identify the processes involved. To accomplish this, Egeth and coworkers used the condition outlined at the bottom of figure 11–3. In the response competition condition, the subjects once again responded SAME and DIFFERENT. However, in this condition the words SAME or DIFFERENT rather than neutral symbols or color names appeared in the colored patches. The experimenters reasoned that if response competition is important, then mismatches between SAME or DIFFERENT and the stimulus information should result in slower responding than in the neutral condition. In other words, if conflict among responses causes the Stroop effect, then responding should be slower in the response competition condition than in the neutral condition. This is exactly what they found. The Stroop effect returned: Now the responses SAME and DIFFERENT took longer when they conflicted with the response in the stimulus. Recall that the identical response words did not produce a Stroop effect in the perceptual inhibition condition. Thus, the converging operations removed the perceptual process as an explanation for the results, leaving us to conclude that a response process accounts for the Stroop effect. Other studies on the Stroop phenomenon also lead to the conclusion that response competition is an important contributing factor to Stroop interference (see Keele, 1973, for an excellent review).

**Personal space.** The concept of **personal space** implies that people are surrounded by invisible bubbles designed to protect them from a wide variety of social encroachments. How do psychologists know that such a bubble exists? It cannot be sensed directly by vision, smell, touch and the other senses, so the concept must be evaluated indirectly. The next two experiments demonstrate that there is a personal-space bubble; they use two different kinds of spatial invasion and yield similar results.

Ironically, the personal-space bubble that helps a person maintain privacy is best studied by invasions that violate the privacy it affords. A simple experiment conducted by Kinzel (1970) shows one operation that defines personal space. Kinzel was interested in the personal-space bubbles surrounding violent and nonviolent prisoners. Thus one independent variable—more precisely, a subject variable (see chapter 9), because it was not manipulated—was classification of prisoners as violent (having inflicted physical injury on another person) or nonviolent. Each prisoner stood in the center of an empty room 20 feet wide and 20 feet long. The experimenter then approached from one of eight directions (the second independent variable) until the prisoner said "Stop" because the experimenter was too close. The dependent variable was the distance between prisoner and experimenter when the prisoner said "Stop." If there is no personal-space bubble, the experimenter should be able to walk right up to the prisoner (distance = 0 feet). Control variables were the room and the experimenter, which were the same throughout the experiment. Results of this experiment are shown in figure 11–4. It is clear that violent prisoners have larger personal-space bubbles than do nonviolent prisoners.

This experiment may not have entirely convinced you that personal-space bubbles exist. In Kinzel's experiment, the personal-space bubble was operationally defined as the point at which the subject said "Stop." A concept based on only one experiment is just a restatement of that particular experimental finding. You may think that there is something strange about a person walking right up to another person without saying anything. Certainly if this happened to you on the street you would think it unusual, to say the least. The next experiment avoids this potential difficulty.

To avoid actively invading someone's personal-space bubble, Barefoot, Hoople, and McClay (1972) gave subjects the opportunity to invade the experimenter's bubble. The experimenter sat near a water fountain and pretended to read a book. Anyone getting a drink of water had to invade the experimenter's personal space. The independent variable was the distance between the experimenter and the water fountain. This could be either 1 foot, 5 feet, or 10 feet. This last distance is large enough so that it exceeds the bounds of the experimenter's personal space and thus is a control condition. A confederate kept track of the number of persons passing by the fountain in each of the three experimental conditions. The dependent variable was the percentage of passersby who drank from the fountain. When the experimenter was 1 foot away, only 10 percent drank; 5 feet away, 18 percent drank. Finally, at a distance of 10 feet, 22 percent drank from the fountain.

Using a very different operational definition of personal space, these results agree with those of the active-invasion paradigm used by Kinzel. The single concept of a personal-space bubble explains findings of both experiments. Hence, the experiments provide converging operations supporting the personal-space concept.

The examples of converging operations we have just detailed are actually rather simple because only a small number of experiments or conditions were

**FIGURE 11–4**

Looking down on the personal-space bubble of violent and nonviolent prisoners. (After Kinzel, *The American Journal of Psychiatry*, vol. 127, pp. 59–64, 1970. Copyright 1970 by the American Psychiatric Association. Reprinted by permission.)

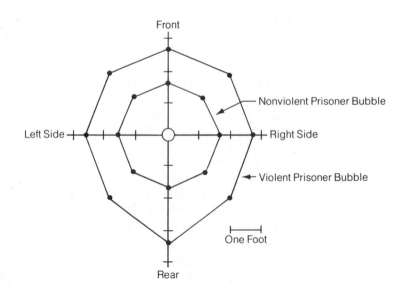

needed to provide validity and generality. In actual practice, many concepts and phenomena require considerable amount of independent evidence before they can be considered valid.

Concepts defined in terms of converging operations are not static. They are modified as we gather additional evidence relevant to the concept. For example, there may be tasks involving incompatible stimuli and responses that place exceptional demands on our perceptual system. Thus, some kinds of Stroop phenomena could result from both input and output effects. In a similar fashion, future research may show that the size of the personal-space bubble differs in active and passive situations: Your bubble may be larger when someone invades it than when you enter the personal space of another person. Because our knowledge is never complete, the meaning of a concept is always open to revision. As we interpret the results of our research, we should therefore keep in mind that our interpretation and conclusions are always tentative: Our words on any issue are unlikely to be the last (see chapter 2).

## CONCEPT SUMMARY

### *CONVERGING OPERATIONS*
Provide **validity** for concepts and hypotheses.
Eliminate **alternative explanations** by two or more operations.

## SUMMARY

1. Several pitfalls may make it difficult for experimenters to interpret the results of their research.

2. Some of these pitfalls pose problems in particular research projects, and others make it difficult to interpret patterns of research. Scale attenuation and regression artifacts can lead to the misinterpretation of the results of a specific project; replications (reliability) and converging operations (validity) are important for interpreting patterns of research.

3. Scale attenuation refers to an inability to observe differences in thought and behavior because performance is either too good (a ceiling effect) or too poor (a floor effect).

4. The scale must be spread out or the task modified in order to handle the attenuation problem.

5. Regression to the mean is likely to occur whenever subjects are selected on the basis of high or low scores on some dependent measure. The regression artifact refers to the tendency of subjects with extreme scores on a first test to have scores closer to the mean on a second test.

6. Random assignment is the best way to guard against regression artifacts.

7. An experiment that can be replicated is a reliable one, as is a test whose results are consistent.

8. The three types of replications are: direct, systematic, and conceptual.

9. Converging operations are several independent procedures that support the meaning of an abstract concept.

10. The need for converging operations demands that scientific research on a problem be varied and extensive.

## Key Concepts

| | |
|---|---|
| ceiling effects | regression artifact |
| conceptual replication | regression to the mean |
| converging operations | replication |
| direct replication | scale-attenuation effects |
| Einstellung | Stroop effect |
| experimental reliability | systematic replication |
| floor effects | test reliability |
| personal space | |

## Exercises

1. [*Special Exercise.*] Here is another design problem for you. Reread the description of Luchins's experiment outlined in table 11–1. There seem to be several problems with that study; see whether you can pinpoint two or three of them. As a hint, consider the following questions: Did Luchins use an appropriate control group? If not, what should be the control condition? Are there points in the study that require counterbalancing? What additional dependent variables might have been informative?

2. Examine figures and tables in several recent journal articles. See whether you can discover any ceiling or floor effects. If you find any—and it may take a while—read the article to determine whether the investigator was aware of the scale-attenuation problem. Can the problem be rectified?

3. Pinpointing regression artifacts may be difficult. However, in an attempt to discover a regression problem, you might find it worthwhile to examine several assessment studies that use subject variables. If you find evidence for a regression artifact, try to determine why the study was published. Remember our discussion of medical research and the difficulty of random assignment. Try these two journals: *Journal of Educational Psychology* and *Journal of Applied Psychology*.

4. Try to find an example of each type of replication in recent journals. You may not find any examples of direct replication, and yet Barber (1976) has asserted that direct replications are crucial to the advancement of psychology. Why do direct replications seldom appear in the literature?

5. More often than not, good examples of converging operations can be found in a single journal article. Papers by Paivio, Mayer, and Thios and D'Agostino, listed in the suggested readings, offer evidence of converging operations at work. You might take a look at these articles.

## Suggested Readings

The following three articles illustrate both reliability and converging operations. Read them carefully. They are also available in the book *Readings in experimental psychology* by Elmes (Chicago: Rand McNally, 1978): Mayer, R. E. (1977). Problem-solving performance with task overload: Effects of self-pacing and trait anxiety. *Bulletin of the Psychonomic Society, 9*, 283–286; Paivio, A. (1975). Perceptual comparisons through the mind's eye. *Memory and Cognition, 3*, 635–667; Thios, S. J., & D'Agostino, P. R. (1976). Effects of repetition as a function of study-phase retrieval. *Journal of Verbal Learning and Verbal Behavior, 15*, 529–536.

## PSYCHOLOGY IN ACTION
### Studying Mental Blocks

*Folk* is pronounced *foke,* with the *l* being silent. *Polk* is pronounced *poke,* again with the *l* being silent.
How is the name of the white of an egg pronounced?

If you just pronounced *yolk* in answering the question, this section is for you. *Yolk* is an erroneous answer; the white part of an egg is the *albumen.* The *yolk,* as you probably know, is the yellow part. The sentences prior to the question featured words that rhyme with *yolk* and therefore primed you for the word *yolk.* When you were asked the question about eggs, *yolk* readily came to you as the answer. If you had not been primed with the two sentences, you probably would not have responded *yolk.* The recent experience of reading the sentences blocked you from giving the correct answer.

Here are two more examples, although you may be more wary now:

Pronounce the word produced by the letters *T-O-P-S.* What does a car do at a green light? Say *tin* out loud ten times. What is an aluminum can made of?

Although you may have answered these questions correctly, if you try them on a friend we think you will find them effective in producing the erroneous answers *stop* and *tin.* You should probably ask the questions aloud, rather than tell your friend to read them.

Such blocks in memory retrieval may play a part in limiting creative thinking (Roediger and Neely, 1982). When people try to solve a problem and fail, they often say that their minds are "in a rut." Usually they mean that when they attempt to solve the problem they are blocked from retrieving a new solution by repeatedly thinking of all the erroneous solutions that previously have been tried. This is the same as the Einstellung effect shown by Luchins's subjects.

You can study the same effect by having some friends read through the priming sentences before the target ones. Compare their behavior with others who do not read the priming sentences. You should consider having the latter group read (or hear) some nonpriming sentences in order to control for the amount of mental work you have your subjects do.

If you are interested in additional ways of studying mental blocks, the following references may be of interest.

Fingerman, P., & Levine, M. (1974). Nonlearning: The completeness of the blindness. *Journal of Experimental Psychology, 102,* 720–721.
Roediger, H. L., & Neely, J. H. (1982). Retrieval blocks in episodic and semantic memory. *Canadian Journal of Psychology, 36,* 213–242.

| **CONDUCTING ETHICAL RESEARCH** Follow the APA's guidelines for research with humans and animals | **Ethical Considerations in Research** |
|---|---|
| | *Is my project designed in accordance with contemporary ethical standards?* |
| | Will my human subjects be treated in a dignified fashion without having their personal freedom violated or their physical or emotional health damaged? |
| | Will I treat my animal subjects in a humane fashion? |
| | Do I understand the ethical principles behind drug research? |
| | Have I read and understood the ethical principles espoused by the American Psychological Association? |

# 12

# CONDUCTING ETHICAL RESEARCH

The scientific enterprise creates ethical dilemmas. Scientific knowledge and techniques that can be used for human betterment can be turned to manipulative and exploitative purposes as well. Just as results of research in atomic physics can be used for the treatment of cancer as well as for destructive weapons, so methods discovered to reduce prejudice toward minority groups, to eliminate troublesome behavior problems, or to facilitate learning in school may also be used to manipulate political allegiance, to create artificial wants, or to reconcile the victims of social injustice to their fate. The double-edged potentiality of scientific knowledge poses ethical problems for all scientists. To the extent that psychological research deals with important problems and potent methods, psychologists must recognize and alert others to the fact that the potential for misuse of research increases its potential for constructive application. (American Psychological Association, 1982, p. 16.)

## RESEARCH WITH HUMAN PARTICIPANTS

The quotation in the introduction to this chapter is from a publication of the American Psychological Association. The quote comes from a preamble to a lengthy discussion of ethical principles covering all aspects of psychology and is presented in abbreviated form here to emphasize the ethical obligations of researchers in all areas of science. These obligations are straightforward in principle but difficult to implement. We will examine both the ethical principles and the problems associated with putting them into practice in psychology. Psychologists are concerned with the ethics of research involving both human participants and animals. Although some of this concern is selfish, owing to fear of restriction of research funds and loss of access to subject populations, most psychologists are ethical persons who have no desire to inflict harm on anyone. The mad researcher, who will do anything to obtain data, is largely fictional.

An experimenter cannot be completely impartial and objective in judging the ethical issues concerning his or her own research, so most universities and research institutions have peer committees that judge the ethicality of proposed research. Indeed, any federally funded research must be approved by such a committee before any funding is granted.

Let us consider a specific experimental situation to illustrate the implementation of ethical principles. Imagine that you are a psychologist interested in determining to what extent depressive feelings influence how well people remember information. One of the major reasons you want to study this topic is that depression is a fairly common emotional problem among college students, and you would like to have some idea how this problem could affect academic performance. You decide to do a tightly controlled laboratory experiment to determine the effects of depression on memory. Your general strategy is to induce depression in some of your subjects, and then compare their memory to that of other subjects who were not induced to be depressed. The manner in which you induce depression in your subjects follows a procedure devised by Velten (1968). To induce a mood by this procedure, the investigator has the subject read aloud sixty self-referent statements that are associated with the mood in question. In this case, the participant reads statements that are supposed to induce depression, beginning with relatively mild statements such as "Today is neither better nor worse than any other day," and progressing to "I feel so bad that I would like to go to sleep and never wake up." This procedure has been shown to induce a mild, temporary depression; participants report feeling depressed, and their behavior suffers on a variety of tasks.

Even though many details of this experiment have not been specified, it should be obvious that the welfare of the research participants in this study could be jeopardized (for complete details of this experiment, see Elmes, Chapman, and Selig, 1984). Inducing a negative mood (such as depression) in college students could have disastrous effects on their social and intellectual functioning. How can you as an ethical researcher try to preserve and protect the fundamental human rights of your participants? What would you do to protect their welfare and at the same time conduct an internally valid experiment?

In a recent review of research on mood and memory, Blaney (1986) listed a number of studies in which depression was induced in college students. In some experiments, a happy mood was induced in subjects. Do the ethical considerations depend on the kind of mood—happy or sad—that is induced in a subject? Also, researchers have used several different mood-induction procedures in their experiments. Besides the Velten (1968) procedure described above, hypnosis and music have been used to induce a depressed or happy mood. Do ethical considerations depend on the mood-induction technique? These questions concerning mood-induction research illustrate how ethical issues associated with psychological research may vary according to the specific circumstances in the experiment.

The American Psychological Association (1981a, 1987, 1989) has provided ethical guidelines for researchers. The association outlined ten general principles governing the conduct of research with human participants. To consider how the welfare of the students was protected in those studies, we will examine the principles that guide research involving human participants. *You should read and understand these ethical principles before you conduct a research project with human participants.*

The decision to undertake research rests upon a considered judgment by the individual psychologist about how best to contribute to psychological science and human welfare. Having made the decision to conduct research, the psychologist considers alternative directions in which research energies and resources might be invested. On the basis of this consideration, the psychologist carries out the investigation with respect and concern for the dignity and welfare of the people who participate and with cognizance of federal and state regulations and professional standards governing the conduct of research with human participants.

1. In planning a study, the investigator has the responsibility to make a careful evaluation of its ethical acceptability. To the extent that the weighing of scientific and human values suggests a compromise of any principle, the investigator incurs a correspondingly serious obligation to seek ethical advice and to observe stringent safeguards to protect the rights of human participants.

2. Considering whether a participant in a planned study will be a "subject at risk" or a "subject at minimal risk," according to recognized standards, is of primary ethical concern to the investigator.

3. The investigator always retains the responsibility for ensuring ethical practice in research. The investigator is also responsible for the ethical treatment of research participants by collaborators, assistants, students, and employees, all of whom, however, incur similar obligations.

4. Except in minimal-risk research, the investigator establishes a clear and fair agreement with research participants, prior to their participation, that clarifies the obligations and responsibilities of each. The investigator has the obligation to honor all promises and commitments included in that agreement. The investigator informs the participants of all aspects of the research that might reasonably be expected to influence willingness to participate and explains all other aspects of the research about which the participants inquire. Failure to make full disclosure prior to obtaining informed consent requires additional safeguards to protect the welfare and dignity of the research participants. Research with children or with participants who have impairments that would limit understanding and/or communication requires special safeguarding procedures.

5. Methodological requirements of a study may make the use of concealment or deception necessary. Before conducting such a study, the investigator has a special responsibility to (i) determine whether the use of such techniques is justified by the study's prospective scientific, educational, or applied value; (ii) determine whether alternative procedures are available that do not use concealment or deception; and (iii) ensure that the participants are provided with sufficient explanation as soon as possible.

6. The investigator respects the individual's freedom to decline to participate in or to withdraw from the research at any time. The obligation to protect this freedom requires careful thought and consideration when the investigator is in a position of authority or influence over the participant. Such positions of authority include, but are not limited to, situations in which research participation is required as part of employment or in which the participant is a student, client, or employee of the investigator.

7. The investigator protects the participant from physical and mental discomfort, harm, and danger that may arise from research procedures. If risks of such consequences exist, the investigator informs the participant of that fact. Research procedures likely to cause serious or lasting harm to a participant are not used unless the failure to use these procedures might expose the participant to risk of greater harm, or unless the research has great potential benefit and fully informed and voluntary consent is obtained from each participant. The participant should

be informed of procedures for contacting the investigator within a reasonable time period following participation should stress, potential harm, or related questions or concerns arise.

8. After the data are collected, the investigator provides the participant with information about the nature of the study and attempts to remove any misconceptions that may have arisen. Where scientific or humane values justify delaying or withholding this information, the investigator incurs a special responsibility to monitor the research and to ensure that there are no damaging consequences for the participant.

9. Where research procedures result in undesirable consequences for the individual participant, the investigator has the responsibility to detect and remove or correct these consequences, including long-term effects.

10. Information obtained about a research participant during the course of an investigation is confidential unless otherwise agreed upon in advance. When the possibility exists that others may obtain access to such information, this possibility, together with the plans for protecting confidentiality, is explained to the participant as part of the procedure for obtaining informed consent.

Principles 9 and 10 are the ones most relevant to protecting welfare, and they can be summarized by noting that the experimenter has an obligation to minimize harm to the participant. The subject should be warned ahead of time if there is potential harm, the subject should be able to withdraw if he or she chooses, and deception should be used carefully. The experimenter is obligated to undo any harm, and the results should remain confidential with regard to a particular participant unless agreed otherwise. These principles need to be reckoned with in any research project.

## Informed Consent and Deception

The ethical researcher tells the subjects, prior to participation, of "all aspects of the research that might reasonably be expected to influence willingness to participate and explains all other aspects of the research about which participants inquire." This means that the participants must be forewarned about those aspects of the research that may have detrimental effects.

In most psychological research, participants are fully informed as to what they will be asked to do during the course of an experiment, so that they can, indeed, give **informed consent**. It is rare that participants are mislead as to the nature of the experiences that they will have during the experiment. Furthermore, when an experimenter states the purpose of the experimental procedure, this statement is usually truthful. Nonetheless, experimenters sometimes mislead participants as to the true purpose of an experiment. This false description is often referred to as a "cover story." As discussed in chapter 10, this kind of **deception** is usually done to control subject reactivity. For instance, a researcher interested in whether people behave more assertively in same-gender groups than in mixed-gender groups tells participants that they will be working on various problems that require group cooperation. He or she also tells them that the purpose of the experiment is to evaluate the difficulty of these tasks. The researcher was concerned that participants' behavior might change if they knew the real purpose of the experiment.

In this case, information regarding the hypothesis under test is unlikely to change anyone's decision as to whether or not to participate, but this information might change performance on the task. Deception of this sort, although usually harmless, must be considered carefully because the participant's consent is not fully informed. A person might choose not to participate in a particular experiment because he or she does not approve of the purpose of the experiment.

Even more rare than deception concerning the purpose of an experiment is deception concerning the experiences that the participant will have during the course of the experiment. Such deception is, unfortunately, necessary in order to answer some research questions. For example, if an investigator were interested in how well people recall information that they are not actively trying to remember, he or she could not inform participants that the experiment would require a memory test. Obviously, the omission of information prevents participants from giving fully informed consent.

Thus, whenever a research question requires that participants be deceived in some way, the ethical researcher faces a dilemma. Obviously, participants must be warned if the procedure will place them in serious danger of physical or psychological harm; deception in such cases is clearly unethical. When a procedure involves only minor risks, the decision regarding full disclosure to participants is more difficult. In all cases, the potential benefits of the research must be weighed against the actual and potential costs to the participant. It is only when the potential benefits of the experiment far exceed any risks to the participant that deception can be justified. Even then, participants should always be given as much information as possible, and it should be made clear to them that they can end their participation at any time without negative consequences.

Let us reexamine the depression and memory experiment we discussed earlier, focusing on the question of informed consent. The people who signed up to participate were told that some of the things they were going to do in the experiment might make them feel unhappy, and they were given the opportunity to refuse to participate. The specific nature of the manipulation, such as the Velten technique and who was going to serve in the experimental group, was not disclosed ahead of time. Complete disclosure might have resulted in reactivity. Because the effects of the mood induction were known to be temporary, the researchers believed that partial information was enough to permit informed consent. Here, although some information was omitted, participants were not misled as to the kind of experiences they could expect in the experiment.

The issues surrounding informed consent and deception often require considerable thought and deliberation in order to arrive at ethical solutions. Individual researchers are seldom left to their own devices to make these decisions. Virtually every research institution in this country has a standing committee that must approve any experimental procedure involving human subjects. The central function of these committees is to ensure the ethical treatment of experimental participants. We will discuss these boards in more detail later.

In sum, fully informed consent is the norm in most areas of psychology. Occasionally, some information is withheld or participants are misled so as to prevent subject reactivity. In such cases, the experimenter, as well as members of institutional review boards, take great care in deciding whether the benefits of the procedure outweigh the risks to the participants.

## Freedom to Withdraw

As mentioned briefly in the previous section, participants should be allowed to decline to participate or to withdraw at any time. Everyone would agree that the mad scientist who straps participants to the chair is unethical. Moreover, few people would deny that people who are unhappy about participating should have the **freedom to withdraw.** Where, then, is the ethical dilemma? The major problem revolves around the definition of a willing volunteer participant. Consider the subject pool for the depression and memory experiment: undergraduate students (mostly freshmen and sophomores) taking introductory psychology. They sign up to participate in experiments, and they usually receive some sort of course credit for their service. Are they volunteering when they sign up, or are they under some sort of coercion that they have inferred from the situation? If the students actually receive extra credit, they are likely to be acting on their own volition. If they must participate as part of a course requirement, then the freedom to participate or not is less obvious. When students are required to participate, they should have some optional way of fulfilling the requirement, such as writing a paper or attending a special lecture. The point, then, is to provide freedom to the potential subjects, so they can participate or not as they choose.

Generally, when the pool of potential participants is a captive audience, such as students, prisoners, military recruits, and employees of the experimenter, then the researcher needs to consider the individual's freedom to withdraw or to participate. In the depression and memory experiment, volunteer students were recruited with the lure of extra credit (participation was not mandatory). When they signed up, they were forewarned about the possibility of unhappiness (they could agree to participate or not). In the instructions at the beginning of the experiment, the students were advised that they had the option of quitting any time they wanted and they would still receive the full extra credit that had been promised (they were free to withdraw).

## Protection from Harm and Debriefing

One additional safeguard that provides research participants with **protection from harm** is suggested by the American Psychological Association: a way for the subjects to contact the investigator following their participation in the research. Even the most scrupulously ethical project of the minimal-risk sort may have unintended aftereffects. Thus, the participant should be able to receive help or advice from the researcher if problems should arise. We have had participants cry (out of frustration and embarrassment) during what was supposed to be a standard, innocuous memory experiment. Those subjects may have carried away from the experiment a negative self-image or strong feelings of resentment toward the experimenter in particular or research in general.

Because of such unintended effects, the prudent researcher provides for subsequent consultation, or what is called **debriefing.** Debriefing means that the investigator explains the general purposes of the research and the nature of the manipulations so that any questions or misunderstandings the subjects may have are removed.

Let us apply the principles of debriefing and protection from harm to the depression and memory experiment. At the end of that project, the participants were given a list of phone numbers of people who could be contacted in the unlikely event that the subjects felt depressed following the experiment. The list of contacts included the principal investigator, a counselor, and the dean of student affairs and his assistant. Also, the day after participation, each subject who had read the depression-inducing statements was phoned by one of the experimenters, who tried to determine whether the participant was having any negative aftereffects.

The participants were also thoroughly debriefed. They were told about the mood-induction procedure, and how its effects were temporary. In addition, other details of the experimental design and rationale were outlined, and any questions the participants had were answered.

## Removing Harmful Consequences

Debriefing subjects and giving them phone numbers may not be sufficient in a risky project. If a participant could indeed suffer long-term consequences as a result of serving in a research project, the investigator has the responsibility for **removing harmful consequences.** It may be difficult to reverse the feelings of resentful subjects, because the resentment may be unintended and undetected. However, where the risks are known, the ethical investigator must take steps to minimize them.

Prior to the debriefing in the depression and memory experiment, the participants read a series of self-referent statements designed to induce elation. This exercise was supposed to counteract the effects of the negative mood induced earlier. Then the participants were questioned about their current feelings, and they were also asked to sign a statement that said they left the experiment feeling no worse than when they began it. All participants signed the statement, but had they not, a contingent plan was to keep them in the laboratory under the supervision of one of the experimenters until they felt better.

## Confidentiality

What a subject does in an experiment should be confidential unless otherwise agreed. An ethical researcher does not run around saying things like: "Bobby Freshman is stupid; he did more poorly than anyone else in my experiment." Also, personal information about particular participants, such as their attitudes toward premarital sex or their family income, should not be revealed without the subjects' permission. The principle of **confidentiality** seems straightforward, but a researcher can be faced with an ethical dilemma when trying to uphold confidentiality.

This dilemma arose in the depression and memory experiment. The experimenter was confronted with an ethical problem, because he believed it was necessary to violate the principle of confidentiality in order to uphold the principle of protection from harm. Let us see how this problem developed. One of the first tasks of the participants was to answer some questions concerning their mental health. They were to indicate whether they were currently seeking professional help for a personal problem, and to give some details about the problem and the therapeutic procedure. The participants were assured that their answers were confidential. Then the subjects completed a clinical test that assessed their current level of depression. If a participant indicated that he or she was being treated for depression and scored high on the test, the experiment was discontinued at that point. Confidentiality was promised so that honest responses could be obtained, and the test was administered to prevent a depressed person from becoming even more depressed by the mood-induction procedure. Thus, the intent was to minimize harm. In the course of the experiment, two students scored very high on the depression test, and one of them was not undergoing therapy. Because the test was known to be a reliable and valid predictor of clinically serious depression, the principal investigator believed that it was necessary to warn one of the college's counselors about the two students who appeared to have very high levels of depression. Then, under the guise of a routine interview, the counselor talked to these students.

## Further Ethical Considerations

The type of dilemma faced in the depression and memory study occurs frequently in research. To adhere to one ethical principle may necessitate violating another. There are no easy choices when this happens. In the case we mentioned, if the highly depressed students had suspected that the investigator had betrayed their confidence, permanent resentment and mistrust could have resulted. On the other hand, the investigator could not ignore the fact that these students, particularly the one not undergoing therapy, were in severe distress. At that time, ensuring that the students received help seemed much more important than upholding their right to confidentiality.

As our example illustrates, ethical decisions must sometimes be made on the basis of pragmatic concerns. In other words, people involved in making decisions about a research project must focus on how best to protect the participants and at the same time conduct a meaningful, valid project. Imagine that you are on an ethics committee, and you must decide whether to allow the following examples of proposed research:

1. An environmental psychologist sits in a crowded library and keeps detailed records of seating patterns.

2. An environmental psychologist takes videotapes of seating patterns in a library. These tapes are maintained indefinitely, and library patrons do not know they have been filmed.

3. An experimental psychologist tells students that she is interested in their reading comprehension when in reality she is recording the speed of their responses rather than their comprehension.

4. A social psychologist is studying bystander intervention in a liquor store. Permission has been obtained from the store manager. In clear view of a patron, an experimenter "steals" a bottle of liquor. A second experimenter approaches the patron and asks, "Did you see him steal that bottle?"

5. A social psychologist connects surface electrodes to male participants, with their prior approval. These subjects are told that the electrodes are

connected to a meter in front of them that measures sexual arousal. In reality, the meter is controlled by the experimenter. Participants are then shown slides of nude males and females. The meter gives high readings for pictures of males, leading the participants to believe that they have latent homosexual tendencies.

Not everyone would agree as to which of these examples constitute ethical or unethical research, and we will not presume to provide definitive answers for you. We have, however, had informal discussions with our colleagues about these examples; only the first example was unequivocally considered ethical. Because the psychologist was merely observing and did not know the people, informed consent was not deemed necessary. Any individual, psychologist or not, could easily observe these same people in the library. The potential harm to participants was extremely small.

You may be surprised that for every other example, there were at least some people who raised objections. Number 2 was thought to invade personal privacy because the tapes were not erased after the data had been abstracted. Some believed that number 3 would be acceptable only if the experimenter carefully debriefed participants by explaining the nature and reasons for this minor deception. Number 4 was actually performed; a patron denied seeing the theft and then called the police as soon as she left the store. The investigator had to go down to the police station to bail out the experimenters. Number 5 was also performed and it too was considered unethical, even with debriefing. It is not clear whether the potential psychological harm of leading the participant to think he had hidden homosexual tendencies could be removed by even immediate extensive debriefing.

These examples show that there is no clear answer as to what is ethical. The responsibility rests on the researcher, review committees, and also journal editors who review research for publication. Although deception and concealment may be justified in limited instances, great caution is demanded in such research. One of the first things to do when designing a project is to consider the ethics of your procedure. Seek advice from your friends and instructor. Deceit and danger are not prerequisites of good research; they should be avoided as much as possible.

## CONCEPT SUMMARY

When conducting research with human subjects, an ethical researcher

- *ensures that participants are fully informed as to the experimental procedure and give their consent before beginning the experiment.*
- *uses deception only when there is no other way to answer the research question and only when the potential benefit of the experiment far exceeds any risk to the participants.*
- *ensures that participants feel free to withdraw from the experiment at any time without fear of penalty.*
- *removes any harmful consequences resulting from the experiment, including long-term consequences.*
- *maintains confidentiality regarding information about participants acquired during the course of the experiment.*

# ETHICS IN RESEARCH WITH ANIMALS

Although the majority of research in contemporary psychology focuses on humans, there are an appreciable number of studies that focus on animals (Miller, 1985); hence, ethical issues specific to animal participants should be discussed. Animals are often used to answer questions that would be impossible or impractical to answer by using human beings. Some people believe, however, that animals should not be used in various kinds of research (Bowd, 1980). For example, Rollin (1985) has argued that if the concept of legal and moral rights can be applied to human research, it can also be applied in the same way to animal research. He suggested that the status of research with animals needs to be elevated to that of human subjects, with many of the same rules that currently govern human research applied to animals. Recently, many reports in the media have discussed the purported mistreatment of laboratory animals and the attempts of animal-rights advocates to limit the use of animals in research. Therefore, a consideration of why animals are used in research is important, and an understanding of the ethical safeguards for animals is necessary.

Animals are often the subjects of research because they are interesting and because they form an important part of the natural world. The number of bird-watchers and other amateur naturalists, as well as the numerous comparative psychologists and ethologists, readily attest to the interest. More important in terms of ethical concerns, however, is that animals serve as convenient, highly controlled models for humans *and* other animals.

Ethics prohibit experimentally induced brain damage in human beings, preclude deliberate separation of a human infant from its parents, forbid testing of unknown drugs on human beings, and generally exclude dangerous and irreversible manipulations on human beings. Animal-rights advocates believe that research on animals should have the same prohibitions. According to the animal-rights advocates, researchers need to uphold the rights of both human beings and animals because, for example, they believe that experimental destruction of a monkey's brain is as ethically reprehensible as the destruction of the brain of a human being. Three points summarize the animal-rights advocates' position: (1) animals feel pain and their lives can be destroyed, as is true of humans (Roberts, 1971); (2) destroying or harming any living thing is dehumanizing to the human scientist (Roberts, 1971); and (3) claims about scientific progress being helped by animal research are a form of racism, called **speciesism,** by Singer (1978), and, like interracial bigotry, are completely unwarranted and unethical. Most experimental psychologists, especially psychobiologists, have strong reservations about the validity of these points. Let us consider each in turn.

The first point is that animals feel pain and suffering. Certainly, this is true, but ethical standards exist in all scientific disciplines that use animals as research subjects. A major portion of these principles concerns the proscription of undue pain and inhumane treatment. No ethical psychologist would deliberately mistreat research animals, nor would an ethical psychologist deliberately inflict undue harm on an animal. When pain and suffering are inflicted on an animal, it is only after considerable deliberation by the scientist and the appropriate ethics review boards. Such deliberations weigh the suffering of the animal against the potential benefits of the experiment. Only when the benefits far exceed the harm is the experiment approved and conducted. Finally, an important point to make about behavioral research on animals is that much of it does not involve pain or physical harm to the animals being studied.

The second plank of the animals-rights platform is that the destruction of any living thing is dehumanizing to the human scientist. Presumably, plants are not meant to be included here, for as human beings, we must destroy plants to survive, if not animals. Even if this proscription against killing living things is limited to animals, it has a number of serious implications beyond eliminating animal research. If one uses this argument against animal research, then one should not eat meat of any kind. Likewise, one should not use any products derived from the destruction of animals (e.g., leather). Finally, if the destruction of animals is dehumanizing, then is it not also dehumanizing to benefit from the destruction of animals? If so, then a true believer in animal rights should forsake most of the wonders of modern medicine because virtually all of it benefited from animal research. The animal-rights position on the sanctity of animal life is a matter of belief, not an arguable point. Nevertheless, to avoid hypocrisy, this belief should be followed consistently and not applied exclusively to the case against animal research.

Finally, there is the charge that scientific progress at the expense of animals is simply speciesism, the belief that the sacrifice of members of other species is justified if our species is benefited. As a criticism against animal research, this argument ignores the fact that a significant amount of animal research benefits the welfare of animals. For example, Miller (1985) points out that research on learned taste aversion in rats has led to new, nonlethal means of keeping coyotes away from sheep and crows away from crops. Similarly, research on how hatchling ducks imprint on human caretakers has been used to better prepare artificially incubated condor chicks for the wild.

In any case, even if using animals for the benefit of human beings is a form of speciesism, it is doubtful that many people would give up the benefits already achieved or even give up the possible future benefits to be derived from animal research. Consider this quote from Robert J. White, an eminent neuroscientist and neurosurgeon, who conducted research on monkeys that involved removing the brain of the animal: "As I write this article, I relive my vivid experiences yesterday when I removed at operation a large tumor from the cerebellum and brain stem of a small child. This was a surgical undertaking that would have been impossible a few decades ago, highly dangerous a few years ago, but is today thanks to extensive experimentation on the brains of lower animals, routinely accomplished with a high degree of safety" (1971, p. 504).

Aside from such clear benefits of experimental surgery on animals, there are numerous benefits derived from behavioral research with animals. Miller (1985) points out that psychological experiments with animals have led directly to benefits in the treatment of such diverse psychological problems as bed-wetting, phobias, compulsive disorders such as anorexia nervosa, and depression. Moreover, animal experiments have given rise to behavioral technologies such as biofeedback that have been used to help individuals with neuromuscular disorders regain control over their bodies. Psychological research with animals has also demonstrated experimentally the link between psychological stress and physical health. Similarly, it has demonstrated that the detrimental effects of physically separating an infant from its parents—as is necessary when a newborn must be placed in an incubator to sustain its life—can be largely reversed simply by stroking the infant during three 15-minute periods during the day. Miller describes a variety of other benefits that have arisen from behavioral research on animals, his point being that the benefits of psychological experimentation on animals are substantial, contrary to the claims made by some animal-rights activists.

Gallup and Suarez (1985) reviewed the rationale, extent, and use of animals in psychological research. They considered the possible alternatives and concluded that in many cases there is no viable alternative to the use of animals in psychological research.

The American Psychological Association (1981a) has provided guidelines governing animal research. As a general principle,

> An investigator of animal behavior strives to advance understanding of basic behavioral principles and/or to contribute to the improvement of human health and welfare. In seeking these ends, the investigator ensures the welfare of animals and treats them humanely. Laws and regulations notwithstanding, an animal's immediate protection depends upon the scientist's own conscience.

As in virtually any human enterprise, abuses sometimes occur in the use of animals in research. It would be erroneous, however, to consider these abuses to be the standard practice of animal researchers. Ethical researchers treat animals humanely. When unethical treatment of animals is uncovered, the researchers in question should be punished accordingly. It does not follow, however, that because abuses occur, animal research should be prohibited. To be fair, animals-rights activists do not use this argument against animal research. Rather, their objection is based on a philosophical position, and this position prohibits the use of animals for human benefit as a general rule, not just where research is concerned. You must decide for yourself what attitude to take toward animal research, but the importance of the issue necessitates that you critically consider each side of the debate and its implications.

The five primary considerations for researchers using animal subjects are listed below.

1. The acquisition, care, use, and disposal of all animals are in compliance with current federal, state or provincial, and local laws and regulations.

2. A psychologist trained in research methods and experienced in the care of laboratory animals closely supervises all procedures involving animals and is responsible for ensuring appropriate consideration of their comfort, health, and humane treatment.

3. Psychologists ensure that all individuals using animals under their supervision have received explicit instruction in experimental methods and in the care, maintenance, and handling of the species being used. Responsibilities and activities of individuals participating in a research project are consistent with their respective competencies.

4. Psychologists make every effort to minimize discomfort, illness, and pain of animals. A procedure subjecting animals to pain, stress, or privation is used only when an alternative procedure is unavailable and the goal is justified by its prospective scientific, educational, or applied value. Surgical procedures are performed under appropriate anesthesia;

techniques to avoid infection and minimize pain are followed during and after surgery.

5. When it is appropriate that the animal's life be terminated, it is done rapidly and painlessly.

The above guidelines were designed for experienced researchers. The APA (1981b) has also provided guidelines for the student researcher, which follow.

## Guidelines for the Use of Animals in School Science Behavior Projects

1. In the selection of science behavior projects, students should be urged to select animals that are small and easy to maintain as subjects for research.

2. All projects *must* be preplanned and conducted with humane considerations and respect for animal life. Projects intended for science fair exhibition must comply with these guidelines as well as with additional requirements of the sponsor.

3. Each student undertaking a school science project using animals *must have a qualified supervisor.* Such a supervisor shall be a person who has had training and experience in the proper care of the species and the research techniques to be used in the project. The supervisor *must* assume the primary responsibility for all conditions of the project and must ensure that the student is trained in the care and handling of the animals as well as in the methods to be used.

4. The student shall do relevant reading about previous work in the area. The student's specific purpose, plan of action, justification of the methodology, and anticipated outcome for the science project shall be submitted to and approved by a qualified person. Teachers shall maintain these on file for future reference.

5. No student shall inflict pain, severe deprivation, or high stress levels or use invasive procedures such as surgery, the administration of drugs, ionizing radiation, or toxic agents *unless* facilities are suitable both for the study and for the care and housing of the animals and *unless* the research is carried out under the extremely close and rigorous supervision of a person with training in the specific area of study. These projects must be conducted in accordance with the APA *Principles for the Care and Use of Animals.*

6. Students, teachers, and supervisors *must* be cognizant of current federal and state legislation and guidelines for specific care and handling of their animals (e.g., the Animal Welfare Act). Copies of humane laws are available from local or national humane organizations. A recommended reference is the *Guide for the Care and Use of Laboratory Animals,* available from the Superintendent of Documents, U.S. Government Printing Office, Washington, D.C. 20402, Stock Number 017-040-00427-3.

7. The basic daily needs of each animal shall be of prime concern. Students *must* ensure the proper housing, food, water, exercise, cleanliness, and gentle handling of their animals. Special arrangements *must* be made for care during weekends, holidays, and vacations. Students must protect their animals from sources of disturbance or harm, including teasing by other students.

8. When the research project has been completed, the supervisor is responsible for proper disposition of the animals. If it is appropriate that the animal's life be ter-

minated, it shall be rapid and painless. *Under no circumstances should students be allowed to experiment with such procedures.*

9. Teachers and students are encouraged to consult with the Committee on Animal Research and Experimentation of the American Psychological Association for advice on adherence to the guidelines. In cases where facilities for advanced research by qualified students are not available, the Committee on Animal Research and Experimentation will try to make suitable arrangements for the students.

10. A copy of these guidelines shall be posted conspicuously wherever animals are kept and projects carried out, including displays at science fairs.

Both sets of guidelines emphasize decent care and treatment. Both also mention additional regulations. Before using animal subjects, you should understand the contents of both sets of guidelines, and you should become familiar with relevant state and local humane regulations. *An ethical psychologist does not mistreat animal subjects, nor does an ethical psychologist submit animal subjects to undue pain or harm.*

## CONCEPT SUMMARY

When deciding whether to engage in research with animals, you should consider
- *whether you accept the proposal that animals deserve to be treated as equivalent to humans and the full implications of this philosophical position.*

When conducting research with animal subjects, an ethical researcher
- *ensures that the research is supervised by a trained psychologist.*
- *subjects animals to pain or discomfort only when no alternative procedure is available and the knowledge to be gained justifies the suffering of the animal.*
- *makes every effort to minimize any pain or discomfort associated with the experiment.*

## ETHICS IN DRUG RESEARCH

The APA guidelines for the use of drugs in research involving both humans and animals are printed below. The primary purpose for reprinting these guidelines is to discourage most undergraduate research on drugs, especially projects using human beings. Special government permits are required for research with controlled substances (including marijuana), and most student projects neglect to include appropriate **aftercare** for their human participants. You are responsible for accidents, antisocial behavior, and worse yet, addiction that could result from an experimentally induced high. If you are compelled to engage in drug research, use animals as your subjects and use legal substances. If you do, be sure that you understand the following rules as well as the other legal documents that are mentioned therein.

## APA Guidelines for Psychologists on the Use of Drugs in Research

General Principle: A psychologist or psychology student who performs research involving the use of drugs shall have adequate knowledge and experience of each drug's action or shall work in collaboration with or under the supervision of a qualified researcher. Any psychologist or psychology student doing research with drugs must comply with the procedural guidelines below. Any supervisor or collaborator has the responsibility to see that the individual he supervises or collaborates with complies with the procedural guidelines.

### Definition of a Qualified Researcher

1. A qualified researcher possesses a Ph.D. degree based in part upon a dissertation that is experimental in nature and in part upon training in psychology, pharmacology, physiology, and related areas, and that is conferred by a graduate school of recognized standing (listed by the United States Office of Education as having been accredited by a recognized regional or national accrediting organization).

2. A qualified researcher has demonstrated competence as defined by research involving the use of drugs which has been published in scientific journals; or continuing education; or equivalent experience ensuring that the researcher has adequate knowledge of the drugs, their actions, and of experimental design.

### Definition of a Drug

In these Guidelines, the term drug includes (a) all substances as defined by the term drug in the "Federal Food, Drug, and Cosmetic Act" (21 USC 321) and (b) all substances, Schedules I–V, as listed in the "Comprehensive Drug Abuse Prevention and Control Act of 1970" (21 USC 812; PL 91-513, Sec. 202) in its present form or as amended (Federal Food, Drug and Cosmetic Act, 21 USC, Sec. 201 (g), Appendix A). Copies of these acts are available from the Superintendent of Documents, United States Government Printing Office, Washington, DC 20402.

### Procedural Guidelines

1. All drugs must be legally obtained and used under conditions specified by state and federal laws. Information concerning these laws should be obtained from federal or state authorities.

2. Proper precautions must be taken so that drugs and drug paraphernalia that are potentially harmful are available only to authorized personnel. All such drugs used in experiments should be kept in locked cabinets and under any additional security prescribed by law.

3. All individuals using or supervising the use of drugs in research must be familiar with PL 91-513, the "Comprehensive Drug Abuse Prevention and Control Act of 1970," and its implementing regulations as well as all amendments to the act and other drug laws relevant to their research.

4. The use of drugs must be justified scientifically.

5. All individuals using or supervising the use of drugs in research must familiarize themselves with available information concerning the mode of action, toxicity, and methods of administration of the drugs they are using.

6. In any experiment involving animals, the welfare of the animal should be considered as specified in APA's "Precautions and Standards for the Care and Use of Animals."

7. Research involving human subjects is governed by additional guidelines as set forth in APA's "Ethical Standards for Psychological Research."

8. The present Guidelines should be brought to the attention of all individuals conducting research with drugs.

9. The present Guidelines should be posted conspicuously in every laboratory in which psychologists use drugs.

Source: American Psychological Association Ad Hoc Committee on Guidelines for the Use of Drugs and Other Chemical Agents in Research. From *American Psychologist*, Vol 27, 1972. Copyright 1972 by the American Psychological Association. Reprinted by permission of the publisher.

## MONITORING ETHICAL PRACTICES

The American Psychological Association provides ethical guidelines for psychological research. Acceptance of membership in the Association commits the member to adherence to these principles. The principles are also intended for nonmembers, including students of psychology and others who work on psychological research under the supervision of a psychologist.

The American Psychological Association established an Ethics Committee that fulfills a number of purposes. Through publications, educational meetings, and convention activities, the Ethics Committee educates psychologists and the public about ethical issues related to psychological research. The committee also investigates and adjudicates complaints concerning unethical research practices. Examples of these cases can be found in an APA (1987) publication titled, *Casebook on ethical issues*. The Ethics Committee also publishes an annual report in *American Psychologist*.

In addition to the ethical guidelines established by APA, any institution that receives money from the federal government—which means virtually every U.S. institution that engages in research—must have an **Institutional Review Board (IRB)** that oversees the protection of human subjects and an Institutional Animal Care and Use Committee that oversees the protection of animal subjects. All experiments must be approved by the members of these committees. Federal regulations require that each IRB have at least five members who are qualified to review the kind of research typically conducted within the institution. Furthermore, if an IRB regularly reviews research involving vulnerable individuals (e.g., children, prisoners, the mentally disabled), the committee should include at least one member whose area of expertise deals with such individuals. There must be at least one member whose primary concern is in a scientific area and one member whose primary concern is in a nonscientific area. There must also be someone on the committee, usually an attorney, who can ascertain whether proposed research violates any laws or federal regulations. Finally, regulations require that at least one member of the committee be otherwise free from affiliation with the institution. This diversity in membership helps to ensure that the rights of individuals participating in research are protected.

How does an IRB make its decision regarding the ethicality of a particular research project? First, there is an assessment of the level of risk involved in the procedure. Many psychological experiments are classified as involving only "minimal risk." Minimal risk means that the experimental procedures involve no greater risk than is associated with daily activities. If greater than minimal risk is deemed necessary for research purposes, then the IRB must decide if these risks are reasonable in relation to the benefits that would be gained from the research. The IRB also ensures that participants are fully informed prior to the experiment and that their safety and confidentiality are safeguarded.

An acquaintance with the institutional review process should help to reassure you that ethical research in psychology, and in other sciences, is the rule, not the exception. Because of safeguards built into the structure of research institutions, scientists cannot simply rely solely on their own judgment to protect the humans and animals participating in their experiments.

## SUMMARY

1. An ethical investigator protects the welfare of research participants by following the ethical standards of the American Psychological Association.

2. Informing the participant about the experiment prior to participation and minimal use of deception on the part of the investigator allow the participant to make a reasoned judgment about whether to participate.

3. The participant has the right to decline to serve in an experiment or to withdraw from an experiment at any time.

4. In an ethical investigation, the participant is protected from physical and mental harm.

5. After the data have been collected, participants should be carefully debriefed to remove any misconceptions that may have arisen.

6. Any harmful consequences resulting from an experiment should be removed by the investigator.

7. Unless the participant otherwise agrees, information relating to his or her participation is confidential.

8. Attempts to uphold ethical principles sometimes lead to a dilemma in that adherence to one principle may violate another.

9. When animal subjects are used, care should be taken to minimize their pain and discomfort.

10. Research with drugs poses special welfare problems, especially those concerned with the aftercare of participants.

### Key Concepts

| | |
|---|---|
| aftercare | informed consent |
| confidentiality | Institutional Review Board |
| debriefing | protection from harm |
| deception | removing harmful consequences |
| freedom to withdraw | speciesism |

## Exercises

Reconsider the ethical principles presented in this chapter and read the list of ethical principles published by American Psychologist Association (1981, 1987).

1. Read selections from the *Casebook on Ethical Issues* published by the American Psychological Association (1987), which is probably available in your library. This book describes the background of different ethical complaints, how the complaints came to be sent to the Ethics Committee, and how the cases were adjudicated. Select two cases and consider the ethical principles involved in the case. Describe why you agree or disagree with the adjudication of the Ethics Committee.

2. Read two of the articles listed below. These articles describe the ethical issues associated with different types of psychological research. Consider the general ethical principles that apply in both cases. Describe how the ethical issues differ between the two types of research discussed in the articles.

## Suggested Readings

Bowd, A. D. (1980). Ethical reservations about psychological research with animals. *Psychological Record, 30,* 201–210.

Devenport, L. D., & Devenport, J. A. (1990). The laboratory animal dilemma: A solution in our backyards. *Psychological Science, 1,* 215–216.

Hoff, C. (1980). Immoral and moral uses of animals. *New England Journal of Medicine, 302,* 115–118.

Imber, S. D., Glanz, L. M., Elkin, I., Sotsky, S. M., Boyer, J. L., & Leber, W. R. (1986). Ethical issues in psychotherapy research: Problems in a collaborative clinical study. *American Psychologist, 41,* 137–146.

Melton, G., & Gray, J. (1988). Ethical dilemmas in AIDS research: Individual privacy and public health. *American Psychologist, 43,* 60–64.

Milgram, S. (1977). Ethical issues in the study of obedience. In S. Milgram (Ed.), *The individual in a social world* (pp. 188–199). Reading, MA: Addison-Wesley.

Miller, N. E. (1985). The value of behavioral research on animals. *American Psychologist, 40,* 423–440.

Scarr, S. (1988). Race and gender as psychological variables: Social and ethical issues. *American Psychologist, 43,* 56–59.

Sieber, J. E., & Stanley, B. (1988). Ethical and professional dimensions of socially sensitive research. *American Psychologist, 43,* 49–55.

Smith, C. P. (1983). Ethical issues: Research on deception, informed consent, and debriefing. In L. Wheeler & P. Shaver (Eds.), *Review of personality and social psychology* (Vol. 4, pp. 297–328). Beverly Hills, CA: Sage.

## RESEARCH REPORTS
How to read and write them

| | | |
|---|---|---|
| **What to Look for in the . . .** | *Abstract:* | What was done to whom, and what was found |
| | *Introduction:* | What the author proposes; the hypotheses tested |
| | *Method:* | Dependent, independent, subject, and control variables; does the method test the hypothesis? |
| | *Results:* | Do the results support or reject the hypothesis? |
| | *Discussion:* | What conclusions are stated? |
| | *References:* | Other reports you might read: Are citations complete? |
| **What to Include in the . . .** | *Abstract:* | What you did to whom and what you found |
| | *Introduction:* | Why are you doing this research; the hypothesis you are testing |
| | *Method:* | A description of all variables; enough detail so that someone else can repeat your project |
| | *Results:* | Tables and/or figures that summarize your results, point the reader to the most pertinent data |
| | *Discussion:* | State how your results relate to the hypotheses tested; include relevant inferences and conclusions |
| | *References:* | All references cited in your paper belong here |

# READING AND
# WRITING RESEARCH REPORTS

Unless you read articles in journals of psychology, you may have difficulty understanding psychological research. The database associated with a particular problem
area resides in journals. Thus, to understand those data, you will need to be able
to comprehend the research reports. The first section of this chapter explains the
format and style of articles and gives you some hints to help you become a critical
reader. Because you will probably have to report the results of your own research,
the second part of this chapter deals with writing a research report.

## HOW TO READ A JOURNAL ARTICLE

Trying to read a psychology journal article for the first time can be a challenging
experience. Researchers write articles for other researchers; consequently, they
use jargon and a terse writing style. These features aid communication among
scholars in a particular field because they can read short reports and understand
them, but this style of writing can be difficult to comprehend for students
beginning their study of a field. This chapter will prepare you for your first
encounter with the psychological literature in two ways. First, the format and
style most often used in journal articles will be explained so that you will know
what to expect in each section of an article. Second, hints will be provided to
help you become a critical reader, skilled at objectively evaluating an article.
The chapter ends with some recommendations for writing a research report.

### The Parts of an Article

The format of journal articles in psychology is governed by the *Publication
Manual of the American Psychological Association*, which was revised in 1983.
This manual is well worth reading, especially when you start to write your own
research reports. The **APA format** for a typical psychology article consists of
seven parts: title and author(s), abstract, introduction, method, results, discussion, and references. The main purpose and content of each section are
summarized below.

**Title and Author(s).**  The **title** gives you an idea of the contents of an article. Because titles must be short, the most common type of title states only the dependent and independent variables—for example, "Rate of bar pressing as a function of quality and quantity of food reward." Although this title is not particularly appealing, it conveys important information.

As you continue to gain knowledge in a particular content area, you will become familiar with many researchers. You may start to pay attention to the authors first; after you have read several articles published by the same author, you will grow in understanding of that writer's viewpoints and how they differ from those of other researchers. Thus, just knowing the **author** of an article will give you some clue as to what kind of information it contains.

So many psychology articles are published each month that no one has the time to read all of them. Each issue of a journal has a table of contents listing the titles and authors of the articles published in that issue. The table of contents is a first step in selecting those articles relevant to your own interests. But an even better decision can be made by consulting the abstract and the references of an article.

**Abstract.**  The **abstract** is a short paragraph (100 to 150 words) that summarizes the key points of an article. According to the *Publication Manual of the American Psychological Association* (1983), it should be "accurate, succinct, quickly comprehensible, and informative" (p. 24). The abstract is the best way to discover quickly what an article is about. If you are new to an area, you can use the abstract to decide if a particular article warrants further reading. As you gain experience and become familiar with authors in the field, you will want to consult the references as well before making this decision.

**References.**  **References** are found at the end of the article. In contrast to journals in other disciplines, psychology journals list full titles of reference articles. This practice helps to inform the reader as to what the article is about. Furthermore, the references are valuable as a guide for related information. They can also be used as an index of the merit of the article. Articles should refer to the most recently published works in the area, as well as to the most important previous publications. The *Social Science Citation Index* (available in most university libraries) is a useful source of additional references (see chapter 1).

**Introduction.**  The **introduction** specifies the problem to be studied and tells why it is important. The purpose of the research should be clearly stated, and, as is usually the case, if any hypotheses are being tested, these should be specified, and the rationale behind any predictions should be given.

Research does not occur in a vacuum: There are many other articles that report research related to the one you are reading. One of the roles of the introduction is to illustrate the connection between the present research and past work on the same topic. Sometimes, the relation to previous research is so strong that it may be necessary to read some of the other articles in order to fully understand the one you are currently reading. For this reason, the introduction will contain short references to these other articles, such as *Brown (1979) found* . . . or *It has been argued that* . . . (*Brown, 1979*). These statements refer to the author of another research article and to the year in which it was published. The complete reference to the research is found in the reference section at the end of the article.

**Method.** The **method** section describes in detail the operations performed by the experimenter. It is usually printed in smaller type to conserve space, but this should not mislead you into believing that it is an unimportant section to be quickly skimmed over. On the contrary, the method section describes exactly what the experimenter did; this description should be explicit enough so that another researcher could replicate the experiment.

It is customary to divide the method section into different subsections that describe subjects, apparatus, and procedure. The **subjects** section tells how many subjects there were, how they were selected (e.g., randomly, haphazardly, only the investigator's relatives, etc.) and who they were (e.g., college under-graduates taking introductory psychology, individuals who had suffered from a specific type of brain injury, a particular strain of rats purchased from a supply house). The **apparatus** section describes any equipment used to test the subjects (e.g., the model number of a computer or the size of the conditioning chamber). In place of an apparatus section, authors will sometimes have a section called *materials* in which they describe such things as the details of a novel set of stimuli or a new personality test. The **procedure** section explains what happened to the subjects and includes instructions (for human subjects). The procedure usually includes statistical design features such as randomization or counter-balancing; however, these features are sometimes described in a separate *design* section.

**Results.** The **results** section tells what happened in the experiment. It is un-usual to find raw data or individual scores reported in a journal article; instead, descriptive statistics such as means and standard deviations are presented that summarize the data. Inferential statistics present the probability that the ob-served differences between the various experimental conditions are merely the result of random, or chance, factors. This information helps the reader to decide whether to believe the data (see appendix B for further explanation and review).

Either **tables** or graphs may be used to describe and summarize data. It is often helpful to draw a graph for yourself from the tabular data. If an article contains several **figures,** check that the scales are comparable so that effects can be easily compared across different figures. The way a graph is drawn can be misleading, as the following example illustrates (also, see chapter 4).

Imagine that a psychologist is interested in how people perceive written English words. Either a word or a nonword—letters that follow the pattern of written English but do not spell a real word, e.g., nale—is presented visually. The participants must press one button if it is a word or press a different button if it is a nonword. This is called a lexical decision. In another condition, the participant must pronounce the word or nonword when it is presented. This is called naming. An experiment to compare naming and lexical decisions was conducted by Frost, Katz, and Bentin (1987). Their results showed how long it took people to respond to high-frequency English words and nonwords.

We have replotted their data in figure 13–1. At first glance, the two panels look quite different. Examining panel (a), we might conclude that naming and lexical decisions are quite similar. From panel (b), on the other hand, we might

FIGURE 13–1(a)

FIGURE 13–1(b)

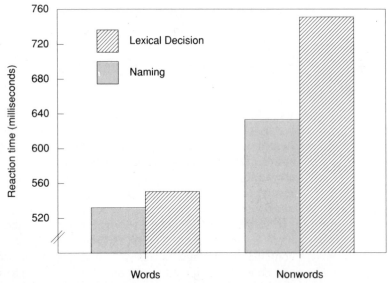

Exaggerated scales. Exactly the same data are presented in the two panels of figure 13–1, but the scale in panel (a) is in seconds and that in panel (b) is in milliseconds (with a scale break indicated, too). Thus the differences appear very small in (a) and very large in (b).

conclude not only that naming is faster, but also that the difference between words and nonwords is greater for lexical decision than for naming. Actually, the same data are presented in both panels. The trick is that the vertical scales are plotted differently. One panel has reaction time (the time between the visual presentation and the participant's response) measured in seconds whereas the other plots reaction time in milliseconds. Because a millisecond is one one-thousandth of a second, the two graphs appear to be different. Also, the scale is "broken" in panel (b), so that measures begin at 520 milliseconds, which further dramatizes the difference. Clearly, the way a graph is drawn can emphasize or conceal results.

But which way of graphing the results is right? In a sense, both are right because both can be argued to portray the data accurately. Nevertheless, if statistical tests indicate that a nonchance difference exists between the two measures, then the graph in panel (b) more accurately captures the relation between measures. This was the scale used by Frost, Katz, and Bentin (1987) to portray their results.

Inferential statistics permit the assessment of whether differences that appear in the results, as in panel (b), can be trusted as real and not due to chance factors. Inferential statistics about the data appear in statements such as "$F(4,60) = 2.03, p<.05$." All this means is that the probability of obtaining an $F$-statistic at least as large as 2.03 by chance is less than 1 in 20. In other words, there is a 5 percent chance that we are accepting differences as real when, in fact, they are merely chance differences. The level of risk one is willing to take in making such an error is set before the experiment is conducted. Any results that yield a probability estimate lower than this preset level are referred to as "significant." Used here, *significant* is a technical term meaning that the results are unlikely to have occurred by chance; it is not meant as a synonym for *important*.

In the results section, the author's specific choice of words is important. Beware of statements such as this: "Although the data just barely missed reaching the proposed level of significance, it appears that a trend in the predicted direction did occur." This kind of statement should be approached with caution for several reasons. First, the word *trend* is a technical term: Existence of a trend can be determined only by appropriate statistical tests. Second, it implies that results that are significant go beyond a trend—that is, they are true and utterly reliable—and that failure to reach a prescribed level only means that "truth" is latent rather than explicit. This implication is false: Even significant results are reliable only in a probabilistic sense—the results may still have occurred by chance.

**Discussion.** The **discussion** section usually includes a brief conceptual summary of the main results and then attempts to relate them to the hypotheses specified in the introduction. The author presents conclusions about the results and often offers a theoretical analysis of them. In the words of the APA publication manual (1983): "In the Discussion section, you are free to examine, interpret, and qualify the results, as well as to draw inferences from them" (p. 27). Authors are given enough rope to hang themselves in the discussion. Hence, although all parts of an article should be approached with caution, an extra degree of skepticism is required for discussion sections. It is for this reason that you should resist the temptation to merely read the discussion section to learn of the outcome of the experiment. The discussion provides the author's view of the results; consequently, evidence supporting the author's hypotheses may be emphasized, whereas problematic results may be downplayed. The author is within his or her rights to interpret the data in this way, but if you fail to read the method and results critically, you may blithely accept this biased view of the data rather than forming your own opinion.

## Exceptions to the Format

Some exceptions to the standard format are common. The exception you are most likely to encounter involves a combination of the results and discussion sections. Fortunately, such combinations are labeled "Results and Discussion." These combined sections often are found in short articles (such as those published in the *Bulletin of the Psychonomic Society*). Combined results and discussion sections are also found in articles that report more than one experiment; each study has its own results and discussion section. When more than one study is reported in an article, there is usually a final section devoted to interpretation of all the results. This last section is generally called "General Discussion" or "Conclusions."

## Order of Reading Sections

Most readers start at the beginning of an article and dutifully plod their way through to the references, except perhaps those who enjoy mystery novels and thus reverse the process. As you become more and more familiar with a research area, it becomes less necessary to follow the order of sections presented in journals. For example, if you are truly an expert in some area, merely reading the results section may be enough for you to infer the rest of the article. After you have read a few articles, do not be afraid to depart from the usual order.

# CHECKLIST FOR THE CRITICAL READER

In this section, we offer some hints to help you become a better consumer of the information presented in psychological journals. Our most important suggestion is that you avoid rushing through the article. Instead, you should stop after each section and write down the answers to the questions we list here. This will be difficult at first, but with practice the process becomes automatic and requires little extra time. We suggest that you write down the answers for several articles. Once you get into the habit of being an active, critical reader, you may omit written answers to all the questions. However, you should keep a written summary of the articles you read (on index cards or in a notebook). The purpose of these notes is to give you ready access to the database relevant to a particular problem. The questions listed here indicate some of the information that should be in your summaries. We have also included some suggestions from an article by M. Anisfeld (1987), which you might want to consult further for additional hints about how to read an empirical research paper critically.

## Introduction

1. *What is the author's goal?* The introduction explains the reasons behind the experiment. If one or more theories are related to the research, the

introduction gives the predictions derived from these theories. As with scientists in other areas, psychologists do not necessarily agree on the theoretical interpretations of data. An author may present several theories that provide a useful explanation of some behavior, but he or she will usually proceed later on to demonstrate that they are not equally successful in explaining the obtained results. Try to figure out which of the several theories the author believes and which are slated for subsequent rejection.

2. *What hypotheses will be tested in the experiment?* The answer to this should be obvious and stated directly in the introduction section.

3. *What assumptions does the author make?* To test hypotheses, it is often necessary to make certain assumptions about the participants' reactions to experimental manipulations. For instance, if a theory predicted that increasing the amount of rehearsal would improve memory and a researcher tested this prediction by allowing experimental participants more time to study, he or she would be assuming that allowing more time leads to increased rehearsal. The assumptions made by an author may often seem quite reasonable, but if you think the author has erred in his or her reasoning, you should treat the results with skepticism. You may want to conduct an experiment testing the validity of the assumption experimentally.

4. *If I had to design an experiment to test this hypothesis, what would I do?* This is the key question for the introduction. You must try to answer this *before* continuing on to the method section of the article. Remember that the writer is frequently biased. Experiments are often done within the context of a systematic investigation of behavior to test and support a particular theoretical framework developed by the author. If the author has any skill as a wordsmith, once you have finished the next section, you are likely to agree with the method that the author has advocated in the article. A clever author will plant the seeds to this answer in the introduction itself; this practice makes it harder for you to state a method independently. Write down the major ideas associated with your method of testing the hypothesis.

## Method

Compare your answer to question 4 with the author's. They probably will differ if you have not peeked. Now answer question 5a.

5a. *Is my proposed method better than the author's?* Regardless of who had the better method, you or the author, this forced comparison will make you think about the method section critically, instead of passively accepting it.

5b. *Does the method actually test the hypothesis?* The hypothesis is sometimes the first casualty, disappearing between the introduction and method sections. Always check that the method used is adequate and relevant to the hypothesis.

5c. *What are the independent, dependent, subject, and control variables?* This is an obvious question and can be answered quickly. Listing the variables helps you avoid passive reading of the method section. After you have resolved differences between your proposed method and the author's, answer the next question.

6. *Using the subjects, apparatus, and procedures described by the author, what results would I predict for the experiment?* You must answer this on your own before reading the results section. To help yourself, review the hypotheses and the independent and dependent variables. You may find it impossible to predict a single outcome. This is not really a problem because the author probably also had more than one prediction originally. He or she may have done some preliminary investigations to narrow down possible outcomes. The results may have been a surprise, forcing the author to rethink the introduction once the results were in. Draw a rough sketch illustrating the most likely outcomes you have predicted.

## Results

Compare the results with your predictions. If they are the same, go on to question 8. If not, answer question 7.

7. *Did the author get the "wrong" results?* After some thought, you will reach one of two conclusions: Either your predictions were wrong, or the results are hard to believe. Perhaps the method the author selected was inappropriate and did not adequately test the stated hypotheses, or it introduced uncontrolled sources of variance. Or perhaps the results would not be obtained again if the experiment were repeated. Keep in mind, however, that hard-to-believe results are sometimes true; it can be exciting to uncover a reliable phenomenon that runs counter to everyone's intuition because such enigmatic findings often lead to a new understanding of what is being studied.

8. *How would I interpret these results?* Try to answer this on your own, before reading the discussion. Carefully scrutinize the data presented in the text, tables, and graphs, and reorganize them in other ways that are meaningful to you. For example, you can retabulate data, or you can graph data that are presented in tables and text. Manipulating the data in this way can help you to generate alternative interpretations of the data, identify interesting results that the author overlooked, or find contradictory trends that the author would rather ignore. Look for biases in both the analysis and the interpretation of the results (Anisfeld, 1987).

## Discussion

Compare your interpretation with the author's. Answer question 9a or 9b, whichever is appropriate.

9a. *Why didn't I think of that?* Conducting experiments and collecting data are ongoing processes. The authors have sometimes already done further research on this topic, but they have not gotten around to reporting it. Furthermore, there is a lag between the date an experiment is completed and the date it is written up for publication. Therefore, in writing up the current work, scientists may already have gained a preview of the results of their next investigation, thereby allowing them to anticipate these findings in their current discussion section. In other words, do not be discouraged because their interpretation seems better than your own: They may know something that you do not.

9b. *Why didn't the author think of that?* Researchers sometimes miss points that, in retrospect, seem obvious. You may occasionally catch such a slip in a journal article. Nevertheless, do not be too hasty in pointing out flaws. Examine the logic of your argument carefully, and be certain that you did not miss any critical details. If you are right in your analysis, you may be able to use your critique as a springboard for a research project of your own.

## Checklist Summary

As you are reading your first article, try to write down the answers to all nine questions. It is hard work the first several times, so do not be discouraged. The following is a typical psychological article. It has been analyzed according to the checklist summarized in table 13–1.

## SAMPLE JOURNAL ARTICLE

In this section, we have reprinted a short article from the *Bulletin of the Psychonomic Society*. The answers to the checklist questions were distilled from answers given in one of the author's classes. Most of those students were college sophomores who had taken two courses in psychology. The article is about

---

**TABLE 13–1   QUESTIONS FOR CRITICAL READERS**

---

Introduction
1. What is the author's goal?
2. What hypotheses will be tested in the experiment?
3. What assumptions does the author make?
4. If I had to design an experiment to test this hypothesis, what would I do?
Method
5a. Is my proposed method better than the author's?
5b. Does the method actually test the hypothesis?
5c. What are the independent, dependent, subject, and control variables?
6. Using the subjects, apparatus, and procedures described by the author, what results would I predict for the experiment?
Results
7. Did the author get the "wrong" results?
8. How would I interpret these results?
Discussion
9a. Why didn't I think of that?
9b. Why didn't the author think of that?

---

experiments that have been interpreted as showing that a particular type of brain wave (alpha waves) can be conditioned in human subjects.

Most articles are written for experts in a particular area, so the authors of a report assume that their readers have some knowledge of the topic under investigation. In addition, most journals set page limitations on articles, which means that some information may be missing or presented very tersely. The assumptions made by the authors and the brevity of many articles pose a problem for the novice reader. The novice may have to read other articles or textbooks in order to understand a particular report. To help you understand the following report, we present some background information.

The article by Lindholm and Lowry (1978) is about learning to control a particular brain wave—the alpha wave. Alpha waves are prominent during meditation and relaxed wakefulness, and these waves are often associated with a pleasant emotional state that is called the alpha experience.

In a typical study about learning to control brain waves, the subject is connected to an electroencephalograph (EEG), a device that measures brain waves. The EEG is constructed so that it can provide a feedback signal to the subject when a particular brain wave, such as the alpha wave, is present. The feedback, usually a tone, is supposed to work as a reinforcer does in operant conditioning; that is, the feedback tells the subject when alpha is occurring. So, when the feedback is contingent on the appearance of alpha waves (feedback occurs only when alpha occurs), the alpha waves should occur more often than when feedback is noncontingent (the occurrence of feedback is unrelated to the occurrence of alpha). The logic here is precisely the same as that of reinforcing a hungry rat with food when the rat makes a particular response. If food is contingent on a particular response, then that response will increase in likelihood. If food is presented noncontingently with respect to that response, then it will not increase in likelihood.

Some earlier alpha-wave studies seemed to show that alpha would increase even when the feedback was noncontingent. Thus, Lindholm and Lowry wanted to examine the effects of false (noncontingent) feedback on alpha-wave production. If alpha waves increase when feedback is noncontingent, then we can conclude that something other than operant conditioning increases the frequency of alpha production.

Lindholm and Lowry also studied the effects of relaxation on the production of alpha. They do not detail the method of inducing relaxation, but we will. The procedure used was Jacobson's (1978) method of progressive relaxation. This technique involves training people to alternately tense and relax small groups of muscles until the entire body is in a state of relaxation. This progressive relaxation usually starts with the toes, works up through the legs, the torso, arms, neck, and finally the face.

The following report is brief. One question you might try to answer is: "Could I replicate this study on the basis of the information presented?"

---

## Alpha production in humans under conditions of false feedback

Ernest Lindholm and Steven Lowry
Arizona State University, Tempe, Arizona 85281

Subjects were pretrained in either Jacobson's relaxation or a control relaxation technique, then served in four daily sessions of biofeedback training. On some days, the feedback was veridical with respect to alpha production, while on other days, the feedback falsely indicated either success or failure at the control task. The results showed that alpha increased over trials, but this increase was independent of feedback contingency. Subjective reports of mood were not influenced by feedback falsely indicating success or failure at the control task, and there were no reliable relationships between mood and amount of alpha actually produced. Prior training on Jacobson's relaxation did not enhance alpha production. It is concluded that alpha production and positive mood states are not systematically related and that neither of these variables is operantly conditioned through biofeedback.

Brown (1970, 1971, 1974), Kamiya (1968, 1969) and others have reported that humans can learn to control their alpha production and that successful learning is accompanied by a variety of positive mood states (e.g., euphoria, well-being) collectively referred to as the "alpha experience." Others (e.g., Lynch, Paskewitz, & Orne, 1974) have argued that alpha production is not learned, that rather, subjects habituate to the strangeness of the experimental environment and over time, engage in fewer activities that tend to block alpha, such as visual fixation on objects in the room. Regarding mood states, Plotkin, Mazer, and Lowey (1976) found no relationship between mood and the amount of alpha produced, although they suggested the possibility that the subjects' perceived success or failure might influence subjective reports of mood; that is, subjects who thought they were successful might report more positive mood states than subjects who thought they were not successful at the control task.

The Lynch et al. (1974) position that alpha enhancement is not learned is questioned by the results of Brolund and Schallow (1976), who showed that combining feedback and reward led to greater alpha enhancement than feedback alone, suggesting that experimental contingencies were controlling the behavior (alpha production) to some reliable degree. Further, Lynch et al. (1974) employed a noncontingent feedback control in which the noncontingent feedback of one subject is a replay of the contingent feedback received by another. This may well be inappropriate for alpha learning experiments, since subjects do (by whatever means) increase alpha over trials, thus the replay of increasing density of feedback over trials might serve to fortuitously reinforce almost anything the control subject does which works in the direction of increasing alpha. This could introduce a bias in the direction of reducing group differences between contingent and noncontingent groups and obscure real differences between groups.

The other type of control group used in alpha experiments is the no-feedback control, which simply requires subjects to sit in a comfortable chair in a quiet room for the duration of the experiment (Browland & Schallow, 1976). The problem here is that these subjects receive less stimulation than subjects receiving feedback (contingent or otherwise) and thus might display enhanced alpha due to a movement toward a sleep or semisleep state. It appears, therefore, that while some argue that alpha enhancement is not a learned phenomenon, the lack of appropriate control groups detracts from the force of these arguments.

There appear to be four important questions that require evaluation before the worth of alpha conditioning experiments can be adequately evaluated: (1) Are alpha increases learned as a result of experimental contingencies? (2) Is the "alpha experience" closely related to the amount of alpha actually produced? (3) Is the intensity of the "alpha experience" influenced by the subject's perceived success or failure? (4) Is the amount of alpha produced and the intensity of the "alpha experience" influenced by the subject's ability to relax? There is an implicit assumption that alpha density and relaxation are closely related, yet this assumption has never been directly tested by manipulating relaxation as an independent variable.

**Question 1.** What is the author's goal? The authors argue that the results of research concerned with learning to control alpha waves are equivocal. Their goal seems to be to show that people cannot learn to control alpha waves.

**Question 2.** What hypotheses will be tested in the experiment? The hypotheses are listed as questions to be answered before one can accept alpha conditioning: (1) Does alpha increase because of the feedback provided? (2) What is the relation between the amount of alpha produced and the alpha experience? (3) What is the relation between the alpha experience and the subject's perceived failure or success? (4) What is the relation between the subject's ability to relax and the production of alpha (and the alpha experience)?

**Question 3.** What assumptions does the author make? The main assumption that the author makes is that the alpha experience is equivalent to a relaxed, positive mood. This assumption is necessary to measure the alpha experience. Without it, the second and third hypotheses could not be tested.

**Question 4.** If I had to design an experiment to test this hypothesis, what would I do? With respect to the first one, you could try to fool the subject in some way so that the feedback provided on the production of alpha is not correct. You could, for example, randomly present feedback to the subject— sometimes when alpha is being produced, and sometimes when it is not being produced. If alpha increases under random feedback, then it is not learned. With regard to the second hypothesis, you could correlate some measure of the subject's mood (the alpha experience) and the amount of alpha that is produced. For the third hypothesis, you could tell some subjects that they are doing well and compare their alpha production to that of subjects who are told that they are not doing well. One way to examine the final hypothesis would be to provide a relaxing atmosphere for some subjects and compare their alpha with the alpha of subjects who are trained in a more tense environment.

## Method

### Subjects

Ten male and 10 female subjects were solicited by advertisement to participate in an experiment in which they could learn self-relaxation techniques and control of brainwaves. All were members of psychology classes regularly offered at Arizona State University.

### Apparatus

Brain activity was recorded from occipital-occipital placements referenced to left mastoid using Grass silver disk electrodes and Grass electrode paste. Signals were amplified by a Beckman Type 411 dynograph, the high-level output of which was fed to the input of a DEC-LAB-8 computer that was programmed to detect alpha activity according to the following criteria: (1) There must be 1½ cycles of activity falling within the 8- to 12-Hz frequency band, and (2) the amplitude of the activity must exceed the Schmitt trigger threshold set for each subject during the baseline sessions. When both criteria were met, the computer software turned on the biofeedback display which consisted of a 61 × 61 cm sheet of milk-white Plexiglas located 61 cm from the subject's face and back-lighted by a 15-W ac bulb. The Plexiglas formed the face of a plywood box, thus providing a diffuse low-intensity glow that covered a large portion of the visual field and minimized focusing.

**Procedure**

Relaxation training. The 20 subjects were divided into two groups of 5 males and 5 females each. The subjects in the Jacobson's group received 3 h of relaxation training, as did the subjects in the control relaxation group; the latter were told only to listen to white noise played at a low intensity and to relax as best they could.

Biofeedback training. Four 54-min sessions of biofeedback training were employed. Subjects were told that each session investigated a different brainwave, and that recent research indicated that relaxation enhanced control of all brain-waves, thus they should use their prior relaxation training to keep the feedback light on as much as possible. This was deception. In fact, the four sessions operated as follows: Contingent Day 1 (CD1) was the first day of feedback for all subjects. Feedback was contingent on alpha production and this was true also for the fourth day (Contingent Day 4, abbreviated (CD4). Days 2 and 3 were either false increasing (FI) or false decreasing (FD) feedback, counterbalanced across subjects. Under FI, the feedback density started at low level and increased over trials while the reverse was true for the FD condition. To make the illusion of "real" feedback convincing, the amounts delivered on Days 2 and 3 were based on individual subject's Day 1 performance, and were programmed for delivery according to an unpredictable computerized schedule, the only constraint being that feedback increased and decreased over trials for the FI and FD groups, respectively. Thus, the amount of feedback presented to each individual subject was both a familiar and credible amount, referenced to his or her Day 1 performance. The rationale for this particular design was as follows: The first day must be contingent to establish baseline performance, and the last day should also be contingent to assess time-dependent changes in alpha production. The middle 2 days were FI and FD to assess perceived success on mood and also to determine whether feedback contingency was systematically related to alpha production.

---

**Question 5a.** Is my proposed method better than the authors'? Their methods are at least as good as ours, if not better.

**Question 5b.** Does the method actually test the hypothesis? Yes, the methods should test the four hypotheses. One problem that does exist is that all subjects receive contingent feedback on the first day. Although that procedure seems necessary to provide a baseline of alpha production, its effects could carry over throughout the next three days and mask the other manipulations. Nevertheless, the effects of false feedback on the second two days probably will not carry over because the order of presenting the two conditions was counterbalanced across subjects. Counterbalancing means that some subjects received false increasing feedback about their brain waves on the second day and decreasing feedback on the third day. The rest of the subjects received those conditions in the reversed order.

**Question 5c.** What are the independent, dependent, subject, and control variables? Independent variables: type of feedback, type of relaxation training, trials, and days. Dependent variables: amount of alpha and mood. It is not clear how or when mood will be assessed. Subject variables: gender. Control variables: amount of feedback on the false feedback days (determined by the subject's alpha level on the first day), session length, and the number of training days.

**Question 6.** Using the subjects, apparatus, and procedures described by the author, what results would I predict for the experiment? Given that previous studies have reported reliable alpha conditioning, we predict that increases in alpha will be observed only on the first and last days—that is, only when the feedback is contingent on alpha production. Furthermore, we expect that alpha will increase with increases in the alpha experience and with perceived success. We expect that the ability to relax will enhance alpha.

## Results and Discussion

The .95 confidence level was adopted throughout as indicating the presence of a reliable difference.

The percent alpha produced during all phases of the experiment are displayed in Figure 1. All functions superficially resemble "learning curves," since performance during Trial 4 was generally superior to performance during Trial 1. An ANOVA revealed main effects for trials and rest vs. feedback. The main effect for sessions approached the .05 level and was therefore further analyzed by comparing CD1 alone with CD2, as a test for extreme differences. This analysis also failed to detect reliable sessions differences. No other main effect or interaction approached significance in either ANOVA.

The interpretation of these results is straightforward: The Jacobson's relaxation and control relaxation groups behaved similarly throughout the experiment. Both displayed more alpha as a function of trials and both displayed more alpha during feedback than during rest periods. However, the amount of alpha produced was not affected by whether the feedback was veridical or false, demonstrating that alpha production was not under the control of the experimental contingencies. We also analyzed the data from the viewpoint of net alpha change, for example, alpha produced during each feedback period minus alpha produced during the preceding rest period. This "change score" produced functions (not shown) that varied in a nonsystematic manner and remained close to 0% change. An ANOVA in this case produced no main effects or interactions that approached reliability.

The mood scores (responses on the Mood Adjective Check List, MACL, Nowlis, 1965) were analyzed by ANOVA, Mann-Whitney U, and parametric and nonparametric correlational methods. None of these analyses even hinted at a reliable relationship among the variables of amount of alpha actually produced, subjective report of mood, prior exposure to relaxation training, or perceived success or failure on the control task. Differences attributable to sex of subject were sought in all of the above analyses, but none were found.

We purposely used visual feedback since the early positive reports of alpha conditioning used visual feedback while more recent, negative findings employed nonvisual feedback designs. Also, we designed control groups that we feel eliminated or circumvented the problems inherent in the control groups used by others. Additionally, we used a computerized system for detecting alpha activity that circumvented the "roll off" problems inherent in the "active filter" systems used by others. Finally, we gathered

**FIGURE 1**

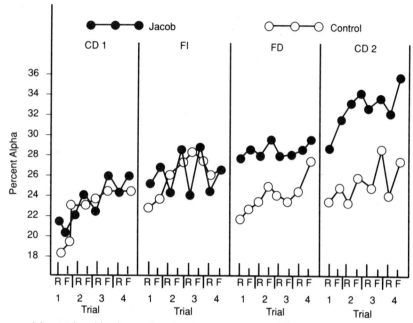

Percent alpha produced by the Jacobson's relaxation group (solid circles) and the control relaxation group (open circles) as a function of sessions and trials. Abbreviations: CD1 and CD2, Contingent Days 1 and 2, respectively; FI and FD, false increasing and false decreasing biofeedback, respectively. R and F, rest and feedback, respectively. The first R period in each session is the mean of the baseline recording period.

data on our subjects over a 4-day period (plus relaxation pretraining) which is longer than other published experiments. Nonetheless, there was no evidence that changes in alpha production were learned through operant conditioning, since the response (alpha production) was not under the control of reinforcement contingencies (biofeedback being veridical or false). We did replicate Brown's (1971) finding that alpha production is greater during feedback than during rest periods. While Brown interpreted this finding as evidence for alpha learning, we point out that feedback need not be contingent to produce this effect, and if alpha is considered to be change scores, no evidence for learning is apparent. Finally, the "alpha experience" appears to be nothing more than suggestibility; empirically, mood was not related to the amount of alpha produced nor to perceived success or failure.

## References

Brolund, J. W., & Schallow, J. R. (1976). The effects of reward on occipital alpha facilitation by biofeedback. *Psychophysiology,* **13,** 236–241.

Brown, B. B. (1970). Recognition of aspects of consciousness through association with EEG activity represented by a light signal. *Psychophysiology,* **6,** 442–452.

Brown, B. B. (1971). Awareness of EEG subjective activity relationships within a closed feedback system. *Psychophysiology,* **7,** 451–464.

Brown, B. B. (1974). *New mind, new body.* New York: Harper & Row.

Kamiya, J. (1968). Conscious control of brainwaves. *Psychology Today,* **1,** 57–60.

Kamiya, J. (1969). Operant control of the EEG alpha rhythm and some of its reported effects on consciousness. In C. Tart (Ed.), *Altered states of consciousness: A book of readings.* New York: Wiley.

Lynch, J. J., Paskewitz, D. A., & Orne, M. T. (1974). Some factors in the feedback control of human alpha rhythm. *Psychosomatic Medicine,* **36,** 399–410.

Nowlis, V. (1965). Research with the mood adjective check list. In S. S. Tomkins & C. E. Izard (Eds.), *Affect, cognition, and personality.* New York: Springer.

Plotkin, W. B., Mazer, C., & Lowey, D. (1976). Alpha enhancement and the likelihood of an alpha experience. *Psychophysiology,* **13,** 466–471.

(Received for publication November 9, 1977.)

---

**Question 7.** Did the author get the "wrong" results? The only prediction of ours that was correct concerned the positive effect of false increasing feedback on the amount of alpha. Nonetheless, this is a small victory because alpha also increased under false decreasing feedback. It looks as if the subjects who received real relaxation training did better on the last day or two than did the control subjects, but the authors report that there was no interaction between relaxation and sessions. This means that the effects of relaxation training did not differ reliably across sessions. "ANOVA" refers to "analysis of variance," a type of statistical test discussed in appendix B.

**Question 8.** How would I interpret these results? Subjects might have increased alpha because they wanted to. In other words, the important variable in an alpha conditioning study is not the relation between feedback and alpha production. Rather, subjects may perceive alpha waves as being desirable, and thus may have tried to have an alpha experience. Because most college students have heard about meditation and brain waves, these subjects may well have tried to relax in order to increase alpha. Furthermore, given that these subjects were introductory psychology students, it is likely that they know quite a bit about alpha waves and the alpha experience.

**Questions 9a and 9b.** Why didn't I think of that/why didn't the author think of that? The authors simply point out that the results are not owing to condition (alternative explanations are mentioned in the introduction). They also argue that the alpha experience is caused by suggestibility, which is somewhat similar to our interpretation of the condition results. The main difference between their explanation and ours is that they seem to be suggesting that because mood was unrelated to alpha production, there may be no such thing as an "alpha experience," whereas our explanation is based on the assumption that the alpha experience is real. The research reported in this article is really insufficient to decide which interpretation is more valid.

## WRITING A RESEARCH REPORT

You have gotten an idea, reviewed the pertinent literature, designed a procedure, collected your data, and analyzed the results. Your course may require a written record of your research. Even if it does not, you are obligated to publicize the results of a carefully done project. We believe that to maintain the self-correcting nature of science, it is important to publish good data. However, this does not mean that journals should be cluttered with information derived from every undergraduate project. If your research is promising, you will receive encouragement from your instructor.

In this section, we will review the format of a typical report and discuss some of the stylistic considerations that make up a comprehensible paper. If you follow our suggestions for reading articles, you will have a pretty good idea about the format of a research report, and you will probably have a good feel for technical writing style. Some aspects of technical writing are not too obvious, so we will discuss them here. What we present are general guidelines. If you need additional information, examine R. J. Sternberg's (1987) book, *The Psychologist's Companion* and D. J. Bem's (1987) chapter, "Writing the Empirical Journal Article." The 1983 revision of the *Publication Manual of the American Psychological Association* (third edition) will also help, because it is the official arbiter of style for almost all of the journals listed in chapter 1, as well as for many other journals in psychology and education.

## Format

The outline of a typical report in figure 13–2 emphasizes the sequence of pages you will have to put together in your APA-style manuscript. This version of the article is known as the *copy* manuscript and is assembled in a particular manner to facilitate the editorial and publication process. A run through that sequence will give you an idea of what you are supposed to include. Your cover page contains the title of your project, your name, and your affiliation (your institution or place of business). The short title that appears at the top of each page of the copy manuscript consists of the first few words of the title and is used to identify the manuscript during the editorial process only. The short title should not be confused with the **running head,** which will appear on each page of the *published* article. The running head is typed near the bottom of the cover page of the copy manuscript. The next page, page 2, contains the head "Abstract" and the abstract itself. On this page and on all subsequent ones (except the figures), you should have an abbreviated title and the page number of the top right-hand corner of the page. Page 3 repeats the whole title and includes your introductory material. Ordinarily, you do not have a heading for the introduction. After your introduction is finished, the method section begins. Note the format shown for the heading on page 4 in figure 13–2. The side headings, such as "Subjects" and "Apparatus," help guide the reader to pertinent information. The results section immediately follows the method. Do not include figures and tables in the body of this section; they come at the end of the report. Instead, indicate the approximate location of each figure as shown in page 5 of figure 13–2. Next comes the discussion, which ends the major textual portion of your report.

The references begin on a separate page. The format for presenting references is complex, and you should use care in preparing them. The article reprinted in this chapter contains most of the different styles of references that you will have to document. Look them over carefully, and, if you have any questions, ask your instructor. You might also study the APA manual and recent journal articles. Any author notes and footnotes appear on separate pages after the references. For most college laboratory reports, footnotes are not

**FIGURE 13–2**

Page sequence for a report in APA format.

necessary. When you prepare something for publication, you may acknowledge financial and intellectual support, which should appear on the author-note page. General acknowledgments are not numbered. Other, perhaps peripheral, information should appear as numbered footnotes on a separate footnote page, but such footnotes are generally discouraged.

If you presented any of your data in tables, these tables would directly follow the footnotes. Each table should appear on a separate page and be numbered consecutively, according to the order in which it was noted in the results section. Make the titles of your tables short but communicative. As with the figures, each table's approximate location should be indicated in the text by breaking the text and stating, "Insert Table 3 about here."

Although the title of each table appears on the same page as the table, the captions identifying and explaining each figure are typed on a separate page, numbered in consecutive order, following the order of their citation in the text. The figure captions page follows the last table. Finally, the figures themselves appear, each on a separate page. No extraneous writing, such as page numbers or short titles, should appear on the front of a figure page because, if published, the figure will be published as it appears on the page. Therefore, to identify these pages as belonging with the rest of manuscript, lightly write your name or the short title on the back of each figure page.

As mentioned before, copy manuscripts are organized in this fashion to accommodate the publisher. However, you should note that there is a special section in the APA publication manual about the accepted format for student papers submitted for a course requirement but not for publication. For example, in student papers, tables and figures may be interspersed in the text. You should check with your professor or department regarding the preferred format for class projects. However, we recommend learning the APA publication format because it provides good practice for preparing your future publications.

A sample manuscript appears on the following pages. You should note the sequence of pages, where typing begins on a new page, and what information is provided in each section. The only aspect missing from this manuscript that may appear in one of yours is a separate footnote page. Note carefully how the references are cited in the reference section.

Recognition of Facial Stimuli

1

Recognition of Facial Stimuli Following an Intervening

Task Involving the Identi-kit

Sara Elizabeth Comish

University of Alberta

Running head:   RECOGNITION OF FACIAL STIMULI

Recognition of Facial Stimuli

2

## Abstract

The Identi-kit is a tool for constructing a facial composite. The types of errors made on a recognition task, following an intervening task involving the Identi-kit, were examined in this study. One hundred and eight introductory psychology students viewed a target composite-face and made an Identi-kit reconstruction. Subsequently, they were required to identify the original composite-face from a lineup of six composite-faces. Subjects who made an Identi-kit reconstruction were prone to make more errors on the recognition task than participants in a control condition, $p < .01$. False alarms were promoted when the subjects saw a lineup containing foils modified to resemble the subjects' own reconstruction errors, $p < .05$. This finding suggests that memory for facial stimuli can be influenced by viewing misleading information.

Recognition of Facial Stimuli Following an Intervening

Task Involving the Identi-kit

There is a commonly held belief that memory for faces is immune to interference; this belief is expressed by the oft heard statement, "I never forget a face." Support for the role of interference in facial memory, however, can be found in experimental studies. Deffenbacher, Carr, and Leu (1981) found that individual's memory for photographs of faces was highly susceptible to retroactive interference, unlike their memory for nouns and objects, which was relatively immune to the interference. Loftus and Greene (1980) examined the extent to which facial memory was influenced by reading misleading descriptions of a previously shown target face. In a later recognition task with the target face absent, the majority of subjects who had read the misleading information picked a face with the misleading information. This finding raises the issue of whether facial memory can be altered by viewing misleading information.

A useful tool for studying this issue is the Identi-kit, a technique that consists of transparencies of line drawings of different facial features that can be superimposed on each other to make a composite-face. A similar system is the Photofit, which consists of actual photographs of features instead of line drawings. Studies that have used composite techniques to examine

Recognition of Facial Stimuli

4

interference in memory for faces have yielded conflicting results.

Mauldin and Laughery (1981) found that use of the Identi-kit to

construct a target face improved recognition of the same target

face in a later recognition task.  On the other hand, Davies,

Ellis, and Shepherd (1978) found different results.  They found a

trend in the opposite direction, which indicated that making a

Photofit reconstruction could interfere with later recognition of

a target face (although this difference failed to attain

statistical significance).  In both of these studies, subjects

viewed a target face and then made a composite reconstruction.

The recognition tasks that were used to assess memory involved

photograph lineups that were not altered to resemble subjects'

composite reconstructions.

It is reasonable to assume, however, that the source of any

interference from Identi-kit reconstruction may result from

viewing one's own errors in Identi-kit reconstruction as a

holistic face and that maximum interference can be expected when

the distractors used during the recognition task are similar to

the individual's errors in Identi-kit reconstruction.  The purpose

of this study was to determine the effect of an intervening task

involving misleading information on later recognition.  In order

to test this, subjects in two conditions made Identi-kit

reconstructions of a target composite-face.  The third condition

was a control condition in which subjects did not make an Identi-kit reconstruction.  For the subsequent recognition task, subjects saw a lineup consisting of the original target composite-face and five foils.  The subjects were yoked on the recognition task to allow for the determination of whether interference was a result of making Identi-kit reconstructions per se or if it occurred only when the distractor foils resembled the participants' own Identi-kit reconstruction errors.

## Method

### Subjects

One hundred and eight introductory psychology students participated in partial fulfillment of a course requirement. Thirty-six subjects were randomly assigned to each of the three conditions.

### Materials

The Identi-kit, available from Smith and Wesson, Inc., is a box containing transparencies of facial features.  It is accompanied by the Identi-kit Handbook, which is a pictorial index of the features available in the kit.

### Design and Procedure

A three-group design was employed.  In the Identi-kit/own-errors condition, subjects made an Identi-kit reconstruction of a target composite-face and, in a later recognition task, encountered foils modified to resemble the subjects' own Identi-kit reconstruction errors. Subjects in the Identi-kit/other-errors conditions also made an Identi-kit reconstruction but were yoked to a subject in the Identi-kit/own-errors condition so that the foils in the recognition task were those of a subject in the Identi-kit/own-errors condition. In the control/other-errors condition, subjects saw the target composite-face but did not make an Identi-kit reconstruction. They were also yoked so that the foils in the recognition task were those of a subject in the Identi-kit/own-errors condition.

Initially, all subjects viewed one of two target composite-faces -- photocopies of an Identi-kit reconstruction of either a man or a woman -- for 10 s until it was removed. Subjects in the Identi-kit/own-errors condition and the Identi-kit/other-errors condition then made an Identi-kit reconstruction that involved an initial choice of facial features from the Identi-kit Handbook. A composite face was made using these features and shown to the subjects, who were allowed to change any of the features. On average, the reconstruction process took 13 min. Following this, subjects performed a filler task in which they were given 7 min to rate two photograph faces on trait dimensions. In order to ensure that the time that elapsed between the initial exposure to the target composition-face and the recognition task was the same for subjects in all conditions, the subjects in the control/other-errors condition spent 20 min rating the two photograph faces.

Finally, the subjects performed the recognition task, in which they were asked to select the original composite-face from a lineup consisting of the original target composite-face and five distractors.  This task was not a forced choice and subjects were allowed to indicate that the target composite-face was not present in the lineup.  In the Identi-kit/own-errors condition, each distractor foil was the same as the original target composite-face except that one error from the individual's Identi-kit reconstruction was substituted for one feature of each distractor.  Thus, the first distractor was the same as the target except for the hair, the second distractor was the same as the target except for the nose, the third differed on the lips, the fourth differed on the eyes, and the fifth differed on the eyebrows (see Figure 1 for an example of a typical lineup). These distractor foils were photocopied and placed in a lineup, counterbalanced to vary the order of the target and the foils.  Using this technique the target appeared in each position six times in each condition, with the positions of the foils randomly determined.  Subjects in the Identi-kit/other-errors condition and control/other-errors condition saw the same lineup in the recognition task as the subject in the Identi-kit/own errors condition to whom they were yoked.

Recognition of Facial Stimuli

8

--------------------------

Insert Figure 1 about here

--------------------------

The data from an additional four participants in the Identi-kit/own-errors condition and from an additional three subjects in the Identi-kit yoked condition were not included in the analyses because one or more features in the Identi-kit reconstruction was identical to the original target composite-face. When the correct feature was selected for the Identi-kit reconstruction, it was not possible to modify the lineup distractor foils in the manner described previously. These subjects were replaced.

The dependent variable was scored as a <u>hit</u>, a <u>miss</u>, or a <u>false alarm</u>. A hit was a correct recognition of the original target composite-face; a miss was an incorrect "not present" decision; and a false alarm was an incorrect selection of a distractor foil. In addition, subjects' satisfaction with their reconstruction and the subjects' certainty with regard to their recognition were obtained on scales from <u>not at all satisfied</u> (1) to <u>totally satisfied</u> (7) and from <u>not at all certain</u> (1) to <u>totally certain</u> (7), respectively.

Results

All data were collapsed over the two target composite-faces and converted to percentages, which are presented by condition in Table 1. A one-way analysis of variance (ANOVA) across the three conditions was performed on the number of overall errors.  A significant difference was found for the overall number of recognition errors, $F(2, 105) = 4.86$, $p < .01$.  A Newman-Keuls comparison revealed that the control/other-errors condition produced significantly fewer errors than either of the Identi-kit reconstruction conditions.  The estimated $\omega^2$ was .065.

-------------------------

Insert Table 1 about here

-------------------------

A further one-way ANOVA was performed on the number of false alarms.  A significant difference was found among the conditions, $F(2, 105) = 4.46$, $p < .05$.  A Newman-Keuls comparison revealed that the Identi-kit/own-errors condition differed significantly from the other two conditions, demonstrating that when the foils resembled subjects' Identi-kit errors, subjects were more prone to incorrectly identify the modified foils.  In this case, the estimated $\omega^2$ was .059.

Although an ANOVA on the number of overall errors and on both of the types of errors is redundant -- because the two types of errors sum to give the number of overall errors -- the effect of Identi-kit use on the different types of errors is of particular interest in this study.  Therefore, an additional ANOVA was performed on the number of "not present" responses (misses). There was a significant different among the conditions, $F(2, 105)$

= 3.75, p < .05, and the Newman-Keuls comparison revealed that the subjects in the Identi-kit/other errors condition made significantly more "not present" responses than subjects in either the Identi-kit/own-errors condition or the control/other-errors condition.  The estimated $\omega^2$ was .047.

An ANOVA was performed on subjects' confidence ratings, and there were no significant differences among the conditions, $F(2, 105) = 1.46$, ns.  Wells and Lindsay (1985) have suggested that confidence ratings of "choosers only" (i.e., those subjects that make a recognition choice rather than those that indicate that the target composite-face was not present) should be analyzed separately to determine whether confidence ratings have predictive use.  No significant differences were found among the conditions when a one-way ANOVA was performed on the confidence ratings of "choosers only," $F(2, 89) = 0.422$, ns.  The low accuracy-confidence correlation, however, is consistent with previous eyewitness studies (see Wells & Murray, 1984).

A point-biserial correlation between confidence and accuracy was performed for "choosers only" by condition and was not significant, highest $r = -.221$.  Further, it was not significant when performed on the data of all subjects, highest $r = -.24$.  A point-biserial correlation between subjects' satisfaction with their Identi-kit reconstruction and accuracy of recognition was also not significant for all subjects ratings nor was it

significant when the analysis was performed on "choosers only,"
highest $r$ = -.27.

### Discussion

The use of the Identi-kit itself promotes overall errors on
the recognition task.  The lineup foils in this study were
modified by only one feature to resemble the Identi-kit
reconstructions.  This was sufficient, however, to bias people in
favor of foils that resembled their own Identi-kit
reconstructions.  When the lineup foils resemble people's own
Identi-kit reconstructions, the errors that are promoted are false
alarms to composite-faces that resemble their Identi-kit
reconstructions.  Errors are promoted even when the composite-
faces in the lineup are not similar to the subject's original
Identi-kit reconstruction.  In these cases, the predominant errors
are misses, that is, failures to correctly identify the original
target composite-face by saying that it is not present.
Therefore, it appears that people who make an Identi-kit
reconstruction are biased away from the original target composite-
face.

The findings in this study appear to conflict with the
results obtained by Davies et al. (1978) and Maudlin and Laughery
(1981).  The differences between the present study and the
experiments of Davies et al. and Mauldin and Laughery are,

however, numerous. Their null results, for example, may be due to
a failure to allow the subject to make a "not present" response.
Alternatively, the high similarity between distractors and target
achieved in the present study, compared with the others, might
account for the different results. Most important, no study prior
to this has used Identi-kit reconstruction errors to build
distractor composite-faces in which the target is embedded. This
contingency between Identi-kit reconstructions and the recognition
task in the Identi-kit/own-errors condition allowed for an optimal
test of the potential interference effects of the Identi-kit task
on subsequent recognition.

What is the source of the recognition errors? It is possible
that the Identi-kit task creates interference because it involves
viewing the misleading errors incorporated into a complete face.
A person making a recognition decision may be easily confused
between the original memory and the memory of the Identi-kit
reconstruction. This is particularly likely to occur when a
composite-face similar to a person's own Identi-kit reconstruction
is present in the lineup.

The distribution of facial features in the foils that
subjects had falsely identified was also examined. In general,
people seem to make more recognition errors when features of less
importance, such as eyebrows and lips, were altered. This is
consistent with previous studies (see Ellis, 1984, for a review).

Recognition errors involving the more important features, hair and eyes, were primarily made only when the altered features resembled the Identi-kit reconstruction.  This suggests that more confusions occur for less important features and for important features that resemble Identi-kit reconstructions.

Although the Identi-kit task was shown to interfere with recognition in this study, there are a number of caveats to consider in generalizing these findings to police lineups.  First, it is not known how representative Identi-kit composite-faces are of photographs of real individuals, let alone the extent to which Identi-kit encoding operations compare with the encoding of live faces.  Thus, performance on an Identi-kit lineup task may not be indicative of performance on a real lineup task.  Second, the lineups used in this experiment consisted of highly similar composite-faces, faces much more similar than a typical police lineup.  In the first condition, the foils were altered so that one feature was precisely the same as the subjects' Identi-kit reconstruction--an occurrence that is highly unlikely in a typical police lineup.  Third, the target stimuli in this study were limited to only two Identi-kit composites that may not be representative of other faces.  Fourth, the reconstructions from which the lineups were created shared no features with the target composite.  Finally, the subjects in this study may have had poorer memories for the target than aroused witnesses to a crime

Recognition of Facial Stimuli

14

and thus made poorer reconstructions.  For these reasons, it is
necessary to be cautious in extrapolating from these results to
police lineups.

## References

Davies, G. M., Ellis, H. D., & Shepherd, J. W. (1978).  Face
   identification:  The influence of delay upon accuracy of
   Photofit construction.  Journal of Police Science and
   Administration, 6, 35-42.

Deffenbacher, K. A., Carr, T. H., & Leu, J. R. (1981).  Memory for
   words, pictures and faces:  Retroactive interference,
   forgetting and reminiscence.  Journal of Experimental
   Psychology:  Human Learning and Memory, 7, 299-305.

Ellis, H. D. (1984).  Practical aspects of face memory.  In G. L.
   Wells & E. F. Loftus (Eds.), Eyewitness testimony:
   Psychological perspectives (pp. 12-37).  New York:  Cambridge
   University Press.

Loftus, E., & Greene, E. (1980).  Warning:  Even memory for faces
   may be contagious.  Law and Human Behavior, 4, 323-334.

Mauldin, M., & Laughery, K. (1981).  Composite production effects
   on subsequent facial identification.  Journal of Applied
   Psychology, 66, 351-357.

Wells, G. L., & Lindsay, R. C. L. (1985).  Methodological notes on
   the accuracy-confidence relation in eyewitness identifications.
   Journal of Applied Psychology, 70, 413-419.

Recognition of Facial Stimuli

16

Wells, G. L., & Murray, D. M. (1984). Eyewitness confidence. In

    G. L. Wells & E. F. Loftus (Eds.), <u>Eyewitness</u> <u>testimony:</u>

    <u>Psychological</u> <u>perspectives</u> (pp. 155-170). New York: Cambridge

    University Press.

## Author Notes

Portions of this article were presented at the meeting of the Canadian Psychological Association held in Toronto, Canada, June 1986.

I am indebted to Gary Wells for the thoughtful help and guidance he provided during the course of this research.  In addition, I am grateful to John Pullyblank, John Turtle, and Brendan Rule for their comments on an earlier version of this article; to Constable Bates of the Royal Canadian Mounted Police for his time and comments; and to two anonymous reviewers for their extremely helpful and meticulous comments.

Correspondence concerning this article should be addressed to Sara Elizabeth Comish, who is now at the Department of Psychology, University of Victoria, P. O. Box 1700, Victoria, British Columbia, Canada, V8W 2Y2.

Recognition of Facial Stimuli

18

Table 1

Performance on the Recognition Task:  Data Converted Into
Percentages by Condition

| | Condition | | |
|---|---|---|---|
| Performance | Identi-kit (own errors) | Identi-kit (yoked) | Control (yoked) |
| Total errors | $86.11_a$ | $77.78_a$ | $56.56_b$ |
| Misses | $8.33_a$ | $27.78_b$ | $8.33_a$ |
| False alarms | $77.78_a$ | $50.00_b$ | $47.22_b$ |
| Correct (hits) | 13.89 | 22.22 | 44.44 |

Note.  Percentages that do not share a common subscript differ at
$p < .05$.

Recognition of Facial Stimuli

19

Figure Caption

<u>**Figure 1**</u>.  **The original target face, a typical Identi-kit**

**reconstruction, and the subsequent lineup.**  **(Foils are identical**

**to the original target face, except for the indicated facial**

**feature obtained from the reconstruction.)**

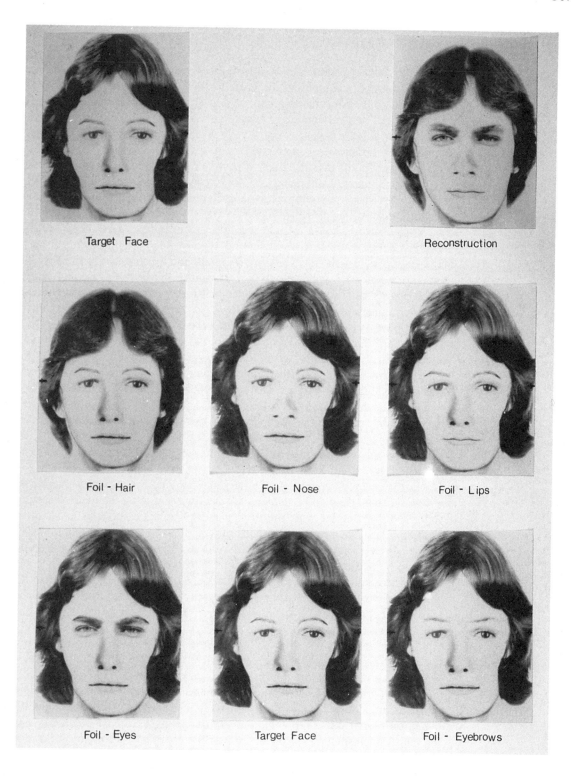

Target Face

Reconstruction

Foil - Hair

Foil - Nose

Foil - Lips

Foil - Eyes

Target Face

Foil - Eyebrows

## Style

Now that you have some idea of format, let us consider style. After you have suffered through some obscurely written article, you will no doubt recognize the advantage of clear, unambiguous writing. The APA format helps standardize the order and general content. However, making sure that the reader understands what you are saying is up to you. We have read many research reports prepared for our classes—some good, some awful, most of them in between—and we have found that the biggest problem is transition, or flow, from one section to the next. Deliberately or not, many students write as if they were composing a surprise-ending short story, even though their report should be as straightforward as possible.

Your abstract should include variables (independent, dependent, and important control variables), number and type of subjects, major results, and important conclusions. Students often include too much detail in the abstract; remember, you have only a few words, so state only the most essential aspects of the project so that a potential reader will have a general, but clear, idea of what was done and what was found. Because the abstract is a summary of the entire report, it is usually easiest to write it last, even though it appears first.

The introduction should first state a broad perspective on the issue you are interested in, then quickly narrow down to the specific question you are interested in. You should lead the reader through the relevant research, always keeping in mind that you are setting up your own research question. Thus, avoid discussion of tangential issues. Toward the end of the introduction, give the reader an overview of your experiment, specifying your hypotheses explicitly and outlining any predictions derived from theories you have discussed. By the end of the introduction, the reader should see your experiment as filling an important gap in our knowledge.

In the method section, state how you examined the variables. Here, it is important to be clear and complete. By the time you write the method section, you are quite familiar with the details and complexities of your experiment. This familiarity makes it difficult to realize that the reader of your report is learning of these details for the first time. As you write, think of what the reader needs to be told in order to get an accurate picture of your research.

In the results section, state what happened when you examined the variables. Clarity is also important here. Avoid simply listing your statistical analyses with minimal comment. Instead, state each finding in plain English first, then support it with statistics.

In your discussion, state what the effects of the variables mean. The biggest danger in this section of the paper is lack of organization. Before you begin writing, you should know the points you want to make. Make them concise and easy to understand. The discussion should follow up the issues pointed out in the introduction. Also, as in the introduction, avoid straying onto tangents. When the reader has completed your report, he or she should be able to state the main conclusions in a sentence or two. Be careful, however, in the conclusions you draw; avoid grandiose statements. Science advances in small steps; your experiment need not be earth-shaking to be scientifically important.

Finally, the body of your report should represent a tight package, not a disjointed essay containing sections that seem independent of each other. You have to tell your readers what you were trying to do, over and over again. Do not be afraid to be somewhat redundant by having each section build on the previous one. If you repeat the purpose of your research often enough, even the dullest reader will have gotten something from your report by the time he or she gets to the reference list. Table 13–2 summarizes the information that should be included in each section of your report.

The APA publication manual outlines style considerations as follows: Use the precise word, avoid ambiguity, order presentation of ideas, and consider the reader. These guidelines warrant some discussion.

Scientific writing demands clarity, so each word has to be chosen carefully. Consider these sentences that regularly appear in undergraduate research reports: "I ran the subjects individually." "The white albino rat was introduced to the Skinner box." Actually, none of the subjects in the study from which the first sentence was pulled did any running during the course of the project. What the author meant to say was, "I tested the subjects individually," or "The subjects were tested individually." From reading about rats introduced to Skinner boxes, you might conclude that the researcher had very clever rats. The rat did not shake hands with a box; all that happened was that the rat was put into the operant-conditioning chambers. Furthermore, "white albino" is redundant. All albino rats are white. The lesson here is that in scientific writing you must be careful to choose the correct word or phrase and avoid ambiguity. Also, be cautious when using pronouns such as *which, this, that, these,* and *those*. Many students find it irresistible to begin a paragraph with one of these pronouns, and more often than not the referent for the pronoun is not very easy to determine. You can usually avoid any ambiguity by including the referent of the pronoun each time it is used.

| TABLE 13–2 | A SUMMARY OF THE INFORMATION IN EACH SECTION OF A RESEARCH REPORT |
|---|---|
| **Section** | **Content** |
| Title | Experiments: State independent and dependent variables— "The effects of X on Y." Other studies: State the relationships examined— "The relation between X and Y." |
| Abstract | In less than 150 words, state what was done to whom and summarize the most important results. |
| Introduction | State what you plan to do and why (you may have to review results from related research). Predicted results may be appropriate. |
| Method | Present enough information to allow someone else to repeat your study exactly the way you did it. For clarity use subheadings (*Subjects, Apparatus,* etc.), and make sure that dependent, independent, subject, and control variables are specified. |
| Results | Summarize important results in tables or figures. Direct the reader to data that seem most relevant to the purpose of the research. |
| Discussion | State how the results relate to the hypotheses or predictions stated in the introduction. Inferences and theoretical statements are appropriate. |
| References | In APA format, list only those references that were cited in your report. |

After you have decided on your words and phrases, put them together carefully. A common problem among some writers is to shift verb tenses abruptly. In general, use the past tense in the review of other studies in your introduction (Smith *found*) and in your method (The subjects *were*). When you are describing and discussing your data, the present tense is usually appropriate (The data *show* that . . ., which *means* that).

Make sure that collective and plural nouns agree with their verbs and pronouns. Plural words that end in *a* are troublesome, such as *data, criteria,* and *phenomena.* Each of these nouns is plural, so they each require plural verbs and pronouns. "These data *are*" is correct, but "this phenomena *is*" is not correct. The singular forms for these nouns are: *datum, criterion,* and *phenomenon* (This phenomenon *is*).

Many scientific writers overuse the passive voice in their reports. Consider this statement: "It is thought that forgetting is caused by interference." Although this sentence is fairly concise (and it is precise), it is also stuffy and less direct than "We think that interference causes forgetting," which is really what was meant. Be careful about using either the active or passive voice too much. If you overuse the passive voice, your report sounds stuffy. If you overuse the active voice, you may take interest away from what you did and place too much emphasis on yourself (I think, I did, and so on). If you want to emphasize what was done and not who did it and why, use the passive construction. On the other hand, if you think that the agent of the activity is also important, or if the reason for the action is important, use the active voice.

The careful writer tries to avoid language that is sexist. The APA recommends that the use of *he* (and *his* and *him*) as a generic pronoun be avoided by changing to a plural construction or by using something like *he or she.* Generally, the writer should strive for accurate, unbiased communication.

Writing a cogent, well-organized research article is a skill that requires considerable effort and practice. More is involved than simply allocating information to the correct sections. There are many fine points of style, usage, and exposition that distinguish lucid, well-written articles from obscure and tortuous ones. While writing your report, you should make frequent use of standard references for points of style and grammar. In addition, consult the APA publication manual regarding aspects of technical writing that are particularly relevant to psychology journal articles, including the organization and content of each section, economy and precision in the expression of ideas, the presentation of data and statistics, and so forth. Finally, we highly recommend the aforementioned book by Sternberg (1987) and the chapter by Bem (1987) for excellent advice and specific examples of good and poor style, phrasing, and organization in psychology articles.

## Sharing Your Results

Assume that your article has been written, proofread, corrected, and the last page has just emerged from a steaming typewriter (or more likely from a steaming printer). Now what? Well, the reason you wrote up your research was to share it with others interested in the same topic. Otherwise, you could have just done the experiment and analyzed the results, content in the knowledge that you have the answer to some scientific puzzle. The question then arises: How do you go about sharing the results of your research?

One avenue for sharing results is psychological conventions. Psychologists gather in groups of varying size to present the results of their most recent research. Some of these conventions are very specific in the type of research reported (e.g., neuropsychological research only), whereas others are much more general, including all areas of psychology. These conferences allow scientists to meet and discuss recent and ongoing research—work that has not yet been published. The results of student research are sometimes presented at such conferences. After conducting a research project, if you think it is worth sharing with the scientific community, you might ask your professors about appropriate conventions in your area. If your professor agrees that the work is good enough to present at such a convention, he or she will explain to you how to submit your research.

Although conventions are often the first place that research is reported, most research is eventually written up to be submitted to a scientific journal. Conventions reach only a small group of scientists. Having a research report published in a journal makes the results available to any interested scientist. Moreover, it makes the results available for researchers many years in the future. Although it is unlikely that your first student effort will produce an article of professional quality, you may nevertheless find it interesting to discover what happens when an article is submitted to a journal by a professional psychologist.

The first step is to send copies of the manuscript (the technical term for an unpublished work) to a small number of trusted associates who can check it over to make sure that it has no obvious or elementary flaws and that it is written clearly. Once the comments come back, the indicated corrections are made and, with some trepidation, the author commits the manuscript to the mail, addressed to the editor of the most appropriate journal. After this, it is necessary to forget about it entirely for the next few months or otherwise exhibit great patience. The review process is slow. (The editor who receives the manuscript is a harried, overworked, tired individual who often regrets accepting the editorship. Editors of journals, like elected politicians, serve a fixed term of office, usually four to six years.) About two or three weeks after submitting the article, the author receives a form letter that thanks him or her for interest in the journal and acknowledges receipt of the manuscript. The manuscript gets a number (like 86–867) and if an associate editor has been assigned to handle it, the author is instructed to direct all future correspondence to that editor.

The editor then sends copies of the manuscript to two or three reviewers. It is unlikely that both of them will be good friends of the author. Some journals allow the author to have blind reviewing, where the author conceals his or her identity. Blind reviewing is for those who do not believe in the impartiality of reviewers. The reviewer, who may also review for several other journals, puts the manuscript in the pile on his or her desk. A conscientious reviewer may take up to a day or two to carefully read and evaluate a manuscript. When each reviewer gets around to it, a summary statement is sent to the editor. When the reviewers are in agreement, the editor's decision is easy. Should the reviewers disagree, the editor must carefully read the manuscript and sometimes may request a third opinion. Finally, an editorial decision is reached and the author receives a letter stating (1) why the manuscript cannot be published, (2) what kind of revisions are needed to make the manuscript acceptable, or (3) that the journal will publish the article. Because rejection rates for manuscripts are quite high in most journals (above 80 percent), editors spend a great deal of time devising tactful letters of rejection.

Whether or not the article was accepted, the comments of the reviewers are most valuable. The best psychologists in the area have provided, free of charge, their careful opinions about the research. Of course, reviewers can also make mistakes. Any author who disagrees with a review has the privilege, even the responsibility, of writing to the editor. Although this action will usually not result in the article being accepted, it is important that rejected authors have the right to appeal or protest. Anyway, there are always other journals.

If the article was accepted for publication, the author is still not yet finished. Some revision of the manuscript may be required. The copyright for the article is signed over to the publisher. Some months later, the author receives galley or page proofs from the publisher. These must be carefully checked to ensure that the words and tables set in type by the printer match those in the original manuscript. After making corrections (and the author is charged for excessive changes that do not result from the printer's errors), the author returns the article to the publisher. Several months later, the article finally appears in the journal. The entire process, from submission of the manuscript until final publication, takes a year or more. Authors do not get paid for articles in journals, but on the other hand, neither do they get charged for the privilege of appearing in print.

As you might expect, it is a great thrill to see your name in print, especially the first time. An even greater thrill, however, is the knowledge that you may have added some small amount to our understanding of why people and animals behave as they do.

## SUMMARY

When you read a research report, you should read actively and critically, so that you can derive maximum benefit from other people's research. The checklist for critical readers is designed to get you into the habit of actively asking questions about the reports you read: What hypotheses are being tested? How are they being tested? Does the method test the hypotheses? How does the author relate the results to the goals of the research? What interpretations and inferences are made by the author? You should also consider these questions when you write your own report. The APA format provides a framework for your report, but it is up to you to write clearly. Several suggestions that help produce a clear, unambiguous style of report writing are provided. The chapter concludes with a brief description of the publication process. For psychological science to progress, reports must be published, and knowledgeable consumers must read them critically.

## Key Concepts

| | |
|---|---|
| abstract | method |
| APA format | procedure |
| apparatus | references |
| author | results |
| checklist for critical readers | running head |
| discussion | subjects |
| figures | tables |
| introduction | title |

# STATISTICAL APPENDIXES

| DESCRIPTIVE STATISTICS Organizing and summarizing | | |
|---|---|---|
| **Useful Computational Formulae** | **Measures of Central Tendency** | **Measures of Dispersion** |
| | *Mode* The most frequent score *Median* The middle score *Mean* $\bar{X} = \Sigma X/n$ | *Variance* $s^2 = \dfrac{\Sigma X^2}{n} - \bar{X}^2$ *Standard Deviation* $s = \sqrt{\dfrac{\Sigma X^2}{n} - \bar{X}^2}$ |
| **Facts about the Normal Distribution** | 1. Of all scores, 68 percent are within $\pm$ 1 standard deviation of the mean. 2. Of all scores, nearly 96 percent are within $\pm$ 2 standard deviations of the mean. 3. Of all scores, 99.74 percent are within $\pm$ 3 standard deviations of the mean. 4. Standard scores ($z$ scores) are differences between individual scores and the mean expressed in units of standard deviations. | |
| **Explanation of Symbols** | 1. $X$ and $Y$ are individual scores (data). 4. $X^2$ is each score squared. | 2. $n$ is the number of observations or subjects. 5. $\Sigma X^2$ refers to adding up the scores after each has been squared. / 3. $\Sigma$ refers to the act of adding (or summing). 6. $(\Sigma X)^2$ means the square of the sum of the raw scores. |

# A

# DESCRIPTIVE STATISTICS

## DESCRIPTIVE STATISTICS: TELLING IT LIKE IT IS

We have conducted research in order to collect data about a psychological topic. What are we going to do with the numbers? First, we need to systematize and organize them. We do not have to look at the whole array of numbers produced by subjects in the different conditions of an experiment. Instead, we can look at a briefer version. Descriptive statistics provide the summarizing and systematizing function. The two main types of descriptive statistics are *measures of central tendency* and *measures of dispersion* (variability).

Let us consider a hypothetical experiment. A drug company has sponsored a test of the effects of LSD on the behavior of rats, so we decide to see how the drug affects the rats' running speed. Forty food-deprived rats have been trained to run a straight-alley maze for a food reward. We randomly assign them to two groups. To one group we administer LSD by injection and observe the effect on the speed with which the rats run the alley for food thirty minutes after the injection. The other group is tested in a similar manner thirty minutes after receiving an injection of an inert substance. The following are the running times (in seconds) for the twenty control subjects: 13, 11, 14, 18, 12, 14, 10, 13, 13, 16, 15, 9, 12, 20, 11, 13, 12, 17, 15, and 14. The running times for the subjects receiving the LSD injections are 17, 15, 16, 20, 14, 19, 14, 13, 18, 18, 26, 17, 19, 13, 16, 22, 18, 16, 18, and 9. Now that we have the running times, what do we do with them? We might want some sort of graphical representation of the numbers. One type of graph is the **histogram** shown in the two panels of figure A–1, where the running speeds in seconds appear along the abscissa (*x*-axis), and the frequency with which each occurred in the two conditions is displayed along the ordinate (*y*-axis). Running times for the control subjects are given in the top histogram, and those for the experimental subjects are shown in the bottom one. Another way to represent the same information is a **frequency polygon.** Its construction is equivalent to that of the histogram; you can visualize this type of graph by connecting the midpoints of the bars in the histogram. (Examples of *frequency polygons* appear in figure A–2.) In both conditions in figure A–1, the greatest number of scores occurs in the middle and the scores tend to decrease in frequency as running times become smaller or larger. Both the histogram and frequency polygon are types of **frequency**

Histograms representing scores for twenty subjects in the control and experimental conditions of the hypothetical LSD experiment.

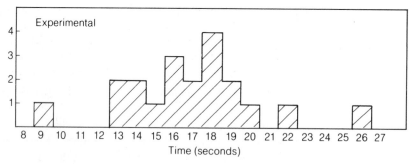

**distributions.** They help systematize the data, but there are more efficient summary descriptions.

## Central Tendency

The most common summary description of data is a measure of central tendency, which indicates the center of the distribution of scores. By far the most common measure of central tendency in psychological research is the **mean**. The mean ($\overline{X}$) is the sum of all the scores ($\Sigma X$) divided by the number of scores ($n$), or $\overline{X} = \Sigma X/n$. It is what most people think of as the average of a set of numbers, although the term *average* technically applies to any measure of central tendency. The sums of the running times for the experimental and control conditions in our hypothetical experiment were 338 and 272 seconds, respectively. Because there were twenty observations in each condition, the means are 16.9 seconds for the experimental condition and 13.6 for the control group.

The mean is by far the most useful measure of central tendency and almost all inferential statistics, which we come to later, are based on it. Therefore, this statistic is used whenever possible. However, two other measures of central tendency are sometimes employed. The second most common measure is the **median**. It is the score above which half of the distribution lies and below which the other half lies. The median, then, is the midpoint of the distribution. When there is an odd number of scores in the distribution, such as 27, the median is the 14th score from the bottom or top, because that score divides the distribution into two groups of thirteen scores. When the number of scores ($n$) is an even number, the median is the arithmetic mean of the two middle scores, if the scores are not tied. So the median of the scores 66, 70, 72, 76, 80, and 96 is

(72 + 76)/2, or 74. When the two middle scores are tied, as in the distribution of scores from the hypothetical LSD experiment, the convention is to designate the median as the appropriate proportion of the distance between the limits of the particular score, where the limits are a half score above and below the tied score. Consider the distributions of scores from our experiment. If we arrange the twenty control running times from lowest to highest, we discover that the eighth, ninth, tenth, and eleventh scores are all 13. Under such conditions, the tenth score is considered the median and it lies three quarters of the distance between the limits of 12.5 and 13.5. So the median would be 12.5 + .75, or 13.25, for the control subjects. By the same reasoning (and you should try it yourself), we find that the median for the experimental subjects is 17.

Why is the median used? The primary reason is that it has the desirable property of being insensitive to extreme scores. In the distribution of scores of 66, 70, 72, 76, 80, and 96, the median of the distribution would remain exactly the same if the lowest score were 1 rather than 66 or the highest score were 1,223 rather than 96. The mean, on the other hand, would differ widely with these other scores. Often this benefit can be extremely useful in summarizing data. In our LSD experiment, suppose that one of the rats given LSD had stopped halfway down the alley to examine a particularly interesting feature of the runway before continuing on its way to the goal box, and its time to complete the runway was 45 minutes or 2,700 seconds. If this score replaced the 26-second score in the original distribution, the mean would go from 16.9 seconds to 150.6, or from 3.30 seconds greater than the control mean to 137.0 seconds greater, because of only one very deviant score. In such cases, researchers frequently use the median score rather than the mean to represent the central tendency. Using the mean seems to give an unrepresentative estimate of central tendency because of the great influence of the one deviant score. However, using the median often severely limits any statistical tests that can be applied to the data.

The final measure of central tendency, almost never reported in psychological research, is the **mode,** or the most frequent score in the distribution. In the distribution of control scores in our experiment, it is 13, and in the distribution of experimental scores, it is 18.

## *Measures of Dispersion: Variability in Data*

Measures of central tendency indicate the center of the scores, whereas measures of dispersion indicate how the scores are spread out about the center. The simplest measure of dispersion is the **range,** which is the difference between the highest and lowest scores in the distribution. For the control rats in the LSD experiment the range is 11 (20 − 9), and for the experimental rats it is 17 (26 − 9). The range indicates only the extreme scores, so it is rarely used.

The most useful measures of dispersion are the **standard deviation** and the **variance** of a distribution. The standard deviation is most useful as a descriptive statistic, whereas the variance of a distribution is employed in inferential statistics. As we shall see, the two are closely related.

One number that reflects the amount of spread that the scores exhibit around some central-tendency measure, usually the mean, is the *mean deviation.* This is calculated by taking the difference between the mean and every score in a distribution, summing these differences, and then dividing by the number of scores. However, we need to take the mean *absolute* difference (that is, to ignore the sign of the difference or whether the score was greater or less than the mean). The reason is that the sum of the deviations of scores about the mean is always zero, a defining characteristic of the mean (see table A–1). Thus, the mean deviation must be the *absolute* mean deviation. The mean deviations for our hypothetical experimental conditions in the LSD experiment are calculated in table A–1. The symbol ‖ indicates the absolute value of a number, so $|-6| = 6$.

The absolute mean deviation of a set of sources is an adequate measure of dispersion and is based on the same logic involved in finding the mean of a distribution. However, the standard deviation and variance are preferred to the mean deviation because they have mathematical properties that make them much more useful in advanced statistical computations. The logic behind their calculation is quite similar to that of the mean deviation, which is why we have considered the mean deviation here. In calculating the mean deviation, we had

**TABLE A–1**   CALCULATION OF THE MEAN DEVIATIONS AND ABSOLUTE MEAN DEVIATIONS FROM TWO SETS OF SCORES. THE SUM OF THE DEVIATIONS (DIFFERENCES) IN CALCULATING THE MEAN DEVIATION IS ZERO, WHICH IS WHY IT IS NECESSARY TO USE THE ABSOLUTE MEAN DEVIATION.

| Control Group | | | Experimental Group | | |
|---|---|---|---|---|---|
| $X$ | $(X - \bar{X})$ | $|X - \bar{X}|$ | $X$ | $(X - \bar{X})$ | $|X - \bar{X}|$ |
| 9 | −4.60 | 4.60 | 9 | −7.90 | 7.90 |
| 10 | −3.60 | 3.60 | 13 | −3.90 | 3.90 |
| 11 | −2.60 | 2.60 | 13 | −3.90 | 3.90 |
| 11 | −2.60 | 2.60 | 14 | −2.90 | 2.90 |
| 12 | −1.60 | 1.60 | 14 | −2.90 | 2.90 |
| 12 | −1.60 | 1.60 | 15 | −1.90 | 1.90 |
| 12 | −1.60 | 1.60 | 16 | − .90 | .90 |
| 13 | − .60 | .60 | 16 | − .90 | .90 |
| 13 | − .60 | .60 | 16 | − .90 | .90 |
| 13 | − .60 | .60 | 17 | + .10 | .10 |
| 13 | − .60 | .60 | 17 | + .10 | .10 |
| 14 | + .40 | .40 | 18 | +1.10 | .10 |
| 14 | + .40 | .40 | 18 | +1.10 | 1.10 |
| 14 | + .40 | .40 | 18 | +1.10 | 1.10 |
| 15 | +1.40 | 1.40 | 18 | +1.10 | 1.10 |
| 15 | +1.40 | 1.40 | 19 | +2.10 | 2.10 |
| 16 | +2.40 | 2.40 | 19 | +2.10 | 2.10 |
| 17 | +3.40 | 3.40 | 20 | +3.10 | 3.10 |
| 18 | +4.40 | 4.40 | 22 | +5.10 | 5.10 |
| 20 | +6.40 | 6.40 | 26 | +9.10 | 9.10 |

| $\Sigma X = 272$ | Total = 0.00 | Total = 41.20 | $\Sigma X = 338$ | Total = 0.00 | Total = 52.20 |
|---|---|---|---|---|---|
| $\bar{X} = 13.60$ | | | $\bar{X} = 16.90$ | | |

Absolute mean deviation $= \dfrac{41.20}{20} = 2.06$     Absolute mean deviation $= \dfrac{52.20}{20} = 2.62$

to determine the absolute value of the difference of each score from the mean so that these differences would not sum to zero. Instead of taking the absolute difference, we could have gotten rid of the troublesome negative numbers by squaring the differences. This is exactly what is done in calculating the variance and standard deviation of a distribution.

The *variance* of a distribution is defined as *the sum of the squared deviations from the mean, divided by the number of scores.* In other words, each score is subtracted from the mean and squared; then all these values are summed and divided by the number of scores. The formula for the variance is

$$s^2 = \frac{\Sigma(X-\bar{X})^2}{n} \tag{A–1}$$

where $s^2$ represents the variance, $X$ the individual scores, $\bar{X}$ the mean, and $n$ the number of scores or observations. The *standard deviation* is simply *the square root of the variance,* and is therefore represented by $s$. So

$$s = \sqrt{\frac{\Sigma(X-\bar{X})^2}{n}} \tag{A–2}$$

Calculation of the standard deviations for the control and experimental conditions in the LSD experiment by the mean-deviation method is illustrated in table A–2.

The formulas for the variance and standard deviation of a distribution shown in equations A–1 and A–2 are rather cumbersome, and in practice, the equivalent computational formulas are used. The standard-deviation formula is

$$s = \sqrt{\frac{\Sigma X^2}{n} - \bar{X}^2} \tag{A–3}$$

where $\Sigma X^2$ is the sum of the squares of all the scores, $\bar{X}$ is the mean of the distribution, and $n$ is the number of scores. Similarly, the formula for variance is

$$s^2 = \frac{\Sigma X^2}{n} - \bar{X}^2 \tag{A–4}$$

The standard deviations for the experimental and control scores are calculated by the computational formula shown in table A–3. The value in each case is the same as when the definitional formula is used.

To describe an array of data, psychologists usually present two descriptive statistics, the mean and the standard deviation. Although there are other measures of central tendency and dispersion, these are most useful for descriptive purposes. Variance is used extensively in inferential statistics (see appendix B).

## THE NORMAL DISTRIBUTION

In the histograms in figure A–1 representing the running times of the rats in the two conditions of our hypothetical experiment, most of the scores pile up in the center and tail off toward the ends (or tails) of the distribution, especially

| TABLE A–2 | CALCULATION OF THE STANDARD DEVIATION, s, FOR THE CONTROL AND EXPERIMENTAL CONDITIONS BY THE MEAN-DEVIATION METHOD. |
|---|---|

| Control Group | | | Experimental Group | | |
|---|---|---|---|---|---|
| $X$ | $(X-\bar{X})$ | $(X-\bar{X})^2$ | $X$ | $(X-\bar{X})$ | $(X-\bar{X})^2$ |
| 9 | −4.60 | 21.16 | 9 | −7.90 | 62.41 |
| 10 | −3.60 | 12.96 | 13 | −3.90 | 15.21 |
| 11 | −2.60 | 6.76 | 13 | −3.90 | 15.21 |
| 11 | −2.60 | 6.76 | 14 | −2.90 | 8.41 |
| 12 | −1.60 | 2.56 | 14 | −2.90 | 8.41 |
| 12 | −1.60 | 2.56 | 15 | −1.90 | 3.61 |
| 12 | −1.60 | 2.56 | 16 | − .90 | .81 |
| 13 | − .60 | .36 | 16 | − .90 | .81 |
| 13 | − .60 | .36 | 16 | − .90 | .81 |
| 13 | − .60 | .36 | 17 | + .10 | .01 |
| 13 | − .60 | .36 | 17 | + .10 | .01 |
| 14 | + .40 | .16 | 18 | + 1.10 | 1.21 |
| 14 | + .40 | .16 | 18 | + 1.10 | 1.21 |
| 14 | + .40 | .16 | 18 | + 1.10 | 1.21 |
| 15 | 1.40 | 1.96 | 18 | + 1.10 | 1.21 |
| 15 | 1.40 | 1.96 | 19 | + 2.10 | 4.41 |
| 16 | 2.40 | 5.76 | 19 | + 2.10 | 4.41 |
| 17 | 3.40 | 11.56 | 20 | + 3.10 | 9.61 |
| 18 | 4.40 | 19.36 | 22 | + 5.10 | 26.01 |
| 20 | 6.40 | 40.96 | 26 | + 9.10 | 82.81 |

$\Sigma X = 272$    Total $= 0.00$    $\Sigma(X-\bar{X})^2 = 138.80$    $\Sigma X = 338$    Total $= 0.00$    $\Sigma(X-\bar{X})^2 = 247.80$

$\bar{X} = 13.60$ $\bar{X} = 16.90$

$$s = \sqrt{\frac{\Sigma(X-\bar{X})^2}{n}}$$ $$s = \sqrt{\frac{\Sigma(X-\bar{X})^2}{n}}$$

$$s = \sqrt{\frac{138.80}{20}}$$ $$s = \sqrt{\frac{247.80}{20}}$$

$$s = 2.63$$ $$s = 3.52$$

for control subjects. Most psychological data tend to look like this when represented graphically; they often approximate the **normal curve** or **standard normal distribution,** where scores are most numerous in the middle, decline in frequency with distance from the middle, and do so in a fairly symmetrical way. A score ten points above the middle is about as common as a score ten points below it. Several examples of normal curves are shown in figure A–2 (see page 324). First note that in all three distributions, the mean, median, and mode are the same. The main difference in the distributions is in their variability. The tall, thin curve A has a smaller variance (and, of course, standard deviation) than the other two, whereas the flat, broad curve C has a larger variance than the others. All three curves, though, are normal curves.

Each side of the normal curve has a point where the curve slightly reverses its direction; it starts bending outward more. This is called the *inflection point*

**TABLE A–3** CALCULATION OF THE STANDARD DEVIATION, s, FOR THE CONTROL AND EXPERIMENTAL CONDITIONS BY USING THE COMPUTATIONAL FORMULA (ALSO CALLED THE RAW-SCORE METHOD). THE SAME VALUES ARE OBTAINED AS WHEN THE DEFINITIONAL FORMULA IS USED (SEE TABLE A–2), BUT THE CALCULATIONS ARE MUCH EASIER TO PERFORM.

| X | X² | X | X² |
|---|---|---|---|
| 9 | 81 | 9 | 81 |
| 10 | 100 | 13 | 169 |
| 11 | 121 | 13 | 169 |
| 11 | 121 | 14 | 196 |
| 12 | 144 | 14 | 196 |
| 12 | 144 | 15 | 225 |
| 12 | 144 | 16 | 256 |
| 13 | 169 | 16 | 256 |
| 13 | 169 | 16 | 256 |
| 13 | 169 | 17 | 289 |
| 13 | 169 | 17 | 289 |
| 14 | 196 | 18 | 324 |
| 14 | 196 | 18 | 324 |
| 14 | 196 | 18 | 324 |
| 15 | 225 | 18 | 324 |
| 15 | 225 | 19 | 361 |
| 16 | 256 | 19 | 361 |
| 17 | 289 | 20 | 400 |
| 18 | 324 | 22 | 484 |
| 20 | 400 | 26 | 676 |

$\Sigma X = 272$     $\Sigma X^2 = 3838$     $\Sigma X = 338$     $\Sigma X^2 = 5960$

$$\bar{X} = 13.60 \qquad\qquad \bar{X} = 16.90$$

$$\bar{X}^2 = 184.96 \qquad\qquad \bar{X}^2 = 285.61$$

$$s = \sqrt{\frac{\Sigma X^2}{n} - \bar{X}^2} \qquad\qquad s = \sqrt{\frac{\Sigma X^2}{n} - \bar{X}^2}$$

$$s = \sqrt{\frac{3838}{20} - 184.96} \qquad\qquad s = \sqrt{\frac{5960}{20} - 285.61}$$

$$s = 2.63 \qquad\qquad s = 3.52$$

and is labeled in the normal curve shown in figure A–3. The inflection point in the curve is always one standard deviation from the mean, and the normal curve has the useful property that specific proportions of the distribution of scores it represents are contained within specific areas of the curve itself. About 68 percent of all scores are contained within one standard deviation of the mean (34 percent on each side). Similarly, almost 96 percent of the scores are contained within two standard deviations of the mean, and 99.74 percent of the scores are within three standard deviations. The percentage of each area is shown in figure A–3. This is true of all normal curves, no matter how sharp or flat they are.

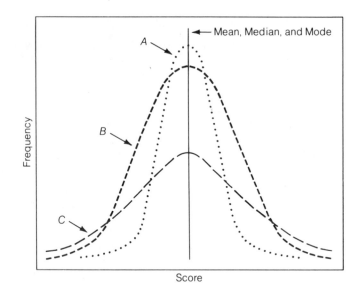

This property of normal curves is extremely useful because if we know an individual's score and the mean and standard deviation in the distribution of scores, we also know the person's relative rank. For example, most IQ tests are devised so that the population mean is 100 and the standard deviation is 15. If a person has an IQ of 115, we know that he or she scored higher than 84 percent of all people on the test (50 percent of the people below the mean and 34 percent above). Similarly, a person with an IQ of 130 scored higher than almost 98 percent of all people, and a person with an IQ of 145 scored higher than 99.87 percent of the population. See whether you can arrive at these percentages by adding up the appropriate areas in figure A–3.

Most distributions of scores in psychological data are, or at least are assumed to be, normal. (Often with small samples, as in our hypothetical data in figure A–1, it is difficult to tell whether the distribution is normal.) Scores are compared across normal distributions with different means and variances in terms of **standard scores** or *z scores*. This score is simply the difference between an individual score and the mean expressed in units of standard deviations. So an

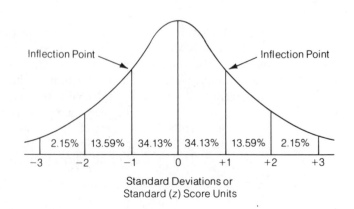

IQ of 115 translates to a $z$ score of 1.00, that is, $(115 - 100)/15$; and an IQ of 78 translates to a $z$ score of $-1.47$, that is, $(78 - 100)/15$. Standard scores are useful because they allow comparison of the relative ranks of scores for a person across distributions in which the means and standard deviations vary greatly. Grades in courses should be calculated in terms of $z$ scores if the means and standard deviations of the scores vary widely from one test to the next. Thus, a person's eventual rank in the class is calculated more faithfully by finding the mean of the $z$ scores than by finding the mean of the raw scores of the tests.

When data in an experiment are said to be *normally distributed*, it means that, if they were graphed, they would form a normal distribution, as in figure A–3. Thus *normal*, as it is used in psychological research, usually refers to a type of distribution (there are many other types of distributions) and is not a value judgment as to the goodness or badness of the scores.

## Correlation Coefficient

In chapter 3, correlational research is described. The purpose of correlational research is to see how two or more attributes of an organism vary together. The strength and direction of a correlation are determined by the calculation of a correlation coefficient. We will consider just one: *Pearson product-moment correlation coefficient* or $r$. Shown in box A–1 is the calculation formula for $r$, using the hypothetical data relating head size to memory performance discussed in chapter 3. Box A–2 repeats this analysis, using the computerized statistical package called MINITAB.

Regardless of how you calculate $r$, you should read the appropriate sections of chapter 3 that discuss the use and interpretation of a correlation coefficient.

---

| **BOX A–1** |
| --- |
| Computing Pearson $r$ |

Let us call one set of numbers in table A–4 $X$ scores and the other set $Y$ scores. For example, head sizes might be $X$ scores and words recalled $Y$ scores. The formula for computing Pearson $r$ from the raw scores in panels (a), (b), or (c) of table 3–1 is as follows:

$$r = \frac{n \Sigma XY - (\Sigma X)(\Sigma Y)}{\sqrt{[n \Sigma X^2 - (\Sigma X)^2][n \Sigma Y^2 - (\Sigma Y)^2]}} \tag{A–5}$$

The $n$ refers to the number of subjects on which observations are taken (here, 10); the terms $\Sigma X$ and $\Sigma Y$ are the totals of the $X$ and $Y$ scores, respectively; $\Sigma X^2$ and $\Sigma Y^2$ are the sum of all the $X$ (or $Y$) values after each is squared; and the $(\Sigma X)^2$ and $(\Sigma Y)^2$ are the total of all the $X$ or $Y$ values with the entire total or sum squared. This leaves the value $\Sigma XY$, or the sum of the cross-products. This is obtained very simply by multiplying each $X$ value by its corresponding $Y$ and then summing these products. You may see other formulas for calculation of Pearson $r$ besides the raw-score formula in equation A–5, but these will be equivalent (in general) to the one presented here. An illustration of how Pearson $r$ is calculated using this raw-score formula is presented in table A–4 using the data from the (a) column of table 3–1 (chapter 3). You should try to work out the values for

Pearson $r$ for the (b) and (c) panels yourself, to make certain you understand how to calculate the values and to gain an intuitive feel for the concept of correlation. The values of $r$ are given below the appropriate columns in table 3–1.

| | $X$ Head Size (cm.) | $X^2$ | $Y$ Words Recalled | $Y^2$ | $X \cdot Y$ |
|---|---|---|---|---|---|
| **Subject Number** | | | | | |
| 1 | 50.8 | 2580.64 | 17 | 289 | 863.60 |
| 2 | 63.5 | 4032.25 | 21 | 441 | 1330.50 |
| 3 | 45.7 | 2088.49 | 16 | 256 | 731.20 |
| 4 | 25.4 | 645.16 | 11 | 121 | 279.40 |
| 5 | 29.2 | 852.64 | 9 | 81 | 262.80 |
| 6 | 49.5 | 2450.25 | 15 | 225 | 742.50 |
| 7 | 38.1 | 1451.61 | 13 | 169 | 495.30 |
| 8 | 30.5 | 930.25 | 12 | 144 | 366.00 |
| 9 | 35.6 | 1267.36 | 14 | 196 | 498.40 |
| 10 | 58.4 | 3410.56 | 23 | 529 | 1343.20 |
| $n = 10$ | $\Sigma X = 426.70$ | $\Sigma X^2 = 19{,}709.21$ | $\Sigma Y = 151$ | $\Sigma Y^2 = 2451$ | $\Sigma XY = 6915.90$ |

**TABLE A–4 CALCULATION OF PEARSON $r$ FOR THE DATA IN THE FIRST (A) COLUMN OF TABLE 3–1, BY THE RAW-SCORE FORMULA (EQUATION A–5).**

$$r = \frac{n\Sigma XY - (\Sigma X)(\Sigma Y)}{\sqrt{[n\Sigma X^2 - (\Sigma X)^2][n\Sigma Y^2 - (\Sigma Y)^2]}}$$

$$r = \frac{10(6915.90) - (426.70)(151)}{\sqrt{[(10)(19{,}709.21) - (426.70)^2][(10)(2451) - (151)^2]}}$$

$$r = \frac{69{,}159.00 - 64{,}431.70}{\sqrt{[197{,}092.10 - 182{,}072.89][24{,}510 - 22{,}801]}}$$

$$r = \frac{4727.30}{\sqrt{[15{,}019.12][1709]}} = \frac{4727.30}{\sqrt{25{,}667{,}829.89}}$$

$$r = \frac{4727.30}{5066.34}$$

$$r = +.93$$

**BOX A–2**

Calculation of $r$ by a Computer

One popular statistical package on many large computers is called MINITAB. The MINITAB program will compute $r$, as well as many other statistics. We have outlined a typical session on a computer in which MINITAB is used to calculate $r$ for the data in box A–1. The entries shaded are what you type into the computer, and the other information is what the computer presents to you. After you have signed on to the computer, you need to gain access to MINITAB, which in this case is done by typing MINITAB. (However, different computer systems may have other ways of accessing MINITAB; check with your computer center before trying to run MINITAB.) Then, you are likely to see some information about the MINITAB program, followed by "MTB." MTB means that you should enter the appropriate MINITAB command, and it is here that you need to tell MINITAB that you are entering data to be "read" for analysis. So, the appropriate command is: "READ INTO C1, C2." This tells MINITAB that you are entering two columns of data (C1 and C2). Then MINITAB asks for the two columns by printing "DATA," next to which you enter the two scores for a particular subject. You continue to enter pairs of scores until the data for all subjects have been entered (ten pairs in this case), after which you type "END." You then enter the command "CORRELATION BETWEEN C1 and C2," which tells MINITAB to compute the *r* between the ten pairs of scores. MINITAB tells you that ten rows of data were read (a handy check that you have entered the correct number of pairs of scores), and then prints out the correlation. The correlation computed by MINITAB is identical to the one in table A–4. Next, MINITAB asks for additional commands. When you enter "STOP," you leave the MINITAB program. You are now ready to sign off the computer. (You could have entered another MINITAB command besides "STOP" if you had additional statistical computations to perform.)

```
MINITAB RELEASE 82.1 *** COPYRIGHT - PENN STATE UNIV. 1982
APRIL 25, 1984 *** CONVERTED AT U. OF WISC. WAISMAN CENTER
STORAGE AVAILABLE   41099

MTB > READ INTO C1, C2
DATA> 50.8 17
DATA> 63.5 21
DATA> 45.7 16
DATA> 25.4 11
DATA> 29.2 9
DATA> 49.5 15
DATA> 38.1 13
DATA> 30.5 12
DATA> 35.6 14
DATA> 58.4 23
DATA> END
     10 ROWS READ
MTB > CORRELATION BETWEEN C1 AND C2

    CORRELATION OF        C1 AND C2       = 0.933

MTB > STOP

*** MINITAB *** STATISTICS DEPT * PENN STATE UNIV. * RELEASE 82.1 *
STORAGE AVAILABLE   41099
```

**The results of a computer session with MINITAB. MINITAB has calculated the *r* for the data presented in box A–1. Shaded entries are typed in by the user, and the other information is printed by the computer program.**

There are several other statistical packages for computers (for exmple, SPSS and BMD) that may be available to you; whichever one is available, we recommend you become familiar with it. Computer analysis is faster and more accurate than doing statistical work by hand or step by step on a calculator.

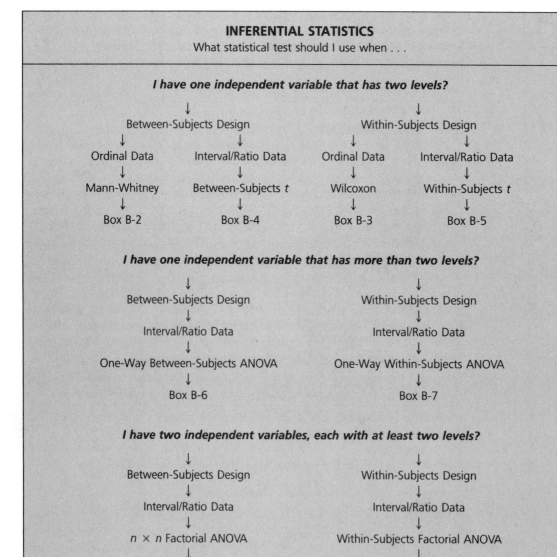

**INFERENTIAL STATISTICS**
What statistical test should I use when . . .

*I have one independent variable that has two levels?*

Between-Subjects Design

| Ordinal Data | Interval/Ratio Data |
| --- | --- |
| Mann-Whitney | Between-Subjects *t* |
| Box B-2 | Box B-4 |

Within-Subjects Design

| Ordinal Data | Interval/Ratio Data |
| --- | --- |
| Wilcoxon | Within-Subjects *t* |
| Box B-3 | Box B-5 |

*I have one independent variable that has more than two levels?*

Between-Subjects Design

Interval/Ratio Data

One-Way Between-Subjects ANOVA

Box B-6

Within-Subjects Design

Interval/Ratio Data

One-Way Within-Subjects ANOVA

Box B-7

*I have two independent variables, each with at least two levels?*

Between-Subjects Design

Interval/Ratio Data

*n* × *n* Factorial ANOVA

Box B-8

Within-Subjects Design

Interval/Ratio Data

Within-Subjects Factorial ANOVA

Box B-9

# B

# INFERENTIAL STATISTICS

## STATISTICAL REASONING

Descriptive statistics are concerned with describing or summarizing data. The results from our LSD experiment (in appendix A) can be summarized by saying that the control group had a mean running time of 13.60 seconds and a standard deviation of 2.63, whereas the experimental rats injected with LSD had a mean of 16.90 seconds and a standard deviation of 3.52 seconds. On average, the experimental rats ran 3.30 seconds slower than the controls, but should we take this difference seriously? Perhaps it resulted from chance factors such as measurement error or a few rats in the control group having a particularly good day and thus feeling like running a bit faster. How can we judge whether the difference between the two conditions is real (reliable) or a fluke? Inferential statistics are used to answer this question.

In actual practice, answering this question is not too complicated. We choose an appropriate statistical test for the experimental situation, perform a few staightforward computations on a calculator (or computer), and then consult a special table. The table informs us of the probability that the difference we found between our conditions is a result of chance factors. If it is sufficiently unlikely to have occurred by chance, we conclude that the difference is statistically significant, or reliable. The computational procedures are often quite simple, but the logic behind them needs to be explained so you will understand how statistical inferences are made.

### Sampling

A **population** is a complete set of measurements (or individuals or objects) having some common observable characteristic (see box B–1). Examples of populations are all U.S. citizens of voting age, all albino rats that have had injections of LSD, and all people asked to remember a list of fifty words. Of course, it is impossible to study the entire population in any of these cases. If we could measure the entire population of rats for running speed after either an injection of LSD or an injection of a chemically inert substance, we would have a better idea of the effects of LSD. (Any difference, of course, might still

Characteristics of a population of scores are called *parameters,* and characteristics of a sample of scores drawn from a larger population are *statistics.* The mean of an entire population of scores is a parameter, and the mean of a sample is a statistic. Different symbols are used for population parameters and sample statistics. Some of the most frequent are listed here. Several of the concepts have already been explained, and the others will be discussed in the next few pages.

$N$ = number of scores in a population

$n$ = number of scores in a sample

$\mu$ = population mean ($\mu$ is pronounced mu)

$\bar{X}$ = sample mean

$\sigma^2$ = population variance ($\sigma$ is pronounced sigma)

$s^2$ = sample variance $\dfrac{\Sigma(X - \bar{X})^2}{n}$

$\hat{s}^2$ = unbiased estimate of population variance $\dfrac{\Sigma(X - \bar{X})^2}{n - 1}$

$\sigma$ = population standard deviation

$s$ = sample standard deviation

$\hat{s}$ = sample standard deviation based on the unbiased variance estimate

$\sigma_{\bar{x}}$ = standard error of the mean $\dfrac{\sigma}{\sqrt{N}}$

$s_{\bar{x}}$ = estimated standard error of the mean $\dfrac{s}{\sqrt{n}}$ or $\dfrac{s}{\sqrt{n - 1}}$

be attributable to measurement error.) But because it is almost always impractical to measure an entire population, we must sample from it. A **sample** is a subset of a population, and it is what we are usually examining when we compare experimental conditions. Thus, we make statistical inferences when we draw a conclusion about an entire population on the basis of only a sample of observations. We really want to know about the effects of LSD and the inert substance on rats in general, but we hope to draw this conclusion from a sample of, say, twenty rats in each condition.

Technically, we can only *generalize* about the population from which we have sampled, but if we took this statement literally, experimental research would hardly be worth doing. If we received fifty rats from a supply house, and we selected a sample of forty and randomly assigned them to the two conditions of our experiment, would our conclusions be true only of the population of fifty rats? Well, perhaps technically, but no one would care about the result if this were so, and we would not have wasted our time doing the experiment. We at least want to assume that the results are characteristic of that strain of rats, and, perhaps, that these results also generalize to other species, including human beings. The problem is the same in research with human beings. Suppose you are a researcher at the University of Toronto interested in some aspect of social behavior. You ready your experiment, which has three conditions, and you plan to use students from introductory psychology courses as subjects, a common practice. You display a sign-up sheet, randomly assign the volunteers to the three experimental conditions when they show up, and collect your data. To whom do your conclusions generalize? To introductory psychology students at the University of Toronto who volunteered for your experiment? If so, who cares about what you found? In practice, psychologists assume that their results generalize more widely than to the limited population from which they sampled for their experiment.

**The distribution of sample means.**  One way we could check on the reliability of our hypothetical LSD experiment would be to perform the experiment repeatedly using new groups of rats. Of course, obtaining exactly the same mean running times for the experimental and control conditions in these replications would be unlikely. The means in seconds for the experimental and control conditions in four replications might be 17.9 and 12.5, 16.0 and 13.4, 16.6 and 14.5, and 15.4 and 15.1. Because the experimental rats that receive the LSD always run slower than the control rats, we would have more confidence in our original finding, although the difference is rather small in the last replication. If we repeated the experiment like this and plotted the distribution of the sample means obtained in the two conditions, the distributions would tend to be normal, and they would have all the characteristics of a normal distribution, such as a certain proportion of the scores falling under a certain part of the curve. A plot of the difference between the sample means in each experiment would also be normally distributed.

To give you a better idea of the **distribution** of sample means concept, let us borrow an example from a class demonstration by Horowitz (1974, pp. 179–182). Horowitz manufactured a population of 1,000 normally distributed scores so that the mean and standard deviation of the entire population would be known, which is almost never the case in actual research situations. His 1,000 scores ranged from 0 to 100 and had a mean of 50 and a standard deviation of 15.8. The scores were listed on 1,000 slips of paper and placed in a container. Horowitz had ninety-six students take samples of ten slips from the container and calculate the mean. On each draw from the container, the student took out a slip, noted its number, and then replaced the slip. The slips were then somewhat mixed up in the container, another slip was drawn, and so on. After each student calculated the mean of the ten scores in his or her sample, Horowitz collected all ninety-six sample means and plotted their distribution, which is represented in table B–1. The intervals between which means might fall are on the left and the number of means falling within each interval is on the right. Notice that the distribution is almost perfectly symmetrical, with almost as many scores in any interval a certain distance below the true mean of the population (50) as above it. Also, the mean of the ninety-six sample means (49.99) is quite close to the actual mean of the population (50). The main thing you should notice in table B–1 is the great variability among the sample means. Although each sample of ten was presumably random, not biased in any way, and came from the same population, one sample had a mean of 37.8, while another had a mean of 62.3. If you did an experiment and found two very different sample means, and you tried to decide whether they came from the same underlying distribution or two different distributions, you might think that such a large difference indicated that they came from different distributions.

| TABLE B–1 | THE DISTRIBUTION OF SAMPLE MEANS FOR THE 96 SAMPLES TAKEN BY STUDENTS IN HOROWITZ'S CLASS. EACH SAMPLE MEAN WAS BASED ON 10 OBSERVATIONS. (AFTER HOROWITZ, 1974, *ELEMENTS OF STATISTICS FOR PSYCHOLOGY AND EDUCATION*, TABLE 8.1. COPYRIGHT 1974 BY McGRAW-HILL. REPRINTED WITH PERMISSION.) |
|---|---|

| Interval | Frequency | |
|---|---|---|
| 62.0–63.9 | 1 | |
| 60.0–61.9 | 1 | |
| 58.0–59.9 | 3 | |
| 56.0–57.9 | 7 | |
| 54.0–55.9 | 9 | |
| 52.0–53.9 | 12 | |
| 50.0–51.9 | 15 | Mean of sample means = 49.99 |
| 48.0–49.9 | 15 | Standard deviation ($s$) of |
| 46.0–47.9 | 13 | sample means = 5.01 |
| 44.0–45.9 | 9 | |
| 42.0–43.9 | 6 | |
| 40.0–41.9 | 3 | |
| 38.0–39.9 | 1 | |
| 36.0–37.9 | 1 | |
| | 96 samples | |

In other words, you would think that the experimental treatment produced scores reliably different (from a different distribution) than the control scores. Usually this is a good rule—the larger the difference between means in the conditions, the more likely the means are to be reliably different—but as we have seen, even random sampling from a known distribution can produce sample means that differ greatly from each other and from the true population mean, which is known in this case. While pondering small differences between means, keep this lesson in mind. Is the 3.30-second difference between experimental and control means in our hypothetical LSD experiment really reliable?

**The standard error of the mean.** The **standard error of the mean** is the standard deviation of a distribution of sample means. In the data in table B–1, it is 5.01. The standard error of the mean gives us some idea as to the amount of variability in the distribution of sample means, or how likely it is that the value of any particular sample mean is in error. Large standard errors indicate great variability, whereas small ones tell us that a particular sample mean is likely to be quite close to the actual population mean. Thus, the standard error of the mean is a very useful number.

You might be wondering why we bother to tell you about the standard error of the mean if in order to calculate it you must repeat an experiment numerous times to get the distribution of sample means and then calculate its standard deviation. Fortunately, you do not. The formula for finding the standard error of the mean (represented by $\sigma_{\bar{x}}$) is simply the standard deviation of the population ($\sigma$) divided by the square root of the number of observations ($\sqrt{n}$). Or

$$\sigma_{\bar{x}} = \frac{\sigma}{\sqrt{n}} \qquad \text{(B–1)}$$

Now, if you are still with us you might well be thinking, "Terrific. What good does this do me if the standard deviation of the population, the numerator in equation B–1, is never known?" That question has occurred to statisticians, too, so they have devised a method for estimating the standard deviation of the population from the standard deviation of a sample. If you look back at equation A–2, in appendix A, where the formula for the standard deviation of a sample ($s$) appears, and simply replace the $n$ in the denominator by $n - 1$, you have the formula for getting an unbiased estimate of $\sigma$, the standard deviation of the population. The equation for finding the standard error of distribution of sample means (called the standard error of the mean, or $s_{\bar{x}}$) is

$$\text{Estimated } \sigma_{\bar{x}} = s_{\bar{x}} = \frac{s}{\sqrt{n - 1}} \qquad (B-2)$$

Because the standard error of the mean indicates our error in assuming that our sample mean represents the population mean, we want it to be as small as possible. Equations B–1 and B–2 tell us how to do this: Increase the size of the sample, $n$, which increases the denominator in the equation. The greater is $n$, the sample size, the smaller will be the standard error of the mean, $s_{\bar{x}}$. In a population involving 1,000 scores, the sample mean should be closer to the population mean if there are 500 observations in the sample rather than only 10.

Horowitz drove this point home to the ninety-six students in his class by having them repeat the exercise of drawing slips from the population of 1,000 scores and calculating the mean again, but this time he had them sample fifty slips rather than only ten. The resulting distribution of sample means is shown in table B–2. This time, with larger samples, there is much less variability in the sample means. They are much closer to the actual population mean of 50. The standard deviation of the distribution of sample means, or the standard

TABLE B–2 THE DISTRIBUTION OF SAMPLE MEANS FOR THE 96 SAMPLES TAKEN BY STUDENTS WHEN SAMPLE SIZE ($n$) = 50. THE DISTRIBUTION IS AGAIN NORMAL, AS IN TABLE B–1, BUT WHEN EACH SAMPLE IS BASED ON A LARGER SAMPLE SIZE, AS IT IS HERE, THE VARIABILITY OF THE DISTRIBUTION (REPRESENTED BY THE STANDARD ERROR OF THE MEAN) IS MUCH SMALLER. (AFTER HOROWITZ, 1974, *ELEMENTS OF STATISTICS FOR PSYCHOLOGY AND EDUCATION*, TABLE 8.2. COPYRIGHT 1974 BY McGRAW-HILL. REPRINTED WITH PERMISSION.)

| Interval | Frequency |
|---|---|
| 55.0–55.9 | 1 |
| 54.0–54.9 | 3 |
| 53.0–53.9 | 5 |
| 52.0–52.9 | 9 |
| 51.0–51.9 | 13 |
| 50.0–50.9 | 17 |
| 49.0–49.9 | 16 |
| 48.0–48.9 | 14 |
| 47.0–47.9 | 9 |
| 46.0–46.9 | 6 |
| 45.0–45.9 | 2 |
| 44.0–44.9 | 1 |
| | 96 samples |

Mean of sample means = 49.95
Standard deviation ($s$) of sample means = 2.23

error of the mean, is 2.23, as opposed to 5.01 when the sample size was only 10. If $n = 100$ in a sample from the 1,000 scores, the standard error of the mean would be 1.59; with a sample of 500 it would be .71, and with 1,000 scores in a sample it would be only .50. (These were calculated from equation B–1 because the standard deviation, $\sigma$, is known for the entire population.) The reason we might not get the population mean even with a sample of 1,000 is that the sampling was done with *replacement;* that is, after a slip was drawn it was returned to the container and it might have been drawn again and again, but some slips were ever drawn.

The lesson to be learned is that we should always try to maximize the number of observations—the sample size—in experimental conditions so that the statistics obtained will be as close as possible to the population parameters.

## Testing Hypotheses

Scientists set up experiments to test hypotheses. The conventional statistical logic for testing hypotheses goes something like this. An experimenter arranges conditions, such as the experimental (LSD) and control (placebo) in our experiment with rats in order to test an *experimental hypothesis.* The experimental hypothesis in this case is that LSD will have some effect on running speed. This is tested against the *null hypothesis,* which maintains that the two conditions do not differ in their effects on running speed. In other words, the experimental hypothesis holds that the samples of running speeds come from two different underlying populations (that is, populations with different distributions), and the null hypothesis maintains that the two samples come from the same distribution. Statistical tests allow us to find the likelihood with which the null hypothesis can be rejected. How unlikely must a null hypothesis be to be rejected? If an experimental result differs from that to be expected by the null hypothesis (so much so that a difference that great would be expected on the basis of chance only 5 times in 100), we conclude that the null hypothesis can be rejected. This .05 *level of significance* is just a convention; many psychologists prefer a more conservative .01 level for rejection, so that a null hypothesis is rejected only if the experimental result is likely to occur by chance in one case in 100. At any rate, the experimental hypothesis is tested, in a sense, indirectly. It is not affirmed, but the null hypothesis is rejected.

The logic of pitting an experimental hypothesis against the null hypothesis has come under attack in recent years for several reasons. Some argue that it gives a misleading idea about how scientists operate. For one thing, not many researchers wander about the world losing any sleep over or investing any thought into the null hypothesis. In general, experiments are set up to test our theories, and what is of primary concern is how the results can be interpreted or accounted for by our theories. Of special interest is the case in which important experimental results seem irreconcilable with the major theories of a phenomenon. Experiments are important because of what they tell us about our theories and ideas—this is why we designed them in the first place—and not about rejection of the null hypothesis. But the logic of testing hypotheses against the null hypothesis is widely used as an introduction, however oversimplified to the way scientific inference proceeds. Thus we present it here.

**Testing hypotheses: Parameters known.** The logic of testing hypotheses against the null hypothesis can be aptly illustrated in cases in which the parameters of a population are known and we wish to determine whether a particular sample comes from the population. Such cases are quite unusual in actual research, of course, because population parameters are rarely known. Suppose you were interested in whether the members of your experimental-psychology class were reliably above the national mean in intelligence as measured by IQ tests (or reliably below, as the case may be). We know the population parameters in this case; the mean is 100 and the standard deviation is 15. You could test your class easily enough by giving them the short form of some intelligence test, such as the Otis, developed for group testing. Suppose you randomly sampled 25 people from your class of 100 and found the mean IQ of the sample to be 108 with a standard deviation of 5.

How do we go about testing the experimental hypothesis that the class is reliably brighter than the population as a whole? First let us consider the hypotheses. The experimental hypothesis is that the students are brighter than people in the nation as a whole, or that the IQ scores of the students sampled come from a different population than randomly selected people. The null hypothesis is that there is no reliable difference between our sample and the national mean, or that the students in the class are a sample from the same national population. If the null hypothesis were actually the case, the difference between the sample mean of 108 and the population parameter mean ($\mu$) of 100 would result from random factors. Certainly this is not implausible, because we have seen from our discussion of the distribution of sample means how much a sample mean can differ from a population parameter, even when the sample is selected in an unbiased manner. Remember Horowitz's classroom demonstration, the results of which are portrayed in tables B–1 and B–2.

The normal curve, the distribution of sample means, and $z$ scores can help us determine how likely it is that the null hypothesis is false. When unbiased samples are taken from a larger population, the means of these samples are normally distributed. With normal distributions we can specify what proportion of the distribution falls under each part of the curve (as shown in figure A–3 in appendix A). Remember also that the $z$ scores are the calculation of any score in a normal distribution in standard deviation units from the mean.

All this by way of review. Now how does this help us? What we do in testing the hypothesis that the sample is actually from a population with a mean IQ greater that the population at large is to treat the sample mean as an individual score (in terms of our earlier discussion) and calculate a $z$ score on the basis of the deviation of the sample mean from the population mean. In our case, we know the population mean is 100 and the class mean of the randomly selected students is 108. To calculate the $z$ score, we also need to know the standard error of the mean, the standard deviation of the distribution of sample means. The equation for the $z$ score here is

$$z = \frac{\bar{X} - \mu}{\sigma_{\bar{x}}} \tag{B–3}$$

The standard error of the mean ($\sigma_{\bar{x}}$) is found by dividing the standard deviation of the population ($\sigma$) by $\sqrt{n}$ (see equation B–1), so $\sigma_{\bar{x}}$ is $15/\sqrt{25}$, or 3. Thus $z$ is $(108 - 100)/3$, or 2.67. This result, 2.67, allows us to reject the null hypothesis with reasonable confidence and conclude in favor of the alternative hypothesis, that the class is actually superior in IQ to the population at large. We establish this by asking the question: How likely is a *z* score of 2.67 when a sample mean is drawn from a larger population whose mean is actually 100? The answer is that it will occur only .0038 of the time, or 38 times in 10,000. (In the next paragraph we will discuss how this was calculated.) The custom in rejecting the null hypothesis is that if it could only occur 1 time in 20 by chance, we would reject it, so the difference in the class sample mean is *reliably different* or **significantly different** from the mean of the population.

To explain how this rather remarkable conclusion is reached, we need to refer again to the special property of the normal curve, which is that a certain proportion of cases fall under each part of the curve. Looking at figure B–1, we see that having a *z* score of ±2.00 is highly improbable. Greater scores in either direction occur only 2.15 percent of the time. In other words, the probability of such an occurrence is .0215. This is also below the 5 percent or .05 level of significance, so any mean score two or more standard deviations from the population mean is considered, using the logic we have outlined here, significantly different from the population mean. In fact, the critical *z* value for rejecting the null hypothesis at the .05 level of significance, is ±1.96. Table C–1 (in appendix C) presents (1) *z* scores from zero to four, with (2) the amount of area between the mean and *z*, and (3) most important, the amount of area beyond *z*. The amount of area beyond *z* is the probability of finding a score that distant from the mean on the basis of chance alone. Once again, when this probability falls below .05, as it does with *z* scores of ±1.96 (or more), we reject the null hypothesis. Notice that with a *z* of 2.67, as in our IQ example, the probability of such a rare occurrence is only .0038 (see figure B–1).

The statistical problem we have just considered—comparing a sample mean to a population parameter to see whether the sample came from that population—is rather artificial, because population parameters are rarely known. But

**FIGURE B–1**

Standard Normal Distribution.

This is the standard normal distribution shown in figure A–3 (in appendix A). There are two sides or tails to the distribution, positive and negative. If an experimenter simply asserts that there should be a difference between an experimental and control condition but does not specify the direction of the difference, this is called a nondirectional hypothesis. If a *z* = 2.67 is found, it is necessary to look up the probability that this will occur in both the positive and negative tails of the distribution and add the two, since the experimenter did not specify whether the difference should be positive or negative. When the experimenter has specified the direction of difference, we need only look up the probability in one tail. Because the distribution is symmetrical, the probability that the null hypothesis can be rejected is half as great with a one-tailed as with a two-tailed test. The less certain we are about the outcome of an experiment, the greater the difference between conditions must be for us to decide that it is not a result of chance.

this example does exhibit characteristics of most common statistical tests. In all tests, some computations are performed on the data or raw scores, a value is found as in the $z$ score just calculated, and then this value is compared with a distribution of values so that we can determine the likelihood that such a value could be obtained if the null hypothesis were in fact true. This distribution tells us, then, with what probability our result could be attributed to random variation. If the probability is less than 5 cases in 100 ($p < .05$), then we say the null hypothesis can be rejected. This probability is sometimes called the **alpha ($\alpha$) level** and, as already mentioned, some psychologists prefer values of .01 or even smaller so that they can be more certain that the null hypothesis should be rejected.

Our $z$-score test can also serve to introduce you very briefly to other important statistical concepts. First, let us consider two types of errors that can be made by applying statistical tests to experimental data. A **type 1 error** is rejection of the null hypothesis when it is actually true, and the probability that this error will occur is indexed by the alpha level, which the experimenter selects. If the alpha level is $p = .05$, then we shall mistakenly reject the null hypothesis in 5 cases in 100. This illustrates the probabilistic nature of inferential statistics; we are not absolutely certain that a null hypothesis can be rejected, only reasonably certain. Thus the lower $\alpha$ level or $p$ level we use in determining statistical significance, the less chance we have of making a type 1 error. However, this increases the probability of a **type 2 error,** which occurs when we *fail* to reject the null hypothesis when it is actually *false*. Thus by setting $\alpha$ levels at different points we systematically decrease and increase the two types of errors.

Scientists are generally conservative in such matters, so the $\alpha$ level is usually kept fairly small, such as .05 or .01 (rather than, say, .10 or .15). Thus we minimize the error of rejecting the null hypothesis when it is true, or claiming a difference in our results when a difference is not there. As a consequence, though, we increase the probability of type 2 errors. A *conservative* statistical test minimizes type 1 errors, whereas more *liberal* statistical tests increase the probability of a type 1 error but decrease that of a type 2 error.

Unfortunately, we can never know positively in our experimental situations whether we are committing type 1 or type 2 errors. We find this out primarily by doing experimental replications of our results, but also by calculating the power of a statistical test. The *power* of a test is the probability of rejecting the null hypothesis when it is actually false; thus we always want to maximize the power of our statistical tests. This is not the place to describe how the power of tests is calculated, but we will note the two main factors that influence power. Look back to the $z$-score formula in equation B–3. Whatever would make the $z$ score larger would increase the power of the statistical test, or the likelihood of rejecting the null hypothesis. The value $\mu$, the population mean, is fixed. Thus only two changes in the values of equation B–3 can affect $z$. One is the difference between the sample mean and the population mean ($\overline{X} - \mu$) and the other is $n$, the size of the sample. If the discrepancy between $\mu$ and $\overline{X}$ is increased (or in other cases, if the difference between sample means in an experimental comparison is increased), the probability of rejecting the null hypothesis is also increased.

However, there is nothing we can do about the size of the difference between means; it is fixed. We can increase the power of our statistical tests by increasing the sample size. The reason is that with larger samples we can be more confident that our sample means represent the mean of the populations from which they are drawn, and thus we can be more confident that any difference between a sample mean and a population mean (or between two sample means) is reliable. Sample size can have a great effect on the power of a test, as shown in table B–3. Presented there are the $z$ scores and $p$ values for our difference between a sample mean of 108 IQ points and the population mean of 100 as the sample size varies. As the sample size varies, so will our conclusion as to whether the sample came from a national population or a more restricted, high-IQ population. If we assume that the null hypothesis is actually false here, then by increasing sample size we decrease the probability of a type 2 error, or increase the power of the test we are using.

One final issue to consider is the *directionality* of statistical tests. According to conventional logic involved in testing an alternative hypothesis against the null hypothesis, the alternative hypothesis may be **directional** or **nondirectional.** If an experimental and a control group are in an experiment, a nondirectional alternative hypothesis would be that the two groups differ in performance on the dependent variable. A directional hypothesis would, in addition, state the predicted direction of the difference; for example, the experimental group might be predicted to do better than the control.

This distinction is important, because if the alternative hypothesis is directional, a **one-tailed** (or *one-sided*) **statistical test** is used, but if the alternative hypothesis is nondirectional, a **two-tailed** (*two-sided*) **test** is used. One versus two "tails" refers to whether we consider one or both tails of the distribution

| TABLE B–3 | HOW VARYING SAMPLE SIZE ($n$) AFFECTS THE POWER OF A STATISTICAL TEST, OR HOW LIKELY IT IS THAT THE NULL HYPOTHESIS CAN BE REJECTED WHEN THE TEST IS USED. THE EXAMPLE IS FROM THE $z$ SCORE (CALCULATED IN THE TEXT) ON A MEAN SAMPLE IQ OF 108, WHERE |
|---|---|

$$z = \frac{\bar{X} - \mu}{\sigma_{\bar{x}}}$$

IF THE MEAN DIFFERENCE REMAINS THE SAME BUT $n$ INCREASES, $z$ INCREASES BECAUSE

$$\sigma_{\bar{x}} = \frac{\sigma}{\sqrt{n}}$$

| $n$ | $\bar{X} - \mu$ | $\sigma_{\bar{x}}$ | $z$ | $p^{\dagger}$ |
|---|---|---|---|---|
| 2 | 8 | 13.14 | .61 | .2709 |
| 5 | 8 | 6.70 | 1.19 | .1170 |
| 7 | 8 | 5.67 | 1.41 | .0793 |
| 10 | 8 | 4.74 | 1.69 | .0455* |
| 12 | 8 | 4.33 | 1.85 | .0322* |
| 15 | 8 | 3.88 | 2.06 | .0197* |
| 17 | 8 | 3.64 | 2.20 | .0139* |
| 20 | 8 | 3.35 | 2.38 | .0087* |
| 25 | 8 | 3.00 | 2.67 | .0038* |
| 50 | 8 | 2.12 | 3.77 | .0001* |
| 75 | 8 | 1.73 | 4.62 | <.00003* |
| 100 | 8 | 1.50 | 5.33 | <.00003* |

*All these values meet the conventional level of statistical significance, $p < .05$ (one-tailed).
$^{\dagger}p$ values are one-tailed.

when we look up a $p$ level associated with the result of a statistical test (say, $z = 1.69$).

Examine figure B–1 once again. We took a sample ($n = 25$) of students, determined that the mean IQ of the sample was 108, and calculated a $z = +2.67$ in testing to see whether this was different from the mean population IQ of 100. If we had no prior expectation of how the sample IQ should deviate from the normal population—if we thought it could be either higher or lower—this would have a nondirectional hypothesis. In fact, we did expect the sample IQ to be greater than 100, so we tested a directional hypothesis and thus used a one-tailed test. This means we looked up the resulting $z$ score in only one tail of the normal distribution, that greater than zero. A $z = +2.67$ leads to a one-tailed $p$ value of .0038. If the hypothesis were nondirectional, then we have no a priori right to expect the resultant $z$ score to be greater instead of less than zero. The $z$ score could be in the positive or negative tail. Because the difference could have occurred in either direction, we use a two-tailed test. In practice, the two tails of the distribution are symmetrical, so we simply double the $p$ level for the one-tailed test. In our example, if the hypothesis had been non-directional, $p$ would equal $2 \times .0038$, or .0076, still well below .05.

Two-tailed tests are more conservative and less powerful than one-tailed tests: it is harder to reject the null hypothesis. If we are uncertain about the outcome of an experiment, we need a greater value of the statistic to allow us to declare a difference. In practice, most investigators prefer to use the more conservative two-tailed test with sufficient power ensured by fairly large sample sizes.

In the remainder of this appendix, we show you how to calculate several statistical tests. We believe it is important for you to do some of these calculations by hand or with a calculator. When you carefully work through the calculations, you become familiar with the logic and components of the statistical test. However, as we noted in appendix A (see box A–2), many statistical tests can be done automatically by sophisticated calculators and computers. All you need to do is access a particular statistical program and then enter your data. Most of the statistical tests outlined in this appendix can be done by the computer package, MINITAB. We suggest you become familiar with the statistical capabilities of the computing equipment available to you. Computers can conduct statistical tests faster and more accurately than you can, and they relieve some of the tedium associated with the more complex statistical tests that require numerous complicated calculations.

## Tests for Differences Between Two Groups

A variety of statistical tests exist for almost every purpose. At present, we are interested in discussing tests that assess the reliability of a difference between two groups or conditions. How do we pick an appropriate test from all those available? There is no hard-and-fast rule. Tests vary in the assumptions they make, their power, and the types of situation for which they are appropriate. Perhaps the most popular test for the difference between two means in psychological research is the *t* **test**. Because the *t* test provides the same estimate of reliability as does the simple analysis of variance (discussed next), we will first concentrate on two other tests, the Mann-Whitney *U* test and the Wilcoxon signed-ranks test. These tests also are useful in introducing yet another type of statistical test.

The Mann-Whitney and Wilcoxon tests are **nonparametric statistics** as opposed to **parametric statistics.** Parametric statistical tests, such as analysis of variance and $t$, are those that make assumptions about the underlying population parameters of the samples on which the tests are performed. Common assumptions of parametric tests are that the variances of the underlying populations being compared are equivalent, that the underlying distributions are normal, and that the level of measurement is at least an interval scale. If these assumptions are not met, the test may be inappropriate. But how can we ever know whether the assumptions underlying the test are met if we do not know the population parameters? Usually we cannot, except by estimating population parameters from sample statistics. However, if we turn to nonparametric statistical tests, the problem does not arise, because these tests make no assumptions about the underlying population parameters. This is why these tests are often called distribution-free statistics. Because the parameters cannot be known anyway, this provides an important reason for using nonparametric tests. Another reason is that these tests are generally very easy to calculate and can often

---

| BOX B–2 |
|---------|

Calculation of a Mann-Whitney U Test

These data are from our hypothetical experiment involving the effects of LSD on the running speeds of rats. Using the Mann-Whitney $U$ test to test the reliability of the difference between our two samples, we follow these steps:

*Step 1.* Rank all the numbers for *both groups* together, beginning with the smallest number. Assign it the lowest rank.

| CONTROL (PLACEBO) | | EXPERIMENTAL (LSD) | |
|---|---|---|---|
| Latency (sec.) | Rank | Latency (sec.) | Rank |
| 9 | 1.5 | 9 | 1.5 |
| 10 | 3 | 13 | 11.5 |
| 11 | 4.5 | 13 | 11.5 |
| 11 | 4.5 | 14 | 17 |
| 12 | 7 | 14 | 17 |
| 12 | 7 | 15 | 21 |
| 12 | 7 | 16 | 24.5 |
| 13 | 11.5 | 16 | 24.5 |
| 13 | 11.5 | 16 | 24.5 |
| 13 | 11.5 | 17 | 28 |
| 13 | 11.5 | 17 | 28 |
| 14 | 17 | 18 | 32 |
| 14 | 17 | 18 | 32 |
| 14 | 17 | 18 | 32 |
| 15 | 21 | 18 | 32 |
| 15 | 21 | 19 | 35.5 |
| 16 | 24.5 | 19 | 35.5 |
| 17 | 28 | 20 | 37.5 |
| 18 | 32 | 22 | 39 |
| 20 | 37.5 | 26 | 40 |
| | $\Sigma$ rank$_1$ 295.5 | | $\Sigma$ rank$_2$ 524.5 |

Note: When scores are tied, assign the mean value of the tied ranks to each. Thus, for both 9-second times in this example, the rank 1.5 is assigned (the mean of 1 and 2).

*Step 2.* The equations for finding $U$ and $U'$ are as follows, where $n_1$ is the size of the smaller sample, $n_2$ is the size of the larger sample, $\Sigma R_1$ is the sum of the ranks of the smaller sample, and $\Sigma R_2$ is the sum of the ranks of the larger sample. The subscripts are important only if the sample sizes are unequal, which is not the case here.

$$U = n_1 n_2 + \frac{n_1(n_1 + 1)}{2} - \Sigma R_1$$

$$U = (20)(20) + \frac{(20)(21)}{2} - 295.5$$

$$U = 400 + 210 - 295.5$$

$$U = 314.5$$

$$U' = n_1 n_2 + \frac{n_2(n_2 + 1)}{2} - \Sigma R_2$$

$$U' = (20)(20) + \frac{(20)(21)}{2} - 524.5$$

$$U' = 85.5$$

Actually, it is only necessary to compute $U$ or $U'$, because the other can be found according to the equation:

$$U = n_1 n_2 - U'$$

or

$$U' = n_1 n_2 - U.$$

*Step 3.* Take $U$ or $U'$, whichever value is *smaller*, and look at table C–2 (in appendix C) to see whether the difference between the two groups is reliable. The values in the table are recorded by different sample sizes. In this case, both sample sizes are 20, so the critical value from the table is 88. For the difference between the two groups to be judged reliable, the $U$ or $U'$ from the experiment must be *less than* the appropriate value shown in table C–2. Because 85.5 is less than 88, we can conclude that the difference between the two groups is reliable at the .001 level of significance.

Note: Table C–2 is only appropriate when the sizes of the two samples are between 8 and 21. For other cases, consult an advanced text.

---

even be done by hand. However, nonparametric tests are usually less powerful than parametric tests used in the same situation; that is, they are less likely to allow the null hypothesis to be rejected.

The **Mann-Whitney U test** is used when we want to compare two samples and decide whether they come from the same or different underlying populations. It is used when the two samples are composed of different subjects— between-subjects designs. The underlying rationale for the Mann-Whitney test will not be discussed here. The logic is the same as in other statistical tests in which a value is computed from the test and compared with a distribution of values to determine whether the null hypothesis should be rejected. The way in which the Mann-Whitney test is applied to data is outlined in box B–2, where the reliability of the difference between the two samples in our hypo- thetical LSD experiment is tested.

The **Wilcoxon signed-ranks test** is also used in testing for the difference between two samples, but in this case the design must be a *related-measures design*. In other words, either the same subjects must serve in both the experimental and control groups (a within-subjects design), or the subjects must be matched in some way. Of course, precautions must be taken in within-subjects designs to ensure that a variable such as practice or fatigue is not confounded with the variable of interest.

Before considering the signed-ranks test, let us examine its simpler cousin, the sign test, which is appropriate in the same situations. The sign test is the essence of simplicity. Suppose we have twenty-six subjects serving in both conditions of an experiment, and we predict that when subjects are in the experimental condition they will do better than when they are in the control condition. Now suppose that nineteen subjects actually do better in the experimental condition than in the control, and the reverse is true for the other seven. Is this difference reliable? The sign test yields an answer to this question without our needing to know what the actual scores were. Under the null hypothesis, we might expect thirteen subjects to perform better in the experimental condition and thirteen to perform better in the control. The sign test allows us to compute the exact probability that the null hypothesis is false when there are nineteen cases in the predicted direction but also seven reversals or exceptions. The null hypothesis can be rejected in this case with a .014 significance level (one-tailed); with a nondirectional prediction, $p$ equals .028 (two-tailed). In table C–3 (in appendix C) are the $\alpha$ levels (one-tailed) for situations with sample sizes from three to forty-two when there are $x$ number of exceptions to the predicted hypothesis. So, for example, when there are sixteen subjects in the experiment (remember, in both conditions) and thirteen show the predicted pattern of results whereas three exhibit reversals, we can reject the null hypothesis at the .011 level of significance (one-tailed).

The sign test uses very little of the data from an experiment, just whether the subjects performed better or worse in one condition than in another. For the sign test, the direction of the difference and not its magnitude is what matters. The sign test therefore wastes much of the information gathered in an experiment and is not a very powerful statistical test. The Wilcoxon signed-ranks test is used as the sign test in situations where the same (or matched) subjects are in two conditions and the direction of the difference is taken into account, too. For this reason it is also called the *sized sign test*. The Wilcoxon test is more powerful than the sign test. Box B–3 shows how the Wilcoxon signed-ranks test is used.

In boxes B–4 and B–5 we present the corresponding $t$ tests for the analyses presented in the previous two boxes. The $t$ test is a parametric test, which means that we assume that the underlying distributions are roughly normal in

---

| **BOX B–3** | Imagine an experiment designed to test whether Professor von Widget's memory |
|---|---|
| Calculation of the Wilcoxon Signed-Ranks Test | course really works. A group of thirty subjects is presented with fifty words to remember. Then the subjects are randomly separated into two groups, and a check indicates that the groups do not differ reliably in terms of the mean number of words recalled. The experimental group is given Professor von Widget's |

three-week course, and the control group is not. Then all thirty subjects are tested again on another fifty-word list. The controls show no improvement from one list to another. The question is whether the experimental subjects' memories were reliably improved. (Note: We could—and should—also compare the experimental subjects' performance on the second test with that of the controls. The Mann-Whitney test is appropriate for this comparison. Do you know why?) We use the Wilcoxon signed-ranks test to assess whether the experimental subjects improved reliably from the first test to the second.

*Step 1.* Place the data in a table (such as the one that follows) where both scores for each subject (before and after the memory course) are paired together. Find and record the difference between the pairs.

| MEAN NUMBER OF WORDS RECALLED | | | | |
|---|---|---|---|---|
| **Subject** | **Before** | **After** | **Difference** | **Rank** |
| 1 | 11 | 17 | + 6 | 14 |
| 2 | 18 | 16 | − 2 | 5.5 |
| 3 | 9 | 21 | +12 | 15 |
| 4 | 15 | 16 | + 1 | 2.5 |
| 5 | 14 | 17 | + 3 | 8.5 |
| 6 | 12 | 15 | + 3 | 8.5 |
| 7 | 17 | 16 | − 1 | 2.5 |
| 8 | 16 | 17 | + 1 | 2.5 |
| 9 | 15 | 20 | + 5 | 13 |
| 10 | 19 | 16 | − 3 | 8.5 |
| 11 | 12 | 13 | + 1 | 2.5 |
| 12 | 16 | 14 | − 2 | 5.5 |
| 13 | 10 | 14 | + 4 | 11.5 |
| 14 | 17 | 20 | + 3 | 8.5 |
| 15 | 6 | 10 | + 4 | 11.5 |
| | $\bar{X} = 13.80$ | $\bar{X} = 16.07$ | | |

*Step 2.* Rank the values of the differences according to size, beginning with the smallest. *Ignore the sign.* Use the absolute values of the numbers. For tied ranks, assign each the mean value of the ranks. (See the right-hand column of the table here.)

*Step 3.* Add the ranks for all the difference values that are negative (5.5 + 2.5 + 8.5 + 5.5 = 22.0) and positive (14 + 15 + 2.5 + 8.5 + 8.5 + 2.5 + 13 + 2.5 + 11.5 + 8.5 + 11.5 = 98.0). These are the signed-rank values.

*Step 4.* Take the signed-rank value that is smallest (22) and go to table C−4 in appendix C. Look up the number of pairs of observations (listed as *n* on the left). There are 15 in this case. Then look at the number under the desired level of significance. The direction of the outcome was predicted (we expected the memory course to help rather than hurt recall of words), so let us choose the value under the .025 level of significance for a one-tailed test. This value is 25. If the smaller of the two values from the experiment is *below* the appropriate value in the table, then the result is reliable. Since 22 is below 25, we can conclude that Professor von Widget's course really did help subjects recall words.

Note: Remember that the controls showed no improvement in performance from one test to the other. This is a crucial bit of information, for otherwise we could not rule out two plausible competing hypotheses—one is that the improvement on the second list was simply owing to practice on the first, and the other is that the second list was easier than the first.

These are hypothetical experimental data previously discussed (see box B–2). The calculation formula is

$$t = \frac{\bar{X}_1 - \bar{X}_2}{\sqrt{\left[\dfrac{\Sigma X_1^2 - \dfrac{(\Sigma X_1)^2}{n_1} + \Sigma X_2^2 - \dfrac{(\Sigma X_2)^2}{n_2}}{n_1 + n_2 - 2}\right]\left[\dfrac{1}{n_1} + \dfrac{1}{n_2}\right]}}$$

$\bar{X}_1$ = mean of group 1
$\bar{X}_2$ = mean of group 2
$n_1$ = number of scores in group 1
$n_2$ = number of scores in group 2

$\Sigma X_1^2$ = sum of squared scores in group 1
$\Sigma X_2^2$ = sum of squared scores in group 2
$(\Sigma X_1)^2$ = square of group-1 sum
$(\Sigma X_2)^2$ = square of group-2 sum

| CONTROL (PLACEBO) | | | | EXPERIMENTAL (LSD) | | | |
|---|---|---|---|---|---|---|---|
| X | X² | X | X² | X | X² | X | X² |
| 9 | 81 | 13 | 169 | 9 | 81 | 17 | 289 |
| 10 | 100 | 14 | 196 | 13 | 169 | 18 | 324 |
| 11 | 121 | 14 | 196 | 13 | 169 | 18 | 324 |
| 11 | 121 | 14 | 196 | 14 | 196 | 18 | 324 |
| 12 | 144 | 15 | 225 | 14 | 196 | 18 | 324 |
| 12 | 144 | 15 | 225 | 15 | 225 | 19 | 361 |
| 12 | 144 | 16 | 256 | 16 | 256 | 19 | 361 |
| 13 | 169 | 17 | 289 | 16 | 356 | 20 | 400 |
| 13 | 169 | 18 | 324 | 16 | 356 | 22 | 484 |
| 13 | 169 | 20 | 400 | 17 | 289 | 26 | 676 |

$\Sigma X = 272$     $\Sigma X^2 = 3838$     $\Sigma X = 338$     $\Sigma X^2 = 5960$
$\bar{X} = 13.60$                              $\bar{X} = 16.90$

Step 1. After calculating $\Sigma X$, $\Sigma X^2$, and $\bar{X}$ for each group (by the way, there is no need to rank order our data), we need to calculate $(\Sigma X)^2/n$ for each group: $(272)^2/20 = 3699.20$ and $(338)^2/20 = 5712.20$. Then we need to determine $\Sigma X^2 - (\Sigma X)^2/n$ for each group: $3838 - 3699.2 = 138.8$ and $5960 - 5712.2 = 247.8$.

Step 2. Now we add the two group figures we obtained in the last step: $247.8 + 138.8$, and divide this sum by $n_1 + n_2 - 2$: $386.6/38 = 10.17$.

Step 3. The quotient obtained in Step 2 (10.17) is multiplied by

$$\left[\frac{1}{n_1} + \frac{1}{n_2}\right]: (10.17)(2/20) = 1.02.$$

Step 4. We now take the square root of the product obtained in Step 3: $\sqrt{1.02} = 1.01$.

Step 5. We find the absolute difference between the mean scores of the two groups (by subtracting one from the other, and ignoring the sign): $16.90 - 13.60 = 3.30$.

Step 6. $t$ = the difference between means (Step 5) divided by the results of Step 4: $3.30/1.01 = 3.27$. So, our $t = 3.27$. To evaluate this, we look in the tabled values of $t$ in table C–5 in appendix C. We enter this table with the number of degrees of freedom ($df$) in our experiment, which means the number of scores that are free to vary. For a between-subjects $t$, the degrees of freedom are $n_1 + n_2 - 2$, in this case $df = 38$. For $p = .05$ and $df = 38$, the critical value of $t$ is 2.04 in our table (always take the next lowest $df$ to calculate the critical value). Our obtained $t$ exceeds the critical value, so we can reject the hypothesis that our two groups have the same running scores; that is, LSD had an effect on the behavior of our subjects.

---

**BOX B–5**

Calculation of a
Within-Subjects $t$
Test

The hypothetical data are from Professor Widget's experiment (see box B–3). The computational formula for the within-subjects $t$ test is as follows:

$$t = \sqrt{\frac{n - 1}{[n\Sigma D^2/(\Sigma D)^2] - 1}}$$

where $n$ = number of subjects; and $D$ = difference in the scores of a given subject (or matched subject pair) in the two conditions.

| | MEAN NUMBER OF WORDS RECALLED | | | |
|---|---|---|---|---|
| **Subject** | **Before** | **After** | **Difference** | **$D^2$** |
| 1 | 11 | 17 | + 6 | 36 |
| 2 | 18 | 16 | − 2 | 4 |
| 3 | 9 | 21 | +12 | 144 |
| 4 | 15 | 16 | + 1 | 1 |
| 5 | 14 | 17 | + 3 | 9 |
| 6 | 12 | 15 | + 3 | 9 |
| 7 | 17 | 16 | − 1 | 1 |
| 8 | 16 | 17 | + 1 | 1 |
| 9 | 15 | 20 | + 5 | 25 |
| 10 | 19 | 16 | − 3 | 9 |
| 11 | 12 | 13 | + 1 | 1 |
| 12 | 16 | 14 | − 2 | 4 |
| 13 | 10 | 14 | + 4 | 16 |
| 14 | 17 | 20 | + 3 | 9 |
| 15 | 6 | 10 | + 4 | 16 |
| | $\bar{X} = 13.80$ | $\bar{X} = 16.07$ | $\Sigma D = 35$ | $\Sigma D^2 = 285$ |
| | | | $(\Sigma D)^2 = 1,225$ | |

*Step 1.* After you arrange the scores for each subject in pairs as shown in this table, record the difference between each pair and then square each of these difference scores.

*Step 2.* Add the difference scores across subjects, which yields $\Sigma D$, then square this sum to get $(\Sigma D)^2$: $\Sigma D = 35$; and $(\Sigma D)^2 = 1,225$.

*Step 3.* Calculate the sum of the squared difference scores to get $\Sigma D^2 = 285$.

*Step 4.* Multiply $\Sigma D^2$ (Step 3) by the number of subjects: $285 \times 15 = 4,275$.

*Step 5.* Divide the product found in Step 4 by $(\Sigma D)^2$: $4,275/1,225 = 3.49$, and then subtract 1 from the result: $3.49 - 1 = 2.49$.

*Step 6.* Divide the number of subjects less 1 ($n - 1$) by the result of Step 5: $14/2.49 = 5.62$.

*Step 7.* $t = \sqrt{5.62} = 2.37$.

*Step 8.* To evaluate $t$, compare it to the critical values shown in table C–5 in appendix C. Enter the table with $n - 1$ $df$, and for this study $df = 14$. With $df = 14$, the critical value of $t$ is 2.145 for $p = .05$. The obtained $t$ exceeds the critical value, so we can conclude that von Widget's course really did affect word recall.

shape. Furthermore, the $t$ test and other parametric tests were designed to be used on data that are at least interval in nature. The $U$ test and the sign test require only ordinal data. The $t$ tests are essentially based on $z$ scores having to do with the standard error of the difference between means. Thus, even if the computational formulas appear unusual at first, the underlying logic is the same as that discussed earlier in this chapter.

**Magnitude of effect.** In summary, calculating a statistic such as $z$ or $t$ allows us to determine whether the results are owing to chance factors. Determining the $\alpha$ level of a difference, as in box B–4, tells us that the difference is significant statistically, and we can reject the null hypothesis. An interesting characteristic of $t$ (and the $F$ test that we discuss next) is that the value of $t$ needed to reject the null hypothesis decreases as the degrees of freedom increase. This means that the power of $t$ increases with sample size just as $z$ (see table B–3). It is also the case, as the formula for the independent groups $t$ in box B–4 indicates, that as we hold the difference between means constant, increasing the sample size ($n$) will increase the value of $t$ by making the denominator smaller. This too will allow us to have more power and reject more null hypotheses. In some cases, then, it is possible that very small differences between means will be statistically significant. Usually when we do an experiment, we want substantial differences between means—a big effect of the independent variable. With a very powerful experiment, however, we can detect differences between means that are exceptionally small. In the latter instance, we may not know whether the difference is owing to a powerful independent variable or a very powerful statistical test.

How do we know when we have a powerful independent variable? To determine the **magnitude of effect** of the independent variable, we need a way of showing the degree to which belonging in a particular group predicts the behavior. In the example in box B–4, we would like to have a calculation that would allow us to have some idea as to whether a rat had received a placebo or LSD. The information we need is a correlation coefficient, because we want to predict what happened to a rat in much the same way we would want to predict a memory score based on head size as in box A–1. After we have conducted a $t$ test, we can then calculate a correlation to assess the magnitude of the effect. The correlation coefficient that would be appropriate here is $r_{pb}$, which is called the **point-biserial** correlation. The formula is

$$r_{pb} = \sqrt{t^2/(t^2 + df)} \tag{B–4}$$

The value of $r_{pb}$ can be between 0 and $+1.00$. By convention, values up to .3 are considered to be small, a value from .31 to .5 is moderate, and values over .5 are appreciable (Thompson & Buchanan, 1979). For the data in box B–4, $t = 3.27$ and $df = 38$, which yields by formula B–4, $r_{pb} = .47$. This would be deemed a moderate effect. The same formula for $r_{pb}$ could be used for the results in box B–5. Why don't you determine what it is?

There are other measures of magnitude of effect, but we will not present the ones that are used with the $F$ test, a discussion of which follows. The logic is the same regardless of the statistical test: the inferential statistics tell us how sure we may be that the null hypothesis is wrong. On the other hand, the correlation coefficients, such as $r_{pb}$, measure the magnitude of the effect of the independent variable—the degree to which the null hypothesis is wrong (Thompson & Buchanan, 1979).

Measures of magnitude of effect have another important use, which is also related to the fact that rejecting the null hypothesis is dependent on sample size. Suppose we conduct an experiment and discover that the value of $t$ is not large enough to reject the null hypothesis even though the difference between means is not zero (that is, they differ). One reason that the $t$ value is small could be owing to a sample size that is too small to detect a statistically significant difference between the means. In this case, a prudent researcher would calculate the appropriate measure of magnitude of effect, such as $r_{pb}$. If the coefficient yields a moderate or appreciable value, then it might be wise to increase the sample size in the experiment in order to reject the null hypothesis. Getting statistically significant results is important, but it is really only "half the battle." Significant results that are very small are not particularly exciting. Appreciable effects that are not statistically significant probably mean that you are on to something, and an increase in statistical power is warranted.

## The Analysis of Variance

Most psychological research has progressed beyond the stage where there are only two conditions, an experimental and a control that are compared with each other. Investigators typically have more than two conditions in psychological research. In our example of the effects of LSD on running speed of rats, it may be quite useful to vary the amount of LSD administered to the rats. Perhaps low dosages and high dosages produce different effects. We could not determine this from the two-group design where one group received LSD in some amount and the other did not. To evaluate the results of such an experiment with multiple groups, we must use the analysis of variance. A simple analysis of variance is used in situations where one factor or independent variable (such as amount of LSD) is varied systematically, and thus is usually called a *one-factor analysis of variance*.

Often researchers are interested in varying more than one factor. They may want to vary two or more factors simultaneously. In such complex or multifactor experimental designs, the analysis of variance is also appropriate, but it is more complex. In this section, we introduce you to the logic of both simple and multifactor analyses of variance (abbreviated *ANOVA*).

**Simple analysis of variance.** The heart of the analysis-of-variance procedure is a comparison of variance estimates. We have already discussed the concept of variance and how it is estimated from one particular sample of observations. You should refer back to the section on measures of dispersion if the concept of variance is unclear. Recall that the equation for the unbiased estimate of the population variance is

$$\hat{s}^2 = \frac{\Sigma(X - \bar{X})^2}{n - 1} \tag{B–5}$$

and that when the deviation of scores from the mean is large, the variance will be great. Similarly, when the deviations from the mean are small, the variance will be small.

In the analysis of variance, two independent estimates of variance are obtained. One is based on the variability between the different experimental groups—how much the means of the different groups differ from one another. Actually, the variance is computed as to how much the individual group means differ from the overall mean of all scores in the experiment. The greater the difference among the means of the groups, the greater will be the **between-groups variance**.

The other estimate of variance is the **within-groups variance**. This is the concept we discussed in considering estimates of variance from individual samples. Now we are concerned with finding an estimate of within-groups variance that is representative of all the individual groups, so we take the mean of the variances of these groups. The within-groups variance gives us an estimate of how much the subjects in the groups differ from one another (or the mean of the group). Two variance estimates are obtained, one for the variance within groups and one for the variance between groups. Now what good does this do?

The basic logic of testing to see whether the scores of the different groups or conditions are reliably different is as follows. The null hypothesis is that all the subjects in the various conditions are drawn from the same underlying population; the experimental variable has no effect. If the null hypothesis were true and all the scores in the different groups came from the same population, then the between-groups variance should be the same as the within-groups variance. The means of the different groups should differ from one another no more nor less than do the scores within the groups. For us to reject the null hypothesis, then, the means of the different groups must vary from one another more than the scores vary within the groups. The greater the variance (differences) between the groups of the experiment, the more likely the independent variable is to have had an effect, especially if the within-groups variance is low.

The person who originated this logic was the eminent British statistician R. A. Fisher, and the test is referred to as an $F$ test in his honor. The $F$ test is simply a ratio of the between-groups variance estimate to the within-groups variance estimate, so

$$F = \frac{\text{between-groups variance}}{\text{within-groups variance}} \tag{B–6}$$

According to the logic just outlined, the $F$ ratio under the null hypothesis should be 1.00, because the between-groups variance should be the same as the within-groups variance. The greater the between-groups variance is than the within-groups variance and, consequently, the greater the $F$ ratio is than 1.00, the more confident we can be in rejecting the null hypothesis. Exactly how much greater the $F$ ratio must be than 1.00 depends on the **degrees of freedom** in the experiment, or how free the measures are to vary. This depends both on the number of groups or conditions in the experiment and on the number of observations in each group. The greater the number of degrees of freedom, the smaller need be the value of the $F$ ratio to be judged a reliable effect, as you can see from examining table C–6 in appendix C. Follow the computational example in box B–6 carefully to get a feel for the analysis of variance.

---

| **BOX B–6** |
|---|
| Computing Simple Analysis of Variance: One Variable— Between Subjects |

This ANOVA is often called a *one-way ANOVA* because there is only *one* independent variable. Imagine you have just performed an experiment testing the effects of LSD on the running speeds of rats, but that there were three levels of LSD administered, rather than two as in our earlier example. Ten rats received no LSD, ten others received a small amount, and a third group received a great amount. Thus the experiment uses a between-subjects design where amount of LSD (none, small, large) is the independent variable and running time is the dependent variable. First calculate the sum of the scores ($\Sigma X$) and the sum of the squared values of the scores ($\Sigma X^2$).

| | AMOUNT OF LSD | | |
|---|:---:|:---:|:---:|
| | **None** | **Small** | **Large** |
| | 13 | 17 | 26 |
| | 11 | 15 | 20 |
| | 14 | 16 | 29 |
| | 18 | 20 | 31 |
| | 12 | 13 | 17 |
| | 14 | 19 | 25 |
| | 10 | 18 | 26 |
| | 13 | 17 | 23 |
| | 16 | 19 | 25 |
| | 12 | 21 | 27 |
| $\Sigma X$ = | 133 | 175 | 249 |
| $\bar{X}$ = | 13.30 | 17.50 | 24.90 |
| $\Sigma X^2$ = | 1819 | 3115 | 6351 |
| $\Sigma\Sigma X$ = | 557 | $\Sigma\Sigma X^2 = 11285$ | |

A basic quantity in calculating analysis of variance is the *sum of squares,* which is an abbreviation for the *sum of squared deviations from the mean.* If you look back to equation A–1 (in appendix A), which defines the variance of a sample, you will see that the sum of squares is the numerator. Three sum of squares are of interest. First, there is the total sum of squares (*SS* Total), which is the sum of the squared deviations of the individual scores from the grand mean or the mean of all scores in all groups in the experiment. Second, there is the sum of squares between groups (*SS* Between), which is the sum of the squared deviations of the group means from the grand mean. Third, the sum of squares within groups (*SS* Within) is the mean of the sum of the squared deviations of the individual scores within groups or conditions from the group means. It turns out that *SS* Total = *SS* Between + *SS* Within, so that in practice only two sums of squares need be calculated; the third can be found by subtraction.

These sums of squares could be calculated by taking the deviations from the appropriate means, squaring them, and then finding the sum, but such a method would take much time and labor. Fortunately, there are computational formulas that allow the calculations to be done more easily, especially if the values of $\Sigma X$

and $\Sigma X^2$ have been found for each group, as in the present data. The formula for finding the total sum of squares is

$$SS \text{ Total} = \Sigma\Sigma X^2 - \frac{T^2}{N} \qquad\qquad (B-7)$$

where $\Sigma\Sigma X^2$ means that each score within each group is squared ($X^2$) and all these squared values are added together, so $\Sigma X^2$. There are two summation signs, one for summing the squared values within groups and one for then summing these $\Sigma X^2$ across the different groups. The $T$ is the total of all scores, and $N$ is the total number of scores in the experiment. So $SS$ Total in our example is calculated in the following way:

$$SS \text{ Total} = \Sigma\Sigma X^2 - \frac{T^2}{N}$$

$$SS \text{ Total} = 1819 + 3115 + 6351 - \frac{(133 + 175 + 249)^2}{30}$$

$$SS \text{ Total} = 11{,}285 - \frac{310{,}249}{30}$$

$$SS \text{ Total} = 11{,}285 - 10{,}341.63$$

$$SS \text{ Total} = 943.37$$

The between-groups sum of squares is calculated with the following formula:

$$SS \text{ Between} = \Sigma\frac{(\Sigma X)^2}{n} - \frac{T^2}{N} \qquad\qquad (B-8)$$

The first part of the formula means that the sum of the values for each group is squared and then divided by the number of observations on which it is based, or $(\Sigma X)^2/n$; then these values are summed across groups, so $\Sigma(\Sigma X)^2/n$. The second part of the formula is the same as the the $SS$ Total:

$$SS \text{ Between} = \Sigma\frac{(\Sigma X)^2}{n} - \frac{T^2}{N}$$

$$SS \text{ Between} = \frac{17{,}689}{10} + \frac{30{,}625}{10} + \frac{62{,}001}{10} - 10{,}341.63$$

$$SS \text{ Between} = 11{,}031.50 - 10{,}341.63$$

$$SS \text{ Between} = 689.87$$

The sum of squares within groups can be found by subtracting $SS$ Between from $SS$ Total, so $SS$ Within $= 943.37 - 689.87 = 253.50$. As a check, we should also calculate it directly. This is done by computing an $SS$ Total (as in equation B–7) for each group and summing all these sums of squares for the individual groups. Unless we have made an error, this quantity should equal $SS$ Within obtained by subtraction. Note that

$$\frac{(\Sigma\Sigma X)^2}{N} \text{ or } \frac{T^2}{N}$$

is called the *correction term* because it is taken out of most $SS$.

After we have obtained the various sums of squares, it is convenient to construct an analysis-of-variance table such as the one that follows. In the far left column appears the source of variance, or source. Keep in mind that there are two primary sources of variance we are interested in comparing—between groups and within groups.

In the next column are the number of degrees of freedom (*df*). These can be thought of as the number of scores that are free to vary, given that the total is fixed. For the degrees of freedom between groups, if the overall total is fixed, all groups are free to vary except one. Thus, the between-groups $df$ is the number of groups minus one. In our example, then, it is $3 - 1 = 2$. The within-groups $df$ is equal to the total number of scores minus the number of groups, because there is one score in each group that cannot vary if the group total is fixed. So within-groups $df$ is $30 - 3 = 27$. The total $df =$ between-groups $df +$ within-groups $df$.

The third column includes the **sum of squares** ($SS$), which have already been calculated. The fourth column represents the *mean squares* ($MS$), which are found by dividing the $SS$ by the $df$ for each row. Each mean square is an estimate of the population variance if the null hypothesis is true. But if the independent variable had an effect, the between-groups mean square should be larger than the within-groups mean square.

As discussed in the text, these two values are compared by computing an $F$ ratio, which is found by dividing the $MS$ Between by the $MS$ Within. Once the $F$ value is calculated, it is necessary to determine whether the value reaches an acceptable level of statistical significance. By looking at table C–6 in appendix C, we can see that for 2 and 26 degrees of freedom (the closest we can get to 2 and 27), an $F$ value of 9.12 is needed for the .001 level of significance. Our $F$ value surpasses 9.12, so we can conclude that the groups varied reliably in running speed because of variation in the independent variable—amount of LSD injected.

| Source | df | SS | MS | F | P |
|---|---|---|---|---|---|
| Between-groups | 2 | 689.87 | 344.94 | 36.73 | <.001 |
| Within-groups | 27 | 253.50 | 9.39 | | |
| Total | 29 | 943.37 | | | |

Note: If you compute analyses of variance with the aid of a calculator, watch out for errors. If you come up with a negative sum of squares within-groups (by subtracting $SS$ Between from $SS$ Total), you will know you made an error. You cannot have a negative sum of squares. You should compute $SS$ Within both by subtraction and directly, anyway, as a check. One common error is to confuse $\Sigma X^2$ (square each number and then sum the squares) with $(\Sigma X)^2$, which is the square of the total of the scores.

---

| **BOX B–7** |
|---|
| Within-Subjects (Treatments × Subjects) ANOVA— One Variable (One-way ANOVA) |

We could have conducted the previous three-level LSD study with a within-subjects rather than a between-subjects design. Of course, we would have counterbalanced the order of administering dosages across subjects. Let us assume that we used nine subjects in our within-subjects LSD study: Three subjects received the dose order None-Large-Small; three received the doses in the Small-None-Large order; and three were dosed in the order Large-Small-None. After each dose of LSD, the rats' running time in the straight alley was recorded. We could analyze the effects of order by a two-factor, within-subjects ANOVA (see box B–9), but for the purposes of this illustration, we will ignore the effects of treatment order.

In a within-subjects ANOVA, we need to calculate the following kinds of variability:

**SS Total**—This is the variation about the mean of all the scores. *SS* Total is the sum of the remaining sums of squares.

**SS Treatment**—This is the difference among the treatment conditions and is calculated like SS Between in the previous ANOVA.

**SS Subjects**—This estimates the differences among individuals in our experiment and is used to calculate the next SS.

**SS Error** or **SS Treatment × Subject**—This represents the random variability that would occur in the scores of the same individuals in the same conditions. This interaction gives the ANOVA the name **Treatments × Subjects.** Usually, this SS is called *error variance,* and it is the denominator of the F ratio of the treatment effect.

We will use the hypothetical data from the first nine subjects of the LSD study shown in box B–6. We will assume the ordering of treatments as mentioned earlier. You should set up your data table as follows, so that the scores for each subject are in a row. Leave room so that a given subject's total score summed across treatments can appear in the table. You might also want to leave room for the squares of the scores and the squares of the subjects' totals.

RUNNING TIMES

| Subject | None | Amount of LSD Small | Large | Subject Total | Subject Total Squared |
|---|---|---|---|---|---|
| 1 | 13 | 17 | 26 | 56 | 3136 |
| 2 | 11 | 15 | 20 | 46 | 2116 |
| 3 | 14 | 16 | 29 | 59 | 3481 |
| 4 | 18 | 20 | 31 | 69 | 4761 |
| 5 | 12 | 13 | 17 | 42 | 1764 |
| 6 | 14 | 19 | 25 | 58 | 3364 |
| 7 | 10 | 18 | 26 | 54 | 2916 |
| 8 | 13 | 17 | 23 | 53 | 2809 |
| 9 | 16 | 19 | 25 | 60 | 3600 |
| $\Sigma X =$ | 121 | 154 | 222 | 497 | |
| $\Sigma X^2 =$ | 1675 | 2674 | 5622 | | 27497 |

$\Sigma\Sigma X = 497$     $\Sigma\Sigma X^2 = 9971 (1675 + 2674 + 5622)$

*Step 1.* When you calculate $\Sigma\Sigma X$ by adding the three treatment totals (121 + 154 + 222), you can check your accuracy by adding up the subject totals, the sum of which should equal $\Sigma\Sigma X$. Calculate $\Sigma X^2$ for each treatment, $\Sigma\Sigma X^2$, and the sum of the squares of the subject totals (last column).

*Step 2.* Calculation of the correction term, C

$C = (\Sigma\Sigma X)^2/N$, where N = the total number of scores in the table (9 subjects × 3 scores for each subject)
= $497^2/27$
= 247009/27
= 9148.48

*Step 3.* SS Total = $\Sigma\Sigma X^2$ − Step 2
= 9971 − 9148.48
= 822.52

*Step 4.* SS Treatments = SS Dose. SS Dose is calculated by summing the squares of the treatment totals, dividing that sum by the number of scores in each treatment, and then subtracting C (Step 2).

$$SS \text{ Dose} = \frac{121^2 + 154^2 + 222^2}{9} - \text{Step 2}$$

$$= 87419/9 - \text{Step 2}$$

$$= 9737.89 - 9148.48$$

$$= 589.41$$

*Step 5.* $SS$ Subject = Sum of the squared subject totals (final column in the table) divided by the number of scores per subject (3) minus $C$.

$$= 27947/3 - \text{Step 2}$$

$$= 9315.67 - 9148.48$$

$$= 167.19$$

*Step 6.* $SS$ Error = $SS$ Total $-$ $SS$ Dose $-$ $SS$ Subject

$$= \text{Step 3} - \text{Step 4} - \text{Step 5}$$

$$= 822.52 - 589.41 - 167.19$$

$$= 65.92$$

*Step 7.* Determination of $df$

$$df \text{ Total} = \# \text{ scores} - 1 = 26$$

$$df \text{ Dose} = \# \text{ treatments} - 1 = 2$$

$$df \text{ Subject} = \# \text{ subjects} - 1 = 8$$

$$df \text{ Error} = (df \text{ Dose})(df \text{ Subject}) = 16$$

*Step 8.* Determination of $MS$

$$MS \text{ Dose} = SS \text{ Dose}/df \text{ Dose} = 589.41/2 = 294.71$$

$$MS \text{ Error} = SS \text{ Error}/df \text{ Error} = 65.92/16 = 4.12$$

*Step 9.* $F = MS \text{ Dose}/MS \text{ Error} = 294.71/4.12 = 71.53$

*Step 10.* Summary Table

| Source | SS | df | MS | F |
|--------|-----|-----|--------|-------|
| Subjects | 167.19 | 8 | | |
| Dose | 589.41 | 2 | 294.71 | 71.53 |
| Error | 65.92 | 16 | 4.12 | |
| Total | 822.52 | 26 | | |

We determine the significance of the $F$ ratio by entering table C–6 (in appendix C) with 2 and 16 degrees of freedom. Our obtained $F$ greatly exceeds those needed for significance with 2 and 16 $df$, so we can conclude that dose level of LSD influenced the running times of our rats.

If the simple analysis of variance yields a significant $F$ ratio, there is still more we would like to know, in particular, which of the individual conditions vary among themselves. This is especially important in cases where manipulation of the independent variable is qualitative in nature. *Quantitative* variation of an independent variable is when the quantity of an independent variable is manipulated (for example, amount of LSD), whereas *qualitative* variation is when conditions vary but not in some easily specified quantitative manner. An example of qualitative variation is an instructional manipulation in which the different conditions vary in terms of the instructions given at the beginning of the experiment. In such situations, it is not enough simply to say that the conditions vary reliably from one to another. It is of interest to know which particular conditions differ. To answer this question, we need to perform tests after the simple analysis of variance. In these follow-up tests (generally called post hoc tests), the conditions of the experiment are taken two at a time and compared so that we can see which pairs are reliably different. There are several statistical tests for this purpose. We could perform analyses of variance on groups taken as pairs, which is equivalent to performing $t$ tests, but usually other tests are done. These include the Newman-Keuls test, the Scheffé test, Duncan's multiple-range test, Tukey's HSD (Honestly Significant Differences) test, and Dunnett's test. These tests vary in their assumptions and their power. You should consult statistical texts when you need to use a follow-up test. Follow-up tests are also used when manipulation of the independent variable is quantitative in nature. These are called *trend tests* (we will not discuss them here).

**Multifactor analysis of variance.** To discover the multiple determinants of behavior and how they interact, we must perform experiments in which more than one factor is varied simultaneously. The appropriate procedure for analyzing results of such experiments is the *multifactor analysis of variance*. There may be any number of factors in the experiment, but it is rare to find more than four variables of interest manipulated simultaneously. When there are two factors, the analysis is referred to as a two-way ANOVA; when there are three factors, it is a three-way ANOVA; and so on.

The importance of such complex designs involving more than one factor is that they allow the experimenter to assess how different factors may *interact* to produce a result. Recall that an interaction occurs when the effect of one experimental variable is influenced by the level of the other experimental variable. When performing a complex analysis of variance, we find out the separate effects of each factor in the experiment (called **main effects**), and also how the variables affect one another (called **interaction effects,** or simply *interactions*).

In the following two boxes, we present some recipes for complex ANOVAs. Because of space limitations, we have refrained from presenting much of the logic behind these tests. However, you should find the examples useful in analyzing your own results even if you have not had a formal course in statistics.

---

| BOX B–8 | This is a between-subjects design. The data are from a memory experiment in which subjects had to remember words of either high imagery (cigar) or low imagery (democracy). Some subjects simply said the words to themselves as they were presented (rote rehearsal), and the other subjects tried to get a mental image of the words (elaborative rehearsal). |
|---|---|
| Calculation of a 2 × 2 ANOVA | |

| | HIGH-IMAGERY WORDS | | LOW-IMAGERY WORDS | |
|---|---|---|---|---|
| | Rote Rehearsal | Elaborative Rehearsal | Rote Rehearsal | Elaborative Rehearsal |
| | 5 | 8 | 4 | 7 |
| | 7 | 8 | 1 | 6 |
| | 6 | 9 | 5 | 3 |
| | 4 | 7 | 6 | 3 |
| | 4 | 10 | 4 | 5 |
| | 9 | 10 | 3 | 6 |
| | 7 | 8 | 4 | 2 |
| | 5 | 9 | 4 | 4 |
| | 5 | 8 | 5 | 5 |
| | 6 | 9 | 3 | 4 |
| $\Sigma X$ = | 58 | 86 | 39 | 45 |
| $\Sigma X^2$ = | 358 | 748 | 169 | 225 |

$$\Sigma\Sigma X^2 = (358 + \ldots + 225) = 1500 \quad \Sigma\Sigma X = 228$$

*Step 1.* Square the grand sum ($\Sigma\Sigma X = 228$) and divide by the total number of scores (40). $(\Sigma\Sigma X)^2/N = (228)^2/40 = 1299.6$. This is the correction term.

*Step 2.* SS Total $= \Sigma\Sigma X^2 - (\Sigma\Sigma X)^2/N$. Subtract the results of Step 1 from 1500. SS Total $= 200.4$.

*Step 3.* SS Imagery. Get the sum of all scores in each imagery condition, square each sum, then divide each sum by the number of scores yielding each sum, add the two quotients, and then subtract the results of Step 1 from the last sum.

$$SS \text{ Imagery} = (58 + 86)^2/20 + (39 + 45)^2/20 - \text{Step 1}$$

$$= \frac{144^2 + 84^2}{20} - 1299.6$$

$$= 1389.6 - 1299.6$$

$$= 90$$

*Step 4.* SS Rehearsal. This is calculated in the same manner as Step 3, except that you base your calculations on the grand sum of each type of rehearsal.

$$SS \text{ Rehearsal} = \frac{(86 + 45)^2 + (58 + 39)^2}{20} - \text{Step 1}$$

$$= 1328.5 - 1299.6$$

$$= 28.9$$

*Step 5.* SS Imagery $\times$ Rehearsal. Square each group sum and add the squares. Then divide each sum by the number of scores in each sum. From the last result, subtract the SS Imagery (Step 3), SS Rehearsal (Step 4), and Step 1.

$$SSI \times R = \frac{58^2 + 86^2 + 39^2 + 45^2}{10} - \text{Step 1} - \text{Step 3} - \text{Step 4}$$

$$= 14306/10 - 1299.6 - 90 - 28.9$$

$$= 12.1$$

*Step 6. SS* Error. Subtract each of your treatments *SS* from *SS* Total.

*SS* Error = 200.4 − 90 − 28.9 − 12.1

          = 69.4

*Step 7.* Determining degrees of freedom

$df$ Total = the number of measures less one (40 − 1) = 39
$df$ Imagery = number of levels of Imagery less one (2 − 1) = 1
$df$ Rehearsal = number of levels of Rehearsal less one (2 − 1) = 1
$df$ I × R = $df$ Imagery × $df$ Rehearsal (1 × 1) = 1
$df$ Error = $df$ Total − $df$ Imagery − $df$ Rehearsal − $df$ I × R
          (39 − 1 − 1 − 1) = 36

*Step 8.* Summary table. Calculate mean squares (*MS*) by dividing *SS* by the number of *df*. Then calculate the *F* ratios by dividing the treatment *MS* by the *MS* Error.

| SUMMARY TABLE OF A 2 × 2 ANOVA | | | | | |
|---|---|---|---|---|---|
| **Source** | **SS** | **df** | **MS** | **F** | **P** |
| Imagery | 90.0 | 1 | 90.0 | 46.6 | <.05 |
| Rehearsal | 28.9 | 1 | 28.9 | 15.0 | <.05 |
| Imagery × Rehearsal | 12.1 | 1 | 12.1 | 6.3 | <.05 |
| Error | 69.4 | 36 | 1.9 | | |

*Step 9.* To determine the significance of the *F* ratio, enter statistical table C–6 with the *df* for the numerator (in this case it is always 1), and with the *df* for the denominator (*df* Error), which is 36, for any effect you are interested in.

We can conclude that the type of words and type of rehearsal both influenced recall. But we should note that the effects of word type were dependent on the type of rehearsal (that is, we obtained an interaction).

---

**BOX B–9**

Factorial ANOVA with
Repeated Measures
(Within-Subjects)

In a within-subjects ANOVA, we need to calculate both column (treatment) and row (subject) totals, because subjects are serving as their own control condition. In fact, our error variance is estimated by the interaction of subjects within treatments (see box B–7). Arrange your data table so that the scores of a single subject are in a row. It is usually a good idea to leave room so that treatment totals for a single subject may be placed in the table. We will analyze the data from Experiment 1 by Elmes and Bjork (1975). In their study, subjects either rote or elaboratively rehearsed words, and then they performed a distracting math task for 2 or 12 seconds before attempting to recall the words. Thus, this is a 2 × 2 within-subjects design. The individual subjects' total recall scores are shown in the following table.

| Subject | ROTE REHEARSAL Retention Interval | | ELABORATE REHEARSAL Retention Interval | | SUBJECT TOTAL | REHEARSAL TOTAL | | RETENTION TOTAL | |
|---|---|---|---|---|---|---|---|---|---|
| | 2 sec | 12 sec | 2 sec | 12 sec | | Rote | Elab. | 2 sec | 12 sec |
| 1 | 15 | 3 | 11 | 11 | 40 | 18 | 22 | 26 | 14 |
| 2 | 20 | 15 | 19 | 18 | 72 | 35 | 37 | 39 | 33 |
| 3 | 18 | 2 | 18 | 19 | 57 | 20 | 37 | 36 | 21 |
| 4 | 15 | 13 | 16 | 15 | 59 | 28 | 31 | 31 | 28 |
| 5 | 10 | 1 | 17 | 12 | 40 | 11 | 29 | 27 | 13 |
| 6 | 14 | 5 | 16 | 13 | 48 | 19 | 29 | 30 | 18 |
| 7 | 17 | 6 | 19 | 18 | 60 | 23 | 37 | 36 | 24 |
| 8 | 19 | 12 | 16 | 19 | 66 | 31 | 35 | 35 | 31 |
| 9 | 11 | 4 | 9 | 12 | 36 | 15 | 21 | 20 | 16 |
| 10 | 17 | 10 | 14 | 7 | 48 | 27 | 21 | 31 | 17 |
| 11 | 18 | 11 | 18 | 10 | 57 | 29 | 28 | 36 | 21 |
| 12 | 18 | 4 | 20 | 19 | 61 | 22 | 39 | 38 | 23 |
| 13 | 16 | 9 | 19 | 18 | 62 | 25 | 37 | 35 | 27 |
| 14 | 18 | 6 | 19 | 17 | 60 | 24 | 36 | 37 | 23 |
| 15 | 10 | 5 | 10 | 7 | 32 | 15 | 17 | 20 | 12 |
| 16 | 16 | 5 | 19 | 18 | 58 | 21 | 37 | 35 | 23 |
| $\Sigma X =$ | 252 | 111 | 260 | 233 | 856 | 363 | 493 | 512 | 344 |
| $\Sigma X^2 =$ | 4114 | 1033 | 4408 | 3669 | 47776 | 24820 | | 24910 | |

$$\Sigma\Sigma X = 856 \qquad \Sigma\Sigma X^2 = 13224$$

*Step 1.* Determine the total score/subject (row) and total score/treatment combination (column). Find each subject's total score for every independent variable. The subject totals for a particular independent variable (for example, subject #1 has rehearsal totals of 18 and 22) should add up to that subject's total score (in this case, 40). Determine each treatment total by adding the appropriate column sums; check your answer by also adding the subject totals for that level of the independent variable. For example, the Rote Rehearsal total = 252 + 111 = 363 (sum of columns 1 and 2, which is equal to the sum of column 6).

*Step 2.* Determine the correction term ($C$). $C = (\Sigma\Sigma X)^2/N$, where $N =$ the number of measures in the table. $N = 16$ subjects $\times$ 4 scores = 64.

$$C = 856^2/64$$
$$= 732736/64$$
$$= 11449$$

*Step 3.* SS Total $= \Sigma\Sigma X^2 -$ Step 2
$$= 13224 - 11449$$
$$= 1775$$

*Step 4.* SS Subjects. Square each subject's total score (column 5), add the squares, and divide that total by the number of scores for each subject (4), then subtract the results of Step 2.

SS Subject $= 47776/4 -$ Step 2
$$= 11944 - 11449$$
$$= 495$$

*Step 5.* SS Rehearsal $= (363^2 + 493^2)/32 -$ Step 2
$$= 374818/32 - \text{Step 2}$$
$$= 11713.06 - 11449$$
$$= 264.06$$

*Step 6. MS* Rehearsal. Divide the *SS* Rehearsal by the *df* for Rehearsal. The *df* Rehearsal = the number of levels of Rehearsal − 1.

$df$ Rehearsal = 2 − 1.
$MS$ Rehearsal = 264.06/1
$\qquad$ = 264.06

*Step 7. SS* Error Rehearsal. The error term for Rehearsal is the interaction of subjects with rehearsal. Square the subject totals for each level of Rehearsal (columns 6 and 7), add the squares, divide by the number of scores needed to get each sum (2 in this case), then subtract *C* (Step 2), *SS* Subject (Step 4), and *SS* Rehearsal (Step 5).

$$SS \text{ Error Rehearsal} = \frac{18^2 + 22^2 + \dots + 21^2 + 37^2}{2} - \text{Steps 2, 4, and 5}$$

$\qquad$ = 24820/2 − Steps 2, 4, and 5
$\qquad$ = 12410 − 11449 − 495 − 264.06
$\qquad$ = 201.94

*Step 8. MS* Error Rehearsal. Divide *SS* Error Rehearsal by *df* Error Rehearsal.

$df$ = (#Subject − 1)($df$ Rehearsal) = (15)(1)
$MS$ Error Rehearsal = 201.94/15
$\qquad$ = 13.46

*Step 9. F* Rehearsal = *MS* Rehearsal/*MS* Error Rehearsal
$\qquad$ = Step 6/Step 8
$\qquad$ = 264.06/13.46
$\qquad$ = 19.62

*Step 10.* Repeat Steps 5–9 to find the *F* for Retention Interval (RI)

$SS$ RI = $(512^2 + 344^2)/32$ − Step 2
$\qquad$ = 441.00
$MS$ RI = 441.00/(2 − 1)
$\qquad$ = 441.00

$$SS \text{ Error RI} = \frac{26^2 + 14^2 + \dots + 35^2 + 23^2}{2} - \text{Step 2, Step 4, and } SS \text{ RI}$$

$\qquad$ = 24910/2 − C − SS Subject − SS RI
$\qquad$ = 12455 − 11449 − 495 − 441
$\qquad$ = 70

$MS$ Error RI = $SS$ Error RI/(16 − 1)(2 − 1)
$\qquad$ = 70/15
$\qquad$ = 4.67

$F$ RI = 441.00/4.67
$\qquad$ = 94.43

$$\textit{Step 11. } SS \text{ Rehearsal} \times RI = \frac{252^2 + 111^2 + 260^2 + 233^2}{16} - C$$

$\qquad$ − SS Reh − SS RI
$\qquad$ = 12357.13 − 11449 − 264.06 − 441.00
$\qquad$ = 203.07

*Step 12. MS* Rehearsal × RI = 203.07/(*df* Rehearsal)(*df* RI)
$\qquad$ = 203.07/1
$\qquad$ = 203.07

*Step 13. SS* Error Rehearsal $\times$ RI. Calculate this triple interaction by subtracting all the *SS* you have calculated from *SS* Total.

$$
\begin{aligned}
\text{SS Error Rehearsal} \times \text{RI} &= \text{SS Total} - \text{SS Subject} - \text{SS Rehearsal} - \text{SS RI} \\
&\quad - \text{SS Rehearsal} \times \text{RI} - \text{SS Error Rehearsal} \\
&\quad - \text{SS Error RI} \\
&= 1775 - 495 - 264.06 - 441 - 203.07 - 204.94 \\
&\quad - 70 \\
&= 99.93
\end{aligned}
$$

*Step 14.* MS Error Rehearsal $\times$ RI

$$
\begin{aligned}
\text{MS Error Rehearsal} \times \text{RI} &= 99.93/(\#\text{Subject} - 1)(df\ \text{Rehearsal})(df\ \text{RI}) \\
&= 99.93/15 \\
&= 6.66
\end{aligned}
$$

*Step 15.* F Rehearsal $\times$ RI

$$
\begin{aligned}
\text{F Rehearsal} \times \text{RI} &= \text{MS Rehearsal} \times \text{RI}/\text{MS Error Rehearsal} \times \text{RI} \\
&= 203.07/6.66 \\
&= 30.49
\end{aligned}
$$

*Step 16.* Summary table of 2 $\times$ 2 within-subjects ANOVA

| Source | SS | df | MS | F |
|---|---|---|---|---|
| Subjects | 495.00 | 15 | | |
| Rehearsal | 264.06 | 1 | 264.06 | 19.62 |
| Error Reh | 201.94 | 15 | 13.46 | |
| Retention Interval | 441.00 | 1 | 441.00 | 94.43 |
| Error RI | 70.00 | 15 | 4.67 | |
| Reh $\times$ RI | 203.07 | 1 | 203.07 | 30.49 |
| Error Reh $\times$ RI | 99.93 | 15 | 6.66 | |
| Total | 1775.00 | 63 | | |

To determine significance, enter table C–6 with the appropriate degrees of freedom for each *F* ratio. (In this case, the $df = 1$ and 15). Note that both rehearsal and retention interval had significant effects on recall, and that the effects of type of rehearsal are dependent on the length of the retention interval.

| TABLE C–1 (Continued) | (A) z | (B) area between mean and z | (C) area beyond z | (A) z | (B) area between mean and z | (C) area beyond z | (A) z | (B) area between mean and z | (C) area beyond z |
|---|---|---|---|---|---|---|---|---|---|
| | 1.50 | .4332 | .0668 | 2.00 | .4772 | .0228 | 2.50 | .4938 | .0062 |
| | 1.51 | .4345 | .0655 | 2.01 | .4778 | .0222 | 2.51 | .4940 | .0060 |
| | 1.52 | .4357 | .0643 | 2.02 | .4783 | .0217 | 2.52 | .4941 | .0059 |
| | 1.53 | .4370 | .0630 | 2.03 | .4788 | .0212 | 2.53 | .4943 | .0057 |
| | 1.54 | .4382 | .0618 | 2.04 | .4793 | .0207 | 2.54 | .4945 | .0055 |
| | 1.55 | .4394 | .0606 | 2.05 | .4798 | .0202 | 2.55 | .4946 | .0054 |
| | 1.56 | .4406 | .0594 | 2.06 | .4803 | .0197 | 2.56 | .4948 | .0052 |
| | 1.57 | .4418 | .0582 | 2.07 | .4808 | .0192 | 2.57 | .4949 | .0051 |
| | 1.58 | .4429 | .0571 | 2.08 | .4812 | .0188 | 2.58 | .4951 | .0049 |
| | 1.59 | .4441 | .0559 | 2.09 | .4817 | .0183 | 2.59 | .4952 | .0048 |
| | 1.60 | .4452 | .0548 | 2.10 | .4821 | .0179 | 2.60 | .4953 | .0047 |
| | 1.61 | .4463 | .0537 | 2.11 | .4826 | .0174 | 2.61 | .4955 | .0045 |
| | 1.62 | .4474 | .0526 | 2.12 | .4830 | .0170 | 2.62 | .4956 | .0044 |
| | 1.63 | .4484 | .0516 | 2.13 | .4834 | .0166 | 2.63 | .4957 | .0043 |
| | 1.64 | .4495 | .0505 | 2.14 | .4838 | .0162 | 2.64 | .4959 | .0041 |
| | 1.65 | .4505 | .0495 | 2.15 | .4842 | .0158 | 2.65 | .4960 | .0040 |
| | 1.66 | .4515 | .0485 | 2.16 | .4846 | .0154 | 2.66 | .4961 | .0039 |
| | 1.67 | .4525 | .0475 | 2.17 | .4850 | .0150 | 2.67 | .4962 | .0038 |
| | 1.68 | .4535 | .0465 | 2.18 | .4854 | .0146 | 2.68 | .4963 | .0037 |
| | 1.69 | .4545 | .0455 | 2.19 | .4857 | .0143 | 2.69 | .4964 | .0036 |
| | 1.70 | .4554 | .0446 | 2.20 | .4861 | .0139 | 2.70 | .4965 | .0035 |
| | 1.71 | .4564 | .0436 | 2.21 | .4864 | .0136 | 2.71 | .4966 | .0034 |
| | 1.72 | .4573 | .0427 | 2.22 | .4868 | .0132 | 2.72 | .4967 | .0033 |
| | 1.73 | .4582 | .0418 | 2.23 | .4871 | .0129 | 2.73 | .4968 | .0032 |
| | 1.74 | .4591 | .0409 | 2.24 | .4875 | .0125 | 2.74 | .4969 | .0031 |
| | 1.75 | .4599 | .0401 | 2.25 | .4878 | .0122 | 2.75 | .4970 | .0030 |
| | 1.76 | .4608 | .0392 | 2.26 | .4881 | .0119 | 2.76 | .4971 | .0029 |
| | 1.77 | .4616 | .0384 | 2.27 | .4884 | .0116 | 2.77 | .4972 | .0028 |
| | 1.78 | .4625 | .0375 | 2.28 | .4887 | .0113 | 2.78 | .4973 | .0027 |
| | 1.79 | .4633 | .0367 | 2.29 | .4890 | .0110 | 2.79 | .4974 | .0026 |
| | 1.80 | .4641 | .0359 | 2.30 | .4893 | .0107 | 2.80 | .4974 | .0026 |
| | 1.81 | .4649 | .0351 | 2.31 | .4896 | .0104 | 2.81 | .4975 | .0025 |
| | 1.82 | .4656 | .0344 | 2.32 | .4898 | .0102 | 2.82 | .4976 | .0024 |
| | 1.83 | .4664 | .0336 | 2.33 | .4901 | .0099 | 2.83 | .4977 | .0023 |
| | 1.84 | .4671 | .0329 | 2.34 | .4904 | .0096 | 2.84 | .4977 | .0023 |
| | 1.85 | .4678 | .0322 | 2.35 | .4906 | .0094 | 2.85 | .4978 | .0022 |
| | 1.86 | .4686 | .0314 | 2.36 | .4909 | .0091 | 2.86 | .4979 | .0021 |
| | 1.87 | .4693 | .0307 | 2.37 | .4911 | .0089 | 2.87 | .4979 | .0021 |
| | 1.88 | .4699 | .0301 | 2.38 | .4913 | .0087 | 2.88 | .4980 | .0020 |
| | 1.89 | .4706 | .0294 | 2.39 | .4916 | .0084 | 2.89 | .4981 | .0019 |
| | 1.90 | .4713 | .0287 | 2.40 | .4918 | .0082 | 2.90 | .4981 | .0019 |
| | 1.91 | .4719 | .0281 | 2.41 | .4920 | .0080 | 2.91 | .4982 | .0018 |
| | 1.92 | .4726 | .0274 | 2.42 | .4922 | .0078 | 2.92 | .4982 | .0018 |
| | 1.93 | .4732 | .0268 | 2.43 | .4925 | .0075 | 2.93 | .4983 | .0017 |
| | 1.94 | .4738 | .0262 | 2.44 | .4927 | .0073 | 2.94 | .4984 | .0016 |
| | 1.95 | .4744 | .0256 | 2.45 | .4929 | .0071 | 2.95 | .4984 | .0016 |
| | 1.96 | .4750 | .0250 | 2.46 | .4931 | .0069 | 2.96 | .4985 | .0015 |
| | 1.97 | .4756 | .0244 | 2.47 | .4932 | .0068 | 2.97 | .4985 | .0015 |
| | 1.98 | .4761 | .0239 | 2.48 | .4934 | .0066 | 2.98 | .4986 | .0014 |
| | 1.99 | .4767 | .0233 | 2.49 | .4936 | .0064 | 2.99 | .4986 | .0014 |

**TABLE C–1**
**(Continued)**

| (A) z | (B) area between mean and z | (C) area beyond z | (A) z | (B) area between mean and z | (C) area beyond z | (A) z | (B) area between mean and z | (C) area beyond z |
|---|---|---|---|---|---|---|---|---|
| 3.00 | .4987 | .0013 | 3.15 | .4992 | .0008 | 3.50 | .4998 | .0002 |
| 3.01 | .4987 | .0013 | 3.16 | .4992 | .0008 | 3.60 | .4998 | .0002 |
| 3.02 | .4987 | .0013 | 3.17 | .4992 | .0008 | 3.70 | .4999 | .0001 |
| 3.03 | .4988 | .0012 | 3.18 | .4993 | .0007 | 3.80 | .4999 | .0001 |
| 3.04 | .4988 | .0012 | 3.19 | .4993 | .0007 | 3.90 | .49995 | .00005 |
| 3.05 | .4989 | .0011 | 3.20 | .4993 | .0007 | 4.00 | .49997 | .00003 |
| 3.06 | .4989 | .0011 | 3.21 | .4993 | .0007 | | | |
| 3.07 | .4989 | .0011 | 3.22 | .4994 | .0006 | | | |
| 3.08 | .4990 | .0010 | 3.23 | .4994 | .0006 | | | |
| 3.09 | .4990 | .0010 | 3.24 | .4994 | .0006 | | | |
| 3.10 | .4990 | .0010 | 3.25 | .4994 | .0006 | | | |
| 3.11 | .4991 | .0009 | 3.30 | .4995 | .0005 | | | |
| 3.12 | .4991 | .0009 | 3.35 | .4996 | .0004 | | | |
| 3.13 | .4991 | .0009 | 3.40 | .4997 | .0003 | | | |
| 3.14 | .4992 | .0008 | 3.45 | .4997 | .0003 | | | |

**TABLE C–2    Critical Values of the $U$ Statistic of the Mann-Whitney $U$ Test**

To use these four subtables, first decide what level of significance you want with either a one- or a two-tailed test. For example, if you want $p = .05$, two-tailed, use subtable c. Then locate the number of cases or measures ($n$) in both groups in the particular subtable you have chosen. The $U$ value you have calculated must be *less* than that at the appropriate place in the table. For example, if you had 18 subjects in each group of an experiment, and calculated $U = 90$, you could conclude that the null hypothesis can be rejected because the critical $U$ value with groups of these sizes is 99 (see subtable c).

*(a)* Critical Values of $U$ for a One-Tailed Test at .001 or for a Two-Tailed Test at .002

| $n_1$ \ $n_2$ | 9 | 10 | 11 | 12 | 13 | 14 | 15 | 16 | 17 | 18 | 19 | 20 |
|---|---|---|---|---|---|---|---|---|---|---|---|---|
| 1 | | | | | | | | | | | | |
| 2 | | | | | | | | | | | | |
| 3 | | | | | | | | | 0 | 0 | 0 | 0 |
| 4 | | 0 | 0 | 0 | 1 | 1 | 1 | 2 | 2 | 3 | 3 | 3 |
| 5 | 1 | 1 | 2 | 2 | 3 | 3 | 4 | 5 | 5 | 6 | 7 | 7 |
| 6 | 2 | 3 | 4 | 4 | 5 | 6 | 7 | 8 | 9 | 10 | 11 | 12 |
| 7 | 3 | 5 | 6 | 7 | 8 | 9 | 10 | 11 | 13 | 14 | 15 | 16 |
| 8 | 5 | 6 | 8 | 9 | 11 | 12 | 14 | 15 | 17 | 18 | 20 | 21 |
| 9 | 7 | 8 | 10 | 12 | 14 | 15 | 17 | 19 | 21 | 23 | 25 | 26 |
| 10 | 8 | 10 | 12 | 14 | 17 | 19 | 21 | 23 | 25 | 27 | 29 | 32 |
| 11 | 10 | 12 | 15 | 17 | 20 | 22 | 24 | 27 | 29 | 32 | 34 | 37 |
| 12 | 12 | 14 | 17 | 20 | 23 | 25 | 28 | 31 | 34 | 37 | 40 | 42 |
| 13 | 14 | 17 | 20 | 23 | 26 | 29 | 32 | 35 | 38 | 42 | 45 | 48 |
| 14 | 15 | 19 | 22 | 25 | 29 | 32 | 36 | 39 | 43 | 46 | 50 | 54 |
| 15 | 17 | 21 | 24 | 28 | 32 | 36 | 40 | 43 | 47 | 51 | 55 | 59 |
| 16 | 19 | 23 | 27 | 31 | 35 | 39 | 43 | 48 | 52 | 56 | 60 | 65 |
| 17 | 21 | 25 | 29 | 34 | 38 | 43 | 47 | 52 | 57 | 61 | 66 | 70 |
| 18 | 23 | 27 | 32 | 37 | 42 | 46 | 51 | 56 | 61 | 66 | 71 | 76 |
| 19 | 25 | 29 | 34 | 40 | 45 | 50 | 55 | 60 | 66 | 71 | 77 | 82 |
| 20 | 26 | 32 | 37 | 42 | 48 | 54 | 59 | 65 | 70 | 76 | 82 | 88 |

**TABLE C−2
(Continued)**

*(b)* Critical Values of *U* for a One-Tailed Test at .01 or for a Two-Tailed Test at .02

| n₁\n₂ | 9 | 10 | 11 | 12 | 13 | 14 | 15 | 16 | 17 | 18 | 19 | 20 |
|---|---|---|---|---|---|---|---|---|---|---|---|---|
| 1 | | | | | | | | | | | | |
| 2 | | | | | 0 | 0 | 0 | 0 | 0 | 0 | 1 | 1 |
| 3 | 1 | 1 | 1 | 2 | 2 | 2 | 3 | 3 | 4 | 4 | 4 | 5 |
| 4 | 3 | 3 | 4 | 5 | 5 | 6 | 7 | 7 | 8 | 9 | 9 | 10 |
| 5 | 5 | 6 | 7 | 8 | 9 | 10 | 11 | 12 | 13 | 14 | 15 | 16 |
| 6 | 7 | 8 | 9 | 11 | 12 | 13 | 15 | 16 | 18 | 19 | 20 | 22 |
| 7 | 9 | 11 | 12 | 14 | 16 | 17 | 19 | 21 | 23 | 24 | 26 | 28 |
| 8 | 11 | 13 | 15 | 17 | 20 | 22 | 24 | 26 | 28 | 30 | 32 | 34 |
| 9 | 14 | 16 | 18 | 21 | 23 | 26 | 28 | 31 | 33 | 36 | 38 | 40 |
| 10 | 16 | 19 | 22 | 24 | 27 | 30 | 33 | 36 | 38 | 41 | 44 | 47 |
| 11 | 18 | 22 | 25 | 28 | 31 | 34 | 37 | 41 | 44 | 47 | 50 | 53 |
| 12 | 21 | 24 | 28 | 31 | 35 | 38 | 42 | 46 | 49 | 53 | 56 | 60 |
| 13 | 23 | 27 | 31 | 35 | 39 | 43 | 47 | 51 | 55 | 59 | 63 | 67 |
| 14 | 26 | 30 | 34 | 38 | 43 | 47 | 51 | 56 | 60 | 65 | 69 | 73 |
| 15 | 28 | 33 | 37 | 42 | 47 | 51 | 56 | 61 | 66 | 70 | 75 | 80 |
| 16 | 31 | 36 | 41 | 46 | 51 | 56 | 61 | 66 | 71 | 76 | 82 | 87 |
| 17 | 33 | 38 | 44 | 49 | 55 | 60 | 66 | 71 | 77 | 82 | 88 | 93 |
| 18 | 36 | 41 | 47 | 53 | 59 | 65 | 70 | 76 | 82 | 88 | 94 | 100 |
| 19 | 38 | 44 | 50 | 56 | 63 | 69 | 75 | 82 | 88 | 94 | 101 | 107 |
| 20 | 40 | 47 | 53 | 60 | 67 | 73 | 80 | 87 | 93 | 100 | 107 | 114 |

**TABLE C−2
(Continued)**

*(c)* Critical Values of *U* for a One-Tailed Test at .025 or for a Two-Tailed Test at .05

| n₁\n₂ | 9 | 10 | 11 | 12 | 13 | 14 | 15 | 16 | 17 | 18 | 19 | 20 |
|---|---|---|---|---|---|---|---|---|---|---|---|---|
| 1 | | | | | | | | | | | | |
| 2 | 0 | 0 | 1 | 1 | 1 | 1 | 1 | 1 | 2 | 2 | 2 | 2 |
| 3 | 2 | 3 | 3 | 4 | 4 | 5 | 5 | 6 | 6 | 7 | 7 | 8 |
| 4 | 4 | 5 | 6 | 7 | 8 | 9 | 10 | 11 | 11 | 12 | 13 | 13 |
| 5 | 7 | 8 | 9 | 11 | 12 | 13 | 14 | 15 | 17 | 18 | 19 | 20 |
| 6 | 10 | 11 | 13 | 14 | 16 | 17 | 19 | 21 | 22 | 24 | 25 | 27 |
| 7 | 12 | 14 | 16 | 18 | 20 | 22 | 24 | 26 | 28 | 30 | 32 | 34 |
| 8 | 15 | 17 | 19 | 22 | 24 | 26 | 29 | 31 | 34 | 36 | 38 | 41 |
| 9 | 17 | 20 | 23 | 26 | 28 | 31 | 34 | 37 | 39 | 42 | 45 | 48 |
| 10 | 20 | 23 | 26 | 29 | 33 | 36 | 39 | 42 | 45 | 48 | 52 | 55 |
| 11 | 23 | 26 | 30 | 33 | 37 | 40 | 44 | 47 | 51 | 55 | 58 | 62 |
| 12 | 26 | 29 | 33 | 37 | 41 | 45 | 49 | 53 | 57 | 61 | 65 | 69 |
| 13 | 28 | 33 | 37 | 41 | 45 | 50 | 54 | 59 | 63 | 67 | 72 | 76 |
| 14 | 31 | 36 | 40 | 45 | 50 | 55 | 59 | 64 | 67 | 74 | 78 | 83 |
| 15 | 34 | 39 | 44 | 49 | 54 | 59 | 64 | 70 | 75 | 80 | 85 | 90 |
| 16 | 37 | 42 | 47 | 53 | 59 | 64 | 70 | 75 | 81 | 86 | 92 | 98 |
| 17 | 39 | 45 | 51 | 57 | 63 | 67 | 75 | 81 | 87 | 93 | 99 | 105 |
| 18 | 42 | 48 | 55 | 61 | 67 | 74 | 80 | 86 | 93 | 99 | 106 | 112 |
| 19 | 45 | 52 | 58 | 65 | 72 | 78 | 85 | 92 | 99 | 106 | 113 | 119 |
| 20 | 48 | 55 | 62 | 69 | 76 | 83 | 90 | 98 | 105 | 112 | 119 | 127 |

**TABLE C–2 (Continued)**

(d) Critical Values of $U$ for a One-Tailed Test at .05 or for a Two-Tailed Test at .10

| $n_1$ \ $n_2$ | 9 | 10 | 11 | 12 | 13 | 14 | 15 | 16 | 17 | 18 | 19 | 20 |
|---|---|---|---|---|---|---|---|---|---|---|---|---|
| 1 | | | | | | | | | | | 0 | 0 |
| 2 | 1 | 1 | 1 | 2 | 2 | 2 | 3 | 3 | 3 | 4 | 4 | 4 |
| 3 | 3 | 4 | 5 | 5 | 6 | 7 | 7 | 8 | 9 | 9 | 10 | 11 |
| 4 | 6 | 7 | 8 | 9 | 10 | 11 | 12 | 14 | 15 | 16 | 17 | 18 |
| 5 | 9 | 11 | 12 | 13 | 15 | 16 | 18 | 19 | 20 | 22 | 23 | 25 |
| 6 | 12 | 14 | 16 | 17 | 19 | 21 | 23 | 25 | 26 | 28 | 30 | 32 |
| 7 | 15 | 17 | 19 | 21 | 24 | 26 | 28 | 30 | 33 | 35 | 37 | 39 |
| 8 | 18 | 20 | 23 | 26 | 28 | 31 | 33 | 36 | 39 | 41 | 44 | 47 |
| 9 | 21 | 24 | 27 | 30 | 33 | 36 | 39 | 42 | 45 | 48 | 51 | 54 |
| 10 | 24 | 27 | 31 | 34 | 37 | 41 | 44 | 48 | 51 | 55 | 58 | 62 |
| 11 | 27 | 31 | 34 | 38 | 42 | 46 | 50 | 54 | 57 | 61 | 65 | 69 |
| 12 | 30 | 34 | 38 | 42 | 47 | 51 | 55 | 60 | 64 | 68 | 72 | 77 |
| 13 | 33 | 37 | 42 | 47 | 51 | 56 | 61 | 65 | 70 | 75 | 80 | 84 |
| 14 | 36 | 41 | 46 | 51 | 56 | 61 | 66 | 71 | 77 | 82 | 87 | 92 |
| 15 | 39 | 44 | 50 | 55 | 61 | 66 | 72 | 77 | 83 | 88 | 94 | 100 |
| 16 | 42 | 48 | 54 | 60 | 65 | 71 | 77 | 83 | 89 | 95 | 101 | 107 |
| 17 | 45 | 51 | 57 | 64 | 70 | 77 | 83 | 89 | 96 | 102 | 109 | 115 |
| 18 | 48 | 55 | 61 | 68 | 75 | 82 | 88 | 95 | 102 | 109 | 116 | 123 |
| 19 | 51 | 58 | 65 | 72 | 80 | 87 | 94 | 101 | 109 | 116 | 123 | 130 |
| 20 | 54 | 62 | 69 | 77 | 84 | 92 | 100 | 107 | 115 | 123 | 130 | 138 |

## TABLE C–3  Distribution for the Sign Test

This table shows alpha levels of the sign test for pairs of observations ranging from 3 to 42. The symbol $x$ denotes the number of exceptions (the number of times the difference between conditions is in the unexpected direction), and the $p$ level indicates the probability that that number of exceptions could occur by chance. If, out of 28 paired observations, 20 are ordered in the expected direction and only 8 are exceptions, the probability that this could occur by chance is .018.

**n = 3**
| x | p |
|---|---|
| 0 | .125 |

**n = 4**
| x | p |
|---|---|
| 0 | .062 |
| 1 | .312 |

**n = 5**
| x | p |
|---|---|
| 0 | .031 |
| 1 | .188 |

**n = 6**
| x | p |
|---|---|
| 0 | .016 |
| 1 | .109 |
| 2 | .344 |

**n = 7**
| x | p |
|---|---|
| 0 | .008 |
| 1 | .062 |
| 2 | .227 |

**n = 8**
| x | p |
|---|---|
| 0 | .004 |
| 1 | .035 |
| 2 | .145 |

**n = 9**
| x | p |
|---|---|
| 0 | .002 |
| 1 | .020 |
| 2 | .090 |
| 3 | .254 |

**n = 10**
| x | p |
|---|---|
| 0 | .001 |
| 1 | .011 |
| 2 | .055 |
| 3 | .172 |

**n = 11**
| x | p |
|---|---|
| 0 | .000 |
| 1 | .006 |
| 2 | .033 |
| 3 | .113 |
| 4 | .274 |

**n = 12**
| x | p |
|---|---|
| 1 | .003 |
| 2 | .019 |
| 3 | .073 |
| 4 | .194 |

**n = 13**
| x | p |
|---|---|
| 1 | .002 |
| 2 | .011 |
| 3 | .016 |
| 4 | .133 |

**n = 14**
| x | p |
|---|---|
| 1 | .001 |
| 2 | .006 |
| 3 | .029 |
| 4 | .090 |
| 5 | .212 |

**n = 15**
| x | p |
|---|---|
| 1 | .000 |
| 2 | .004 |
| 3 | .018 |
| 4 | .059 |
| 5 | .151 |

**n = 16**
| x | p |
|---|---|
| 2 | .002 |
| 3 | .011 |
| 4 | .038 |
| 5 | .105 |
| 6 | .227 |

**n = 17**
| x | p |
|---|---|
| 2 | .001 |
| 3 | .006 |
| 4 | .025 |
| 5 | .072 |
| 6 | .166 |

**n = 18**
| x | p |
|---|---|
| 3 | .004 |
| 4 | .015 |
| 5 | .048 |
| 6 | .119 |
| 7 | .240 |

**n = 19**
| x | p |
|---|---|
| 3 | .002 |
| 4 | .010 |
| 5 | .032 |
| 6 | .084 |
| 7 | .180 |

**n = 20**
| x | p |
|---|---|
| 3 | .001 |
| 4 | .006 |
| 5 | .021 |
| 6 | .058 |
| 7 | .132 |

**n = 21**
| x | p |
|---|---|
| 4 | .004 |
| 5 | .013 |
| 6 | .039 |
| 7 | .095 |
| 8 | .192 |

**n = 22**
| x | p |
|---|---|
| 4 | .002 |
| 5 | .008 |
| 6 | .026 |
| 7 | .067 |
| 8 | .143 |

**n = 23**
| x | p |
|---|---|
| 4 | .001 |
| 5 | .005 |
| 6 | .017 |
| 7 | .047 |
| 8 | .105 |
| 9 | .202 |

**n = 24**
| x | p |
|---|---|
| 5 | .008 |
| 6 | .011 |
| 7 | .032 |
| 8 | .076 |
| 9 | .154 |

**n = 25**
| x | p |
|---|---|
| 5 | .002 |
| 6 | .007 |
| 7 | .022 |
| 8 | .051 |
| 9 | .115 |
| 10 | .212 |

**n = 26**
| x | p |
|---|---|
| 6 | .005 |
| 7 | .014 |
| 8 | .038 |
| 9 | .084 |
| 10 | .163 |

**n = 27**
| x | p |
|---|---|
| 6 | .003 |
| 7 | .010 |
| 8 | .026 |
| 9 | .061 |
| 10 | .124 |
| 11 | .221 |

**n = 28**
| x | p |
|---|---|
| 6 | .002 |
| 7 | .006 |
| 8 | .018 |
| 9 | .044 |
| 10 | .092 |
| 11 | .172 |

**n = 29**
| x | p |
|---|---|
| 7 | .004 |
| 8 | .012 |
| 9 | .031 |
| 10 | .068 |
| 11 | .132 |

**n = 30**
| x | p |
|---|---|
| 7 | .003 |
| 8 | .008 |
| 9 | .021 |
| 10 | .049 |
| 11 | .100 |
| 12 | .181 |

**n = 31**
| x | p |
|---|---|
| 7 | .002 |
| 8 | .005 |
| 9 | .015 |
| 10 | .035 |
| 11 | .075 |
| 12 | .141 |

**n = 32**
| x | p |
|---|---|
| 8 | .004 |
| 9 | .010 |
| 10 | .025 |
| 11 | .055 |
| 12 | .108 |
| 13 | .189 |

**n = 33**
| x | p |
|---|---|
| 8 | .002 |
| 9 | .007 |
| 10 | .018 |
| 11 | .040 |
| 12 | .081 |
| 13 | .148 |

**n = 34**
| x | p |
|---|---|
| 9 | .005 |
| 10 | .012 |
| 11 | .029 |
| 12 | .061 |
| 13 | .115 |
| 14 | .196 |

**n = 35**
| x | p |
|---|---|
| 9 | .003 |
| 10 | .008 |
| 11 | .020 |
| 12 | .045 |
| 13 | .088 |
| 14 | .155 |

**n = 36**
| x | p |
|---|---|
| 9 | .002 |
| 10 | .006 |
| 11 | .014 |
| 12 | .033 |
| 13 | .066 |
| 14 | .121 |
| 15 | .203 |

**n = 37**
| x | p |
|---|---|
| 10 | .004 |
| 11 | .010 |
| 12 | .024 |
| 13 | .049 |
| 14 | .094 |
| 15 | .162 |

**n = 38**
| x | p |
|---|---|
| 10 | .003 |
| 11 | .007 |
| 12 | .017 |
| 13 | .036 |
| 14 | .072 |
| 15 | .128 |

**n = 39**
| x | p |
|---|---|
| 11 | .005 |
| 12 | .012 |
| 13 | .027 |
| 14 | .054 |
| 15 | .100 |
| 16 | .168 |

**n = 40**
| x | p |
|---|---|
| 11 | .003 |
| 12 | .008 |
| 13 | .019 |
| 14 | .040 |
| 15 | .077 |
| 16 | .134 |

**n = 41**
| x | p |
|---|---|
| 11 | .002 |
| 12 | .006 |
| 13 | .014 |
| 14 | .030 |
| 15 | .059 |
| 16 | .106 |
| 17 | .174 |

**n = 42**
| x | p |
|---|---|
| 12 | .004 |
| 13 | .010 |
| 14 | .022 |
| 15 | .044 |
| 16 | .082 |
| 17 | .140 |

**TABLE C–4  Critical Values of Wilcoxon's _T_ Statistic for the Matched-Pairs Signed-Ranks Test**

In using this table, first locate the number of *pairs* of scores in the _n_ column. The critical values for several levels of significance are listed in the columns to the right. For example, if _n_ were 15 and the computed value 19, we could conclude that since 19 is less than 25, the difference between conditions is significant beyond the .02 level of significance for a two-tailed test.

| | Level of significance for one-tailed test | | |
| | .025 | .01 | .005 |
| | Level of significance for two-tailed test | | |
| _n_ | .05 | .02 | .01 |
|---|---|---|---|
| 6 | 1 | — | — |
| 7 | 2 | 0 | — |
| 8 | 4 | 2 | 0 |
| 9 | 6 | 3 | 2 |
| 10 | 8 | 5 | 3 |
| 11 | 11 | 7 | 5 |
| 12 | 14 | 10 | 7 |
| 13 | 17 | 13 | 10 |
| 14 | 21 | 16 | 13 |
| 15 | 25 | 20 | 16 |
| 16 | 30 | 24 | 19 |
| 17 | 35 | 28 | 23 |
| 18 | 40 | 33 | 28 |
| 19 | 46 | 38 | 32 |
| 20 | 52 | 43 | 37 |
| 21 | 59 | 49 | 43 |
| 22 | 66 | 56 | 49 |
| 23 | 73 | 62 | 55 |
| 24 | 81 | 69 | 61 |
| 25 | 90 | 77 | 68 |

## TABLE C–5   Critical Values of *t*

To find the appropriate value of *t*, read across the row that contains the number of degrees of freedom in your experiment. The columns are determined by the level of significance you have chosen. The value of *t* you obtain must be *greater* than that in the table in order to be significant. For example, with $df = 15$ and $p = .05$ (two-tailed test), your *t* value must be greater than 2.131.

| | Level of significance for one-tailed test | | | | | |
| | .10 | .05 | .025 | .01 | .005 | .0005 |
| | Level of significance for two-tailed test | | | | | |
| df | .20 | .10 | .05 | .02 | .01 | .001 |
|---|---|---|---|---|---|---|
| 1 | 3.078 | 6.314 | 12.706 | 31.821 | 63.657 | 636.619 |
| 2 | 1.886 | 2.920 | 4.303 | 6.965 | 9.925 | 31.598 |
| 3 | 1.638 | 2.353 | 3.182 | 4.541 | 5.841 | 12.941 |
| 4 | 1.533 | 2.132 | 2.776 | 3.747 | 4.604 | 8.610 |
| 5 | 1.476 | 2.015 | 2.571 | 3.365 | 4.032 | 6.859 |
| 6 | 1.440 | 1.943 | 2.447 | 3.143 | 3.707 | 5.959 |
| 7 | 1.415 | 1.895 | 2.365 | 2.998 | 3.449 | 5.405 |
| 8 | 1.397 | 1.860 | 2.306 | 2.896 | 3.355 | 5.041 |
| 9 | 1.383 | 1.833 | 2.262 | 2.821 | 3.250 | 4.781 |
| 10 | 1.372 | 1.812 | 2.228 | 2.764 | 3.169 | 4.587 |
| 11 | 1.363 | 1.796 | 2.201 | 2.718 | 3.106 | 4.437 |
| 12 | 1.356 | 1.782 | 2.179 | 2.681 | 3.055 | 4.318 |
| 13 | 1.350 | 1.771 | 2.160 | 2.650 | 3.012 | 4.221 |
| 14 | 1.345 | 1.761 | 2.145 | 2.624 | 2.977 | 4.140 |
| 15 | 1.341 | 1.753 | 2.131 | 2.602 | 2.947 | 4.073 |
| 16 | 1.337 | 1.746 | 2.120 | 2.583 | 2.921 | 4.015 |
| 17 | 1.333 | 1.740 | 2.110 | 2.567 | 2.898 | 3.965 |
| 18 | 1.330 | 1.734 | 2.101 | 2.552 | 2.878 | 3.922 |
| 19 | 1.328 | 1.729 | 2.093 | 2.539 | 2.861 | 3.883 |
| 20 | 1.325 | 1.725 | 2.086 | 2.528 | 2.845 | 3.850 |
| 21 | 1.323 | 1.721 | 2.080 | 2.518 | 2.831 | 3.819 |
| 22 | 1.321 | 1.717 | 2.074 | 2.508 | 2.819 | 3.792 |
| 23 | 1.319 | 1.714 | 2.069 | 2.500 | 2.807 | 3.767 |
| 24 | 1.318 | 1.711 | 2.064 | 2.492 | 2.797 | 3.745 |
| 25 | 1.316 | 1.708 | 2.060 | 2.485 | 2.787 | 3.725 |
| 26 | 1.315 | 1.706 | 2.056 | 2.479 | 2.779 | 3.707 |
| 27 | 1.314 | 1.703 | 2.052 | 2.473 | 2.771 | 3.690 |
| 28 | 1.313 | 1.701 | 2.048 | 2.467 | 2.763 | 3.674 |
| 29 | 1.311 | 1.699 | 2.045 | 2.462 | 2.756 | 3.659 |
| 30 | 1.310 | 1.697 | 2.042 | 2.457 | 2.750 | 3.646 |
| 40 | 1.303 | 1.684 | 2.021 | 2.423 | 2.704 | 3.551 |
| 60 | 1.296 | 1.671 | 2.000 | 2.390 | 2.660 | 3.460 |
| 120 | 1.289 | 1.658 | 1.980 | 2.358 | 2.617 | 3.373 |
| ∞ | 1.282 | 1.645 | 1.960 | 2.326 | 2.576 | 3.291 |

Table C–5 is taken from Table III of Fisher & Yates': *Statistical Tables for Biological, Agricultural and Medical Research*. Published by Longman Group UK Ltd. London (previously published by Oliver and Boyd Ltd. Edinburgh) and by permission of the authors and publishers.

## TABLE C–6   Critical Values of the F Distribution

Find the appropriate values in the table by looking up the degrees of freedom in the numerator and denominator of the $F$ ratio. After you have decided on the level of significance desired, the obtained $F$ ratio must be *greater* than that in the table. For example, with $p = .05$ and 9 $df$ in the numerator and 28 in the denominator, your $F$ value must be greater than 2.24 to be reliable.

| df for denom. | α | 1 | 2 | 3 | 4 | 5 | 6 | 7 | 8 | 9 |
|---|---|---|---|---|---|---|---|---|---|---|
| 3 | .25 | 2.02 | 2.28 | 2.36 | 2.39 | 2.41 | 2.42 | 2.43 | 2.44 | 2.44 |
|  | .10 | 5.54 | 5.46 | 5.39 | 5.34 | 5.31 | 5.28 | 5.27 | 5.25 | 5.24 |
|  | .05 | 10.1 | 9.55 | 9.28 | 9.12 | 9.01 | 8.94 | 8.89 | 8.85 | 8.81 |
|  | .025 | 17.4 | 16.0 | 15.4 | 15.1 | 14.9 | 14.7 | 14.6 | 14.5 | 14.5 |
|  | .01 | 34.1 | 30.8 | 29.5 | 28.7 | 28.2 | 27.9 | 27.7 | 27.5 | 27.4 |
|  | .001 | 167 | 148 | 141 | 137 | 135 | 133 | 132 | 131 | 130 |
| 4 | .25 | 1.81 | 2.00 | 2.05 | 2.06 | 2.07 | 2.08 | 2.08 | 2.08 | 2.08 |
|  | .10 | 4.54 | 4.32 | 4.19 | 4.11 | 4.05 | 4.01 | 3.98 | 3.95 | 3.94 |
|  | .05 | 7.71 | 6.94 | 6.59 | 6.39 | 6.26 | 6.16 | 6.09 | 6.04 | 6.00 |
|  | .025 | 12.2 | 10.6 | 9.98 | 9.60 | 9.36 | 9.20 | 9.07 | 8.98 | 8.90 |
|  | .01 | 21.2 | 18.0 | 16.7 | 16.0 | 15.5 | 15.2 | 15.0 | 14.8 | 14.7 |
|  | .001 | 74.1 | 61.2 | 56.2 | 53.4 | 51.7 | 50.5 | 49.7 | 49.0 | 48.5 |
| 5 | .25 | 1.69 | 1.85 | 1.88 | 1.89 | 1.89 | 1.89 | 1.89 | 1.89 | 1.89 |
|  | .10 | 4.06 | 3.78 | 3.62 | 3.52 | 3.45 | 3.40 | 3.37 | 3.34 | 3.32 |
|  | .05 | 6.61 | 5.79 | 5.41 | 5.19 | 5.05 | 4.95 | 4.88 | 4.82 | 4.77 |
|  | .025 | 10.0 | 8.43 | 7.76 | 7.39 | 7.15 | 6.98 | 6.85 | 6.76 | 6.68 |
|  | .01 | 16.3 | 13.3 | 12.1 | 11.4 | 11.0 | 10.7 | 10.5 | 10.3 | 10.2 |
|  | .001 | 47.2 | 37.1 | 33.2 | 31.1 | 29.8 | 28.8 | 28.2 | 27.6 | 27.2 |
| 6 | .25 | 1.62 | 1.76 | 1.78 | 1.79 | 1.79 | 1.78 | 1.78 | 1.78 | 1.77 |
|  | .10 | 3.78 | 3.46 | 3.29 | 3.18 | 3.11 | 3.05 | 3.01 | 2.98 | 2.96 |
|  | .05 | 5.99 | 5.14 | 4.76 | 4.53 | 4.39 | 4.28 | 4.21 | 4.15 | 4.10 |
|  | .025 | 8.81 | 7.26 | 6.60 | 6.23 | 5.99 | 5.82 | 5.70 | 5.60 | 5.52 |
|  | .01 | 13.8 | 10.9 | 9.78 | 9.15 | 8.75 | 8.47 | 8.26 | 8.10 | 7.98 |
|  | .001 | 35.5 | 27.0 | 23.7 | 21.9 | 20.8 | 20.0 | 19.5 | 19.0 | 18.7 |
| 7 | .25 | 1.57 | 1.70 | 1.72 | 1.72 | 1.71 | 1.71 | 1.70 | 1.70 | 1.69 |
|  | .10 | 3.59 | 3.26 | 3.07 | 2.96 | 2.88 | 2.83 | 2.78 | 2.75 | 2.72 |
|  | .05 | 5.59 | 4.74 | 4.35 | 4.12 | 3.97 | 3.87 | 3.79 | 3.73 | 3.68 |
|  | .025 | 8.07 | 6.54 | 5.89 | 5.52 | 5.29 | 5.12 | 4.99 | 4.90 | 4.82 |
|  | .01 | 12.2 | 9.55 | 8.45 | 7.85 | 7.46 | 7.19 | 6.99 | 6.84 | 6.72 |
|  | .001 | 29.2 | 21.7 | 18.8 | 17.2 | 16.2 | 15.5 | 15.0 | 14.6 | 14.3 |
| 8 | .25 | 1.54 | 1.66 | 1.67 | 1.66 | 1.66 | 1.65 | 1.64 | 1.64 | 1.63 |
|  | .10 | 3.46 | 3.11 | 2.92 | 2.81 | 2.73 | 2.67 | 2.62 | 2.59 | 2.56 |
|  | .05 | 5.32 | 4.46 | 4.07 | 3.84 | 3.69 | 3.58 | 3.50 | 3.44 | 3.39 |
|  | .025 | 7.57 | 6.06 | 5.42 | 5.05 | 4.82 | 4.65 | 4.53 | 4.43 | 4.36 |
|  | .01 | 11.3 | 8.65 | 7.59 | 7.01 | 6.63 | 6.37 | 6.18 | 6.03 | 5.91 |
|  | .001 | 25.4 | 18.5 | 15.8 | 14.4 | 13.5 | 12.9 | 12.4 | 12.0 | 11.8 |
| 9 | .25 | 1.51 | 1.62 | 1.63 | 1.63 | 1.62 | 1.61 | 1.60 | 1.60 | 1.59 |
|  | .10 | 3.36 | 3.01 | 2.81 | 2.69 | 2.61 | 2.55 | 2.51 | 2.47 | 2.44 |
|  | .05 | 5.12 | 4.26 | 3.86 | 3.63 | 3.48 | 3.37 | 3.29 | 3.23 | 3.18 |
|  | .025 | 7.21 | 5.71 | 5.08 | 4.72 | 4.48 | 4.32 | 4.20 | 4.10 | 4.03 |
|  | .01 | 10.6 | 8.02 | 6.99 | 6.42 | 6.06 | 5.80 | 5.61 | 5.47 | 5.35 |
|  | .001 | 22.9 | 16.4 | 13.9 | 12.6 | 11.7 | 11.1 | 10.7 | 10.4 | 10.1 |

**TABLE C-6**
**(Continued)**

| df for denom. | α | \multicolumn{9}{c}{df for numerator} |
|---|---|---|---|---|---|---|---|---|---|---|
| | | 1 | 2 | 3 | 4 | 5 | 6 | 7 | 8 | 9 |
| 10 | .25 | 1.49 | 1.60 | 1.60 | 1.59 | 1.59 | 1.58 | 1.57 | 1.56 | 1.56 |
| | .10 | 3.29 | 2.92 | 2.73 | 2.61 | 2.52 | 2.46 | 2.41 | 2.38 | 2.35 |
| | .05 | 4.96 | 4.10 | 3.71 | 3.48 | 3.33 | 3.22 | 3.14 | 3.07 | 3.02 |
| | .025 | 6.94 | 5.46 | 4.83 | 4.47 | 4.24 | 4.07 | 3.95 | 3.85 | 3.78 |
| | .01 | 10.0 | 7.56 | 6.55 | 5.99 | 5.64 | 5.39 | 5.20 | 5.06 | 4.94 |
| | .001 | 21.0 | 14.9 | 12.6 | 11.3 | 10.5 | 9.92 | 9.52 | 9.20 | 8.96 |
| 11 | .25 | 1.47 | 1.58 | 1.58 | 1.57 | 1.56 | 1.55 | 1.54 | 1.53 | 1.53 |
| | .10 | 3.23 | 2.86 | 2.66 | 2.54 | 2.45 | 2.39 | 2.34 | 2.30 | 2.27 |
| | .05 | 4.84 | 3.98 | 3.59 | 3.36 | 3.20 | 3.09 | 3.01 | 2.95 | 2.90 |
| | .025 | 6.72 | 5.26 | 4.63 | 4.28 | 4.04 | 3.88 | 3.76 | 3.66 | 3.59 |
| | .01 | 9.65 | 7.21 | 6.22 | 5.67 | 5.32 | 5.07 | 4.89 | 4.74 | 4.63 |
| | .001 | 19.7 | 13.8 | 11.6 | 10.4 | 9.58 | 9.05 | 8.66 | 8.35 | 8.12 |
| 12 | .25 | 1.46 | 1.56 | 1.56 | 1.55 | 1.54 | 1.53 | 1.52 | 1.51 | 1.51 |
| | .10 | 3.18 | 2.81 | 2.61 | 2.48 | 2.39 | 2.33 | 2.28 | 2.24 | 2.21 |
| | .05 | 4.75 | 3.89 | 3.49 | 3.26 | 3.11 | 3.00 | 2.91 | 2.85 | 2.80 |
| | .025 | 6.55 | 5.10 | 4.47 | 4.12 | 3.89 | 3.73 | 3.61 | 3.51 | 3.44 |
| | .01 | 9.33 | 6.93 | 5.95 | 5.41 | 5.06 | 4.82 | 4.64 | 4.50 | 4.39 |
| | .001 | 18.6 | 13.0 | 10.8 | 9.63 | 8.89 | 8.38 | 8.00 | 7.71 | 7.48 |
| 13 | .25 | 1.45 | 1.55 | 1.55 | 1.53 | 1.52 | 1.51 | 1.50 | 1.49 | 1.49 |
| | .10 | 3.14 | 2.76 | 2.56 | 2.43 | 2.35 | 2.28 | 2.23 | 2.20 | 2.16 |
| | .05 | 4.67 | 3.81 | 3.41 | 3.18 | 3.03 | 2.92 | 2.83 | 2.77 | 2.71 |
| | .025 | 6.41 | 4.97 | 4.35 | 4.00 | 3.77 | 3.60 | 3.48 | 3.39 | 3.31 |
| | .01 | 9.07 | 6.70 | 5.74 | 5.21 | 4.86 | 4.62 | 4.44 | 4.30 | 4.19 |
| | .001 | 17.8 | 12.3 | 10.2 | 9.07 | 8.35 | 7.86 | 7.49 | 7.21 | 6.98 |
| 14 | .25 | 1.44 | 1.53 | 1.53 | 1.52 | 1.51 | 1.50 | 1.49 | 1.48 | 1.47 |
| | .10 | 3.10 | 2.73 | 2.52 | 2.39 | 2.31 | 2.24 | 2.19 | 2.15 | 2.12 |
| | .05 | 4.60 | 3.74 | 3.34 | 3.11 | 2.96 | 2.85 | 2.76 | 2.70 | 2.65 |
| | .025 | 6.30 | 4.86 | 4.24 | 3.89 | 3.66 | 3.50 | 3.38 | 3.29 | 3.21 |
| | .01 | 8.86 | 6.51 | 5.56 | 5.04 | 4.69 | 4.46 | 4.28 | 4.14 | 4.03 |
| | .001 | 17.1 | 11.8 | 9.73 | 8.62 | 7.92 | 7.43 | 7.08 | 6.80 | 6.58 |
| 15 | .25 | 1.43 | 1.52 | 1.52 | 1.51 | 1.49 | 1.48 | 1.47 | 1.46 | 1.46 |
| | .10 | 3.07 | 2.70 | 2.49 | 2.36 | 2.27 | 2.21 | 2.16 | 2.12 | 2.09 |
| | .05 | 4.54 | 3.68 | 3.29 | 3.06 | 2.90 | 2.79 | 2.71 | 2.64 | 2.59 |
| | .025 | 6.20 | 4.77 | 4.15 | 3.80 | 3.58 | 3.41 | 3.29 | 3.20 | 3.12 |
| | .01 | 8.68 | 6.36 | 5.42 | 4.89 | 4.56 | 4.32 | 4.14 | 4.00 | 3.89 |
| | .001 | 16.6 | 11.3 | 9.34 | 8.25 | 7.57 | 7.09 | 6.74 | 6.47 | 6.26 |
| 16 | .25 | 1.42 | 1.51 | 1.51 | 1.50 | 1.48 | 1.47 | 1.46 | 1.45 | 1.44 |
| | .10 | 3.05 | 2.67 | 2.46 | 2.33 | 2.24 | 2.18 | 2.13 | 2.09 | 2.06 |
| | .05 | 4.49 | 3.63 | 3.24 | 3.01 | 2.85 | 2.74 | 2.66 | 2.59 | 2.54 |
| | .025 | 6.12 | 4.69 | 4.08 | 3.73 | 3.50 | 3.34 | 3.22 | 3.12 | 3.05 |
| | .01 | 8.53 | 6.23 | 5.29 | 4.77 | 4.44 | 4.20 | 4.03 | 3.89 | 3.78 |
| | .001 | 16.1 | 11.0 | 9.00 | 7.94 | 7.27 | 6.81 | 6.46 | 6.19 | 5.98 |
| 17 | .25 | 1.42 | 1.51 | 1.50 | 1.49 | 1.47 | 1.46 | 1.45 | 1.44 | 1.43 |
| | .10 | 3.03 | 2.64 | 2.44 | 2.31 | 2.22 | 2.15 | 2.10 | 2.06 | 2.03 |
| | .05 | 4.45 | 3.59 | 3.20 | 2.96 | 2.81 | 2.70 | 2.61 | 2.55 | 2.49 |
| | .025 | 6.04 | 4.62 | 4.01 | 3.66 | 3.44 | 3.28 | 3.16 | 3.06 | 2.98 |
| | .01 | 8.40 | 6.11 | 5.18 | 4.67 | 4.34 | 4.10 | 3.93 | 3.79 | 3.68 |
| | .001 | 15.7 | 10.7 | 8.73 | 7.68 | 7.02 | 6.56 | 6.22 | 5.96 | 5.75 |

**TABLE C–6**
**(Continued)**

| df for denom. | α | \multicolumn{9}{c}{df for numerator} |
|---|---|---|---|---|---|---|---|---|---|---|
| | | 1 | 2 | 3 | 4 | 5 | 6 | 7 | 8 | 9 |
| 18 | .25 | 1.41 | 1.50 | 1.49 | 1.48 | 1.46 | 1.45 | 1.44 | 1.43 | 1.42 |
| | .10 | 3.01 | 2.62 | 2.42 | 2.29 | 2.20 | 2.13 | 2.08 | 2.04 | 2.00 |
| | .05 | 4.41 | 3.55 | 3.16 | 2.93 | 2.77 | 2.66 | 2.58 | 2.51 | 2.46 |
| | .025 | 5.98 | 4.56 | 3.95 | 3.61 | 3.38 | 3.22 | 3.10 | 3.01 | 2.93 |
| | .01 | 8.29 | 6.01 | 5.09 | 4.58 | 4.25 | 4.01 | 3.84 | 3.71 | 3.60 |
| | .001 | 15.4 | 10.4 | 8.49 | 7.46 | 6.81 | 6.35 | 6.02 | 5.76 | 5.56 |
| 19 | .25 | 1.41 | 1.49 | 1.49 | 1.47 | 1.46 | 1.44 | 1.43 | 1.42 | 1.41 |
| | .10 | 2.99 | 2.61 | 2.40 | 2.27 | 2.18 | 2.11 | 2.06 | 2.02 | 1.98 |
| | .05 | 4.38 | 3.52 | 3.13 | 2.90 | 2.74 | 2.63 | 2.54 | 2.48 | 2.42 |
| | .025 | 5.92 | 4.51 | 3.90 | 3.56 | 3.33 | 3.17 | 3.05 | 2.96 | 2.88 |
| | .01 | 8.18 | 5.93 | 5.01 | 4.50 | 4.17 | 3.94 | 3.77 | 3.63 | 3.52 |
| | .001 | 15.1 | 10.2 | 8.28 | 7.26 | 6.62 | 6.18 | 5.85 | 5.59 | 5.39 |
| 20 | .25 | 1.40 | 1.49 | 1.48 | 1.47 | 1.45 | 1.44 | 1.43 | 1.42 | 1.41 |
| | .10 | 2.97 | 2.59 | 2.38 | 2.25 | 2.16 | 2.09 | 2.04 | 2.00 | 1.96 |
| | .05 | 4.35 | 3.49 | 3.10 | 2.87 | 2.71 | 2.60 | 2.51 | 2.45 | 2.39 |
| | .025 | 5.87 | 4.46 | 3.86 | 3.51 | 3.29 | 3.13 | 3.01 | 2.91 | 2.84 |
| | .01 | 8.10 | 5.85 | 4.94 | 4.43 | 4.10 | 3.87 | 3.70 | 3.56 | 3.46 |
| | .001 | 14.8 | 9.95 | 8.10 | 7.10 | 6.46 | 6.02 | 5.69 | 5.44 | 5.24 |
| 22 | .25 | 1.40 | 1.48 | 1.47 | 1.45 | 1.44 | 1.42 | 1.41 | 1.40 | 1.39 |
| | .10 | 2.95 | 2.56 | 2.35 | 2.22 | 2.13 | 2.06 | 2.01 | 1.97 | 1.93 |
| | .05 | 4.30 | 3.44 | 3.05 | 2.82 | 2.66 | 2.55 | 2.46 | 2.40 | 2.34 |
| | .025 | 5.79 | 4.38 | 3.78 | 3.44 | 3.22 | 3.05 | 2.93 | 2.84 | 2.76 |
| | .01 | 7.95 | 5.72 | 4.82 | 4.31 | 3.99 | 3.76 | 3.59 | 3.45 | 3.35 |
| | .001 | 14.4 | 9.61 | 7.80 | 6.81 | 6.19 | 5.76 | 5.44 | 5.19 | 4.99 |
| 24 | .25 | 1.39 | 1.47 | 1.46 | 1.44 | 1.43 | 1.41 | 1.40 | 1.39 | 1.38 |
| | .10 | 2.93 | 2.54 | 2.33 | 2.19 | 2.10 | 2.04 | 1.98 | 1.94 | 1.91 |
| | .05 | 4.26 | 3.40 | 3.01 | 2.78 | 2.62 | 2.51 | 2.42 | 2.36 | 2.30 |
| | .025 | 5.72 | 4.32 | 3.72 | 3.38 | 3.15 | 2.99 | 2.87 | 2.78 | 2.70 |
| | .01 | 7.82 | 5.61 | 4.72 | 4.22 | 3.90 | 3.67 | 3.50 | 3.36 | 3.26 |
| | .001 | 14.0 | 9.34 | 7.55 | 6.59 | 5.98 | 5.55 | 5.23 | 4.99 | 4.80 |
| 26 | .25 | 1.38 | 1.46 | 1.45 | 1.44 | 1.42 | 1.41 | 1.39 | 1.38 | 1.37 |
| | .10 | 2.91 | 2.52 | 2.31 | 2.17 | 2.08 | 2.01 | 1.96 | 1.92 | 1.88 |
| | .05 | 4.23 | 3.37 | 2.98 | 2.74 | 2.59 | 2.47 | 2.39 | 2.32 | 2.27 |
| | .025 | 5.66 | 4.27 | 3.67 | 3.33 | 3.10 | 2.94 | 2.82 | 2.73 | 2.65 |
| | .01 | 7.72 | 5.53 | 4.64 | 4.14 | 3.82 | 3.59 | 3.42 | 3.29 | 3.18 |
| | .001 | 13.7 | 9.12 | 7.36 | 6.41 | 5.80 | 5.38 | 5.07 | 4.83 | 4.64 |
| 28 | .25 | 1.38 | 1.46 | 1.45 | 1.43 | 1.41 | 1.40 | 1.39 | 1.38 | 1.37 |
| | .10 | 2.89 | 2.50 | 2.29 | 2.16 | 2.06 | 2.00 | 1.94 | 1.90 | 1.87 |
| | .05 | 4.20 | 3.34 | 2.95 | 2.71 | 2.56 | 2.45 | 2.36 | 2.29 | 2.24 |
| | .025 | 5.61 | 4.22 | 3.63 | 3.29 | 3.06 | 2.90 | 2.78 | 2.69 | 2.61 |
| | .01 | 7.64 | 5.45 | 4.57 | 4.07 | 3.75 | 3.53 | 3.36 | 3.23 | 3.12 |
| | .001 | 13.5 | 8.93 | 7.19 | 6.25 | 5.66 | 5.24 | 4.93 | 4.69 | 4.50 |
| 30 | .25 | 1.38 | 1.45 | 1.44 | 1.42 | 1.41 | 1.39 | 1.38 | 1.37 | 1.36 |
| | .10 | 2.88 | 2.49 | 2.28 | 2.14 | 2.05 | 1.98 | 1.93 | 1.88 | 1.85 |
| | .05 | 4.17 | 3.32 | 2.92 | 2.69 | 2.53 | 2.42 | 2.33 | 2.27 | 2.21 |
| | .025 | 5.57 | 4.18 | 3.59 | 3.25 | 3.03 | 2.87 | 2.75 | 2.65 | 2.57 |
| | .01 | 7.56 | 5.39 | 4.51 | 4.02 | 3.70 | 3.47 | 3.30 | 3.17 | 3.07 |
| | .001 | 13.3 | 8.77 | 7.05 | 6.12 | 5.53 | 5.12 | 4.82 | 4.58 | 4.39 |

| TABLE C−6 (Continued) | df for denom. | α | df for numerator | | | | | | | | |
|---|---|---|---|---|---|---|---|---|---|---|---|
| | | | 1 | 2 | 3 | 4 | 5 | 6 | 7 | 8 | 9 |
| | 40 | .25 | 1.36 | 1.44 | 1.42 | 1.40 | 1.39 | 1.37 | 1.36 | 1.35 | 1.34 |
| | | .10 | 2.84 | 2.44 | 2.23 | 2.09 | 2.00 | 1.93 | 1.87 | 1.83 | 1.79 |
| | | .05 | 4.08 | 3.23 | 2.84 | 2.61 | 2.45 | 2.34 | 2.25 | 2.18 | 2.12 |
| | | .025 | 5.42 | 4.05 | 3.46 | 3.13 | 2.90 | 2.74 | 2.62 | 2.53 | 2.45 |
| | | .01 | 7.31 | 5.18 | 4.31 | 3.83 | 3.51 | 3.29 | 3.12 | 2.99 | 2.89 |
| | | .001 | 12.6 | 8.25 | 6.60 | 5.70 | 5.13 | 4.73 | 4.44 | 4.21 | 4.02 |
| | 60 | .25 | 1.35 | 1.42 | 1.41 | 1.38 | 1.37 | 1.35 | 1.33 | 1.32 | 1.31 |
| | | .10 | 2.79 | 2.39 | 2.18 | 2.04 | 1.95 | 1.87 | 1.82 | 1.77 | 1.74 |
| | | .05 | 4.00 | 3.15 | 2.76 | 2.53 | 2.37 | 2.25 | 2.17 | 2.10 | 2.04 |
| | | .025 | 5.29 | 3.93 | 3.34 | 3.01 | 2.79 | 2.63 | 2.51 | 2.41 | 2.33 |
| | | .01 | 7.08 | 4.98 | 4.13 | 3.65 | 3.34 | 3.12 | 2.95 | 2.82 | 2.72 |
| | | .001 | 12.0 | 7.76 | 6.17 | 5.31 | 4.76 | 4.37 | 4.09 | 3.87 | 3.69 |
| | 120 | .25 | 1.34 | 1.40 | 1.39 | 1.37 | 1.35 | 1.33 | 1.31 | 1.30 | 1.29 |
| | | .10 | 2.75 | 2.35 | 2.13 | 1.99 | 1.90 | 1.82 | 1.77 | 1.72 | 1.68 |
| | | .05 | 3.92 | 3.07 | 2.68 | 2.45 | 2.29 | 2.17 | 2.09 | 2.02 | 1.96 |
| | | .025 | 5.15 | 3.80 | 3.23 | 2.89 | 2.67 | 2.52 | 2.39 | 2.30 | 2.22 |
| | | .01 | 6.85 | 4.79 | 3.95 | 3.48 | 3.17 | 2.96 | 2.79 | 2.66 | 2.56 |
| | | .001 | 11.4 | 7.32 | 5.79 | 4.95 | 4.42 | 4.04 | 3.77 | 3.55 | 3.38 |
| | ∞ | .25 | 1.32 | 1.39 | 1.37 | 1.35 | 1.33 | 1.31 | 1.29 | 1.28 | 1.27 |
| | | .10 | 2.71 | 2.30 | 2.08 | 1.94 | 1.85 | 1.77 | 1.72 | 1.67 | 1.63 |
| | | .05 | 3.84 | 3.00 | 2.60 | 2.37 | 2.21 | 2.10 | 2.01 | 1.94 | 1.88 |
| | | .025 | 5.02 | 3.69 | 3.12 | 2.79 | 2.57 | 2.41 | 2.29 | 2.19 | 2.11 |
| | | .01 | 6.63 | 4.61 | 3.78 | 3.32 | 3.02 | 2.80 | 2.64 | 2.51 | 2.41 |
| | | .001 | 10.8 | 91 | 5.42 | 4.62 | 4.10 | 3.74 | 3.47 | 3.27 | 3.10 |

### TABLE C–7    Random Numbers

|    | 1 | 2 | 3 | 4 | 5 | 6 | 7 | 8 | 9 |
|----|-----|-----|-----|-----|-----|-----|-----|-----|-----|
| 1  | 32942 | 95416 | 42339 | 59045 | 26693 | 49057 | 87496 | 20624 | 14819 |
| 2  | 07410 | 99859 | 83828 | 21409 | 29094 | 65114 | 36701 | 25762 | 12827 |
| 3  | 59981 | 68155 | 45673 | 76210 | 58219 | 45738 | 29550 | 24736 | 09574 |
| 4  | 46251 | 25437 | 69654 | 99716 | 11563 | 08803 | 86027 | 51867 | 12116 |
| 5  | 65558 | 51904 | 93123 | 27887 | 53138 | 21488 | 09095 | 78777 | 71240 |
| 6  | 99187 | 19258 | 86421 | 16401 | 19397 | 83297 | 40111 | 49326 | 81686 |
| 7  | 35641 | 00301 | 16096 | 34775 | 21562 | 97983 | 45040 | 19200 | 16383 |
| 8  | 14031 | 00936 | 81518 | 48440 | 02218 | 04756 | 19506 | 60695 | 88494 |
| 9  | 60677 | 15076 | 92554 | 26042 | 23472 | 69869 | 62877 | 19584 | 39576 |
| 10 | 66314 | 05212 | 67859 | 89356 | 20056 | 30648 | 87349 | 20389 | 53805 |
| 11 | 20416 | 87410 | 75646 | 64176 | 82752 | 63606 | 37011 | 57346 | 69512 |
| 12 | 28701 | 56992 | 70423 | 62415 | 40807 | 98086 | 58850 | 28968 | 45297 |
| 13 | 74579 | 33844 | 33426 | 07570 | 00728 | 07079 | 19322 | 56325 | 84819 |
| 14 | 62615 | 52342 | 82968 | 75540 | 80045 | 53069 | 20665 | 21282 | 07768 |
| 15 | 93945 | 06293 | 22879 | 08161 | 01442 | 75071 | 21427 | 94842 | 26210 |
| 16 | 75689 | 76131 | 96837 | 67450 | 44511 | 50424 | 82848 | 41975 | 71663 |
| 17 | 02921 | 16919 | 35424 | 93209 | 52133 | 87327 | 95897 | 65171 | 20376 |
| 18 | 14295 | 34969 | 14216 | 03191 | 61647 | 30296 | 66667 | 10101 | 63203 |
| 19 | 05303 | 91109 | 82403 | 40312 | 62191 | 67023 | 90073 | 83205 | 71344 |
| 20 | 57071 | 90357 | 12901 | 08899 | 91039 | 67251 | 28701 | 03846 | 94589 |
| 21 | 78471 | 57741 | 13599 | 84390 | 32146 | 00871 | 09354 | 22745 | 65806 |
| 22 | 89242 | 79337 | 59293 | 47481 | 07740 | 43345 | 25716 | 70020 | 54005 |
| 23 | 14955 | 59592 | 97035 | 80430 | 87220 | 06392 | 79028 | 57123 | 52872 |
| 24 | 42446 | 41880 | 37415 | 47472 | 04513 | 49494 | 08860 | 08038 | 43624 |
| 25 | 18534 | 22346 | 54556 | 17558 | 73689 | 14894 | 05030 | 19561 | 56517 |
| 26 | 39284 | 33737 | 42512 | 86411 | 23753 | 29690 | 26096 | 81361 | 93099 |
| 27 | 33922 | 37329 | 89911 | 55876 | 28379 | 81031 | 22058 | 21487 | 54613 |
| 28 | 78355 | 54013 | 50774 | 30666 | 61205 | 42574 | 47773 | 36027 | 27174 |
| 29 | 08845 | 99145 | 94316 | 88974 | 29828 | 97069 | 90327 | 61842 | 29604 |
| 30 | 01769 | 71825 | 55957 | 98271 | 02784 | 66731 | 40311 | 88495 | 18821 |
| 31 | 17639 | 38284 | 59478 | 90409 | 21997 | 56199 | 30068 | 82800 | 69692 |
| 32 | 05851 | 58653 | 99949 | 63505 | 40409 | 85551 | 90729 | 64938 | 52403 |
| 33 | 42396 | 40112 | 11469 | 03476 | 03328 | 84238 | 26570 | 51790 | 42122 |
| 34 | 13318 | 14192 | 98167 | 75631 | 74141 | 22369 | 36757 | 89117 | 54998 |
| 35 | 60571 | 54786 | 26281 | 01855 | 30706 | 66578 | 32019 | 65884 | 58485 |
| 36 | 09531 | 81853 | 59334 | 70929 | 03544 | 18510 | 89541 | 13555 | 21168 |
| 37 | 72865 | 16829 | 86542 | 00396 | 20363 | 13010 | 69645 | 49608 | 54738 |
| 38 | 56324 | 31093 | 77924 | 28622 | 83543 | 28912 | 15059 | 80192 | 83964 |
| 39 | 78192 | 21626 | 91399 | 07235 | 07104 | 73652 | 64425 | 85149 | 75409 |
| 40 | 64666 | 34767 | 97298 | 92708 | 01994 | 53188 | 78476 | 07804 | 62404 |
| 41 | 82201 | 75694 | 02808 | 65983 | 74373 | 66693 | 13094 | 74183 | 73020 |
| 42 | 15360 | 73776 | 40914 | 85190 | 54278 | 99054 | 62944 | 47351 | 89098 |
| 43 | 68142 | 67957 | 70896 | 37983 | 20487 | 95350 | 16371 | 03426 | 13895 |
| 44 | 19138 | 31200 | 30616 | 14639 | 44406 | 44236 | 57360 | 81644 | 94761 |
| 45 | 28155 | 03521 | 36415 | 78452 | 92359 | 81091 | 56513 | 88321 | 97910 |
| 46 | 87971 | 29031 | 51780 | 27376 | 81056 | 86155 | 55488 | 50590 | 74514 |
| 47 | 58147 | 68841 | 53625 | 02059 | 75223 | 16783 | 19272 | 61994 | 71090 |
| 48 | 18875 | 52809 | 70594 | 41649 | 32935 | 26430 | 82096 | 01605 | 65846 |
| 49 | 75109 | 56474 | 74111 | 31966 | 29969 | 70093 | 98901 | 84550 | 25769 |
| 50 | 35983 | 03742 | 76822 | 12073 | 59463 | 84420 | 15868 | 99505 | 11426 |

# REFERENCES

Adams, J. A. (1972). Research and the future of engineering psychology. *American Psychologist, 27*, 615–622.

Alsip, J. E., & Chezik, D. D. (1974). *Research guide in psychology*. Morristown, NJ: General Learning Press.

American Psychological Association. (1972). Guidelines for psychologists for the use of drugs in research. *American Psychologist, 27*, 336.

American Psychological Association. (1981a). Ethical principles of psychologists. *American Psychologist, 36*, 633–638.

American Psychological Association. (1981b). Guidelines for the use of animals in school-science behavior projects. *American Psychologist, 36*, 686.

American Psychological Association. (1982). *Ethical principles in the conduct of research with human behavior*. Washington, DC: Author.

American Psychological Association. (1983). *Publication manual of the American Psychological Association* (3rd ed.). Washington, DC: Author.

American Psychological Association. (1987). *Casebook on ethical issues*. Washington, DC: Author.

American Psychological Association. (1989). Ethical principles of psychologists. *American Psychologist, 45*, 390–395.

Anderson, N. H. (1981). *Foundations of information integration theory*. New York: Academic Press.

Anisfield, M. (1987). A course to develop competence in critical reading of empirical research in psychology. *Teaching of Psychology, 14*, 224–227.

Atkinson, R. C. (1975). Mnemotechnics and second-language learning. *American Psychologist, 30*, 821–828.

Bachman, J. D., & Johnston, L. D. (1979). The freshman. *Psychology Today, 13*, 78–87.

Banaji, M. R., & Crowder, R. G. (1989). The bankruptcy of everyday memory. *American Psychologist, 44*, 1185–1193.

Barber, T. X. (1976). *Pitfalls in human research: Ten pivotal points*. New York: Pergamon.

Barefoot, J. C., Hoople, H., & McClay, D. (1972). Avoidance of an act which would violate personal space. *Psychonomic Science, 28*, 205–206.

Barker, R. G. (1968). *Ecological psychology*. Stanford, CA: Stanford University Press.

Barker, R. G., & Wright, H. F. (1951). *One boy's day*. New York: Harper and Row.

Bem, D. J. (1987). Writing the empirical journal article. In M. P. Zanna & J. M. Darley (Eds.), *The compleat academic: A practical guide for the beginning social scientist*. New York: Random House.

Berkowitz, L., & Donnerstein, E. (1982). External validity is more than skin deep. *American Psychologist, 37*, 245–257.

Best, J. B. (1989). *Cognitive psychology* (2nd ed.). St. Paul, MN: West.

Blaney, R. H. (1986). Affect and memory: A review. *Psychological Bulletin, 99*, 229–246.

Boe, R., & Winokur, S. (1978). A procedure for studying echoic control in verbal behavior. *Journal of the Experimental Analysis of Behavior, 30*, 213–217.

Boice, R. (1983). Observational skills. *Psychological Bulletin, 93*, 3–29.

Boring, E. G. (1950). *A history of experimental psychology*. New York: Appleton-Century-Crofts.

Boring, E. G. (1954). The nature and history of experimental control. *American Journal of Psychology, 67*, 573–589.

Boring, E. G. (1961). The beginning and growth of measurement in psychology. *Isis, 52*, 238–257.

Bowd, A. D. (1980). Ethical reservations about psychological research with animals. *Psychological Record, 30*, 201–210.

Bower, G. H. (1972). Mental imagery and associative learning. In L. Gregg (Ed.), *Cognition in learning and memory*. New York: Wiley.

Brady, J. V. (1958). Ulcers in "executive" monkeys. *Scientific American, 199*, 92–100.

Brady, J. V., Porter, R. W., Conrad, D. G., & Mason, J. W. (1958). Avoidance behavior and the development of gastroduodenal ulcers. *Journal of the Experimental Analysis of Behavior, 1*, 69–72.

Brennan, T., Baguley, T., Bright, J., & Bruce, V. (1990). Resolving semantically induced tip-of-the-tongue states. *Memory & Cognition, 18*, 339–347.

Broad, W., & Wade, N. (1982). *Betrayers of the truth*. New York: Simon and Schuster.

Broadbent, D. E. (1971). *Decision and stress*. London: Academic Press.

Broadbent, D. E. (1973). *In defence of empirical psychology*. London: Methuen.

Brown, R., & McNeill, D. (1966). The "tip-of-the-tongue" phenomenon. *Journal of Verbal Learning and Verbal Behavior, 5*, 325–327.

Butters, N., & Cermak, L. S. (1986). A case study of the forgetting of autobiographical knowledge: Implications for the study of retrograde amnesia. In D. Rubin (Ed.), *Autobiographical memory* (pp. 253–272). New York: Cambridge University Press.

Campbell, D. T., & Erlebacher, A. (1970a). How regression artifacts can mistakenly make compensatory education look harmful. In J. Helmuth (Ed.), *Compensatory education: A national debate: Vol. 3. Disadvantaged child*. New York: Brunner/Mazel.

Campbell, D. T., & Erlebacher, A. (1970b). Reply to the replies. In J. Helmuth (Ed.), *Compensatory education: A national debate: Vol. 3. Disadvantaged child*. New York: Brunner/Mazel.

Campbell, D. T., & Stanley, J. C. (1963). *Experimental and quasi-experimental designs for research*. Chicago: Rand McNally.

Carver, C. S., Coleman, A. E., & Glass, D. C. (1976). The coronary-prone behavior pattern and the suppression of fatigue on a treadmill test. *Journal of Personality and Social Psychology, 33*, 460–466.

Chaplin, J. P. (1968). *Dictionary of psychology*. New York: Dell.

Cicirelli, V. (1970). The relevance of the regression artifact problem to the Westinghouse-Ohio evaluation of Head Start: A reply to Campbell and Erlebacher. In J. Helmuth (Ed.), *Compensatory education: A national debate: Vol. 3. Disadvantaged child*. New York: Brunner/Mazel.

Cicirelli, V. et al. (1969, June). *The impact of Head Start on children's cognitive and affective development*. A report presented to the Office of Economic Opportunity pursuant to Contract B89–4536. Westinghouse Learning Corporation, Ohio University. (Distributed by Clearinghouse for Federal Scientific and Technical Information, U.S. Department of Commerce, National Bureau of Standards, Institute for Applied Technology, PB 184 328.)

Clark, W. C., & Yang, J. C. (1974). Acupunctural analgesia: Evaluation by signal detection theory. *Science, 184*, 1096–1098.

Cohen, J. D., Dunbar, K., & McClelland, J. L. (1990). On the control of automatic processes: A parallel distributed processing account of the Stroop effect. *Psychological Review, 97*, 332–361.

Colasanto, D. (1989, October). Earthquake fails to shake composure of many Bay Area residents. *Gallup Report, 289*, 21–23.

Cole, M., Gay, J., Glick, J. A., & Sharp, D. W. (1971). *The cultural context of learning and thinking*. New York: Basic Books.

Comish, S. E. (1987). Recognition of facial stimuli following an intervening task involving the Identi-kit. *Journal of Applied Psychology, 72*, 488–491.

Cook, T. D., & Campbell, D. T. (1979). *Quasi-experimentation: Design and analysis for field settings*. Chicago: Rand McNally.

Cornsweet, T. N. (1962). The staircase method in psychophysics. *American Journal of Psychology, 75*, 485–491.

Crowder, R. G. (1982). *The psychology of reading*. New York: Oxford University Press.

D'Amato, M. R. (1970). *Experimental psychology: Methodology, psychophysics, and learning*. New York: McGraw-Hill.

DeGreene, K. B. (Ed.). (1970). *Systems psychology*. New York: McGraw-Hill.

Dewing, K., & Hetherington, P. (1974). Anagram solving as a function of word imagery. *Journal of Experimental Psychology, 102*, 764–767.

Dipboye, R. L., & Flanagan, M. F. (1979). Research settings in industrial and organizational psychology. *American Psychologist, 34*, 141–150.

Dollard, J., & Miller, N. E. (1950). *Personality and psychotherapy*. New York: McGraw-Hill.

Edwards, A. L. (1953). The relationship between the judged desirability of a trait and the probability that the trait will be endorsed. *Journal of Applied Psychology, 37*, 90–93.

Edwards, A. L. (1957). *The social desirability variable in personality research*. New York: Dryden.

Egeth, H., Blecker, D. L., & Kamlet, A. S. (1969). Verbal interference in a perceptual comparison task. *Perception & Psychophysics, 6*, 355–356.

Eibl-Eibesfeldt, I. (1970). *Ethology: The biology of behavior*. New York: Holt, Rinehart & Winston.

Eibl-Eibesfeldt, I. (1972). Similarities and differences between cultures in expressive movements. In R. A. Hinde (Ed.), *Non-verbal communication*. Cambridge, England: Cambridge University Press.

Elmes, D. G. (1978). *Readings in experimental psychology*. Chicago: Rand McNally.

Elmes, D. G. (1988, May 8). Cheap-shot prize goes to Proxmire. *Roanoke Times & World News*, p. F3.

Elmes, D. G., & Bjork, R. A. (1975). The interaction of encoding and rehearsal processes in the recall of repeated and nonrepeated items. *Journal of Verbal Learning and Verbal Behavior, 14*, 30–42.

Elmes, D. G., Chapman, P. F., & Selig, C. W. (1984). Role of mood and connotation in the spacing effect. *Bulletin of the Psychonomic Society, 22*, 186–188.

Eron, L. D. (1982). Parent-child interaction, television violence, and aggression of children. *American Psychologist, 37*, 197–211.

Eron, L. D., Huesmann, L. R., Leftkowitz, M. M., & Walder, L. O. (1972). Does television violence cause aggression? *American Psychologist, 27*, 253–263.

Evans, J. W., & Schiller, J. (1970). How preoccupation with possible regression artifacts can lead to a faulty strategy for the evaluation of social action programs: A reply to Campbell and Erlebacher. In J. Helmuth (Ed.), *Compensatory education: A national debate: Vol. 3. Disadvantaged child.* New York: Brunner/Mazel.

Eysenck, H. J., & Eaves, L. J. (1981). *The cause and effects of smoking.* New York: Gage.

Fechner, G. (1860/1966). *Elements of psychophysics*, Vol. 1. (H. E. Adler, D. H. Howes, and E. G. Boring, Eds. and Trans.). New York: Holt, Rinehart and Winston.

Feingold, B. F. (1975). Hyperkinesis and learning disabilities linked to artificial food flavors and colors. *American Journal of Nursing, 75*, 797–803.

Festinger, L. (1957). *A theory of cognitive dissonance.* Stanford, CA: Stanford University Press.

Festinger, L., Riecken, H. W., & Schachter, S. (1956). *When prophecy fails.* Minneapolis: University of Minnesota Press.

Ficken, M. S. (1990). Acoustic characteristics of alarm calls associated with predation risk in chickadees. *Animal Behaviour, 39*, 400–401.

Fingerman, P., & Levine, M. (1974). Nonlearning: The completeness of the blindness. *Journal of Experimental Psychology, 102*, 720–721.

Fossey, D. (1972). Living with mountain gorillas. In T. B. Allen (Ed.), *The marvels of animal behavior.* Washington, DC: National Geographic Society.

Frost, R., Katz, L., & Bentin, S. (1987). Strategies for visual word recognition and orthogonal depth: A multilingual comparison. *Journal of Experimental Psychology: Human Perception and Performance, 13*, 104–115.

Frye v. United States, 293F.1013 (D.C. Cir. 1923).

Gabrenya, W. K., Latané, B., & Wang, Y. (1983). Social loafing in cross-cultural perspective: Chinese on Taiwan. *Journal of Cross-Cultural Psychology, 14*, 368–384.

Gallup, G. G., & Suarez, S. D. (1985). Alternatives to the use of animals in psychological research. *American Psychologist, 40*, 1104–1111.

Garner, W. R., Hake, H., & Eriksen, C. W. (1956). Operationism and the concept of perception. *Psychological Review, 63*, 149–159.

Gescheider, G. A. (1976). *Psychophysics: Method and theory.* Hillsdale, NJ: Erlbaum.

Glenberg, A. M. (1988). *Learning from data.* San Diego: Harcourt Brace Jovanovich.

Graessle, O. A., Ahbel, K., & Porges, S. W. (1978). Effects of mild prenatal decompressions on growth and behavior in the rat. *Bulletin of the Psychonomic Society, 12*, 329–331.

Gregory, R. (1970). *The intelligent eye.* New York: McGraw-Hill.

Guilford, J. P. (1967). *The nature of human intelligence.* New York: McGraw-Hill.

Hanson, N. R. (1958). *Patterns of discovery.* Cambridge: Cambridge University Press.

Hardy, J. D., Wolff, H. G., & Goodell, H. (1952). *Pain reactions and sensations.* Baltimore: Williams & Wilkins.

Harkins, S. G., Latané, B., & Williams, K. (1980). Social loafing: Allocating effort or taking it easy? *Journal of Experimental Social Psychology, 16*, 457–465.

Harlow, H. F., Gluck, J. P., & Suomi, S. J. (1972). Generalization of behavioral data between nonhuman and human animals. *American Psychologist, 27*, 709–716.

Harré, R. (1983). *Great scientific experiments.* Oxford: Oxford University Press.

Hart, B. M., Allen, K. E., Buell, J. S., Harris, F. R., & Wolf, M. M. (1964). Effects of social reinforcement on operant crying. *Journal of Experimental Child Psychology, 1*, 145–153.

Hicks, E. A., & Kilcourse, J. (1983). Habitual sleep duration and the incidence of headaches in college students. *Bulletin of the Psychonomic Society, 21*, 119.

Hintzman, D. L., Carre, F. A., Eskridge, V. L., Owens, A. M., Shaff, S. S., & Sparks, M. E. (1972). "Stroop" effect: Input or output phenomenon? *Journal of Experimental Psychology, 95*, 458–459.

Hoff, C. (1980). Immoral and moral uses of animals. *New England Journal of Medicine, 302*, 115–118.

Homans, G. C. (1965). Group factors in worker productivity. In H. Proshansky and L. Seidenberg (Eds.), *Basic studies in social psychology.* New York: Holt.

Horowitz, L. M. (1974). *Elements of statistics for psychology and education.* New York: McGraw Hill.

Huesmann, L. R., Eron, L. D., Leftkowitz, M. M., & Walder, L. O. (1973). Television violence and aggression: The causal effect remains. *American Psychologist, 28*, 617–620.

Huff, D. (1954). *How to lie with statistics.* New York: Norton.

Hyman, R. (1964). *The nature of psychological inquiry.* Englewood Cliffs, NJ: Prentice-Hall.

Imber, S. D., Glanz, L. M., Elkin, I., Sotsky, S. M., Boyer, J. L., & Leber, W. R. (1986). Ethical issues in psychotherapy research: Problems in a collaborative clinical study. *American Psychologist, 41*, 137–146.

Jacobson, E. (1978). *You must relax* (5th ed.). New York: McGraw-Hill.

Jarrard, L. E. (1963). Effects of d-lysergic acid diethylamide on operant behavior in the rat. *Psychopharmacologia, 5*, 39–46.

Jensen, A. R. (1969). How much can we boost I.Q. and scholastic achievement? *Harvard Educational Review, 39*, 1–123.

Johnson-Laird, P. N. (1988). *The computer and the mind: An introduction to cognitive science.* Cambridge: Harvard University Press.

Jones, R. F. (1982). *Ancients and moderns.* New York: Dover.

Judd, C. M., Smith, E. R., & Kidder, L. H. (1991). *Research methods in social relations* (6th ed.). Fort Worth: Holt, Rinehart and Winston.

Kantowitz, B. H. (1974). Double stimulation. In B. H. Kantowitz (Ed.), *Human information processing—Tutorials in performance and cognition*. Hillsdale, NJ: Erlbaum.

Kantowitz, B. H., Roediger, H. L., & Elmes, D. G. (1991). *Experimental psychology: Understanding behavioral research* (4th ed.). St. Paul, MN: West.

Kaplan, R. M., & Saccuzzo, D. P. (1982). *Psychological testing: Principles, applications, and issues*. Monterey, CA: Brooks/Cole.

Katz, D. (1979, February 7). Paying the price for drug development. *Roanoke Times & World News*.

Keele, S. W. (1973). *Attention and human performance*. Pacific Palisades, CA: Goodyear.

Kendler, H. H. (1981). *Psychology: A science in conflict*. New York: Oxford.

Kerlinger, F. (1986). *Foundations of behavioral research*. New York: Holt, Rinehart & Winston.

Kinsey, A. C., Pomeroy, W. B., & Martin, C. E. (1953). *Sexual behavior in the human female*. Philadelphia: Saunders.

Kinzel, A. F. (1970). Body-buffer zone in violent prisoners. *The American Journal of Psychiatry, 127*, 59–64.

Kirk, R. R. (1982). *Experimental design: Procedures for the behavioral sciences*. (2nd ed.). Belmont, CA: Brooks/Cole.

Kohn, A. (1986). *False prophets*. New York: Basil Blackwell.

Kravitz, D. A., & Martin, B. (1986). Ringelmann rediscovered: The original article. *Journal of Personality and Social Psychology, 50*, 936–941.

Kuhn, T. S. (1962). *The structure of scientific revolutions*. Chicago: University of Chicago Press.

Latané, B. (1981). The psychology of social impact. *American Psychologist, 36*, 343–356.

Latané, B., & Darley, J. M. (1970). *The unresponsive bystander—Why doesn't he help?* New York: Appleton-Century-Crofts.

Latané, B., Williams, K., & Harkins, S. (1979). Many hands make light the work: Causes and consequences of social loafing. *Journal of Personality and Social Psychology, 37*, 822–832.

Leon, G. R. (1990). *Case histories of psychopathology* (4th ed.). Boston: Allyn and Bacon.

Lester, B. M., & Brazelton, T. B. (1982). Cross-cultural assessment of neonatal behavior. In D. A. Wagner & H. W. Stevenson (Eds.), *Cultural perspectives on child development*. San Francisco: Freeman.

Levin, I. P., Louviere, J. J., & Schepanski, A. A. (1983). External validity tests of laboratory studies of information integration. *Organizational Behavior and Human Performance, 31*, 173–193.

Lindholm, E., & Lowry, S. (1978). Alpha production in humans under conditions of false feedback. *Bulletin of the Psychonomic Society, 11*, 106–108.

Lovelace, E. A., & Twohig, P. T. (1990). Healthy older adult's perception of their memory function and use of mnemonics. *Bulletin of the Psychonomic Society, 28*, 115–118.

Luchins, A. S. (1942). Mechanization in problem solving: The effect of Einstellung. *Psychological Monographs, 54* (6, Whole No. 181).

MacLeod, C. M. (1991). Half a century of research on the Stroop effect: An integrative review. *Psychological Bulletin, 109*, 163–203.

Marks, L. E. (1974). *Sensory processes: The new psychophysics.* New York: Academic Press.

Marriot, P. (1949). Size of working groups and output. *Occupational Psychology, 23,* 47–57.

Masling, J. (1966). Role-related behavior of the subject and psychologist and its effects upon psychological data. *Nebraska symposium on motivation* (Vol. 14). Lincoln: University of Nebraska Press.

Massaro, D. W. (1975). *Experimental psychology and information processing.* Chicago: Rand McNally.

Mayer, R. E. (1977). Problem-solving performance with task overload: Effects of self-pacing and trait anxiety. *Bulletin of the Psychonomic Society, 9,* 283–286.

Mayr, E. (1982). *The growth of biological thought.* Cambridge, MA: Belknap Press.

Mayzner, M. S., & Tresselt, M. E. (1966). Anagram solution times: A function of multiple solution anagrams. *Journal of Experimental Psychology, 71,* 66–73.

McCall, R. B. (1990). *Fundamentals of statistics for the behavioral sciences* (5th ed.). San Diego: Harcourt Brace.

McSweeny, A. J. (1978). The effects of response cost on the behavior of a million persons: Charging for directory assistance in Cincinnati. *Journal of Applied Behavior Analysis, 11,* 47–51.

Melton, G., & Gray, J. (1988). Ethical dilemmas in AIDS research: Individual privacy and public health. *American Psychologist, 43,* 60–64.

Milgram, S. (1963). Behavioral study of obedience. *Journal of Abnormal and Social Psychology, 67,* 371–378.

Milgram, S. (1977). Ethical issues in the study of obedience. In B. Milgram (Ed.), *The individual in a social world* (pp. 188–199). Reading, MA: Addison-Wesley.

Mill, J. S. (1930). *A system of logic.* London: Longmans Green. (Original work published 1843).

Miller, D. B. (1977). Roles of naturalistic observation in comparative psychology. *American Psychologist, 32,* 211–219.

Miller, N. E. (1959). Liberalization of basic S-R concepts: Extensions to conflict behavior, motivation, and social learning. In S. Koch (Ed.), *Psychology: A study of a science* (Vol. 2, pp. 196–292). New York: McGraw-Hill.

Miller, N. E. (1985). The value of behavioral research on animals. *American Psychologist, 40,* 423–440.

Mook, D. G. (1983). In defense of external invalidity. *American Psychologist, 38,* 379–387.

Morin, R. E., & Grant, D. A. (1954). Learning and performance of a key-pressing task as a function of the degree of spatial stimulus-response correspondence. *Journal of Experimental Psychology, 49,* 39–47.

Moscovitch, M. (1982). Multiple dissociations of functions in the amnesic syndrome. In L. Cermak (Ed.), *Human memory and amnesia.* Hillsdale, NJ: Erlbaum.

Neisser, U. (1976). *Cognition and reality: Principles and implications of cognitive psychology.* San Francisco: Freeman.

Neisser, U. (1978). Memory: What are the important questions? In M. M. Gruneberg, P. E. Morris, & R. N. Sykes (Eds.), *Practical aspects of memory* (pp. 3–24). London: Academic Press.

Neisser, U. (1981). John Dean's memory. *Cognition, 9,* 1–22.

Neisser, U. (1982). *Memory observed: Remembering in natural contexts.* San Francisco: Freeman.

Nissen, M. J., Ross, J. L., Willingham, D. B., MacKenzie, T. B., & Schacter, D. L. (1988). Memory and awareness in a patient with multiple personality disorder. *Brain and Cognition, 8,* 117–134.

Notterman, J. M., & Mintz, D. E. (1965). *Dynamics of response.* New York: Wiley.

Orne, M. T. (1962). On the social psychology of the psychological experiment: With particular reference to demand characteristics and their implications. *American Psychologist, 17,* 776–783.

Orne, M. T. (1969). Demand characteristics and the concept of quasi-controls. In R. Rosenthal & R. L. Rosnow (Eds.), *Artifact in behavioral research.* New York: Academic Press.

Orne, M. T., & Evans, T. J. (1965). Social control in the psychological experiment: Antisocial behavior and hypnosis. *Journal of Personality and Social Psychology, 1,* 189–200.

Paivio, A. (1975). Perceptual comparisons through the mind's eye. *Memory & Cognition, 3,* 635–647.

Parsons, H. M. (1974). What happened at Hawthorne? *Science, 183,* 922–931.

Pavlov, I. P. (1963). *Lectures on conditioned reflexes.* New York: International Publishers.

Peirce, C. S. (1877). The fixation of belief. *Popular Science Monthly, 12,* 1–15. Reprinted in E. C. Moore (Ed.). (1972). *Charles S. Peirce: The essential writings.* New York: Harper & Row.

Phillips, D. P. (1972). Deathday and birthday: An unexpected connection. In J. Tanur, F. Mosteller, W. H. Kruskal, R. F. Link, R. S. Peters, & G. R. Rising (Eds.), *Statistics: A guide to the unknown.* San Francisco: Holden Day.

Phillips, D. P. (1977). Motor vehicle fatalities increase just after publicized suicide stories. *Science, 196,* 1464–1465.

Phillips, D. P. (1978). Airplane accident fatalities increase just after stories about murder and suicide. *Science, 201,* 148–150.

Phillips, D. P. (1983). The impact of mass media violence on U.S. homicides. *American Sociological Review, 48,* 560–568.

Piaget, J., & Inhelder, B. (1969). *The psychology of the child.* London: Routledge & Kegan Paul.

Piliavin, I. M., Piliavin, J. A., & Rodin, J. (1975). Costs, diffusion, and the stigmatized victim. *Journal of Personality and Social Psychology, 32,* 429–438.

Platt, J. R. (1964). Strong inference. *Science, 146,* 347–353.

Plotkin, W. B. (1979). The alpha experience revisited: Biofeedback in the transformation of psychological state. *Psychological Bulletin, 86,* 1132–1148.

Popper, K. R. (1961). *The logic of scientific discovery.* New York: Basic Books.

Poulton, E. C. (1982). Influential companions: Effects of one strategy on another in the within-subjects designs of cognitive psychology. *Psychological Bulletin, 9,* 673–690.

Pratkanis, A. R., Greenwald, A. G., Leippe, M. R., & Baumgardner, M. H. (1988). In search of reliable persuasion effects: The sleeper effect is dead. Long live the sleeper effect. *Journal of Personality and Social Psychology, 54,* 203–218.

Putnam, F. W., Guroff, J. J., Silberman, E. K., Barban, L., & Post, R. M. (1986). The clinical phenomenology of multiple personality disorder: 100 recent cases. *Journal of Clinical Psychiatry, 47*, 285–293.

Read, J. D. (1983). Detection of Fs in a single statement: The role of phonetic recoding. *Memory & Cognition, 11*, 390–399.

Richman, C. L., Mitchell, D. B., & Reznick, J. S. (1979). Mental travel: Some reservations. *Journal of Experimental Psychology: Human Perception and Performance, 5*, 13–18.

Ringelmann, M. (1913). Recherches sur les moteurs animes: Travail de l'homme. *Annales de l'Institut National Agronomique*, 2e series-tome XII, 1–40.

Roberts, C. (1971). Debate I. Animal experimentation and evolution. *American Scholar, 40*, 497–503.

Roediger, H. L., & Neely, J. H. (1982). Retrieval blocks in episodic and semantic memory. *Canadian Journal of Psychology, 36*, 213–242.

Rogosa, D. (1980). A critique of the cross-lagged correlation. *Psychological Bulletin, 88*, 245–248.

Rollin, B. E. (1985). The moral status of research animals in psychology. *American Psychologist, 40*, 920–926.

Rose, T. L. (1978). The functional relationship between artificial food colors and hyperactivity. *Journal of Applied Behavior Analysis, 11*, 439–446.

Rosenberg, M. J. (1969). The conditions and consequences of evaluation apprehension. In R. Rosenthal & R. L. Rosnow (Eds.), *Artifact in behavioral research*. New York: Academic Press.

Rosnow, R. L., & Rosenthal, R. (1970). Volunteer effects in behavioral research. In *New directions in psychology 4*. New York: Holt, Rinehart & Winston.

Rowland, L. W. (1939). Will hypnotized persons try to harm themselves or others? *Journal of Abnormal and Social Psychology, 34*, 114–117.

Saari, L. M., & Latham, G. P. (1982). Employee reactions to continuous and variable ratio reinforcement schedules involving a monetary incentive. *Journal of Applied Psychology, 67*, 506–508.

Sacks, O. (1985). *The man who mistook his wife for a hat and other clinical tales*. New York: Summit.

Sanders, G. S., & Simmons, W. L. (1983). Use of hypnosis to enhance eyewitness accuracy: Does it work? *Journal of Applied Psychology, 68*, 70–77.

Scarborough, D. L. (1972). Stimulus modality effects on forgetting in short-term memory. *Journal of Experimental Psychology, 95*, 285–289.

Scarr, S. (1988). Race and gender as psychological variables: Social and ethical issues. *American Psychologist, 43*, 56–59.

Schachter, S. (1982). Don't sell habit-breakers short. *Psychology Today, 16*, 27–33.

Schaie, K. W. (1977). Quasi-experimental designs in the psychology of aging. In J. E. Birren & K. W. Schaie (Eds.), *Handbook of the psychology of aging*. New York: Van Nostrand.

Sellin, T., & Wolfgang, M. E. (1964). *The measurement of delinquency*. New York: Wiley.

Sidman, M. (1960). *Tactics of scientific research*. New York: Basic Books.

Sieber, J. E., & Stanley, B. (1988). Ethical and professional dimensions of socially sensitive research. *American Psychologist, 43*, 49–55.

Singer, P. (1978). Animal experimentation: Philosophical perspectives. In W. T. Reich (Ed.), *Encyclopedia of bioethics*. New York: Free Press.

Skinner, B. F. (1938). *The behavior of organisms: An experimental analysis*. New York: Appleton-Century-Crofts.

Smith, C. P. (1983). Ethical issues: Research on deception, informed consent, and debriefing. In L. Wheeler & P. Shaver (Eds.), *Review of personality and social psychology* (Vol. 4, pp. 297–328). Beverly Hills, CA: Sage.

Smith, M. C. (1983). Hypnotic memory enhancement: Does it work? *Psychological Bulletin, 94*, 387–407.

Sternberg, R. J. (1987). *The psychologist's companion: A guide to scientific writing for students and researchers*. Cambridge: Cambridge University Press.

Stevens, S. S. (1961). The psychophysics of sensory functions. In W. A. Rosenblith (Ed.), *Sensory communication*. Cambridge: M.I.T. Press.

Stevens, S. S. (1966). A metric for the social consensus. *Science, 151*, 530–541.

Stroop, J. R. (1935). Studies of interference in serial verbal reactions. *Journal of Experimental Psychology, 18*, 643–662.

Swensson, R. G. (1980). A two-stage detection model applied to skilled visual search by radiologists. *Perception & Psychophysics, 27*, 11–16.

Thios, S. J., & D'Agostino, P. R. (1976). Effects of repetition as a function of study–phase retrieval. *Journal of Verbal Learning and Verbal Behavior, 15*, 529–536.

Thompson, J. B., & Buchanan, W. (1979). *Analyzing psychological data*. New York: Scribner's.

Tulving, E., & Pearlstone, Z. (1966). Availability versus accessibility of information in memory for words. *Journal of Verbal Learning and Verbal Behavior, 5*, 381–391.

Tversky, B., & Teiffer, E. (1976). Development of strategies for recall and recognition. *Developmental Psychology, 12*, 406–410.

Underwood, B. (1957). *Psychological research*. New York: Appleton.

Underwood, B. J. (1975). Individual differences as a crucible in theory construction. *American Psychologist, 30*, 128–134.

Uttal, W. R. (1978). *The psychology of mind*. Hillsdale, NJ: Erlbaum.

Velten, E. A. (1968). A laboratory task for the induction of mood states. *Behavior Research and Therapy, 6*, 473–478.

Walters, C., Shurley, J. T., & Parsons, O. A. (1962). Differences in male and female responses to underwater sensory deprivation: An exploratory study. *Journal of Nervous and Mental Disease, 135*, 302–310.

Warren, R. M. (1963). Are loudness judgments based on distance estimates? *Journal of the Acoustical Society of America, 35*, 613–614.

Wason, P. C. (1977). 'On the failure to eliminate hypotheses . . .'—A second look. In P. N. Johnson-Laird & P. C. Wason (Eds.), *Thinking: Readings in cognitive science*. Cambridge: Cambridge University Press.

Webb, E. J., Campbell, D. T., Schwartz, R. D., & Sechrist, L. (1981). *Unobtrusive measures: Nonreactive research in the social sciences*. Chicago: Rand McNally.

Weber, S. J., & Cook, T. D. (1972). Subject effects in laboratory research: An examination of subject roles, demand characteristics, and valid inference. *Psychological Bulletin, 77*, 273–295.

Weinstock, S. (1958). Acquisition and extinction of a partially reinforced running response at a 24-hour intertrial interval. *Journal of Experimental Psychology, 56*, 151–158.

Weiss, J. M. (1968). Effects of coping responses on stress. *Journal of Comparative and Physiological Psychology, 65*, 251–260.

Weiss, J. M. (1971). Effects of coping behavior in different warning signal conditions on stress pathology in rats. *Journal of Comparative and Physiological Psychology, 77*, 1–13.

White, R. J. (1971). Debate II. Antivivisection: The reluctant hydra. *American Scholar, 40*, 503–512.

Wildman, B. G., & Erickson, M. T. (1977). Methodological problems in behaviorial observation. In J. D. Cone and R. P. Hawkins (Eds.), *Behaviorial assessment*. New York: Brunner/Mazel.

Williams, K., Harkins, S., & Latané, B. (1981). Identifiability as a deterrent to social loafing: Two cheering experiments. *Journal of Personality and Social Psychology, 40*, 303–311.

Williams, R. D., & Long, J. D. (1979). *Toward a self-managed life style* (2nd ed.). Boston: Houghton-Mifflin.

Windes, J. D. (1968). Reaction time for numerical coding and naming of numerals. *Journal of Experimental Psychology, 78*, 318–322.

Wohwill, J. F. (1970). Methodology and research strategy in the study of developmental change. In L. R. Goulet & P. B. Baltes (Eds.), *Life-span developmental psychology: Research and theory*. New York: Academic Press.

Wolf, M. M., & Risley, T. R. (1971). Reinforcement: Applied research. In R. Glaser (Ed.), *The nature of reinforcement*. New York: Academic Press.

Woods, P. J. (1976). *Career opportunities for psychologists*. Washington, DC: American Psychological Association.

Woolfolk, M. E. (1981). The eye of the beholder: Methodological considerations when observers assess nonverbal communication. *Journal of Nonverbal Behavior, 5*, 199–204.

Woolfolk, M. E., Castellan, W., & Brooks, C. I. (1983). Pepsi versus Coke: Labels, not tastes, prevail. *Psychological Reports, 52*, 185–186.

Wright, L. (1988). The Type A behavior pattern and coronary artery disease. *American Psychologist, 43*, 2–14.

Young, P. C. (1952). Antisocial uses of hypnosis. In L. M. LeCron (Ed.), *Experimental hypnosis*. New York: Macmillan.

Zajonc, R. B., & Marcus, N. (1975). Birth order and intellectual development. *Psychological Review, 82*, 74–88.

# GLOSSARY

**ABA and ABAB designs** see *reversal design*

**Abscissa** the horizontal axis (or *x*-axis) in a graph

**Absolute threshold** the average point on a sensory continuum (such as light intensity) at which an observer detects a stimulus

**Aftercare** the need for experimenters to guard the welfare of their subjects subsequent to the research manipulation; especially important in drug research

**Alpha level** see *significance level*

**Analysis of variance** a statistical test appropriate for analyzing reliability from experiments with any number of levels on one or more independent variables

**Anthropomorphizing** attributing human characteristics or emotions, such as happiness, to animals

**APA format** the journal article format specified by the American Psychological Association (APA)

**Applied research** research whose focus is on solving a practical problem

**A priori method** according to Peirce, a way of fixing belief due to the reasonableness of the event (see *method of tenacity, method of authority,* and *empirical*)

**Apprehensive-subject role** a presumed role taken by a research subject who dislikes being evaluated; see *evaluation apprehension* and *reactivity*

**Balanced Latin square** counterbalancing scheme in which each condition is preceded and followed equally often by every other condition

**Baseline** the "normal" or typical behavior used as a standard of comparison in an experiment

**Basic research** research whose focus is on understanding rather than on the immediate solution to a problem

**Behavior** the basic dependent variable of psychology

**Beta** the criterion of the decision process in signal detection measured by the slope of the receiver-operating-characteristic (ROC) function at the point of interest

**Between-groups variance** a measure of the dispersion among groups in an experiment

**Between-subjects design** an experimental design in which each subject is tested under only one level of each independent variable

**Blind experiment** experiment in which subjects do not know whether or not they are in the treatment condition (see *double-blind design*)

**Block randomization** a counterbalancing technique in which the treatment orders are randomized in successive blocks of presenting those conditions

**Carryover effect** relatively permanent effect that testing subjects in one condition has on their later behavior in another condition

**Case study** intensive investigation of a particular instance, or cases, of some behavior; does not allow inferences of cause and effect but is merely descriptive

**Ceiling effect** see *scale-attenuation effects*

**Central tendency** descriptive statistics indicating the center of a distribution of scores; see *mean, median,* and *mode*

**Computerized literature search** a method of searching the data base in a library that uses a computer

**Conceptual replication** attempt to demonstrate an experimental phenomenon with an entirely new paradigm or set of experimental conditions (see *converging operations*)

**Confidence level** see *significance level*

**Confidentiality** information obtained about subjects should remain confidential unless otherwise agreed

**Confounding** simultaneous variation of a second variable with an independent variable of interest so that any effect on the dependent variable cannot be attributed with certainty to the independent variable; inherent in correlational research

**Construct validity** when several measures fit sensibly with other results, we are measuring an underlying psychological concept

**Control** the technique of producing comparisons and holding other variables constant

**Control condition** the comparison condition in a within-subjects design (compare to *control group*)

**Control group** the group in a between-subjects experiment that receives a comparison level of the independent variable

**Control variable** a potential independent variable that is held constant in an experiment

**Converging operations** a set of related lines of investigation that all bolster a common conclusion

**Correlation** a measure of the extent to which two variables are related, not necessarily causally

**Correlation coefficient** a number that can vary from $-1.00$ to $+1.00$ and indicates the degree of relation between two variables

**Counterbalancing** refers to any technique used to vary systemically the order of conditions in an experiment to distribute the effects of time of testing (e.g., practice and fatigue) so they are not confounded with conditions

**Criterion** an independent means of determining the validity of an observation, experiment, or judgment; and the decision point in a signal-detection experiment at which an observer decides to say yes or no

**Critic** a person who makes an informed judgment

**Critical thinker** a person who approaches scientific procedures and results with a critical attitude

**Cross-lagged panel correlation** calculating several correlation coefficients across time on the same participants to increase the internal validity of correlational research

**Cross-over interaction** when the effect of one independent variable on a dependent variable reverses at different levels of a second independent variable

**Cross-sectional method** taking a large sample of the population of various ages at one time and testing them (contrast with *longitudinal method*)

**Cross-sequential design** a quasi-experimental design used when age is a subject variable to try to control for cohort and time of testing effects; involves testing several different age groups at several different time periods (see *longitudinal method* and *cross-sectional method*)

**d'** the sensitivity of an observer in a signal-detection experiment; the distance between signal and noise distributions

**Data** the scores obtained on a dependent variable

**Debriefing** when subjects are told all details of an experiment after they have participated; an ethical obligation of the researcher

**Deception** a research technique in which the participant is mislead about some aspect of the project; may be unethical (see *double-blind design*)

**Decision process** evaluation of the sensory impression of a stimulus

**Deduction** reasoning from the general to the particular

**Degrees of freedom** the number of values free to vary if the total number of values and their sum are fixed

**Demand characteristics** those cues available to subjects in an experiment that may enable them to determine the purpose of the experiment, or what is expected by the experimenter

**Dependent variable** the variable measured and recorded by the experimenter

**Descriptive observation** a determination of the quantity (frequency, magnitude) of behavior resulting from observation, case study, survey, and testing methods

**Descriptive statistics** methods of organizing and summarizing data

**Deviant-case analysis** investigation of similar cases that differ in outcome in an attempt to specify the reasons for the different outcomes

**Difference** a basic property of all measurement scales, such that objects or their attributes can be categorized as different from each other

**Difference threshold** the average point at which two stimuli are judged to be different (half of the interval of uncertainty)

**Directional/nondirectional statistical tests** see *one-* and *two-tailed tests*

**Direct scaling** the observer applies his or her scale in assigning numbers (see *indirect scaling*)

**Direct replication** repeating an experiment as closely as possible to determine whether the same results will be obtained

**Discounting cue** a message, signal, or pertinent fact that makes you doubt the accuracy or credibility of a persuasive message

**Dispersion** the amount of spread in a distribution of scores

**Distribution** a set of values of a variable

**Double-blind design** experimental technique in which neither the subject nor the experimenter knows which subjects are in which treatment conditions

**Ecological validity** the extent to which a research setting matches the environment of the problem under investigation; a threat to the external validity of experiments

**Einstellung** the effect of expectancy on cognition; for example, if the people solve problems in one particular way, they will often approach new problems in the same way even when the original strategy is no longer effective

**Empirical** relying on or derived from observation or experiment

**Equal interval** a property of measurement scales such that a one-unit change is equivalent throughout the range of the scale

**Ethogram** a data sheet providing categories for making naturalistic observations

**Ethology** the systematic study of behavior; usually animal behavior in natural settings

**Evaluation apprehension** a source of reactivity in which subjects are uneasy about being evaluated in an experiment (see *reactivity*)

**Experiment** the systematic manipulation of some environment in order to observe the effect of this manipulation on behavior; a particular comparison is produced

**Experimental control** holding constant extraneous variables in an experiment so that any effect on the dependent variable can be attributed to manipulation of the independent variable

**Experimental group** the group in an experiment that receives the level of interest of the independent variable

**Experimental reliability** see *replication*

**Explanation** a causal statement about why or when a particular event occurs resulting from experimental methods (see *joint method of agreement and difference*)

**Ex post facto** literally, "after the fact"; refers to conditions in an experiment that are not determined prior to the experiment, but only after some manipulation has occurred naturally

**External validity** refers to the generality of research; externally valid research is representative of real life and does not distort the question under investigation

**Factorial design** an experimental design in which each level of every independent variable occurs with all levels of the other independent variable

**Faithful-subject role** when subjects do their utmost to follow the demands of the experimenter (see *reactivity*)

**False alarm** saying yes when a signal is not present (in contrast to a hit)

**Falsifiability view** the assertion by Popper that negative results are more informative than positive results

**Fechner's law $\Psi = K$ log stimulus** an ordinal scale specifying the relation between psychological judgment and stimulus intensity

**Field research** research conducted in natural settings in which subjects typically do not know that they are in an experiment

**Floor effect** see *scale-attenuation effects*

**Forced-choice tests** tests in which the participant must select between two or more statements; often used to control response styles

**$F$ ratio** a ratio of between-groups variance to within-groups variance; forms the basis of the analysis of variance

**Freedom to withdraw** experimenter is ethically obligated to allow subjects to discontinue participation in the research

**Frequency distribution** a set of scores arranged in order along a distribution indicating the number of times each score occurs

**Frequency polygon** a frequency distribution in which the height of the curve indicates the frequency of scores (see *histogram*)

**Generalizability** the issue of whether a particular experimental result will be obtained under different circumstances, such as with a different subject population or in a different experimental setting

**Good-subject role** when a subject attempts to determine the purposes of an experiment and reacts accordingly (see *demand characteristics* and *reactivity*)

**Hawthorne effect** refers to conditions under which performance in an experiment is affected by the knowledge of participants that they are in an experiment (see *demand characteristics*)

**Histogram** a frequency distribution in which the height of bars in the graph indicates the frequency of a class of scores; also called a bar graph

**History** a possible confound in research that inadvertently takes place between measurements because of historical changes in the participant

**Hit** saying yes when a signal is presented (see *false alarm*)

**Independent variable** the variable manipulated by the experimenter

**Indirect scaling** the observer limits judgments to a small set of categories in order to scale the attribute in question (contrast with *direct scaling*)

**Individual differences** a problem that may confound the results of a between-subjects experiment

**Induction** reasoning from the particular to the general

**Inferential statistics** procedures for determining the reliability and generality of a particular experimental finding

**Informed consent** potential subjects must be in a position to decide whether to participate in an experiment

**Institutional Review Board (IRB)** a board in nearly every United States institution conducting research that oversees the protection of human subjects

**Interactions** experimental results that occur when the effects of one independent variable depend on the levels of other independent variables

**Internal distribution** the presumed sensory impressions in signal-detection theory

**Internal validity** allows straightforward statements about causality; experiments are usually internally valid because the joint method of agreement and difference is employed

**Interrupted-time-series design** a quasi-experiment that involves examination of a naturally occurring treatment on the behavior of a large number of participants

**Interval of uncertainty** the difference between the upper and lower thresholds in the determination of a difference threshold

**Interval scale** a scale with equal intervals but without a true zero point (for example, temperature)

**Intervening variable** an abstract concept that links independent variables to dependent variables

**Joint method of agreement and difference** in Mill's system a situation, such as an experiment, in which $X$ always follows $A$ and never occurs when $A$ is not present

**Just-noticeable difference (JND)** the smallest perceptible difference between two stimuli

**Latin-square design** a counterbalancing procedure in which each conditioning occurs equally often during each time period of the experiment (see *balanced Latin square*)

**Longitudinal method** testing one group of people repeatedly as they age (contrast with *cross-sectional method*)

**Magnitude** a property of measurement scales having to do with the fact that scale values can be ordered on the basis of magnitude—if A > B and B > C, then A > C

**Magnitude estimation** observers assign numbers to attributes usually without restriction except that the numbers be assigned proportionately to the judged magnitude (a ratio scale)

**Magnitude of effect** a calculation such as $r_{pb}$ that reveals the magnitude of the effect of the independent variable—how wrong the null hypothesis is

**Main effect** when the effect of one independent variable is the same at all levels of another independent variable

**Mann-Whitney *U* test** a nonparametric test to determine whether the behavior of two independent groups is statistically different

**Matched-groups design** experimental design in which subjects are matched on some variable assumed to be correlated with the dependent variable and then randomly assigned to conditions

**Matching** see *subject variable* and *matched-groups design*

**Maturation** changes in people over time because of growth and other historical factors; may be a source of confounding in quasi-experiments

**Mean** measure of central tendency; the sum of all the scores divided by the number of scores

**Measurement** the systematic assignment of numbers to objects or attributes of objects

**Measurement scales** in order of increasing power; nominal, ordinal, interval, and ratio

**Median** measure of central tendency; the middle score of a distribution, or the one that divides a distribution in half

**Method of authority** a method of fixing belief in which an authority's word is taken on faith (contrast with *empirical*)

**Method of limits** a psychophysical procedure for determining thresholds in which ascending and descending sequences of stimuli are presented

**Method of tenacity** a way of fixing belief involving a steadfast adherence to a particular belief, regardless of contrary arguments (see *empirical*)

**Mixed design** an experimental design that contains both between-subjects and within-subjects manipulations of the independent variables

**Mode** a measure of central tendency; the most frequent score

**Mortality** a possible source of confounding in research resulting from subjects dropping out either because they will not participate or because they cannot participate

**Motivated forgetting** distortions of past events reported retrospectively because of the emotional nature of those events

**Naturalistic observation** description of naturally occurring events without intervention on the part of the investigator

**Negativistic-subject role** when a subject deliberately attempts to sabotage an experiment

**Noise** a random disturbance that can be confused with signals in a signal-detection experiment

**Nominal scale** a scale in which objects are named or categorized—the weakest measurement scale

**Nonequivalent control group** in quasi-experiments a control group that is not determined by random assignment but is usually selected after the fact and is supposed to be equivalent to the naturally treated group

**Normal curve** a distribution of events that, when plotted, results in a bell-shaped curve; in a normal curve the mean, the median, and the mode are all equal

**Normal distribution** one producing a symmetric bell-shaped curve

**Nonparametric statistics** statistical tests that do not make any assumptions about the underlying distribution of scores; ordinarily require just ordinal-level data (see *parametric statistics*)

**Null hypothesis** states that the independent variable will have no effect on the dependent variable

**Null result** an experimental outcome where the dependent variable was not influenced by the independent variable

**Observation-treatment-observation** a quasi-experimental design; usually includes a nonequivalent control group

**One-shot case study** (see *case study*) a quasi-experiment in which the behavior of a single individual is studied and "explained" in terms of life events (see also *deviant-case analysis*)

**One-tailed test** test that places the rejection area at one end of a distribution

**Operational definition** a definition of a concept in terms of the operations that must be performed to demonstrate the concept

**Ordinal scale** a measurement scale in which objects or attributes are ordered but in which the intervals between points are not equal

**Ordinate** the vertical axis (or *y*-axis) in a graph

**Organize** one function of a theory is to collect or organize what is known into a coherent statement

**Parallel forms** two alternative forms of a test

**Parametric statistics** statistical tests that make assumptions about the distribution of scores (e.g., normally distributed); require interval or ratio data

**Parsimony** a good, powerful theory should explain many events with few statements or explanatory concepts; thus, refers to simplicity

**Participant observation** an observation procedure in which the observer participates with those being observed; e.g., living with gorillas in the wild

**Pearson** *r* one form of correlation coefficient

**Personal space** the "invisible bubble" surrounding a person

**Pilot research** preliminary research undertaken to discover problems of method and design for a subsequent full-scale project

**Point biserial** *r* a correlation coefficient often used in two group experiments to determine the magnitude of effect of the independent variable

**Point of subjective equality** the mean of the upper and lower thresholds in a difference-threshold experiment

**Population** the total set of potential observations from which a sample is drawn

**Power (of a statistical test)** the probability of rejecting the null hypothesis in a statistical test when it is in fact false

**Precision** a good theory should be precise in its predictions

**Prediction** a specification of relationships resulting from correlational methods; also one aim of a theory

**Predictive validity** when a test can predict a particular outcome

**Protection from harm** ethical researchers protect their subjects from any harm

**Protocol** a recipe to be followed exactly in conducting a research project

**Proximate cause** the immediate causes of an event, such as the independent variable in an experiment (see *ultimate cause*)

**Psychological Abstracts** a journal produced by the APA that lists abstracts of most of the journal articles relevant to psychological topics

**Psychophysical methods** procedures such as the method of limits used to determine absolute and difference thresholds

**Psychophysics** judgment of stimuli along a known physical dimension; e.g., the perceived brightness of lights of different intensities

**Quasi-experiment** an experiment in which the independent variable occurs naturally and is not under direct control of the experimenter (see *ex post facto*)

**Random assignment** a crucial tool in experimentation whereby subjects are assigned to conditions in an unbiased fashion

**Randomization** see *random assignment*

**Random-groups design** when subjects are randomly assigned to conditions in a between-subjects design

**Random sample** a sample from a population that has been selected in an unbiased way

**Random sampling** (see *random sample*)

**Range** descriptive measure of dispersion; the difference between the largest and smallest score in a distribution

**Ratio scale** the highest form of scale in which there is a true zero and in which it is meaningful to consider multiplicative differences among attributes

**Reactivity** term to describe observations that are influenced by (or may be, in part, a reaction to) the detected presence of the investigator

**Realism** the extent to which a research procedure matches the characteristics of the real world (contrast with *generality of results*)

**Receiver-operating-characteristic (ROC)** a plot of hits against false alarms in signal-detection experiments

**Regression artifacts** an artifact in the measurement of change on a variable when groups of subjects who scored at the extremes on the variable are tested again (see *regression to the mean*)

**Regression to the mean** tendency for extreme measures on some variable to be closer to the group mean when remeasured, due to unreliability of measurement

**Relational observation** research that tries to determine how two or more variables are related

**Reliability** refers to the repeatability of an experimental result; inferential statistics provide an estimation of how likely it is that a finding is repeatable; also refers to the consistency of a test or measuring instrument determined by computing a correlation between scores obtained by subjects taking the test twice (test-retest reliability), or taking two different parallel forms of the test, or scores obtained on each half of the test (split-half reliability)

**Removing harmful consequences** ethical researchers remove any harmful consequences that their subjects may have incurred

**Repeated-measures design** several measures are taken on the same subject, such as several learning trials or numerous psychophysical judgments; a type of within-subject experiment

**Replication** the repetition of an earlier experiment to duplicate (and perhaps extend) its findings (see also *systematic replication*)

**Researcher bias** deliberate or inadvertent bias in which data are misanalyzed or participants are differentially treated over and above any planned differences in treatment

**Response acquiescence** a habitual way of responding on tests that involves frequently responding "yes" (see *response styles*)

**Response deviation** a habitual way of responding on tests that involves frequently responding "no" (see *response styles*)

**Response styles** habitual ways of responding on a test that are independent of the particular test item (see *response deviation, response acquiescence,* and *social desirability*)

**Retrospective** in case studies when the person has to report on events that occurred in the distant past; subject to ordinary and motivated forgetting

**Reversibility** an assumption made in research that the characteristics of different populations and species of subjects have the same underlying process; the behavioral "equation" can be determined from the behavior that is observed

**Reversal (ABA) design** small-$n$ design in which a subject's behavior is measured under a baseline (A) condition, then an experimental treatment is applied during the B phase and any changes in behavior are observed; finally, the original baseline (A) conditions are reinstituted to ensure that the experimental treatment was responsible for any observed change during the B phase

**Sample** observations selected from a population

**Scale-attenuation effects** difficulties in interpreting results when performance on the dependent variable is either nearly perfect (a ceiling effect) or nearly lacking altogether (a floor effect)

**Scatter diagrams** a graphical relationship indicating degree of correlation between two variables made by plotting the scores of individuals on two variables

**Scientific method** according to Peirce, this method fixes belief on the basis of experience (see *empirical*)

**Selection bias** occurs when subjects are not selected randomly (see *subject attrition* and *matching*)

**Self-correcting** science is self-correcting because it relies on public, empirical observation; old beliefs are discarded if they do not fit the empirical data

**Sensory impression** a hypothetical process that depends on the intensity of the stimulus in a signal-detection experiment

**Setting representativeness** see *ecological validity*

**Significance level** probability that an experimental finding is due to chance, or random fluctuation, operating in the data

**Simulated experiment** a fake experiment in which subjects are told to simulate the behavior of real subjects in a particular experiment

**Skewed distribution** a nonsymmetrical distribution

**Sleeper effect** an improvement in the effect of a persuasive message with the passage of time

**Small-$n$ design** research design utilizing a small number of subjects

**Social desirability** a habitual way of responding on tests that involves making socially desirable responses (see *response styles*)

**Social loafing** the decrease in individual effort that sometimes occurs when other people are present and when group performance is measured

**Social Science Citation Index** a journal containing lists of articles that cite a particular author or work

**Speciesism** a term used to describe the view that animal life is qualitatively different from human life and, therefore, a form of bigotry

**Split-half reliability** determining reliability of a test by dividing the test items into two arbitrary groups and correlating the scores obtained on the two halves of the test

**Staircase method** an abbreviated version of the method of limits in which only stimuli around the threshold value are presented

**Standard deviation** descriptive measure of dispersion; square root of the sum of squared deviations of each score from the mean divided by the number of scores

**Standard error of the mean** the standard deviation of the distribution of sample means

**Standard normal distribution** a distribution of events that, when plotted, results in a bell-shaped curve; in a standard normal distribution the mean, the median, and the mode are all equal

**Standard scores** also called z scores; differences between individual scores and the mean score expressed in units of standard deviations

**Statistical reliability** rejecting the null hypothesis on the basis of a statistical test that yields an alpha level of less than .05

**Stevens' law** $\Psi = k$ **stimulus**$^n$ the law derived from the method of magnitude estimation that says that psychological judgments grow exponentially with increments in stimulus intensity

**Strong inference** Platt's view that scientific progress comes about through a series of tests of alternative theoretical outcomes

**Stroop effect** difficulty in naming the color of an object when the color conflicts with the name of the object (when the word *blue* is printed in red ink)

**Subject attrition** when a subject fails to complete an experiment, which may destroy the basis of matching subjects across groups

**Subject representativeness** determination of generality of results across different subject populations

**Subject roles** how a subject reacts in an experiment (see *apprehensive-subject role, faithful-subject role, good subject role,* and *negativistic-subject role*)

**Subject variable** some characteristics of people that can be measured or described but cannot be varied experimentally (e.g., height, weight, sex, IQ, etc.)

**Sum of squares (SS)** sum of the squared scores used to calculate effects via analysis of variance

**Survey research** the technique of obtaining a limited amount of information from a large number of people, usually through random sampling

**Synergism** a term used in medical research to describe an interaction (see *interactions*)

**Systematic replication** repeating an experiment while varying numerous factors considered to be irrelevant to the phenomenon to see if it will survive these changes

**Test reliability** see *test-retest reliability* and *split-half reliability*

**Testability** a good theory needs to be capable of disproof

**Testable hypothesis** a hypothesis that specifies what can be measured and manipulated to test a theory

**Test-retest reliability** giving the same test twice in succession over a short interval to see if the scores are stable, or reliable; generally expressed as a correlation between scores on the tests

**Theory** a collection of ideas whose purpose is to describe and predict

**Theory of signal detection** states that sensory impressions and decision processes control our detection of signals

**Threshold** in psychophysics the hypothetical barrier a stimulus must cross to be detected

**Time-lag design** a quasi-experimental design used when age is a subject variable in order to control time of testing effects; subjects of a particular age (e.g., 19-year-olds) are tested at different time periods

**Treatment × treatment × subjects design** a within-subjects factorial design with two independent variables

**True zero** the absence of a physical property (zero weight in grams) as opposed to an arbitrary zero such as 0° Centigrade

**Truncated range** a problem in interpreting low correlations; the amount of dispersion (or range) of scores on one variable may be small, thus leading to the low correlation found

*t* **tests** parametric tests for testing differences between two groups

**Two by two factorial design (2 × 2)** a design in which there are two levels of each of two independent variables yielding four conditions

**Two-tailed test** test that places the rejection area at both ends of a distribution

**Type 1 error** probability that the null hypothesis is rejected when it is in fact true; equals the significance level

**Type 2 error** failure to reject the null hypothesis when it is in fact false

**Ultimate cause** the basic or final cause of an event, such as a "big bang" or evolution (contrast with *proximate cause*)

**Unobtrusive measures** measures taken from the results of behavior not the behavior itself

**Unobtrusive observations** observations not resulting in reactivity

**Validity** refers to whether an observation or procedure is sound or genuine

**Variable representativeness** determination of generality of results across different manipulations of an independent variable or different dependent variables

**Variance** measure of dispersion; the standard deviation squared

**Volunteer problem** volunteer subjects differ from those less eager to participate; may be a source of bias in research

**Weber's law** $\Delta I/I = K$ the just-noticeable difference is a constant fraction of the base intensity

**Wilcoxon signed-ranks test** a nonparametric test for two related groups

**Within-groups variance** a measure of the dispersion among subjects in the same group in an experiment

**Within-subjects design** an experimental design in which each subject is tested under more than one level of the independent variable

# NAME INDEX

# SUBJECT INDEX